SCHOOL HISTORIES AT WAR

LONDON: HUMPHREY MILFORD

OXFORD UNIVERSITY PRESS

SCHOOL HISTORIES AT WAR

A STUDY OF THE TREATMENT OF OUR WARS
IN THE SECONDARY SCHOOL HISTORY BOOKS
OF THE UNITED STATES AND IN THOSE OF ITS
FORMER ENEMIES

By ARTHUR WALWORTH

With an Introduction by
ARTHUR M. SCHLESINGER
Professor of American History
Harvard University

CAMBRIDGE, MASSACHUSETTS
HARVARD UNIVERSITY PRESS
1938

17341

PRINTED AT THE HARVARD UNIVERSITY PRESS

CAMBRIDGE, MASS., U.S.A.

To

M. L. W.
who fights
for civilization

PREFACE

ONCE upon a time — in September, 1814, to be exact — a Yankee fleet under the command of Lieutenant Macdonough defeated a Canadian fleet on Lake Champlain.

So much for the bare fact. It is not a fact of great importance; yet authors of school history textbooks make a good deal of it.

In his Canadian history for secondary schools, Duncan McArthur writes:

> Captain Downie attacked the *superior* [italics inserted] American naval force [that of Macdonough] and gave his life in the unsuccessful encounter.

In his American history for secondary schools, David Saville Muzzey writes:

> . . . young Lieutenant Thomas Macdonough . . . stationed his *inferior* [italics inserted] fleet at the entrance of the bay and so skillfully outmaneuvred and outfought the British squadron that he gained as decisive a victory as Perry's on Lake Erie.

Other American historians also insist that Macdonough fought against odds, one of them stating that he gained his victory against "twice his force."

This and many similar instances of contradiction in the history textbooks of former enemy nations make one wonder just where the truth does lie, and, more than that, whether it is necessary, more than a hundred years after the events, to call the attention of school children to such unimportant and controversial questions — whether it is necessary for a writer of school histories to be to some extent glory-monger as well as historian.

That fairness and objectivity in school histories is no Utopian dream is suggested by the extent to which the "drum and trumpet" school of history already has lost caste. Yet from the instances of prejudice resulting from emphasis, omission, and insinuation that are revealed by this study, it appears clear that, despite a change of emphasis in the newer books, the historians of former enemy nations have still to find a height on Parnassus from which they can look down without nationalistic bias upon the wars of their native lands.

It is not the purpose of this study to arrive at one essential and eternal Truth about the history of the foreign wars in which the United States has taken part. The writer lacks sufficient training in history to fortify him for such an undertaking. By contrasting parallel treatments of past wars that now appear in the history textbooks currently used in the secondary schools of the United States and of the countries with which we have fought, it is intended merely to direct lay and professional attention to the extremes of national prejudice to which the youth of the world are being exposed at the present time.

If, in addition to guiding the work of writers of history textbooks, this study may help teachers and other citizens to turn a spotlight upon hidden bias and also provide passages from foreign textbooks in a form that is convenient for the use of pupils in progressive secondary schools, possibly this new and lighter approach to an old and weighty problem will add something of value to the substantial volume of scholarly work that has already been done under the auspices of the International Committee on Intellectual Coöperation and other public-spirited bodies.

Secondary school histories, rather than college or elementary textbooks, have been examined in this study because, for reasons that are set forth fully in the Bibliography, it seems probable that they exert a greater influence on public opinion.

The author wishes to express his hearty appreciation of the sympathetic and stimulating assistance of Arthur Meier Schlesinger through the years during which this study has been developing. He wishes also to record his gratitude for their reading of the manuscript, at the same time absolving them of responsibility for its shortcomings, to President Charles Seymour, W. G. Kimmel, and George Bell Dyer. To Hubert Herring, Frederick Bliss Luquiens, and John Insley Coddington, thanks are given for assistance in securing the textbooks of foreign countries; and to Edwin Deeks Harvey, Southard Menzel, and M. I. Raphael, acknowledgment of valuable aid in translating certain passages.

Acknowledgment is made of the coöperation of the following in granting permission to quote from their respective books, the titles of which are listed in the Bibliography of this study: Allyn and Bacon; the American Book Company; Blackie and Son, Ltd.; The Clarendon Press, Oxford; W. G. Gage and Company; Ginn and Company; Harper and Brothers; Houghton Mifflin Company; Longmans, Green and Company; The Macmillan Company; the Minister of Education for Ontario Province; John Murray; Oxford University Press; Thomas Nelson and Sons, Ltd.; George Philip & Son, Ltd.; Row, Peterson and Company; Charles Scribner's Sons.

ARTHUR WALWORTH

Newton Center, Massachusetts
November 1, 1937

CONTENTS

INTRODUCTION

THE sources of international misunderstanding are legion. From misunderstanding to armed conflict the road is short, slippery, and straight. A Conference on the Cause and Cure of War several years ago named some twenty-four reasons for war, but no student of the subject would agree that this or any similar list exhausts the possibilities. Commercial rivalry, redundant populations, cultural and religious antagonisms, excessive nationalism, the urge to self-determination, dynastic ambitions — these and a hundred other factors, combining and recombining in unpredictable patterns, drive governments and peoples to the dread ordeal by combat. The attack upon war, if it is to succeed, must be waged along all fronts.

Among the possible causes of war, education holds a particular and significant place. The evil effects of education on national attitudes do not lend themselves to settlement by diplomatic negotiation as do specific economic differences or rival territorial claims. In every country education is a domestic commodity not intended for export. It may consciously be used by special groups or by the government for chauvinistic propaganda; more often perhaps it represents a gradual accretion of national traditions, popular hopes, and hates. In either case, it occupies a central position with reference to all other provocations to war, for in so far as it embodies dangerous nationalistic prejudices, it is the means of disseminating them constantly to all the people. It is a seedbed of international discord for both present and future generations.

Broadly speaking, the term education embraces all the agencies that influence opinion: not only the school and the college, but also the printing press, the public library, the pulpit, the stage, the screen, and the radio. The school, however, belongs in a special category, for to this type of education the youth of the land are continuously exposed during their most impressionable years. The beliefs and emotional attitudes then acquired are difficult, if not impossible, to outgrow or change. It is a common experience of college teachers of the social sciences to find that the basic viewpoints of their students five years or so after graduation have reverted to what they were on entering college. The party bigot resumes his bigotry, the individualist his individualism, the chauvinist his chauvinism.

The child's notions about his country and the outlying world come to him from many subjects in the curriculum. Professor Pierce's painstaking study, *Civic Attitudes in American School Textbooks*, exposes the fundamental assumptions in leading texts in history and other social studies, geography, music, English, and foreign languages. From her analysis of nearly four hundred manuals in these fields she concludes: "Textbooks are permeated with a national or patriotic spirit. . . . On the other hand, the attitudes engendered toward other peoples through a reading of these books must, in many cases, redound to their ignominy in contrast with the glory of America." In order to discover how far the children's viewpoints resembled those expressed in the textbooks, questions were directed to 1,125 pupils in the seventh to twelfth grades in the schools of Pennsylvania and Iowa. The great majority regarded defense of country as the highest attribute of patriotism, with obedience to law a close second. From the number of times other attributes were mentioned, the children apparently considered defense of one's country nine times as important as the obligation to vote and twenty-five times as important as the duty to pay taxes.

Only four pupils out of the entire number asserted that the United States "has carried on some enterprises which we can't be proud of."[1]

These thousand and more children probably represent a typical sample of the school population as a whole. Nowhere in the results of this inquiry does there appear any clear recognition that patriotism entails the obligation to think independently, to criticize, to strive continually for an improvement of conditions. One cannot help recalling the comment of Woodrow Wilson, then a professor at Princeton, to a teachers' convention in 1899:

> We have been told that it is unpatriotic to criticize public action. Well, if it is, then there is a deep disgrace resting upon the origins of this nation. This nation originated in the sharpest sort of criticism of public policy. . . . We have forgotten the very principle of our origin if we have forgotten how to object, how to resist, how to agitate, how to pull down and build up, even to the extent of revolutionary practices if it be necessary, to readjust matters.

Of all the subjects in the school curriculum history probably wields the greatest formative influence on national and international attitudes. This is partly because of the intrinsic nature of the study and partly because, in one form or another, it is taught to children from the first grade to the last. American history texts have greatly improved in the last generation. On the whole, they are less didactic, less given to uncritical hero worship, and more nearly abreast the findings of modern scholarship. That they still lend themselves to the purposes of exaggerated nationalism is owing largely to three conditions.

One is the continued (if somewhat waning) conception of American history as primarily a record of politics, war,

[1] Bessie L. Pierce, *Civic Attitudes in American School Textbooks* (Chicago, 1930), pp. 125–129.

and diplomacy. In so far as other nations are concerned, this directs attention to them only at periods of tension and points of conflict. Great Britain is impressed on youthful minds as an enemy in two wars and a diplomatic antagonist on many other occasions. Germany barely figures in the narrative till she suddenly emerges in the twentieth century as a monster of ruthlessness. Our unfortified boundary with Canada escapes notice in many textbooks, and few of the writers who do mention it dwell on its true significance, whereas our vexatious neighbor to the south receives full and invidious attention. Is it any wonder that school children imbibe the notion that foreign countries exist principally for the sake of causing trouble for the United States?

As American histories turn increasingly from the doings of government to a portrayal of the life of the people, the treatment of international relations will fall into a different and truer perspective. Wars and diplomatic crises will then be seen as a relatively small part of the story: they will appear merely as occasional interruptions of the usual intercourse among nations. Emphasis, rather, will be placed upon normal peace-time relations, on those constant exchanges of ideas, of goods and of people that have contributed greatly to the enrichment of American civilization and have had far-reaching effects on other lands. It will become evident that such characteristic movements in our history as antislavery, the extension of manhood suffrage, popular education, women's rights, and the rise of organized labor were simply American versions of a worldwide striving for human betterment. Nor will any student leave the course without a sharpened awareness, for example, of our indebtedness to France and Italy for leadership in the fine arts, to Germany for fructifying ideas at all levels of education from the kindergarten to the graduate school, and to England for our political ideals, much of our literary inspiration, and a knowledge of how to deal with the perplexing problems of modern industrialism. History so considered involves no belittlement of America's own achievement but simply a better understanding of it, combined with an appreciation of the fundamental interdependence of peoples. If wars and diplomatic controversies sometimes divide them, the children will learn that deeper currents irresistibly draw them together.

Any effort by textbook writers to lessen the nationalistic emphasis of their works encounters at once the second obstacle to which allusion has been made: the resistance, if not persecution, offered by powerful pressure groups. The members of these organizations, unfurling the redoubtable banner of "patriotism," use as their touchstone of historical truth the knowledge which they acquired when they themselves were school children. They want everything but the hurrahs left out of American history. Patriotism they construe not merely as love of one's own country but also as hatred or distrust of other countries. Ignoring the tremendous advances made by modern scholarship in exploring the past, they set up a canon from which any deviation by textbook authors becomes a species of treason. A cynic might suggest that they suspect their country's history of containing episodes so disgraceful that it is unsafe for the young to hear of them.

The number of these organizations is formidable, including in the last two decades groups of such varying membership and diverse purpose as the Sons of the American Revolution, the Daughters of the American Revolution, the Descendants of the Signers of the Declaration of Independence, the United States Daughters of 1812, the Grand Army of the Republic, the United Spanish War Veterans, the American Legion, the Veterans of Foreign

Wars, the Patriotic Order of Sons of America, the Patriot League for the Preservation of American History, the Junior Order of United American Mechanics, the Knights of Pythias, the Knights of Columbus, and the Ku Klux Klan. Supported by the Hearst syndicate of newspapers and certain other members of the press, these groups have exerted their influence in hundreds of communities throughout the land, securing the dismissal of teachers and superintendents and the ejection of "treason texts," providing spurious issues for unscrupulous local politicians, and inducing legislatures to enact statutes of censorship.

Such statutes, it should be noted, have usually been more harmful in their intent than in their phraseology. Thus the Wisconsin law, passed in 1923, forbids the use of any textbook "which falsifies the facts regarding the War of Independence, or the War of 1812, or which defames our nation's founders or misrepresents the ideals for which they struggled and sacrificed, or which contains propaganda favorable to any foreign government." Nothing could be more unexceptionable, but the execution of the act is left not to a board of qualified historical experts, but to the complaint of any five citizens and the final decision of the state superintendent of public instruction. The American Historical Association, condemning such "attempts, however well meant, to foster national arrogance and boastfulness," declared that the result must inevitably be a "ruinous deterioration both of textbooks and of teaching."

The recent deluge of teachers' oath laws is directed less at the books in use than at the teachers who use them, and not simply at the history teachers but at all teachers. Though these statutes, like the Wisconsin act, are usually innocuous as to wording, the purpose underlying them and the means provided for their enforcement obviously erect additional barriers to an honest teaching of history and of current questions. It is clear, therefore, that the textbook author is not free to set down the facts as perhaps a lifetime of study and reflection has caused him to understand them, but must perfume his product to titillate the sensitive nostrils of patrioteering organizations and their legislative allies.

The final deterrent to the textbook writer is the publisher through whose favor his volume reaches the public. The publisher, naturally enough, is in business to get his books sold. Even less than the author can he ignore the wishes of his possible market. The fact is that publishers have gone so far as to issue separate history books for use in Northern and in Southern schools, and some of them continue to publish different texts for Catholic and Protestant schools. It may be noted that the advertisement of a widely used school history sets up five tests of merit in a textbook without naming accuracy as one of them. The prospectus of an American Legion history text, published for school use shortly after the war, announced that the volume would "speak the truth" but would "tell the truth optimistically."

Everything considered, one may marvel that the American history textbooks are not more thoroughly saturated with national vainglory and jingoism than they are. Somehow or other the stream has managed to rise above its source. Yet, as Mr. Walworth's book makes evident, much remains to be done if we are to do our part in bringing about that emotional disarmament which, in the case of every people, constitutes an essential condition of international understanding. Mr. Walworth, wisely, has not undertaken to deal with the whole problem of the relation of school instruction to world peace. His is the rushlight that illumines the entire scene. In a lively and readable narrative he contrasts the manner in which each of our major wars is treated in the leading secondary school histories of our own and the enemy country. The reader will quickly realize that both accounts of these conflicts cannot be right. If he takes offense at what seems to be the distorted emphasis of the foreign textbook, presently he will begin to wonder whether all the misrepresentation is on the one side. Mr. Walworth does not undertake to settle the point: he is content merely to raise the question.

One of the values of the book is the demonstration that what may be only an innocent manifestation of national vanity in one's own texts is a source of international peril when indulged in by the schoolbooks of other countries. Several years ago the Liaison Committee of the Major International Associations recommended that the League's Committee on Intellectual Coöperation "consider the desirability of including in school textbooks to be used in the upper forms of secondary schools the reproduction of chapters of textbooks from different countries, with a view of enabling both teachers and pupils to make comparisons . . . ." Mr. Walworth's study now makes available for Americans such a comparison in regard to one of the most critical matters on which national prejudices operate. The fact that he confines his attention to works that are in general use today, omitting those that have done their damage in the past, gives his treatise added importance as a basis for practical remedial action.

ARTHUR M. SCHLESINGER

SCHOOL HISTORIES AT WAR

CHAPTER I

THE PARTING OF THE WAYS

WHEN the American adult recalls his schoolboy notions of "the times that tried men's souls," he is likely to think of George III as a blundering bigot. The King George of our school history course is remembered as an obstinate and narrow-minded boy who was brought up by his mother to be every inch a king. By toadying to the wealthy English tradesmen he secured the means to buy his way to control of Parliament; and then he and his subservient statesmen used their power in pursuit of a domineering policy that inevitably led to war with the colonies.

Though Patrick Henry of the colony of Virginia gave warning that "Caesar had his Brutus, Charles I his Cromwell, and George III may profit by their example," George stubbornly refused to profit. Instead, he and his Parliament promulgated a succession of acts and orders that encroached upon the liberties of the American colonists beyond all endurance. This series of tyrannical measures was punctuated in England by periods of vacillation and in America by indignation meetings, bonfires, burnings-in-effigy, tar-and-featherings, riots, and the Boston Massacre. Noble American patriots were proclaiming "Down with Tyranny," "No Taxation without Representation," and "Give Me Liberty or Give Me Death."

The leaders of the several colonies, putting aside sectional jealousies, met in solemn conclave to consider concerted action; and the flame needed to weld the colonies together burst out when the redcoats marched upon the munition stores of Concord. Yankee minutemen forced Britain's dapper veterans to breathe deeply of humiliation and Massachusetts dust. Herded into Boston town, the redcoats were checked later at Bunker Hill and were bottled up in the city until they slipped away by sea.

Then appeared George Washington, commissioned by the Continental Congress to take command of poorly equipped but stout-hearted militia who had rallied to their country's call. Forsaking their firesides, these doughty forebears plodded through the rigors of military campaigning with unwavering loyalty to their Chief and to the Cause.

Soon the scene of battle shifted to New York and New Jersey. Reduced in numbers and equipment by action near New York, the American troops retreated to New Jersey and Pennsylvania. There they were exposed to the cruel winter weather while their adversaries — the Hessian minions of George III — amused themselves with the effete pleasures of town life. But in the dead of winter our virile men fell upon the Hessians, beer-sodden in Trenton, and slaughtered them.

Meanwhile, General Burgoyne struck into New York State from Canada, but his expedition was conducted with a stupidity that was as characteristic of British military maneuvers as it had been of their prewar diplomacy.

In the Northwest, in the South, and on the high seas other valiant souls rose to support the American cause. George Rogers Clark and Francis Marion are names that deserve well of posterity. John Paul Jones, too, achieved epic heights of courage in bearding the British lion in his own den. Credit is due also to the envoys who secured France's promise of aid. In fact, the French fleet really was of some slight help to our land forces in making the siege of Yorktown effective.

In negotiating the peace treaty, Franklin, Adams, and Jay proved themselves leaders as well as master diplomats by acting beyond their orders, to the everlasting advantage of their country. The terms of the peace were so favorable that the war can be considered a brilliant triumph for America against what had seemed insuperable odds.

* * * * *

So runs the story of the Revolutionary War in the minds of those of us who lack advanced training in American history, but who have retained from our school histories something more than a vision of George Washington, a cherry tree, and a colt. This concept of history fulfills the Napoleonic definition: "History is legend agreed upon." It also fulfills the ideal set up in the preface of a book endorsed by several organizations of war veterans and self-styled "patriots": "The heroic history of a nation is the drum-and-fife music to which it marches. It makes a mighty difference whether America continues to quick-step to *Yankee Doodle* or takes to marking time to *God Save the King*." [1]

To some writers of history textbooks it apparently has seemed desirable to stir the blood of the students so that they will keep step with the mass of their schoolfellows. Although the themes that historians of England and the United States have played for this purpose are as similar as "America" and "God Save the King," the words that are set to the tunes are very different. This the following quotations will show.

* * * * *

Contrary to the view that has become traditional in America, King George III, when he is seen through a monocle, turns out to be a human being with virtues as well as faults. The English historian Mowat presents him thus:

[1] Charles Grant Miller, *The Poisoned Loving-Cup* (Chicago: privately published by the "National Historical Association," 1928), p. viii.

George III was a thorough Englishman, proud of his country, fond of the people, good-natured, respectable, obstinate. Although the early part of his reign was a failure and he had to pass through a period of unpopularity, he lived to be a popular figure in the country. The domestic life of the first two Georges had not been good. Neither was the life of his son, George IV. The third George was an upright man, living a simple life, not extravagant, kindly, affable. He resided a great deal at Windsor Castle, and used to walk much in the forest and in the roads round the town. He was a familiar figure to every one for miles around, and was known especially to the schoolboys of Eton, whom he would often stop at the roadside, pat on the head, and ask kindly questions. Many stories, some true, some made up, have gathered around his personality. It is said that, walking in the grounds of Windsor Castle, he stopped to ask a gardener's boy what he earned. The boy discontentedly said: "Meat and drink, a bed, a fire, and a roof." "Why, that's all I get," said the good-natured king as he walked away.[2]

Where in this Anglicized picture can one find the arrogant monarch whom the American schoolboy has been taught to dislike by such criticism as that in Guitteau's pronouncement: "the new monarch was a narrow-minded, obstinate man filled with those ideas of the royal prerogative which his mother had taught him in early youth";[3] in the Beards' characterization of King George as one who had developed "high and mighty notions";[4] in Adams and VanNest's phrase — "stupid and stubborn as the King was to prove?"[5] Where indeed? The conflicting versions seem to agree on only one attribute of the King — he was

---

[2] R. B. Mowat, *A New History of Great Britain* (1931), p. 508.

[3] W. B. Guitteau, *History of the United States* (1937), p. 107.

[4] Charles and Mary Beard, *The Making of American Civilization* (1937), p. 97.

[5] J. T. Adams and C. G. VanNest, *The Record of America* (1935), p. 114.

"obstinate." But even on this point Muir (of England) prefers to say:

> a young man of moderate ability with a firm will, real courage, and a high sense of public obligation and of his own rights and duties as king.[6]

Though the English writers agree with their American colleagues in criticizing the ineptness of George III and his ministers in administering the imperial policies during the decade before the war, they defend almost to a man the justness of those policies. Rayner writes of the position of the colonies in 1765:

> They [the American colonies] were the freest communities in the world — certainly no other Power allowed overseas possessions anything like such a degree of independence. But they had inherited British ideas of liberty; and those ideas, transplanted into a new country, had developed much farther than in England, where they were tempered by traditional respect for the privileged classes. But the better off people are, the better off they want to be; and bad feeling had long been arising between the colonists and the Home Government. There were two main causes of disagreement. Firstly, the colonists resented having officials sent out, especially as these were usually connected with the "ruling class" in Britain, and therefore men of very different upbringing and outlook from their own. The colonial Assemblies sometimes refused to vote the salaries of these officials, and the result was a good deal of unseemly bickering. Secondly, the colonials did not dispute the right of the Home Government to regulate their trade — they simply ignored it, by carrying on wholesale smuggling.

> Obviously, this law-breaking and tax-dodging could not be allowed to go on forever . . . the Seven Years' War had now brought matters to a head. The colonists

[6] Ramsay Muir, *English History*, Part III: 1688–1815 (1929), p. 398.

had persisted in their illegal trading with the French even during the war, and had gone so far as to sell to the enemy goods that were urgently required for the British forces in America. Moreover, the war had doubled the National Debt, but the colonies had contributed little or nothing towards its cost, despite the fact it had been fought largely to save them from French aggression. Furthermore, Britain had by the Treaty of Paris acquired a vast area between the Alleghany Mountains and the Mississippi, and a permanent armed force would be necessary to protect the colonies from the Indians who inhabited those parts. Of course, it would have been a fine thing if the colonies had undertaken to provide for their own defence.[7]

Brett of England states:

. . . the Seven Years' War had to be paid for, and as it had been fought mainly in the interests of the colonists, justice seemed to indicate that they should share in the cost. It was the attempt to enforce this policy which provoked colonial resistance and hence was the first of the events leading to the outbreak of war.

. . . Though unimaginative and unstatesmanlike, Grenville was a lawyer who loved business routine, and his investigations showed that American customs duties were producing a mere £2,000 per annum and were costing £7,000 for the process! The evident explanation was that the regulations were systematically evaded and that smuggling was taking place on a vast scale. This suggested an obvious way of increasing national revenue. . . .

On the face of things there was nothing unreasonable in Grenville's proposal, which was certainly made in a conciliatory spirit. That a standing army was necessary in America was clearly demonstrated in 1763 by raids of Red Indians on Virginia, Pennsylvania, and Maryland against whom the colonists would have been powerless

[7] R. M. Rayner, *A Concise History of Britain, 1688–1815* (1934), pp. 413–414.

had not British troops been still in the country. More-over, that the French would take the first opportunity to renew their attacks was almost certain. Yet towards the cost of their own protection the colonists were being asked to contribute less than one-third, and the failure of the colonists to propose, during the stipulated twelve months, any alternative to the Stamp Duties seemed a proof that the method suggested for raising the neces-sary money was not irksome.[8]

Even G. M. Trevelyan ventures to call the failure of the colonies to tax themselves, "unfortunate":

As a matter of political expediency it was most desir-able that the colonists should be taxed for imperial purposes by their own representatives rather than by the British Parliament.

Unfortunately they made no move to tax themselves, partly from thrift and partly from indifference to the Imperial connection. When once the French danger had disappeared, the Empire had seemed a far-off ab-straction to the backwoodsman of the Alleghenies, like the League of Nations to the Middle West today. And even on the seacoast, where the Empire was better known, it was not always better loved.[9]

These charges and insinuations tap a sensitive nerve in the American "patriot," a nerve which the majority of our historians have protected by a cloak of indifference. Some, however, have a reply ready for England's demand that the colonists share the expense of the English troops. Guitteau, for example, presents this rebuttal of state-ments made by Rayner and Brett in the passages quoted above:

. . . to Grenville's mind it appeared just and reasonable that the colonies should share the burden of their mili-

---

[8] S. R. Brett, *British History, A School Certificate Course, 1688–1815* (1936), pp. 162–163.
[9] G. M. Trevelyan, *History of England* (1937), p. 550.

tary protection. Undoubtedly the colonists would have agreed with this conclusion if they had accepted the premise; but they emphatically denied the military necessity for a standing army in America, and reasoning from English precedents, they had good grounds to fear that the presence of such an army would be a constant menace to colonial rights.[10]

Wertenbaker and Smith refuse to accept the implication in the English books that the colonies were a liability rather than an asset to the British Empire. Their judgment is:

His [Grenville's] plan was neither wise nor entirely just. It is true that England had always defended her colonies, and that at times the expense had been heavy, but she received a rich compensation. She had grown wealthy and powerful through her colonial trade, a trade in which she had not hesitated to sacrifice the interests of the colonies. Although the Americans had contributed little directly to the British treasury, they had contributed millions of pounds to the development of British prosperity. Thus it was folly for Grenville to incur their resentment by insisting upon a direct tax. . . . This seems so obvious as to arouse the suspicion that the Stamp Act was designed, in part at least, as a blow at colonial liberty.[11]

Some American writers throw responsibility for the beginning of hostilities largely upon the British Parliament's passage of the "Intolerable Acts." Wertenbaker and Smith state that "these harsh measures led to war." [12] And Muzzey writes:

By these "Intolerable Acts," as they were called in America, Parliament thought that it was punishing the

[10] Guitteau, *History of the United States*, p. 109.

[11] T. J. Wertenbaker and D. E. Smith, *The United States of America* (1931), p. 106.

[12] *United States*, p. 114.

colony of Massachusetts, but it soon found that it had stirred a whole people to resistance.[13]

The English historians are more inclined to feel that the acts of violence committed by the radical element in the colonies made military action necessary. Probably Carrington and Jackson make the strongest presentation of this view, in the following passage:

> On March 5th, 1770, Lord North announced in Parliament the repeal of all the duties except that on tea; on the same day in Boston the first shots of the American Revolution were fired. A picket of soldiers, on their way to barracks amid a mob of ruffians jeering and throwing stones, turned in exasperation and shot down two or three of them. This episode was called in America the Boston Massacre. From this time Boston and all New England were in a state of rebellion, and no offer, however reasonable, from the British Government received the slightest attention. In 1772 a British revenue-cutter, the Gaspée, was attacked and burned by a band of rebels whom the colonial government refused to prosecute. In 1773, when the ships of the East India Company arrived, armed men disguised as Red Indians boarded the ships and destroyed the tea. Again the local authorities treated this riot, the "Boston Tea Party," as a mere joke. No government could permit such lawlessness.[14]

Yet the king made one last attempt at conciliation. Most of the American books entirely overlook this final effort for peace. This omission could hardly have been owing to a lack of space, for the accounts of the war are given almost twice as much space in the American books as in the English ones. Carrington and Jackson have found space to treat this matter in these lines:

[13] D. S. Muzzey, *History of the American People* (1936), p. 124.
[14] C. E. Carrington and J. H. Jackson, *A History of England* (1936), p. 536. By permission of The Macmillan Company, publishers.

. . . In the Spring of 1775 the king made a new effort. He offered the colonies a release from all taxation if they would disband the continental congress, and arrange for themselves in each colony some way of contributing to the cost of their defence. In those days when there was no telegraph and it might take three months to get an answer from America it is not surprising that this well-meant offer was not received until too late. Two regular battles had taken place near Boston. . . .

The Declaration [of the Independence of the United States] proceeded with a list of charges against the King of England, who had "burnt our towns, ravaged our coasts," let loose on our frontiers "the merciless Indian savages" and had tried to reduce the colonies to a state of absolute submission. These charges were most unjust, ignoring as they did the long series of riots, brawls, and attacks on royal officials or loyal citizens which had forced King George to declare martial law.[15]

In sentences such as the following from Guitteau, some of the American books suggest that the young colonies were in a sense "bringing up Mother" when they fought with her:

By resisting the arbitrary measures of such a government, Englishmen living in the colonies were really fighting the cause of English liberty in the motherland.[16]

This solicitous interest is not acknowledged in the English books.

The chronicles of the martial events run closely parallel in the books of the two nations, though in general the American writers give far more space to battles, proportionately. There is less of drumbeating than in the old-time school histories. In describing those picturesque

---

[15] *History of England*, pp. 536–538.
[16] *History of the United States*, p. 108.

actions that have been most celebrated in song and story, however, several of the books flaunt their colors.

American books give a paragraph or so to the rout of the Hessians at Trenton. The last sentence of Guitteau's story is:

> This brilliant exploit, at a time when all seemed lost, put new life into the patriot cause.[17]

But half of the English books make no mention of this battle, and the others give only a sentence to it, Muir dismissing it, with perhaps a glance down his nose, thus:

> Though Washington achieved a brilliant little success [sic!] by surprising a detached force of Hessians at Trenton, his position was extremely difficult.[18]

To the assertion of Carrington and Jackson, in their description of the battle of Bunker Hill, that:

> . . . the small English army suffered as heavy losses with as steady courage as has ever been shown on prouder fields of honour.[19]

Muzzey retorts:

> The American defeat at Bunker Hill was a moral victory; for it showed that the raw colonial troops could face the regulars without flinching. . . . Howe's loss of over a thousand men was double that of the Americans.[20]

Wirth adds:

> It was a costly victory for Gage, as more than a thousand British were killed, while the Americans lost only about four hundred. It was really a moral victory for the Americans, for their inexperienced troops had twice proved their ability to hold their own against the well-trained British.[21]

[17] History of the United States, p. 141.
[18] British History, p. 413.   [19] History of England, p. 537.
[20] History of the American People, p. 127.
[21] F. P. Wirth, The Development of America (1936), p. 156.

And Adams and VanNest, explaining that the battle was "an overwhelming victory for American morale," take three lines of text to point out that

> from one-third to a half of the British were killed by the New Englanders who held their deadly fire against the enemy each time until they could see "the whites of their eyes." [22]

Although they pay tribute to the steadfast courage of Washington, English historians are not complimentary in their allusions to the colonial army. Of course in the Land of the Free, the children of the Daughters of the American Revolution are not contaminated by information of the sort that is given by Warner and Marten in this passage:

> The American colonist did not like moving far from his home. Moreover, he only enlisted for short periods, and therefore might leave, and not infrequently did leave, his fellow-colonists in the crisis of a campaign. He was, besides, inclined to be insubordinate, "regarding," said one general, "his officer as no more than a broomstick," especially if serving under the command of officers from any other colony but his own. The Congress, which supervised the generals, was loquacious and incompetent, whilst "peculation and speculation," in the words of the commander-in-chief, were rife amongst the contractors. And finally, a large number of the colonists were either loyal to the mother country or indifferent to the cause of both combatants. [23]

How, then, do the English historians explain the defeat of their country?

Like the American writers, they give much of the credit for America's victory to Washington. But they also offer excuses suggesting that the glory accruing to the American army and its general is not so great as it appears in the

---

[22] *Record of America*, p. 99.

[23] G. T. Warner and C. H. K. Marten, *The Groundwork of British History* (1931), p. 506.

American books. This quotation from Mowat, for example, is hardly pleasing to Americans who like to gloat upon the Yankee grit and resourcefulness of their forebears:

> Broadly considered, however, the defeat of the Mother Country may be said to have been due to three things: to mismanagement at home, to the distance across the Atlantic, and to the vast and roadless spaces of the Colonies.[24]

The one cause for Britain's defeat emphasized above all others in the English books, however, is the pressure brought against Great Britain by other world powers. The last stages of the Revolution are treated in Muir's book under the heading *Brittania contra Mundum* (*1778–1782*) — an exaggeration which even classical phrasing does not conceal from a critical eye. To impress the full significance of this heading upon the pupil, the historian leads up to it with these remarks:

> It is usual to regard the later stages of the American war as a period of unmitigated humiliation. They should rather be regarded as a proof of the strength and courage of the British people even under bad leadership. For never in her history, before or since, has Britain been compelled to face so great a combination of enemies, and to face them without allies.[25]

Though the American books give more or less space to the part that the French fleet played in the defeat of the British army at Yorktown, they do not emphasize the importance of British control of the sea to the British cause, as Brett does in the following typical quotation:

> That British troops and supplies had to cross the Atlantic meant that the effectiveness of British operations in America depended upon uninterrupted control

[24] *History of Great Britain*, p. 521.
[25] Muir, *British History*, p. 415.

of the sea. Once more, the war on land would be decided by the possession of sea-power: if the British lost that control they would lose the war. That, in fact, was precisely what took place: the intervention of European sea-faring nations on the side of the colonists jeopardized the naval supremacy of Britain and henceforward she lost the war in America. . . .

. . . by the close of 1780, Britain was at war, either actually or potentially, not only with the Americans but also with every maritime power of Europe. The critical nature of sea-power was now to show itself; nor was the result long in being seen.[26]

In view of the fact that the intervention of France and the others deprived England of sea power at a time when it was so desperately needed, it is not strange that the British histories not only agree with the American books in attributing the loss of the battle of Yorktown to this calamity, but even ascribe the unsuccessful conclusion of the war to it. In this vein Carrington and Jackson write:

The situation was so hopeless that England was willing to recognise American independence in order to save herself from France and Spain.[27]

And Mowat states:

The intervention of France and Spain, though bringing disaster to those two countries, had made the reduction of the American colonies impossible for England.[28]

To this length the American writers, apparently wishing to preserve something of the halo that has gathered about the heads of the American troops and their leaders in the years since the Revolution, have been unwilling to go.

Most of the American historians either scant or ignore

---

[26] *British History*, pp. 169, 174, respectively.
[27] *History of England*, p. 541.
[28] *History of Great Britain*, p. 531.

a movement growing directly out of the Revolution that profoundly affected the subsequent history of North America — the migration of Loyalists ("Tories," in some American books) from the thirteen colonies to Canada. A few sentences are given to the Loyalists in the British books. A full account of this phase of the war and of the human suffering and national traditions that it engendered is supplied by the histories now in use in the secondary schools of Canada.

In the following passages, Wallace's *A History of the Canadian People* emphasizes the brutality and fanaticism of the American "patriots" and the worthiness of the Loyalists who were ridden out of the colonies on rails:

In their desire for independence, . . . the people of the thirteen colonies had been far from unanimous. It has been estimated that fully one-third of them, if not more, were opposed to the Declaration of Independence. There are historians, indeed, who have maintained that the revolutionists were an organized and energetic minority who imposed their will on an unorganized and uncertain majority. . . .

At one time it was estimated that there were more Loyalists fighting on the British side than there were soldiers in the whole of Washington's armies, which were always "moulting." As was to be expected, the Loyalists were heartily detested by the Revolutionists. After the Declaration of Independence in 1776, they were regarded as traitors and were treated as such. In many of the colonies their property was confiscated, they were fined and heavily taxed, large numbers of them were imprisoned, others were banished, and a number were put to death. A favourite method of dealing with them consisted in "tarring and feathering": the unfortunate victim was stripped of his clothes, was smeared with a coat of tar and feathers, and was thus driven through the streets in a cart for the amusement of the public. Not only the Loyalists, but even their families, were subjected to the most inhuman persecution. . . .

In the Treaty of Versailles, the British government did what it could to protect the interests of the Loyalists. It was agreed that they should meet with no impediment to the recovery of their lawful debts, and that they should suffer no future loss or damage for any part they had taken in the war. The American commissioners promised also that Congress would "earnestly recommend" to the legislatures of the various states the restitution of confiscated Loyalist property. But these promises were worthless . . . In the prevailing mood of public opinion, it was not possible to guarantee the Loyalists even freedom from persecution. Some of them did, it is true, return to their homes; but tens of thousands found themselves driven from the place of their birth, penniless and destitute.

The Loyalist settlement of the Maritime provinces and Ontario was one of the most touching episodes of modern history. The migration to Nova Scotia began with the British evacuation of Boston in 1776. At that time about a thousand Boston Loyalists accompanied the British troops to Halifax. "Neither Hell, Hull, nor Halifax," said one of them, "can afford worse shelter than Boston." It was not, however, until the close of the war that the great influx took place. . . . In all, at least thirty thousand Loyalists were transported to the land of the Acadians. Of these, many belonged to the upper classes of the American colonies before the Revolution. Not a few were graduates of Harvard and Yale colleges; and some belonged to families famous in early American history. Very few had saved anything out of the wreck of their fortunes; and all had to start life afresh in their new home under conditions that were both difficult and unfamiliar. Those who were landed at the mouth of the River St. John, and formed the first settlement in what became the province of New Brunswick, were disembarked on a wild and primeval shore, where they had to clear away the undergrowth before they could pitch their tents or build their shelters. "Nothing but wilderness before our eyes! The women and children did not refrain from tears," wrote one of the exiles, and the mother of one family used to tell her descendants, "Such a feeling of loneliness came over me that, although I had not shed a tear through all the war, I sat down on the damp moss, with my baby in my lap, and cried." There were those whose hearts failed them; and one Loyalist, franker perhaps than the rest, wrote bitterly, "I have made one great mistake in politics in my life, for which reason I intend not to make another." But the majority of the Loyalists were of sterling stock; and they attacked the problem of carving homes for themselves out of the wilderness with such courage and vigour that in a few years those parts of Nova Scotia, New Brunswick, and Prince Edward Island settled by them presented the appearance of flourishing communities.

The Loyalist settlers in Upper Canada were fewer in number. . . . For the first few years they had a severe struggle for existence. . . . When government assistance was cut off, famine stalked through the "western settlements." . . . But here, too, the high qualities of the Loyalists triumphed over difficulties.[29]

Bingay points out that not merely the ignorant mob, but the responsible leaders as well, joined the persecution:

. . . in every State the leaders, the Assembly, and the mob vied with one another in persecuting by legal and illegal methods these now helpless people. . . . Washington said they were only fit for suicide. Adams declared that they ought to be hanged; and in some cases his verdict was executed. On the average, the loyalists belonged to the more substantial class of the country; and in many instances the acts of the States' legislatures directed against them point rather to motives of plunder than to motives of patriotism.[30]

[29] W. S. Wallace, *A History of the Canadian People* (1930), pp. 131–137.
[30] James Bingay, *A History of Canada for High Schools* (1934), p. 195.

Such persecution doubtless left an enduring brand upon the people of North America and reveals much about the origin of contemporary attitudes.

*   *   *   *   *

In attempting to untangle the web of argument that has been spun from school histories, one may find help in a tolerant summary of the significance of the Revolutionary War with which Trevelyan concludes his account:

> It was well that America was made. It was tragic that the making could only be effected by a war with Britain. The parting was perhaps inevitable at some date and in some form, but the parting in anger, and still more the memory of that moment's anger fondly cherished by America as the starting-point of her history, have had consequences that we rue to this day.[31]

Trevelyan's view inclines one to believe that there may have been much truth in a remark that dropped from the pen of Samuel Curwen, an American who wrote in London in 1775: "It is unfashionable and even disreputable to look askew on one another for differences of opinion in political matters; the doctrine of toleration, if not better understood, is, thank God, better practised here than in America." [32]

Yet, on the other hand, the American historians appear to have made greater progress toward objectivity during the last decade than have their English colleagues.

Whichever way the pendulum of toleration may be swinging at the present juncture, it seems desirable that the American school historians join their British colleagues in an effort to play ball (or should one say "play cricket?") in conformity with international rules.

[31] *History of England*, p. 555.
[32] R. B. Mowat, *Americans in England* (Boston: Houghton Mifflin Co., 1935), p. 45.

CHAPTER II

THE SECOND WAR FOR INDEPENDENCE

EVEN after the drubbing that she received in the Revolutionary War, Great Britain did not drop her overbearing attitude toward the United States. Insults were added to injuries during the next thirty years. The English had inspired the Indians of the Northwest to attack our settlers; moreover, they had seized American cargoes upon the high seas, held up American vessels, impressed American seamen, and then refused to give compensation for these wrongs. Finally American patience was exhausted, and in 1812, diplomatic protests having availed nothing, Congress declared war upon Great Britain.

On land the War of 1812 amounted to little more than a series of raids across the Canadian border. By two of their sallies into Canada the Americans gained notable victories — at the battle of the Thames under General Harrison and at Lundy's Lane under General Jacob Brown and General Winfield Scott. The major engagement of the war, fought at New Orleans after the signing of the peace but before the news had crossed the Atlantic, resulted in a triumph for General Jackson against a detachment of England's sturdiest veterans.

It was primarily on the seas, however, that America served notice to the world that she was no longer a nation to be trifled with. Manned by hardy and resourceful seamen, our little frigates and privateers preyed upon British commerce and even swooped down and destroyed some of Britannia's staunch men-of-war.

Shortly after war had been declared, the *Constitution* (affectionately called "Old Ironsides") humbled the arro-

21

gant *Guerrière*, a British ship which had been very active in violating America's rights as a neutral. This was but the first of a series of brilliant engagements on ocean and lakes. On the Atlantic, Captain Lawrence of "don't-give-up-the-ship" fame waged a gallant though losing battle against the British *Shannon*. Lawrence's name and fame were perpetuated by the flagship which later carried Oliver Hazard Perry to immortal deeds on Lake Erie. Hewed out of green timbers on the shores of the lake and commanded by this lad of twenty-seven, the American flotilla outfought a fleet of heavier British vessels and gave its young commodore a chance to send the modest yet stirring message by which he is so well remembered: "We have met the enemy and they are ours — two ships, two brigs, one schooner, and one sloop." A year later on Lake Champlain, Commodore Macdonough overcame great odds to win a significant victory, a Congressional vote of thanks, a gold medal, and a farm overlooking the scene of his triumph!

Alarmed by the presence of American privateers that were harrying British traffic on the high seas, England sent her grim watchdogs to blockade our Atlantic ports. Towns on the coast were plundered; and a large expedition sailed up Chesapeake Bay, marched against Washington, and burned the government buildings. The British fleet then sailed to attack Fort McHenry at Baltimore, bombarding the fort all night. Came the dawn, and the "Star-Spangled Banner" still floated over the ramparts, to the inspiration of Francis Scott Key. Incidentally, Baltimore did not fall.

At length, growing weary of this inconclusive strife, both countries agreed to a peace without annexation or indemnities; and thereafter America's rights on the seas were more scrupulously respected.

*   *   *   *   *

Such is the fabric of fact and fancy that has been woven into the minds of adult American "patriots" in their old-time school histories. Though the story has been somewhat tempered (some would say *emasculated*) in contemporary secondary school histories, enough bitterness still lingers to curdle the narrative here and there.

The most obvious difference between the American and English versions is one of space. To the English historian the War of 1812 apparently was a minor episode in the grapple to the death with Napoleon. Although the slighting of the War of 1812 in the English histories does not necessarily prove that the English historians are ashamed of the part England played in the conflict, it is difficult to believe that they would not have found space for a fuller treatment of this event if it held for the English people the glamor associated with such victories as Trafalgar and Waterloo.

Be that as it may, the fact remains that the American texts give several pages to the War of 1812, whereas the British histories mention it very briefly, usually in association with the Napoleonic Wars. Mowat dismisses the war with these three lines:

> From 1812 to 1814 England had been involved in hostilities with the United States, over the "right of search" at sea. This war was terminated by the Treaty of Ghent, December 24, 1814.[1]

Warner and Marten give only one paragraph to this war. The last half of it reads:

> Disputes [over the impressment of seamen] led to war being declared in 1812. In the earlier stages of the war, though Captain Broke in the *Shannon* upheld our prestige by causing the American frigate *Chesapeake* to surrender in fifteen minutes, the American frigates — so equipped as to be almost ships of the line — won

[1] *History of Great Britain*, p. 592.

many successes over the lighter-armed British frigates; and United States privateers took some five hundred British merchantmen in seven months. The land operations of the United States across the Canadian frontier were, however, a failure. The Canadians, whether of French or of British descent, combined with the British regulars to resist the invasion, and fought with great courage and persistency. Eventually Great Britain, in 1814, after Napoleon's abdication, was able to send a large fleet and her Peninsular veterans to America. Washington was taken, but an attack upon New Orleans failed, and peace was made at the end of the year.[2]

The longest of the English accounts of this war covers only about two pages. The typical English point of view is well expressed by Muir in these sentences:

This was the most futile and wasteful of wars. Its only result was to embitter the relations between the two main groups of English-speaking peoples. To most Englishmen at the time it seemed to be a stab in the back, delivered when Britain was fighting for her life and for the freedom of the world. To most Americans it appeared to be a war in defence of the freedom of traffic on the seas, against the naval tyranny of Britain.[3]

However casual and conciliatory the popular British histories may be in treating the War of 1812, the Canadian writers have not failed to rally to the imperial cause. Though most of the British histories are free from the traditional accusation that the United States was guilty of matricidal intentions at a time when the mother country's back was turned toward America, the Canadian historians emphasize the "stab-in-the-back" idea above all other causes of the war. Wallace writes as follows:

The War of 1812 had its ostensible origin in questions connected with the Napoleonic struggle in Europe. . . .

[2] *Groundwork of British History*, p. 554.
[3] *British History*, p. 505.

But it is by no means certain that the ostensible reasons for the war were the real reasons. The New England states, which were the most vitally affected by the actions of the British navy, were on the whole opposed to war; and the chief demand for war came from the southern and western states, where a strong and very vocal party, known as the *war hawks*, thought that the time was opportune to invade and occupy Canada.[4]

Bingay of Canada summarizes the war in this way:

In 1812, seizing the opportunity of the Napoleonic War, the United States declared war against Great Britain, with the object of taking Canada, which was again invaded unsuccessfully, English and French uniting to repel the aggressor.[5]

In the American version of causes of the war the stab-in-the-back theory is missing and is replaced by a third cause that is entirely ignored by British historians. The American Muzzey, for example, adduces evidence of his countrymen's suspicions of British propaganda among the Indians in the Northwest:

Harrison strengthened the belief of the West that British officials had been inciting the Indians on our frontier ever since St. Clair's defeat of twenty years before, by reporting the capture of new guns and "ample supplies of the best British glazed powder" at Tippecanoe, evidently obtained from the king's stores at Malden.[6]

And Latané writes:

Another grievance against Great Britain arose out of the aid and encouragement given by the Canadian authorities to the Indians of the Northwest. . . . The Indians (those whom Harrison fought) had secured

[4] *History of the Canadian People*, pp. 142–143.
[5] *History of Canada*, p. viii.
[6] *History of the American People*, p. 242.

their arms and ammunition in Canada and it was generally believed that the British authorities had incited
them to acts of hostility.[7]

And the Beards' account is:

> On land no less than on sea, the British were belliger-
> ent toward the United States. They protected the Indian
> chief Tecumseh, who was terrifying the frontier by his
> forays on white settlements. . . . British support of the
> Indians was not only provoking; it was a serious matter
> for the Americans.[8]

This "serious matter" is brushed aside by McArthur of
Canada:

> Some Americans charged the Canadians with actively
> encouraging the Indians to wage war on the white set-
> tlers. It is not necessary to believe such charges to
> understand the hostility of the American frontiersman
> to the Canadian traders. The Canadians made the In-
> dians dangerous. The West could be made secure for
> settlement only by ousting the Canadian traders, and the
> most effective means of accomplishing this end was the
> conquest of Canada. Thus thought many Americans
> who knew western conditions in the Spring of 1812.

> There were other reasons for contemplating the seiz-
> ure of Canada. The people in the Ohio valley who
> needed good agricultural lands were beginning to turn
> to Upper Canada, described by many of the American
> settlers who had already gone there as possessing an
> abundance of excellent timber, numerous waterfalls,
> fertile lands, and a pleasant climate. The vision of
> Canada as a part of the United States was attractive;
> the course of settlement could then be diverted north-
> ward to lands which were more desirable than those of
> the far West, and the St. Lawrence, controlled by the
> Republic, would bring the western farmer nearer to the

[7] J. H. Latané, *History of the American People* (1930), p. 271.

[8] *Making of American Civilization*, p. 230. This and other passages from
this book are quoted by permission of The Macmillan Company, publishers.

markets both of the Atlantic seaboard and of the Old World.

The prospect of enlarging the territory of the United States appealed to many senators and congressmen of the Republic. For some time, there had been a demand in the Southern States for the annexation of Florida, but such an acquisition of territory would have disturbed the balance of political power between the North and the South. In 1812, however, the Southerners seized the opportunity of gaining Northern support for the acquisition of Florida by advocating the conquest of Canada. The South, therefore, was prepared to encourage the designs of the North against Canada in return for Northern aid in securing Florida. The policy of conquering Canada, therefore, found vigorous support in the representatives of the North-western, Western, and Southern States, while the Atlantic States were opposed to war.[9]

Although some of the American textbooks make it clear that Clay and the War Hawks used the prospect of the annexation of Canada to lure the northwestern states into immediate action, the impression is given that America's grievances against England justified a martial move on the part of the United States.

> The impressment question [says Latané] was the main cause of the popular feeling against England, and that alone was enough to justify war.[10]

The most striking difference between the Canadian and American versions of hostilities lies in the relative amount of space that is given to land and water fighting. From reading the American textbooks one gets the impression that the War of 1812 was primarily a marine war. Most of the American texts devote no more than half of their

[9] Duncan McArthur, *History of Canada for High Schools* (1931), pp. 181–182.

[10] *History of the American People*, p. 272.

topics to the activities of the army, and a large part of this space is given to Jackson's victory at New Orleans and the British raid on Washington.

In the Canadian histories, however, emphasis is thrown on the heroic military defense of Canada. Wallace has devoted five topics to land campaigns, one to the sea and lakes. In McArthur's book the ratio is thirteen to two; in Bingay's, eleven paragraphs to two; in Burt's, four to none.

The reason for this difference is transparent: the Canadian writers find the best food for national aplomb in the military exploits of their ancestors; the Americans, in the naval events. For example, three of the four Canadian histories give several lines to the battle of Chateaugay, and none of the American histories covered by this study so much as mentions this battle. Needless to say, the battle was a Canadian victory, against odds. McArthur's story of it is:

> After an initial reverse, the Americans were thrown into great confusion and finally retreated. The Canadians had defeated an army ten times the size of their own with losses of only two killed, sixteen wounded, and four missing.[11]

Bingay writes that

> four hundred and sixty French-Canadians defeated an army seven thousand five hundred strong.[12]

Wallace has fallen short of McArthur's heights of "patriotism" by stating mildly that

> The Americans outnumbered the Canadians by more than three to one.[13]

[11] McArthur, *History of Canada for High Schools*, p. 193.
[12] Bingay, *History of Canada for High Schools*, p. 220.
[13] *History of the Canadian People*, p. 149.

Canadian historians wax more eloquent over the battle of Queenston Heights, where, writes Bingay:

> Thirteen hundred of the enemy attacked the little British force of three hundred. The resulting battle was one of the most desperate of the war. Victory at last swung to the British side, — a result only possible because of the refusal of the bulk of the enemy's militia to cross the river and fight.[14]

But the Canadians have observed a decorous silence over a certain naval battle on Lake Champlain. There is no niche for Macdonough in the Canadian Valhalla. The most glowing account of his exploits to appear in a Canadian history is the following in McArthur's text:

> Urged by Prevost, Captain Downie attacked the *superior* American naval force [that of Macdonough] and gave his life in the unsuccessful encounter. [Italics inserted.] [15]

Yet American histories place Macdonough upon a pedestal.[16] Barker, Dodd, and Commager differ from the Canadian version in writing that

> the invasion of the northern army was stopped by Captain Thomas Macdonough's victory over a *superior* [*sic!*] British fleet on Lake Champlain.[17] [Italics inserted.]

Adams and VanNest characterize Macdonough's fleet as "much weaker than Prevost's." [18]

Canadian historians have skipped quickly over the naval battles on the Great Lakes. In McArthur's text we read of

[14] Bingay, *History of Canada for High Schools*, p. 216.
[15] McArthur, *History of Canada for High Schools*, p. 194.
[16] *History of the American People*, p. 250.
[17] E. C. Barker, W. E. Dodd, and H. S. Commager, *Our Nation's Development* (1934), p. 175.
[18] *Record of America*, p. 205.

the advantage of the American ships *in both numbers and size*; and later, in the same text:

> The American naval squadron, under the command of Captain Perry, included nine vessels of superior armament.[19]

British historians, also, in their brief surveys of the events of the war are inclined to glide over the naval activities on the Great Lakes. Some of them, however, explain their country's reverses on the Atlantic more fully. Warner and Marten, in the passage quoted above on page 24, point out that the British frigates were *lighter-armed*.

But the American Guitteau relegates these historians to the ranks of the journalists by asserting:

> In vain the London papers tried to explain away these defeats by saying that the American vessels carried more men and threw heavier broadsides. The fact was that our gunners were better marksmen than their adversaries, partly owing to the fact that the British government limited the number of shot that could be "wasted" in mere practice.[20]

Several of the American writers find glory for their countrymen in the saga of the *Constitution* and her sister scourges of the Atlantic. Wertenbaker and Smith point out that

> the navy, although led by able captains and manned by crews unsurpassed for seamanship and gunnery, was dwarfed by the mighty British fleet.[21]

After pointing out in two lines that "Except for New Orleans . . . American warfare on land was unsuccessful," Faulkner and Kepner give thirteen lines to praise of our Navy's accomplishments:

[19] *History of Canada for High Schools*, p. 192.
[20] *History of the United States*, p. 244.
[21] *United States*, p. 229.

. . . to the glory of American naval history, the little American navy of sixteen ships repeatedly rebuffed the mistress of the seas with her thousand ships. In a series of sea duels the heroic deeds of Perry and Macdonough on the Lakes were repeated as the self-reliant Yankee seamen, expert in gunnery and with vessels of superior speed, brought renown to America and humiliation to Britain. . . . The daring recklessness of the *Constitution* ("Old Ironsides"), the *President*, and the *Argus* especially stirred American pride.

But these events have been mentioned, apparently, for their effect upon the emotions of the readers rather than because of their bearing upon the outcome of the war; for the authors go on to say

. . . but in the end the war at sea was not determined by naval duels or by the unparalleled success of American privateers

and then explain briefly in four lines that the British navy finally succeeded in destroying or blockading the American boats.[22]

Better marksmen, better sailors, better fighters? Or was it greater gun power that gave victories to America? Apparently the answer depends upon the nationality of the historian. In any event, the argument seems as aimless as that of two boys boasting of whose father can fight better.

Most of the American and English books give a fair account of the major atrocities of the war by stating that the British burned the government buildings in Washington in reprisal for the burning of York (now Toronto) by the Americans. Four of the American books, however, relate the Washington burnings without mention of American incendiarism in Canada. In the following passage

[22] H. U. Faulkner and T. Kepner, *America: Its History and People* (1934), pp. 191–192.

Muzzey makes the British appear as a rather ruthless band of marauders:

> With their control of the sea, the British not only blocked our commerce but landed parties at will to burn towns and pillage farms along the coast. . . . As a climax to their marauding expeditions, Major-General Ross, with four thousand men, landed on the banks of the Potomac and marched on the undefended city of Washington . . . the British set fire to the Capitol, the White House, and several other public buildings.[23]

Guitteau probes this episode even more deeply, writing:

> The British claimed that this action [the burning of the Washington buildings] was justified in retaliation for the burning of York by the Americans in the preceding year.

And in a footnote:

> However, the burning of the Parliament House at York was the work of individual soldiers, and was not ordered or sanctioned by their superiors. The burning of the public buildings at Washington was done by order of the British commander, and is now admitted by British historians to have been an act of vandalism.[24]

Possibly true; but only one of the more popular English secondary-school textbooks makes this admission.[25]

The battle of New Orleans, fought after peace was concluded, is chronicled with a good deal of drumbeating in some of the American books and mentioned only briefly, if at all, in the foreign books. Wertenbaker and Smith give a description that seems needlessly bloodthirsty:

> The English guns opened with a terrific din, but the Americans replied with an intensity and precision that

[23] *History of the American People*, p. 248.
[24] *History of the United States*, p. 246.
[25] Muir, *British History*, p. 504.

amazed General Pakenham. By noon all the British
batteries had been silenced, and most of the gunners
killed or driven away. Despite this failure Pakenham
decided to storm Jackson's position. On the morning of
January 8, 1815, the long columns of redcoats advanced,
with flags flying, and bayonets glistening. A deadly fire
greeted them, Jackson's frontiersmen picking out their
men and taking careful aim. The red lines staggered
and fell back. Pakenham himself was killed, while
stretched out on the sugar fields lay 2,000 men, among
them 85 officers. The American loss was 71.[26]

*   *   *   *   *

The War of 1812 bequeathed unfortunate traditions to
both the United States and Canada; and these have been
nourished by such textbook summaries as Faulkner and
Kepner's statement that "America . . . taught the British
to treat us with respect." (This is followed by this quotation from Professor Morison: 'Confident in their power to
lick all creation, the Americans turned their backs on
Europe and faced West.')[27]

The contribution which the war made to jingoistic tra-
dition is one of the more deplorable results of this unnecessary conflict. This is pointed out in the following
quotation from Trevelyan's single paragraph on the war:

> The next generation of Englishmen forgot the Ameri-
> can War as an unpleasant and unnecessary episode in the
> greater Napoleonic struggle; but Americans remem-
> bered it only too well, as a patriotic landmark in their
> early growth as a nation. From the point of view of
> future Anglo-American relations it was most unfortu-
> nate that the first foreign war of the young Republic
> should have been waged with the motherland, against
> whom also her War of Independence had been fought.[28]

[26] *United States*, p. 235.
[27] *America*, p. 192.   *17341*
[28] *History of England*, p. 582.

The United States, however, was not the only participant to derive nationalistic ardor from the War of 1812. By admission of the Canadian historians themselves, Canadian super-patriotism has depended largely upon the battles of this war for nourishment. Wallace writes, for example:

> . . . the war itself, with its many episodes of gallantry and heroism illustrating the determination of Canadians to be free, has exerted a powerful influence on feeling and opinion in Canada since that time.[29]

After describing those details that can give the most satisfaction to Canadian "feeling and opinion," Wallace concludes his discussion of the war with a panegyric that should convince the average student that the roots of his country are dependent for life upon the glory of battle:

> Neither the British nor the American people have looked back with much pride on the War of 1812. . . . Only in Canada has the war been a source of pride. The Canadians, with the aid of the British regulars stationed in Canada, showed on many stricken fields of battle their ability to defend their own country against overwhelming odds. Wars waged against a foreign invader against such odds — wars such as the War of Scottish Independence or the Italian War of Liberation — have frequently given birth to a strong national feeling; and this the War of 1812 — which might not improperly be called the Canadian War of Independence — did in Canada . . . it gave Canadians memories which are invoked to this day.[30]

Bingay points out that Canada derived material advantages from the war, as well as moral benefits:

> "Out of the eater comes forth meat," and the devouring United States furnished food for its intended victim. Never were times so good in Halifax.[31]

[29] *History of the Canadian People*, pp. 143–144.
[30] *History of the Canadian People*, pp. 151–152.
[31] *History of Canada for High Schools*, p. 221.

There, on the walls of history opposite the traditional American picture that is described at the beginning of this chapter, hang contrasting reproductions of the same subject.

The panel on which the English historians have engraved their versions of the war seems strangely empty. A few words, phrased with the finality of an epitaph, record the skirmishes off on the western flank which America has chosen to dignify by the name of the War of 1812.

Canadian historians, however, have painted a more lurid picture of the war to serve as a crest of honor for their citizens. In this picture, of which a seascape occupies only a tiny corner, a land-hungry United States is met and defeated by inferior numbers of Canadians, to the everlasting glory of the Dominion of Canada.

CHAPTER III

TEXAS AND MEXICO

ONCE upon a time, when Mexico owned the vast region that is now known as the State of Texas, intrepid pioneers from the United States settled there with their families and all their worldly goods. Mexico encouraged this migration, granting land to the settlers and promising political freedom. But it was not long before these bold Americans felt their inbred love of liberty stifled by Mexican rule. When in 1835 the dictator Santa Anna reduced Texas to the status of a mere province and robbed her people of their local political rights, the Texans rose in righteous wrath and declared themselves independent. War followed. At first fortune went against the Texans, despite their heroism and the noble leadership of such beloved characters as Sam Houston, Bowie, Crockett, and the wily "Deaf" Smith. At Goliad and again at the Alamo, hopelessly outnumbered, they were trapped and shot down ruthlessly. But at San Jacinto, maddened by the cry "Remember the Alamo," a band of Texans routed a large Mexican army at the point of the bowie knife. The Mexican losses exceeded the number of the whole Texan army, and many a fugitive fell on his knees with the wail of "Me no Alamo!" Its independence soon recognized by the United States, Texas was known until 1845 as the "Lone Star Republic."

Meanwhile, the people of the United States watched the exploits of their blood-kin with fatherly concern and pride until in 1845, at the urgent request of the Texans themselves, they decided to admit Texas to the Union. Strangely enough, Mexico took offense at this move and ordered her minister to leave Washington. When President Polk sent

General Taylor with an army to protect the boundary that Texas had established at the Rio Grande, Mexico attacked them, killing several men. War was made inevitable by the act of Mexico in shedding American blood on American soil; and Congress made a declaration of war in 1846.

At no time was the outcome of the war in doubt. Shouting "Ho for the halls of Montezuma!" two American armies pierced to the heart of Mexico, one under Taylor defeating Santa Anna's huge force at Buena Vista, and the other following General Scott in an assault on Mexico City. The march from the coast to the Mexican capital was a bold stroke, brilliantly executed. Even rugged mountain trails, bristling fortifications, and ambushes failed to check the gallant little band of Americans. At a pass called Cerro Gordo the Mexican defenders were routed so badly that Santa Anna had to hop away, leaving his wooden leg behind. In Mexico City Santa Anna gathered a tremendous force about him and strengthened the defenses of the city while holding off General Scott with talk of peace; but all his treachery and forts availed little against the resourceful and determined onslaught of the American troops. Scaling the heights of Chapultepec under heavy fire, the Americans with the aid of ladders climbed into the castle before its defenders could blow it up. The capital itself was at the mercy of General Scott.

Mexico was conquered, her territory overrun, her armies helpless, her government broken. She lay prostrate before the United States. Though many Americans wanted to annex Mexico, President Polk stood against this, saying that he had been "falsely charged with a war for the conquest of Mexico." Though the war had cost about $100,-000,000 and many lives, the United States asked only the territory north of the Rio Grande and paid $15,000,000 to Mexico.

This is the story of the Texan and Mexican wars that has lingered in the memories of the present older generation of citizens of the United States.

The Texan Revolt

To see the causes of the Texan Revolt from the Mexican point of view, one may well read volume three of *Historia de México*, by Alfonso Toro, one of the most widely used of the Mexican histories for the secondary school. Toro presents the theme of his song in these paragraphs:

In discussing the Texan war — the root of almost all of our troubles with the United States — we have seen how the latter had been breathing intentions of territorial expansion at our expense ever since the days before we gained our independence [in 1821].

On April 1, 1812, the Spanish minister at Washington, Don Luis de Onís, wrote to the viceroy of New Spain: "Every day one can see the ambitious ideas of this republic unfolding more and more, and its hostile attitude toward Spain manifesting itself. Already your excellency has been apprised by my correspondence that this government has set its mind on nothing less than establishing its boundary at the mouth of the Rio Grande, following the river's course to the 31st parallel of latitude, and thence drawing a line straight across to the Pacific Ocean, — thus seizing the provinces of Texas, Nuevo Santander, Coahuila, New Mexico, and part of the provinces of Nueva Vizcaya and Sonora. These designs will seem to every sane person to be a dream; but it is none the less certain that the scheme exists and that a map of these provinces has been sketched by express order of the government. The map also includes the island of Cuba within the above-mentioned boundaries as a natural possession of this republic."

The territorial expansion of the United States, foreseen by the Count of Aranda or by whoever was responsible for the memorandum found among his papers, had been effected with amazing speed and dexterity since the establishment of the independence of the United States. They had acquired Louisiana by paying Napoleon $15,-000,000 in 1803; Oregon by means of exploration and invasions, and Florida by purchase from Spain in 1819, at $5,000,000; but their insatiable thirst for territory was not satisfied, and the fight for political supremacy between the pro-slavery and anti-slavery factions eventually resulted in the independence of Texas.

This was but the first step. The real aim was the addition of the seething republic of Texas to the United States, an event which was the subject of diplomatic disputes between us and that country in 1844.[1]

Pérez Verdía's *Historia de México* also tells of the relation of the United States to the Texan revolt:

That revolt would not have occurred if the colonists had relied only on their own scant resources; but they were strengthened by the determined support of the United States, which supplied them armament, munitions, and a band of adventurers who took the name of "volunteers." . . . The colonists, united with the volunteers, fell back to the frontier of the United States, whence they received money, munitions, arms, and even soldiers who spoke of themselves as "deserters" from the American army.[2]

Toro further develops the theme of the land hunger of the United States; and, while sympathizing with the Texans in their desire for liberty, he places the blame for hostilities upon the plotting of American imperialists:

Since a time before Mexico became independent, the United States was desirous of extending its territory at the expense of that of New Spain, to the Rio Grande. They alleged so-called rights, invaded the territory often, and gave rise to frequent claims that never were

[1] Alfonso Toro, *Compendio de Historia de México* (1926), III, 390–391.
[2] Luis Pérez Verdía, *Compendio de la Historia de México* (1935), pp. 413–414.

adequately satisfied. All this is proved by the correspondence of Don Luis de Onís, the Spanish ambassador to Washington, and by the proposals made by Secretary of State Monroe to the rebel Gutiérrez de Lara to the effect that the United States government would help the cause of Mexican independence provided that Mexico should be given a republican constitution and should be added to the United States. Later Minister Poinsett, by Jackson's order, proposed to the Mexican government that Texas be purchased for $5,000,000. . . . Perhaps in spite of all their just complaints against Mexican rule, the Texans would have clung to Mexico if it had not been for the political forces put in play in the neighboring country — the struggle for political predominance between the northern states and those of the South. The former were enemies of slavery, while the latter believed the maintenance of such an institution essential to their existence.

. . . The partisans of the South looked toward us to increase their territory, make new slave states out of it, and strengthen their domination; and they resolutely determined to acquire Texas, counting upon the aid of President Jackson, an unscrupulous man who, as a proprietor of slaves, was personally interested in the matter and resorted to every sort of means, even the most immoral, to accomplish his ends. . . .[3]

It is curious to note that, although the first Texas rebellion was the work of the Texan colonists themselves and had as its object the riddance of Mexican troops from the territory, in the subsequent uprising (after their grievances had been satisfied) the colonists took almost no part. This was carried on principally by filibusters sent from the United States. . . . The American filibusterers were the ones who took charge of the civil and military government of the territory.[4]

Wertenbaker and Smith, writing for the United States, tell only the first part of this story and do not describe the activities of the "filibusterers." Their interpretation is:

[3] Toro, *Historia*, pp. 344–346.   [4] Toro, *Historia*, pp. 349–351.

In the early days of the revolution Texas did not demand independence. An agent of Santa Anna "found the people still desirous of maintaining peace with Mexico, yet equally determined to resist with energy the entrance of troops into their country." They were incensed, also, at the overthrow of constitutional government by Mexico, and the "threatened encroachments of military despots." But the treachery of Santa Anna and the barbarities committed by his soldiers drove the province into secession.[5]

Faulkner and Kepner also ascribe the revolt of the Texans to local causes, writing:

It was hardly to be expected that these aggressive Anglo-Saxon frontiersmen could long dwell in peace under the control of a people representing a very different civilization, and under a weak and inefficient government continually changing as one revolution succeeded another.[6]

There is somewhat less ado about the fighting in the Texan revolt than about the causes of hostilities.

Everyone who has had a typical American education remembers the Alamo, for American historians have been in the habit of focusing their school textbook stories of the Texan War upon this epic instance of Texan gallantry and upon the sordid character of the Mexican commander-in-chief. Wertenbaker and Smith give a lurid picture of the battle of the Alamo in this passage:

Suddenly the Mexicans in overwhelming numbers fell on San Patricio and annihilated the garrison. A few days later the main army, perhaps 3,000 strong, closed in on San Antonio. The brave W. B. Travis led his men into an old Spanish mission called the Alamo, and awaited the assault. Here, in desperate hand-to-hand fighting, the last of the Texans were cut down. Not one of the defenders survived. "Thermopylae had its mes-

[5] *United States*, p. 315.   [6] *America*, p. 664.

senger of fate, the Alamo had none." A few days later
a band of four hundred Americans were surrounded at
Goliad, and, though they surrendered on condition that
they should be "treated as prisoners of war," were
slaughtered in cold blood. As the remaining groups of
Texans fell back, they vowed vengeance for the Alamo
and for Goliad.[7]

Muzzey pays his respects to Santa Anna in this way:

Santa Anna, the new Mexican president, a man of perfidious and cruel character, led an army in person to
punish the rebellious province. At the Alamo, a mission
building in San Antonio, he exterminated the garrison of
one hundred and sixty-six Texans, not even sparing the
sick in the hospital ward. A little further on, at Goliad,
the defenders were massacred in cold blood after their
surrender.[8]

Pérez Verdía finds it convenient not to mention the
slaughter at Goliad and passes rapidly over the Alamo
massacre in a short clause:

The seventh of March the Mexican army took the
Alamo after a bitter assault.[9]

Even more glorious (from the point of view of the United
States) and shameful (from the point of view of Mexico)
is the account of the Battle of San Jacinto in the book by
Wertenbaker and Smith. This reads:

. . . here, on April 21, 1836, was fought the deciding
battle of the war. It was late in the afternoon that the
Texans, suddenly leaving their camp, swept forward on
the run. The Mexicans were taken by surprise. Despite
the efforts of their officers, they were thrown into hopeless confusion. Now bowie-knife and musket-butt did
their work, amid screams of terror and the Texan cry of
"Remember the Alamo." Some of the Mexicans fell in

their camp, others perished in a nearby morass, others fled to the prairie only to be cut down by the cavalry. The Mexican army was annihilated. The president himself was overtaken the next morning crawling on all fours in the high grass. He was compelled to sign a treaty recognizing the independence of the province.[10]

Toro, writing for Mexico, matches this instance with a tale of victory against odds; but this time the Mexicans are the heroes (the Texans must have forgotten to sharpen their bowie knives before the fray):

> John Austin organized a band of colonists, and on the second of August, 1832, attacked the garrison at Nacogdoches. . . . About three hundred and fifty Mexicans had remained there; and they repulsed twice as many Texans.[11]

The Annexation of Texas by the United States

In their treatment of the annexation of Texas, which was an underlying, if not the immediate, cause of the Mexican War of 1846, the American books are inclined to regard this event as the consummation of the natural sympathy between the Texans and the citizens of the United States. Wertenbaker and Smith write:

> The people of the United States had watched the heroic struggle of the Texans with interest. To many it seemed a contest of liberal institutions against despotism, of Anglo-Saxons against Spaniards and Indians.[12]

Adams and VanNest remind us that the Texans "clamored for admission to the United States." [13] And Wirth gives this explanation:

> The war with Mexico has been described by earlier historians as a war of aggression on the part of the

---

[10] *United States*, pp. 315–316.
[11] *Historia*, p. 347.
[12] *United States*, p. 316.
[13] *Record of America*, p. 258.

United States for the purpose of acquiring territory for the extension of the institution of slavery. This view, however, in the light of recent investigations, does not seem to be the correct one, for our government tried to remain neutral during the Texas Revolution. Furthermore, since Texas had maintained her independence for nine years, and since she wished to come into the Union, we had a right to annex her without offense to Mexico.[14]

Although other American textbooks apply less whitewash than Wirth has spread over his country's record, they do differ at many points from this partisan Mexican account by Toro:

> After the battle of San Jacinto [marking the end of the Texan revolt], the United States government adopted an aggressive policy toward Mexico in order to compel her to declare war. General Gaines was directed to occupy Nacogdoches at the head of an army corps in 1836; and absurd claims were made for imaginary injuries to American citizens, with the designation of the brief space of two weeks for favorable settlement. The American minister threatened to ask for his passports and, in spite of the fact that the Mexican government replied within the time limit, Minister Ellis withdrew in a huff and President Jackson, in his message of February 6, 1837, called the attention of Congress to the necessity for using the land and sea forces against Mexico. These manoeuvres of the slavery men did not meet with a prompt response in Congress. The Mexican government understood clearly that they were working to involve us in a war in which our country would be defeated, and therefore acted prudently.[15]

Toro's "absurd claims for imaginary injuries to American citizens" take a very real size and shape in the American book by Barker, Dodd, and Commager, and attention is called to the fact that the Mexican government "on one

[14] *Development of America*, p. 317.
[15] *Historia*, p. 391.

pretext or another, evaded settlement," that "though
President Jackson made repeated efforts to bring Mexico
to settle the claims, it was useless," and that a court of
arbitration later "examined claims amounting to about
$6,649,000 and allowed the claimants $2,026,000." [16]

Toro goes on to say that, in spite of Mexico's conciliatory policy,

> Texas was annexed to the United States by treaty on
> the twelfth of April, 1844. The protests of our govern-
> ment were no obstacle, though the American congress
> did reject the treaty.[17]

Pérez Verdía writes that the treaty was rejected because
it was "so iniquitous," [18] whereas the American books
ascribe the rejection to the desire of northern abolitionists to avoid an increase in the number of slave states.

To Toro's statement that, after the treaty of annexation
had later been approved by Congress, "our minister at
Washington considered himself obliged to withdraw," [19]
Guitteau counters with this assertion:

> Texas had been recognized as an independent nation
> by the United States and by the leading nations of
> Europe. The independence of Texas was an accom-
> plished fact, and Mexico's claim to her former province
> had nothing to rest upon.[20]

Wertenbaker and Smith deliver this dictum upon the
cause of the annexation of Texas:

> In the end, it was the fear that if we failed to annex
> Texas, England would establish a protectorate over the
> country which finally forced us to take action.[21]

[16] *Our Nation's Development*, pp. 245–246.
[17] *Historia*, p. 392.
[18] *Compendio*, p. 426.
[19] *Historia*, p. 392.
[20] *History of the United States*, p. 348.
[21] *United States*, p. 329.

The Mexican War

Toro's interpretation of the immediate cause of hostilities between the United States and Mexico is:

Texas, supported by the American government, then pretended that its territory stretched to the Rio Grande, the truth being that the actual boundary of their territory never lay beyond the Nueces River. Here originated a serious quarrel. It was caused by the bad faith of the Americans who, while ordering troops to invade various places in our territory, worked with consummate treachery, pretending that Mexico was invading American possessions. Thus Mexico was made to appear the aggressor. What the United States really wanted was to stir up war — war in which the southern states of the Union were vitally interested in order that they might maintain their supremacy in the American government by acquiring new territory that could be converted into slave states. But since the majority of the people of the United States did not favor slavery and did not approve of a war of conquest, President Polk, foreseeing the opposition that he would meet among his own people, tried to give his first military moves the appearance of defensive measures. Afterward, when he had secured the declaration of war, he pretended to desire no more than the peaceful possession of the territory added; and when finally Mexico City was occupied, he gave his countrymen to understand that they could obtain no other indemnity for the bloodshed and costs of the war than a cession of territory. In this way they succeeded in attaining the objective pursued from the beginning.

The better to conceal its intentions and feign a desire for peace, the American government appointed Mr. John Slidell Minister Plenipotentiary to Mexico; but since diplomatic relations between the two countries had been severed already, the Mexican government refused to recognize him in any capacity but that of Envoy Extraordinary and declined to deal with him until the

American naval forces that had appeared in our ports should have been withdrawn. . . .[22]

Guitteau makes this comment on the Slidell mission:

> The new administration refused to give Slidell an audience. After this rebuff, President Polk concluded that Mexico was not willing to settle the dispute except by resort to arms.[23]

It goes almost without saying that the American books do not accuse Polk of insincerity in sending the Slidell mission, but Pérez Verdía joins his countryman Toro in questioning the good faith of the United States:

> The United States still pretended to want peace, and named Mr. John Slidell Minister Plenipotentiary to Mexico; but because there was no desire to receive him as such, but only as Envoy Special and Extraordinary, considering the break in diplomatic relations between the two countries, it came to be said that the Mexican government did not want peace.[24]

The overt act and the opening of hostilities are recounted thus in the Mexican books by Toro and Pérez Verdía:

> The United States government ordered General Taylor, encamped at Corpus Christi since 1845, to advance over the Rio Grande with his forces. In carrying out that order he arrived at the Frontón de Santa Isabel the 25th of March, 1846, and three days later encamped opposite Matamoras, where he built Fort Brown. . . .

> The president as well as the congress and press of the United States was proclaiming and pretending to believe that Mexico was the aggressor in the war; and so Taylor had orders to await the attack of the Mexicans. At the end of April our troops attacked and captured a detachment of dragoons. This trivial act led

[22] *Historia*, pp. 392–393.
[23] *History of the United States*, p. 349.
[24] *Compendio*, p. 426.

the Washington congress to declare the existence of a state of war between the United States and Mexico on May thirteenth, 1846.[25]

Still not content [with the annexation of Texas] the United States gave to the territory an extent which it never had had geographically or politically, making it contiguous to the Rio Grande so that when, in a manner entirely contrary to international law, the United States violated the Mexican frontiers by taking its army to the banks of the Rio Grande, it hypocritically feigned to believe that it was Mexico that was violating its own frontiers, in order that in this way the United States might convert itself from the aggressor that it was into the attacked party.[26]

The following account by Barker, Dodd, and Commager is typical of the view taken by some of the American histories in analyzing the causes of the war:

Texas really had no sound claim to the territory between the Nueces and the Rio Grande. . . . The troops of the United States, therefore, ought not to have occupied the area. . . . After all, however, it was not the dispute about this particular bit of land that caused the Mexican War. Mexico claimed all of Texas, and at the same time refused to negotiate a settlement of American damage claims. That was the issue.[27]

Some of the American books, however, do not even concede that their country was in the wrong in advancing to the Rio Grande. Muzzey, for example, writes:

When the news of Slidell's rejection reached Washington in January, Taylor was ordered to advance to the Rio Grande, which we insisted was the southern boundary of Texas. Taylor built a fort opposite Matamoras as a warning to the Mexicans not to cross the river.

[25] *Historia*, p. 396.
[26] *Compendio*, p. 426.
[27] *Our Nation's Development*, p. 249.

When he refused to withdraw to the Nueces River at the order of the Mexican commander, a Mexican detachment crossed the Rio Grande and captured a scouting party of Americans under Captain Thornton, killing or wounding sixteen of them. . . . On receiving the news of the attack on Captain Thornton, Polk sent a special message to Congress, declaring that war already existed "by the act of Mexico herself, in spite of all our efforts to prevent it." "After reiterated menaces," he said, "Mexico has passed the boundary of the United States . . . and shed American blood on American soil." [28]

And Wertenbaker and Smith make even a stronger case against Mexico:

. . . war sentiment in the United States was growing. Our relations with Mexico had long been strained. "The United States have borne more insult, abuse, insolence, and injury from Mexico, than one nation ever before endured from another," said the New Orleans *Commercial Bulletin*. . . . In April, 1846, the two armies were facing each other across the Rio Grande near Brownsville. On April 24, the Mexican cavalry crossed the river, ambushed a company of Americans, killing several men and capturing the rest. . . . Polk waited no longer. . . . The message was received with acclaim. Congress, by overwhelming majorities, voted 50,000 men and $10,000,000 for the war.[29]

Pérez Verdía derives a good deal of glory for his nation from the major battle of the war, that of Buena Vista. He writes:

. . . the enemy was obliged to fall back several times, so that at the end of the day they held only one of the central positions and their line of Buena Vista, distant about one league from that which they had occupied at first. At six in the afternoon the battle ended, only the

---

[28] *History of the American People*, p. 330.
[29] *United States*, p. 324.

cannonading continuing, and the Mexican army exhibited, as trophies of its victory, the abandoned positions of the enemy, as well as three cannon, three flags, four carts, a forge, and various prisoners. . . . Their troops, although fewer than the Mexicans (8,000 soldiers with twenty pieces of artillery) made up for our numerical superiority by the advantageous positions that they had chosen.[30]

Faulkner and Kepner contradict this flatly, stating that "Taylor defeated Santa Anna, whose force was four times his own." [31] In this and most of the other American books there is no reference to the "advantageous positions" which the Mexican historian ascribes to the American forces.

Pérez Verdía goes on to say:

If the commander-in-chief had ordered the first brigade of cavalry, made up of 1,400 men under the command of General Niñón, to attack the rear guard of the enemy, it would have sealed the victory; but unfortunately he did not do it, and the brigade confined itself stupidly to threatening Saltillo. . . . Night came and while Taylor, fearing that his defeat would be completed the next day, placed the archives in safety and called to his aid the small force that he had left in Saltillo, Santa Anna unnecessarily, without consulting one of his generals and cruelly abandoning his wounded, gave the order to retreat and shamefully left his positions, falling back on Agua Nueve. In this way the enemy remained master of the field, this sufficing for them to proclaim their victory; but, as Roa Barcena says, "If it is not possible to call the Mexican army the victor, there was no victor on the field of the Angostura." [32]

Muzzey is one of the enemy who still "proclaim their victory," for he writes:

[30] *Compendio*, p. 432.
[31] *America*, p. 668.
[32] *Compendio*, pp. 432–433.

After two days of furious battle the shattered army
left the field under the shadow of night. Buena Vista
was a glorious victory [*sic*!] in the face of tremendous
odds, against the largest army that American troops had
ever met.[33]

Out of other military exploits that have been retold in
glowing song and story in the American textbooks, the
Mexican historians take much of the glory. For example,
Pérez Verdía levels Scott's much-trumpeted march from
the sea to Mexico City to the flatness of a dress parade by
implying that some of his engagements with Santa Anna
were merely sham battles staged to "save face" for the
Mexican generalissimo. This author makes this revelation,
which is startling to one brought up on American histories:

By means of secret agents, Santa Anna made the
enemy secret and shameful proposals, finally asking
for money, which Scott ordered given to him; and although judicious historians assume that the communication with the enemy was intended to gain time and to
deceive rather than to commit treason, others, analyzing the combination of circumstances, find there the key
to great errors, to great obstinacy in constantly displaying our forces in detail, and to all or the greater part
of our defeats.[34]

Moreover, exploits that seem brilliant and amazing to
an American historian lose much of their glamor when,
before recounting the events of the war, Pérez Verdía
points out the handicaps under which his country went to
battle:

The condition of the country, one must say with sorrow, could not be worse to provide for its defense against
the foreigner: unstable governments; complete poverty;
an army demoralized and corrupt, without organization
or discipline and without a single capable leader; the

[33] *History of the American People*, p. 331.
[34] *Compendio*, p. 438.

political parties seething and implacable; the clergy selfish; and the people cold.[35]

Furthermore, in Toro one reads this description of the ragtag and bobtail against which our troops fought:

Although Mexico had an enormous war budget, she really lacked an army; for hardly worthy of the name was the assemblage of drafted men, badly armed, and without chiefs worthy of the name. The invading forces were of superior strength because of their armament, because of their artillery . . . because of the abundance of provisions and money, because of their discipline, because of their trained officers, and because of their recruiting.

Our troops were brave, but were drafted men, without confidence in their leaders; their armament was antiquated; the artillery was old, of short range, and badly equipped; the cavalry was almost useless, its manoeuvres hopelessly slow; there were no ambulances, provisions, hospitals, or transports belonging to the army itself. So in the battle of Molino del Rey the caissons had been dragged back to Mexico by the foremen merely to suit the convenience of the contractors.

The soldiers, who were almost never paid but were maltreated and exploited by their chiefs, deserted whenever they could and even rebelled with arms in their hands when they were ordered to march, as happened in the Texan war. . . .

There were places where the cavalry remained dismounted because they had nothing with which to buy fodder and where the troops were almost destitute, without uniforms or shelter. In San Juan de Ulúa, with the American squadron already in sight, Colonel Cano was obliged to sell five cannon to a foreign vessel in order to feed the garrison.

The little money on hand was hardly enough to placate the pretorian generals, who, it was feared, might revolt. . . . The sluggishness of our generals was manifest in lack of skill in choosing positions, and in negli-

[35] *Compendio*, pp. 427–428.

gence in safeguarding and defending the flanks during the American war. In almost all of the battles our army was on the defensive, which according to the strategists is the worst possible plan to follow. Our generals' strategy was simply to block the progress of the enemy, without ever taking care to organize the war on the ground that remained at the back and on the wings of the enemy. Our armies always marched with a large number of women and children who handicapped the manoeuvres and pillaged whatever they found in their way, leaving a trail of sick and dead men and animals, to whom no one paid any attention.

As one can well imagine, it was not that the soldiers lacked valor, but rather that they were not disposed to shed their blood for a condotiere or for an abstract principle that they did not understand. . . . In a country sunk to the level of demoralization of Mexico at that time, bravery is useless and even a hindrance.[36]

The Peace

Very little is written in the American books about the armistice that was called after Scott's occupation of Churubusco in the course of his march upon Mexico City. Pérez Verdía does not miss this opportunity to remind his readers of the causes of the war and of America's increasing land hunger:

During the armistice peace proposals were made according to which the States of Texas, New Mexico, and Upper California would be ceded as well as the right of transit across the Isthmus of Tehuantepec, in exchange for an indemnity. The Government declined these proposals because . . . , the nation being disposed to cede Texas, which was the cause of the war, the war ought to cease for lack of an object, since it would be wicked and unprecedented for a people to make war upon a neighbor because the neighbor did not wish to sell part of its territory. Yet this was to have a precedent.[37]

[36] *Historia*, pp. 434–437, 439, 442.   [37] *Compendio*, p. 440.

Finally, whether by virtue of its own prowess or through Mexico's helplessness, the United States was in a position to dictate the terms of peace. There is no difference of opinion among the historians upon that point. There is disagreement, however, about the way in which the United States used its advantage.

The Mexican books suggest that the terms of the treaty were far from generous, Toro calling the payment to Mexico "the wretched sum of $15,000,000," [38] and Pérez Verdía writing:

> In spite of its [the treaty's] burdensomeness and the injustice that it involved, resources and troops for keeping up resistance were completely lacking and it was even feared that the enemy would stir up a class war.[39]

Guitteau points out, on the other hand, how much more severe the terms of the treaty might have been, had it not been for the fairness of President Polk. He writes:

> The fact is that Polk withstood the popular clamor which demanded the whole of Mexico. All of the President's cabinet except the Attorney-General favored this course, but Polk steadfastly refused to consent to the extinction of Mexico's nationality.[40]

Latané agrees, writing:

> The unparalleled success of the American arms had led to a demand for the annexation of the whole of Mexico, but Polk adhered to his original purpose.[41]

And Faulkner and Kepner say:

> The completeness of the victory might have warranted additional demands, but Polk's restraint was the part of wisdom.[42]

[38] *Historia*, p. 446.
[39] *Compendio*, p. 444.
[40] *History of the United States*, p. 352.
[41] *History of the American People*, p. 349.
[42] *America*, p. 670.

In summarizing the results of the war, the Mexican historians do not fail to make it clear that America had to pay heavily in man power to conquer even such a disorganized country as they have shown Mexico to be. In this regard Toro says:

> In spite of the fact that the war with the United States caught us in a most disadvantageous condition because of our chronic civil disorders and party feuds, according to Spencer's *History of the United States* the American government was forced during the war to use 27,000 men from the regular army and 71,300 volunteers — in all about 99,000 men — of whom 40,000 withdrew or were sent to the hospital and four or five thousand deserted. The number of those lost through death, sickness, and other causes was not less than 25,000 men. Three thousand wagons, 200 cannon, as many boats, and $150,000,000 were required in addition. Notwithstanding the cost, the war with Mexico was a brilliant stroke skillfully executed by the United States; for the men and money expended upon the unjust annexation were more than repaid by the territorial expansion which made the growth of slave states possible and by the magnificent lands of Texas and California, with ports on both oceans and gold placers in the latter state at that time hardly discovered. That is why Henry Clay wrote to Channing: "There are crimes whose enormity surpasses the ultimate. The seizure of Texas by our countrymen has a right to this honor. Modern times do not offer an example of theft committed by mankind on such a grand scale." [43]

Pérez Verdía concludes:

> The historian Bancroft declared "that the government of the United States did not have justice on its side; such is the verdict of all civilized nations and this has been recognized even by American citizens themselves." [44]

[43] *Historia*, pp. 447–448.   [44] *Compendio*, p. 445.

Yet, whatever prominent American historians may have written on this subject for adults, the writers of secondary school textbooks do not condemn their country's action in this way. Most of those that give any consideration to the morality of the acts of the United States are inclined to take a safe position on the fence and to put such criticisms of their country as they do print in the mouths of those abolitionists and Whigs who opposed the war from the beginning.

Wertenbaker and Smith, however, venture to contradict their elders, Bancroft and Clay, in this passage:

> Certain American historians have condemned the Mexican war as a blot upon the honor of the United States. It was a war forced on Mexico by slaveholders, they say, with the intent of robbing her of California and New Mexico, so that those vast territories could be carved up into new slave states. But this contention does not square with the facts. It was Polk who tried to maintain peace, the Mexicans who insisted on war.[45]

*   *   *   *   *

Of the unpleasantness of 1914 along the Rio Grande not a word is written in the Mexican books, for their narratives do not come down to this date. Therefore no foil for the American accounts of this affair is available.

But the panoramas of the events of 1836–1848 that are spread out by the historians of the two countries are in sharp contrast. The ultra-American picture shows a faithless Mexico, ruled by a tyrant perfidious and cruel, a butcher of sick soldiers. After tolerating insults and acts of bad faith by the succession of Mexican presidents, and failing in sincere attempts to reach a peaceful settlement of all differences, the United States was forced to fight to protect her rights and property. After a series of splendid

[45] *United States*, pp. 328–329.

victories, the United States might well have seized the whole land of Mexico, but they were magnanimous enough to pay for a strip of desert and Indian territory.

On another screen Mexican historians have revealed a Nordic octopus gradually but inexorably wrapping its tentacles around the coveted southwestern territories, plotting cannily to absolve itself of the guilt of precipitating war, squeezing Mexico — crippled and disorganized — into impotency, and then stealing seaports and gold fields that were to contribute to the opulence of the overbearing United States of America.

CHAPTER IV

SPAIN IN THE AMERICAS

MANY a citizen of the United States looks southward with a vague sense of condescension. We seem to have an inbred notion that peoples who are below us in latitude are inferior also in virtue. We habitually look "down" morally as well as geographically when we survey the history of Spanish activities in the Caribbean region.

In reviewing the history of Spanish-America, the Yankee who has been steeped in the best Nordic traditions sees the Inquisition striking Mexico and Peru in the wake of the conquistadors, who ruthlessly carried off native treasure and set dogs upon the Indians just for the joy of seeing them torn to pieces. Moreover, the dastardly character of the Spaniard cropped out again as late as 1895, when General Weyler penned up the Cuban patriots in pest-ridden camps and thereby roused the righteous indignation of the United States. In the subsequent Spanish-American War, the Rough Riders and other spirited volunteer units proved their superiority to the Spanish minions both in wits and in intestinal fortitude.

The superpatriotic creed of Main Street states or insinuates this.

But the authors of Spanish histories that were in use just before the Civil War present quite another picture. Beginning wtih the conquest of the New World, for example, Moreno Espinosa's history of Spain offers a strong presentation of the ultra-Spanish view.

> While the famous regiments of Charles V triumphantly overran Europe, off in the New World Spanish sailors and soldiers were discovering and conquering

vast regions. Our country dedicated itself solely to the great task of Christianizing the trans-Atlantic world, sacrificing to this lofty historical end the ideals of political and religious liberty which the spirit of the times called for. To fulfill this civilizing mission, it was necessary to maintain the traditional monarchy and the Catholic Church as centers of power and guidance. Consequently the soldier who acclaimed the king and enlarged the fatherland was accompanied by the missionary who proclaimed his God and spread the Gospel. . . .

If we compared the scanty means of those explorers with the immense resources which Stanley, Braza, and the rest of the African explorers had at their disposal, we should see how illustrious our magnificent forebears appear. For they were inspired not so much by desire for gold as by a noble yearning for fame and by a generous aspiration to carry the Cross in triumph over all the world. A race of sublime Quixotes, consumed by a passion for the unknown and the great, which made of the sixteenth century a poem of action, eclipsing the most exalted figures of ancient history, Greece would have ranked them among her demigods. . . .

"As a military enterprise," said Prescott, "the conquest of Mexico is little short of miraculous, too unbelievable even for fiction, and without parallel in ancient history. For this reason that generation of heroes who triumphantly carried the Cross of Jerusalem to America will be revered as long as admiration and justice throb in the depths of the human conscience." [1]

But few American boys and girls read Prescott's scholarly works; and in their secondary school histories they often find other ideas mingled with some praise for the military genius of the Spanish conquistadors.

Guitteau, for example, writes:

[1] Alfonso Moreno Espinosa, *Compendio de Historia de España* [n.d.], pp. 339, 341, 343.

It was the lust for gold that led on the Spanish adventurers . . . ; it was the immense treasure from the
New World that became the foundation stone of the
great Spanish Empire of the sixteenth century. This
same golden stream undermined Spanish character and
industry. . . .[2]

Wirth points out that

the Inca, as the ruler of these Indians was known, was
taken prisoner and cruelly murdered, even though he
paid as ransom for his freedom a roomful of gold worth
about $15,000,000.[3]

Muzzey also throws doubt upon the "civilizing mission"
of Cortez and Pizarro. In summary of Spanish penetration
in the North, he writes:

For all their expenditure of money and lives, the
Spaniards, seventy years after Columbus's great voyage,
had not a single settlement in America north of the Gulf
of Mexico. . . . They did not colonize this region as
they did the West Indies, Mexico, and Central and
South America. The provinces, or vice-royalties, which
they set up in New Spain were governed quite despoti-
cally. All the trade was regulated by the "India House"
at Seville and forbidden to foreigners. The Roman
Catholic religion was the only one allowed. The native
Indians and imported Negroes were frightfully treated
under the lash of the slave-drivers. The land was in the
hands of a few wealthy proprietors. There were no
representative assemblies.[4]

Wertenbaker and Smith tell this ghastly tale:

Pizarro, in imitation of Cortes, laid hands on the Inca
Atahualpa, and held him as security for the good behavior of his people. In return for his freedom the Inca
promised to fill a large room with objects of gold to a
depth of nine feet. Almost immediately porters began

[2] *History of the United States*, p. 17.
[3] *Development of America*, p. 34.
[4] *History of the American People*, p. 41.

to come in bearing golden vases, goblets, and jars; miniature gold birds and beasts; golden leaves, flowers, heads, roots. Melted down, this mass yielded 1,326,539 *pesos de oro*, the equivalent of $15,500,000 in American money. Having secured this treasure, the Spaniards treacherously led their prisoner out to the plaza of Caxamarca and strangled him with a bowstring.[5]

A civilizing mission indeed! Were not the conquistadors scourges of the devil, rather than emissaries of the Christian God? Moreno Espinosa has an answer ready:

Accomplished during a century that was as brilliant and hard as the steel of Toledo, the conquest of America lost its adventurous aspect when the clamor of arms ceased. The man to use the most somber colors in painting the violence and excesses inherent in that kind of conquest is Father Las Casas, a priest of Seville.

Foreign authors have depended upon his testimony to loosen their tongues in insults against our country, without considering the fact that similar deeds were committed by the Portuguese in the conquest of the Indies, and by Englishmen, Frenchmen, and other European peoples in the American colonizations.

In the discovery and conquest of the New World, Spain showed herself as she was at the time, a nation with deplorable faults but also great virtues; and thanks to the latter, that continent came soon into the bosom of civilization. If there were crimes, "the crimes were of the times and not Spain's," as the poet said. To expect the discovery and conquest of America without war — and war without violence, ravages, and desolation — is the same as expecting parting without sorrow and life without death. Only the nation that has fought with tactics different from those practiced by Spain is privileged to throw the first stone at Spain.[6]

Rafael Ballester, in one of the more recent Spanish histories, describes Cortez as a man "valiant, long-suffering,

[5] *United States*, pp. 18–19.
[6] *Historia*, p. 350.

cultured, and diplomatic," [7] and narrates the story of his conquests at some length and without apology.

Pedro Aguado Bleye, in his short history of Spain, also tells the story of the exploits of the conquistadors in such a way as to give them their full luster. He emphasizes, too, the ability with which Cortez and Pizarro carried the White Man's Burden of their day.

> After the taking of Mexico, Cortez divided the land among the conquerors, and on the ruins of the Aztec city he began to build the Spanish city of Mexico, proclaiming its future greatness. He organized a city corporation, established markets, repaired the aqueduct of Chapultepec, which had been cut during the siege, laid down moral laws, thus beginning the government of the colony whose wealth he protected by wise measures.
>
> .　.　.　.　.　.　.　.　.　.　.　.　.　.
>
> Then Pizarro showed his admirable gifts as organizer and colonizer; he divided the land into districts, he organized the administration of justice and the working of the mines, . . . and in a short time, thanks to his energy and will, the church, town hall, palaces, and houses formed a beautiful city [Lima] which grew and prospered.[8]

Moreno Espinosa, also, gives much space to Spanish administration and culture in America, making it plain that the mother country poured precious life blood into the New World.

> In order to govern such distant colonies, the mother country laid down the wise Laws of the Indies, a code that gives us a claim to glory because of the noble humanitarian impulse by which it was inspired.
>
> Thanks to the Laws of the Indies, all Spanish-America was covered with universities and other centers of

---

[7] Rafael Ballester, *Curso de Historia de España* (1933), p. 256.

[8] Pedro Aguado Bleye, *Compendio de Historia de España* (1933), II, 115, 123–124.

learning which spread culture among all those peoples, stimulating in some — Mexico and Peru, for instance — a great flowering of literature.

While the colonial systems of other countries are concerned solely with material exploitation of the colonies, ours always was preoccupied especially with moral purposes. We strove to propagate learning in such a way that within a few years of its conquest all Spanish-America was covered with universities and other institutions of learning. In this respect no other colonizing has outdone Spain's; and perhaps this explains why, the culture of the natives having been raised so considerably, Spanish America was so soon able to free herself from our dominion and rule her own destiny. For this reason Señor Barrantes called our colonial system "generous and Christian, without doubt, but also suicidal." Therefore today, now that the old hates are dying out, all Americans of Latin blood are stretching their arms toward the mother country, proud to feel the noble blood of Spain coursing through their veins. . . .

The discovery of America is the most transcendent episode of secular history, since in a way it completed the work of God, making contacts between lands and peoples separated by force of geological cataclysms, and triumphantly carrying them the Gospel of Christ and the Word of Spain. The consequences of this great movement have influenced all peoples and all phases of life: astronomy increased its list of stars by those that shine in the sky of the southern hemisphere; geography doubled its domains with a new continent; medicine was enriched by quinine and other medicinal substances; and agriculture by the potato, coffee, sugar, tobacco, corn, sarsaparilla, cocoa, and other products that have vastly influenced our diet.[9]

The Spanish youth who reads this panegyric of Spanish colonization cannot but be angered by the preying proclivities which are imputed to the United States in the Spanish histories. Bleye, for instance, teaches him that

[9] Moreno Espinosa, *Historia,* pp. 350–351.

the hard-won conquests of his country in the New World
were threatened by the United States long before the War
of 1898. He writes:

> Spain, yielding to the pressure of the North American
> Minister Erving, ceded Florida to the United States [in
> 1819] whence as a matter of fact came constant aid for
> the rebels in the Spanish colonies.[10]
>
> There was danger of a war between Spain and the
> United States. Desiring to prevent it, France and Eng-
> land finally composed a plan of agreement and invited
> the United States to adhere to it. The contracting pow-
> ers were to refrain from taking possession of the island
> of Cuba and were to resist every attempt by any nation
> or individual that was directed toward this end. The
> President of the United States, Fillmore, refused to ac-
> cept the agreement.
>
> President Pierce of the United States, affiliated with
> "Young America," a group which preached territorial
> aggrandizement, alluded in his message to the necessity
> of acquiring Cuba [1853].
>
> The United States did not decide then upon their
> purpose of taking possession of Cuba by force, perhaps
> because they suspected that neither France nor England
> would view the aggression indifferently; but they took
> advantage of an incident, the detention and search of an
> American vessel, *El Dorado*, by the Spanish corvette
> *Ferrolana*, in waters which Spain considered to be under
> her jurisdiction and the United States considered open
> sea, to carry their demands to an extreme and propose
> again, as the only solution of the incident, the purchase
> of the island [December 9, 1856], a measure of which
> President Buchanan also spoke in his message [1858]
> and which Spain rejected with dignity.[11]

Moreno Espinosa states the case against North American imperialism even more strongly in these paragraphs:

> Florida was the only continental territory not to join
> in the emancipation movement [which resulted in the

---

[10] *Compendio de Historia*, II, 481.
[11] Bleye, *Compendio de Historia*, II, 533.

independence of most of Spain's American possessions early in the nineteenth century]; but Ferdinand VII finally ceded Florida to the United States in liquidation of a debt. The illustrious Count of Aranda, who is called with good reason "the first of our modern statesmen," in his famous secret memorandum to Charles III prophesied the annexation of Florida to the United States and the land-grabbing tendency which that republic was soon to show. He said of the United States: "There will come a day when it will grow and become a giant and even a dreadful Colossus in that region. Its first step, after it has succeeded in waxing great, will be to seize control of Florida in order to control the Gulf of Mexico."

The United States, whose proximity to the beautiful islands of Cuba and Porto Rico menaced Spanish dominion, began to sow the spirit of emancipation in Cuba, thus initiating the first insurrectionist movements, which were to result in the total loss of our Antilles.[12]

The American books have little to say about the acquisition of Florida, and less about the sending of aid to revolting Spanish colonists. On the other hand, Muzzey mentions an Indian in the woodpile that the Spanish writers have carefully concealed:

That power [Spain] had promised in the Pinckney Treaty of 1795, to prevent the Indians of Florida from marauding our borders, but had miserably failed to keep its word. Acting on instructions from Washington to pursue the Indians into Spanish territory if necessary, General Jackson swept across East Florida.[13]

In their analyses of the immediate causes of the Spanish-American War, the latest editions of the American histories are notably fairer than some of the older books. Most of them mention both the idealistic and the materialistic forces that were at work. Barker, Dodd, and Com-

---

[12] *Historia*, p. 482.
[13] *History of the American People*, p. 263.

mager, however, are inclined to emphasize the idealistic element, stating flatly that "American sympathy for Cuba, coupled with the mysterious destruction of the battleship Maine in Havana harbor, was the cause of the Spanish-American War." [14] Most of the books censure the cruelties of the Spanish régime, Adams and VanNest characterizing the government of Cuba by Spain as "inefficient, weak, and venal." [15]

In continuation of their treatment of the cession of Florida and the attempts of the United States to purchase Cuba during the nineteenth century, Bleye and Ballester give the impression that the United States was bent upon driving the Spanish from Cuba and persisted in this intention in spite of the fact that Spain offered every concession that a self-respecting and independent nation could give.

Bleye writes:

> The Spanish government published a decree [November 27] granting autonomy to Cuba and Porto Rico. But President McKinley answered this decree [December 6], in his message to Congress, by declaring that the United States was ready to intervene with force when it could undertake this action with assurance of the approval of the civilized world. In view of such statements, it was natural that the insurgents should not accept autonomy.[16]

And Ballester declares:

> The concession of autonomy to Cuba in December of 1897 and the relief of Weyler, did not appease the ardor of the interventionist party [in the United States], which was gaining in public opinion. . . . The American government intimated to the Spanish that if in a

[14] *Our Nation's Development*, p. 572.
[15] *Record of America*, p. 619.
[16] *Compendio de Historia*, II, 584–585.

short time a satisfactory agreement were not reached which would assure the pacification of the island, a *casus belli* would be presented to Congress. The Spanish government appealed to the European powers, offering to submit to the decision of an arbitral tribunal; but the United States insisted upon attributing to the Spanish government the responsibility for the explosion of the Maine and upon requiring immediate pacification, declaring at the same time the freedom of Cuba and armed intervention.[17]

Moreno Espinosa treats the causes of the war very briefly and places major emphasis upon the heroism of the Spanish fighting man in his defense of a lost cause:

. . . Unfortunately, the separatist war . . . broke out anew in Cuba, thanks to the support of the United States. . . . The United States, maintaining that Spain should at last recognize the independence of Cuba, brought on the conflict between our nation and that powerful republic. They carried the struggle not only to our Antilles but also to the Philippine archipelago, which was already in revolt against Spain. Some time previously a huge conspiracy had been brewing in the Philippine archipelago, of which the uprising of Cavite in 1872 was the first spark. This was promptly suppressed. But in 1897 a general movement broke out which would have been suppressed likewise if the United States, already at war with Spain over the Cuban question, had not sent a fleet to the Philippines also and destroyed our fleet at Cavite, obliging us to let the Philippine archipelago fall into the hands of the victor. The last platoon of Spanish soldiers to remain there was the Baler detachment, commanded by the glorious Captain Las Morenas, who died for the Cause along with two other officers and twelve soldiers. The heroes of this glorious epilogue of our Philippine dominion held out for more than a year, without receiving any aid. . . .

The United States destroyed our fleets in the waters

[17] *Curso de Historia*, p. 433.

of Manila and Santiago de Cuba. The battle of Cavite took place the second of May 1898, and that of Santiago de Cuba the third of July of the same year — both dates of sad memory, though not devoid of glory. Even though the North American fleets were far superior to ours in number and strength of ships, the Spanish sailors, who were unable to carry on the fighting to any advantage, proved themselves worthy successors to the glorious losers of Trafalgar and sacrificed their lives heroically as a holocaust for their country. As proof that the indomitable vigor of our race has not been extinguished, there should pass into history the names of Lazaga, Commander of the Oquenda, who, wrapping himself in a flag as a shroud, died on his ship because he was unwilling to abandon it; of midshipman Fajardo who, seeing that one arm had been completely lopped off by a shot, exclaimed coolly, "It doesn't matter; I still have another for my country"; of midshipman Saralequi, who was taken to the hospital with both legs shot to pieces and said to the chaplain who was administering the last rites, "Father, do you think that I have done my duty?"; of the artillery sergeant Zaragoza who, his stomach ripped open by grapeshot, asked for a piece of the flag to cover his mortal wound; and of many other heroes of those horrible tragedies.[18]

Could any pupil of impressionable age be unstirred by this outburst? Sedatives applied years later may not subdue his rancor against the enemy that made his forebears die so desperately.

Ballester gives little space to the war's events, but does emphasize the inferiority of the Spanish fleets and the inevitability of their fate:

> Admiral Cervera, notwithstanding the inferiority of the Spanish fleet, engaged in combat and was destroyed. . . . In the Philippines a Spanish fleet composed of antiquated boats also could not help being destroyed in

[18] *Historia*, pp. 510–511.

a few hours by the Americans who, two months before the declaration of war, were already stationed in Hong-kong.[19]

Bleye's version is:

General Blanco ordered that the Spanish fleet leave Santiago. The order was carried out, and immediately our boats were destroyed by the American squadron, which was immensely superior.[20]

Another squadron of the United States, that of Commodore Dewey, left the port of Hongkong and entered Manila Bay, where there was a Spanish squadron, very inferior, in command of Montojo. The Spanish sailors fought worthily, but our ships were destroyed, and we sustained 356 casualties.[21]

American children usually are not told about the obvious inferiority of the Spanish armaments. They are not informed that the victories at Manila and Santiago were setups, bouts between heavyweights and featherweights. Muzzey points out that in the destruction of the Spanish fleet off Santiago,

only one man was killed and one seriously wounded on the American fleet, while $10,000 repaired all the damage done by the Spanish guns. But the enemy's fleet was completely destroyed, over five hundred men were killed, wounded, or drowned, and 1700 taken.[22]

Surely this ought to satisfy the most bloodthirsty American reader, particularly since it is presented as the outcome of a contest between fleets that, for all the reader knows, are presumably about equal in tonnage and speed.

Wertenbaker and Smith's account of Admiral Dewey's victory seems almost lurid enough to deserve a place in the blood-and-thunder histories of a generation ago:

[19] *Curso de Historia*, p. 434.
[20] *Compendio de Historia*, p. 586.
[21] *Compendio de Historia*, p. 585.
[22] *History of the American People*, p. 540.

At Hong-Kong was Commodore George Dewey, with a squadron of light cruisers. On April 27, he sailed for the Philippines, six hundred and twenty-eight miles away, with orders to attack the Spanish fleet there. Three days later, at nightfall, he moved boldly into Manila Bay, unmindful of the roar of the Spanish batteries and the explosions of hidden mines. The next morning he steamed past the arsenal of Cavite, where Admiral Montojo awaited the attack with seven vessels. As the gray American fighters approached, two more submarine mines hurled water high in the air just ahead of the flagship *Olympia*, and shells began to burst over them. On the cruisers men stood at their posts in the intense heat, stripped to the waist. Suddenly arose the cry: "Remember the *Maine*." An eight-inch gun in the forward turret of the *Olympia* roared forth. Then came the order, "Open all guns," and a shower of shells began to fall on the doomed Spanish cruisers. Five times the American fleet moved past Cavite, each time drawing closer, each time dealing greater havoc among the enemy. Some of the Spanish cruisers went up in flames, others sank, still others were beached. The red-and-yellow flag of Spain now was lowered from the staff over Cavite, and Dewey was master of Manila Bay. None of the American ships was injured, not a man was killed, and but seven wounded.[23]

Equally flamboyant is the account by these authors of the exploits of the Rough Riders:

. . . handicaps were offset by the gallantry of the soldiers. When once they set foot on Cuban soil, they went forward rapidly, through jungles, past tangled wire, over fortified posts, until they planted the Stars and Stripes on the hills above Santiago. The storming of the heights of San Juan and El Caney, in which the volunteer cavalry regiment known as the Rough Riders played an important part, will always remain a bright chapter in American military history.[24]

[23] *United States*, p. 489.
[24] *United States*, p. 492.

A simple statement of numbers from Bleye punctures and deflates this balloon of "patriotic" fancy:

> A division of 6,500 Americans attacked El Caney, defended by 419 soldiers of the regiment of the Constitution, who, led by General Vara de Rey, carried the defense to the extreme of heroism. Vara de Rey died, and the Americans took the position when no more than eighty defenders remained. The enemy also attacked San Juan hill, where Generals Linares and Bustamente were, and Colonel Ordóñez. They were wounded. The resistance likewise was brave; and the losses of the Americans, in one attack or another, very considerable.[25]

Here the Spanish reader may enjoy a little taste of blood!

*   *   *   *   *

If we are to believe the extreme statements of our secondary school histories, then, Spain is a nation whence came ruthless conquistadors; the roots of her empire were sunk in greed and indulgence and soon withered; stupid cruelty in Cuba pricked the moral sensibilities of the United States; and Spain's navy wilted under the superior sailing and gunnery of the American seamen.

But the Spanish histories suggest that these views cast undeserved shadows upon the fair scutcheon of the real Spain — mother of culture, of true religion, and of heroism.

[25] *Compendio de Historia*, II, 586.

CHAPTER V

THE UNITED STATES VERSUS GERMANY

LAST but not least — and freshest in the memories of those of us who were suckled upon it — is the anti-German legend.

After scheming for years to make himself the Napoleon of his era, and building a military machine for this purpose, Kaiser Wilhelm Hohenzollern rattled his saber so loudly in its scabbard that his neighbors could not but take offense. Some of them begged to differ with his egotistic assertion of the superiority of German *Kultur*. But Wilhelm believed that might made right. He forced Europe into war, and his Junkers proceeded with great abandon to kill children, violate women, gas soldiers, and sink neutral merchant ships. It must have been a grave disappointment to the Kaiser to learn that, in spite of all these plain manifestations of the benefits of *Kultur*, the United States was as unwilling as the Allied Powers to accept Junker rule as a dispensation from Providence. Even the most skillful of the Kaiser's envoys to the United States — such men as Von Papen and Bernstorff — through their spying and sabotage and their attempt to align Mexico and Japan against the United States, did not wholly succeed in winning the sympathy of the United States for the German cause. In fact, some good Americans were beginning to wonder whether the Junkers were not just a modern tribe of Huns.

We had at that time a mild and good-hearted President who believed that a soft answer turneth away wrath. He wrote a polite note of protest to the Kaiser. But as the actions of Germany strayed farther and farther from the protestations of friendship that she made in her replies, Wilson's notes became firmer, until finally Wilson and Congress lost patience with Germany and declared war.

It was *Democracy*, Wilson asserted, and not *Kultur*, for which the world was to be made safe. That was the magic word which was to take us to Utopia.

And so our gallant men went abroad — doughboys and devil-dogs — under the protection of our most efficient navy; and in a year and a half they had broken through the famous Hindenburg Line. So sudden and irresistible was their rush in the St. Mihiel salient that German cooks had to serve the American troops the very breakfasts they had cooked for their own men!

In the peace negotiations at Paris, President Wilson adhered as closely as mortal could to the principles for which we had fought; but the greed and secret machinations of the European diplomats made him give way on many points in order to preserve his most precious ideal — the establishment of a League of Nations through which he hoped that *Law*, instead of the *Might* that the Kaiser had championed, would come to rule the world.

*   *   *   *   *

During the World War and afterward, these new articles of faith were added to our patriotic creed. Vindictiveness toward Germany began to creep into the teaching of history, and government propaganda seeped into the writings of our historians. Germanophobia was implanted in our children, covering or obscuring the old Anglophobia. Has this new antagonism all the virility of the old, and will it also be a source of irritation for a century and a half?

The answer is not yet clear; but a clew to it can be found in the history textbooks that were in general use in secondary schools in 1936 — eighteen years after the Armistice. Since the height of the war fever, much heat has been eliminated from school histories in the United States. Since Hitler's rise to power in Germany, new supplements covering the post-war period have been written to replace corresponding sections in two of the standard German textbooks for the secondary school. (See the Bibliography, p. 92.) These supplements cast aspersions upon post-war democracy in Germany at every opportunity; but the Nazi scorn of democracy, interestingly enough, has not led the writers of the new supplements to add bitterness to the tart original accounts of America's part in the World War and Wilson's so-called "betrayal" of the German people in the interests of world democracy.

All in all, a study of the current histories gives evidence that enough embers of war feeling remain to flare up at the first fanning that may come.

The first issue over which American and German histories come to grips is the question of America's conduct as a neutral between 1914 and 1917. Wilmanns, contending for Germany, writes:

> President Wilson had from the beginning held fast to an equivocal neutrality. His inclinations were evidently towards the interests of the Entente. He obstinately and self-righteously belabored Germany, having no comprehension of the justifiable complaints concerning the attacks by England on the rights of neutrals. He had an inexhaustible patience and respect for England and its Allies, and gladly suffered American industry to wax fat out of armament and munition deliveries to the Entente. While he knocked the props out from under the neutral trade with Germany, he opposed submarine warfare and demanded for every American the right to go unmolested through war zones. Bethmann was unable to maintain any clear line of policy towards America. He assented to the submarine warfare, and

afterwards drew back in the face of Wilson's incivil notes.[1]

Ebner, also of Germany, writes:

> Through secret assistance from "neutral" America, . . . the Entente hoped to be able to destroy the German army.[2]

Guitteau the American, however, finds justification for his country's trade with England, stating that

> this theory [the German objection to America's trading with England] was not well founded, for the right of private individuals to sell arms to belligerents was well established under international law; and German firms, notably the Krupp works, had sold munitions during every war of modern times.[3]

American histories also point out that America would have willingly traded with Germany, had this been possible, and they cite America's protests against English interference with trade with Germany. In this connection, the Beards raise a point that German historians overlook, namely,

> She [Great Britain] alleged that the Germans were sowing mines in open waters. To offset this menace, she proclaimed the entire North Sea a military zone.[4]

Faulkner and Kepner remind American pupils that "England promised a fair settlement for legitimate losses," and these authors and others explain carefully why the German violations of our neutrality were more serious than those committed by the allied powers. Faulkner and Kepner write:

[1] E. Wilmanns, *Deutsche Geschichte vom Wiener Kongress bis 1918* (1935), p. 204.

[2] Ebner, *Geschichte der Neuzeit* (1936), p. 196.

[3] *History of the United States*, p. 607.

[4] *Making of American Civilization*, p. 787.

Serious as were England's infractions of neutral rights, they were concerned chiefly with property rights. German violations involved the loss of American lives and were the immediate cause of our entrance into the war.[5]

These ideas are conspicuously absent in the German books.

As a counterattack to the strictures of the German historians upon America's conduct as a neutral, American histories charge Germany with frequent violations of America's neutral status. Almost all of them censure Germany for the sinking of the *Lusitania* and other ships without warning, and for loosing death and destruction upon our industrial plants. Barker, Dodd, and Commager state their country's case clearly in these lines:

> The German submarine policy was the cause of the growth of war sentiment in the United States, but both German and Austrian agents were guilty of acts which also aroused the greatest indignation. They tried to enlist soldiers in the United States and get them out of the country on forged passports. . . . Germany wished the United States to forbid the exportation of arms and munitions to France and England because the British blockade prevented Germany from buying such supplies. Such trade, however, was legal, and the United States declined to forbid it. The German and Austrian agents were trying, therefore, to prevent illegally what they could not stop by legal methods. In doing so they violated both international law and the hospitality of the United States.[6]

Muzzey asserts that

> Emissaries [of Germany and Austria] placed bombs on board munition ships, blew up bridges, and fomented strikes in munition plants.[7]

[5] *America*, p. 706.
[6] *Our Nation's Development*, p. 504.
[7] *History of the American People*, p. 651.

Against these accusations the German books offer no defense except necessity, although Ebner does explain that Germany did yield for a time, to her sorrow:

> In order to avoid war with America, Germany almost completely stopped submarine warfare (April, 1916). Thus England had time to devise effective means of resistance to the U-boats.[8]

To the German assertion that they were forced to use submarines to deal adequately with neutral merchantmen who were carrying munitions and with belligerent merchantmen who masqueraded under a neutral flag, the American texts in their turn make no reply.

In the sounding of America's battle cry, there is more give and take, and sermons of moralizing are uttered on both sides.

In presenting America's reasons for entering the war, all of the American historians quote from the speeches of Wilson on the theme of "making the world safe for democracy." Faulkner and Kepner make it clear that America was justified in her declaration of war, when they write:

> . . . In September Germany pledged that "liners will not be sunk . . . without warning and without safety of the lives of non-combatants, provided that liners do not try to escape or offer resistance." This pledge she broke in March, 1916, when the passenger steamer *Sussex* was torpedoed, injuring several American citizens.[9]

The German historians fail to express appreciation of the spirit of forbearance that is attributed to Wilson in the American books. Wilmanns asserts:

> At the same time that Bethmann was dealing with Wilson, concerning a peace-mediation, the announce-

[8] *Geschichte der Neuzeit*, p. 198.
[9] *America*, p. 706.

ment of unrestricted submarine warfare was made (February 1917). Wilson, personally very offended, feared the consequences of the submarines and the preponderance of a victorious Germany. He declared war against her to hinder her in every way. *Then*, in fact, the decision of war went against Germany.[10]

Ebner makes only this matter-of-fact statement:

The renewed and intensified submarine warfare (February 1917) gave America the ostensible cause for a declaration of war against Germany (April 1917). The real causes were economic necessity: America was war-purveyor and creditor of the Entente.[11]

Schnabel writes:

Wilson was, without doubt, prejudiced against Germany. He was filled with the political theory and cultural views of western Europe and he was also bound by his solicitude for American business interests, which were heavily damaged by the U-boat warfare and which on the other hand wished very much to profit by the war by the delivery of war-supplies.[12]

And Suchenwirth:

Wilson, from the first in sympathy with the Entente, was led on to a declaration of war also by American industry and high finance, which were interested in an English victory.[13]

Moreover, the German writers do not confine themselves to attacks upon America's war platform. Some of them raise a battle cry for Germany. Ebner, for example, describes Germany's attitude at the beginning of the war as follows:

[10] *Deutsche Geschichte*, p. 204.
[11] *Geschichte der Neuzeit*, p. 203.
[12] Franz Schnabel, *Geschichte der Neuesten Zeit von der Französischen Revolution bis zur Gegenwart* (1936), p. 168.
[13] R. Suchenwirth, *Deutsche Geschichte* (1937), p. 550.

Germany fought for her very existence. Consciousness of this united the whole people, in those August
days, in defensive warfare. . . . Strong and firm was
the faith in the righteousness of this inevitable defensive
war; unbreakable the confidence in the power of the
army and in the ability of its leaders; trustworthy the
hope placed upon God and in the final victory.[14]

As long as they are reassured by such paeans, why
should a schoolboy of either nation so much as question
the righteousness of his country's cause?

*   *   *   *   *

And what of the actual fighting? Do the German historians echo Muzzey's account of "another month of steady
hammering against some of the best of the Kaiser's troops"
after "our army never faltered" in clearing the Argonne of
Germans when "the French officers had declared the forest
impenetrable?" [15] Or these passages from Guitteau:

The Germans did not gain any of their objectives,
but for long weeks [in the Spring of 1918] the Allied
armies were in deadly peril. This was because they were
outnumbered two to one, sometimes even three or four
to one, at the point of attack. . . .[16] On September 26
[in the Argonne Forest] American troops fought their
way through the barbed-wire entanglements and across
the shell craters of No Man's Land. Six of the nine
initial attacking divisions had never been in battle before, yet they soon captured the enemy's first line of
defenses. . . . Our soldiers had fought gallantly, and
had made possible the victory in the most stupendous
conflict of history.[17]

The Beards write that "American soldiers distinguished
themselves by dashing action." [18]

[14] *Geschichte der Neuzeit*, pp. 187–188.
[15] *History of the American People*, p. 684.
[16] *History of the United States*, p. 619.
[17] *History of the United States*, p. 622.
[18] *Making of American Civilization*, p. 801.

No, the German writers do not join in these panegyrics. They picture a German army paralyzed by utter exhaustion and overwhelmed by superior mass. Wilmanns writes, for instance:

> The last energy of the German army had been put into these attacks [in the spring and summer of 1918]. At the same time, however, America had finished her preparations. A new opponent stood opposite the exhausted German troops. The starving, completely exhausted German people could do nothing against this. . . .[19]

Chaos ruled in Germany and the army began to suffer from the phenomena of a waxing dissolution at home. Hindenburg and Ludendorff saw . . . that Germany "in spite of military successes would inevitably go to ruin" if inactive leadership at home did not maintain the "will to victory" in people and army. Bethmann hesitated. Ludendorff attacked the problem where the government showed weakness. To all the inner quarrels there was added a battle between the government and the supreme command. . . . Germany went leaderless on the current of events.[20]

Schnabel puts it more succinctly:

> The German army broke on the 8th August, 1918, a day which Ludendorff describes as the "black day of the Germany army." The causes were: "Political strife at home; above all else the dire economic exigencies [among the people and army]; and subtle English propaganda which was based fundamentally on bolshevistic principles. . . . Also the overwhelming superiority of the Entente in men, military supplies, guns, airplanes, etc.[21]

And Breiherr says:

[19] *Deutsche Geschichte*, pp. 198–199.
[20] *Deutsche Geschichte*, p. 204.
[21] *Geschichte der Neuesten Zeit*, p. 172.

For the first time [after the German defeat of August 8, 1918] bands appear which openly resort to mutiny and which call their comrades, sent to make them fight, "strikebreakers" and "war-prolongers." The Marxian poison had now reached the front-line troops. . . .

The enemy superiority in men and material had become ever more evident.[22]

Thus have the German historians conjured up Fate and the ogre of Communism to pluck away the laurel with which some American historians have crowned their "doughboys."

* * * * *

The Peace of Versailles is the subject of much bitterness in the German books.

Wilmanns explains that Germany attempted to end the war before 1918, an idea that does not appear in most of the American books:

In the year 1916, secret peace negotiations had been begun between Germany and Russia. These went to pieces in November when the Central Powers announced the restoration of Poland as a kingdom. Thereupon Germany and Austria made a public declaration to all combatants of their readiness to make a just peace. They were rewarded with scorn and contempt on the part of the Entente, who saw in the offer an indication of weakness and answered it with unmeasured demands. Peace was unattainable.[23]

Except for listing the terms and stating that the Peace was based in general on Wilson's Fourteen Points, the American textbooks give little space to the Treaty of Versailles. Guitteau and Faulkner and Kepner, however,

[22] Max Breiherr, *Die Neueste Zeit von 1789 bis zur Gegenwart für obere Klassen* (1935), pp. 356, 357.
[23] *Deutsche Geschichte*, p. 204.

elevate the peace negotiations into high morality by writing, respectively, that

> the President fought hard for his principles and sometimes prevailed [24]

and

> Wilson fought desperately during the weeks of negotiation to save his Fourteen Points, and in particular the League of Nations. Under terrific pressure, he was time and again forced to give way until the Fourteen Points all but disappeared.[25]

The Beards point out that Germany probably would not have been allowed to join the League of Nations had it not been for Wilson's efforts at the Peace Conference:

> It was mainly for the purpose of carrying out this pledge [to make the constitution of the League a part of the peace settlement] that Wilson went to Paris in person. . . . With the idea of banishing war hatreds Wilson insisted that all nations should finally be included in the League — the former enemy countries by a two-thirds vote of the League Assembly.[26]

But German histories acknowledge no debt to Wilson or to the League of Nations. In fact they have a great deal to say about the Treaty of Versailles that is highly uncomplimentary to the United States and its president.

Ebner goes so far as to characterize Wilson's Fourteen Points as a means of betrayal of the German people. In this passage he shows that Wilson raised German hopes:

> . . . President Wilson asked for a statement of Germany's war aims. He thereby threw an apple of discord amidst the German people and awakened hopes of peace in them. . . . Many, many persons in Germany, driven

[24] *History of the United States*, p. 629.
[25] *America*, p. 724.
[26] *Making of American Civilization*, pp. 805–806.

by an understandable longing for peace, would have been only too happy with a "renunciatory peace" based on the so-called Wilsonian Fourteen Points. . . .[27]

And here Ebner divulges the betrayal at Versailles:

The more important councils were conducted by the representatives of the Great Powers: Germany was completely shut out of the deliberations. The result was a dictated peace [DIKTAT] which completely ignored Wilson's Fourteen Points, through which the German people had been betrayed. The allies demanded, Germany had to accept. In case of refusal there was the threat of a march into and garrisoning of Germany.[28]

Suchenwirth writes:

Here [in Wilson's message on Congress] appear for the first time the Fourteen Points, in which, to the misfortune of our people from now on, the majority of the German Reichstag believed as if in a Gospel. . . .

Viewed more closely, the Fourteen Points already contain the germ of the Versailles treaty of force. . . . In spite of this, the statesmen and politicians of the Central Powers had given another meaning to Wilson's words than they held. So the German people steered toward capitulation because of the hypocritical enemy. Count Hertling assented, but already President Wilson kept his views to himself and "followed suit," so to speak. He declared that Germany had shown in Brest-Litovsk that it was striving for world domination. So he immediately cut off the discussions, calling Germany a danger to the world.[29]

Breiherr finds Wilson not dishonest, but somewhat prejudiced (as Wilson might find Breiherr, were he now alive to confront him):

He [Wilson] proceeds particularly from the thought of the self-determination of nations. One may allow him

[27] *Geschichte der Neuzeit*, p. 204.
[28] *Geschichte der Neuzeit*, p. 207.
[29] *Deutsche Geschichte*, pp. 561, 562.

an inner honesty but there is no doubt that he was out-
wardly one-sided, caught in the assumption of western
national history-writing, which treats problems from the
angle of vision of their own country.[30]

Typical of the severe condemnation of the Treaty of
Versailles which still infects the German books are these
passages. The first is from Edelmann:

They [the Big Four] were in a position to give a
genuine peace to a humanity which, at the conclusion
of four years of a frightful conflict, had in truth de-
served it. But the Conference failed to achieve the goal
in every respect. The whole world today is paying for
the fact that not righteousness and tolerance but rather
hatred, selfishness, and incapacity prevailed there.
When the discussions began it became apparent that
the Fourteen Points were to serve as guiding lines in a
peculiar way. No really well-thought-out plan lay behind them. The American representatives who came to
bring peace to the world according to their own assumptions, were wholly helpless in the face of the actual
demands made. . . .
The first of the Fourteen Points, the demand for the
relinquishment of secret diplomacy, was first destroyed.
Dozens of secret commissions were created in which the
future of Europe and the world was discussed. The work
of these commissions, and the subsequent decisions of
the Big Four upon them, are to be characterized as as
completely irresponsible as any ever . . . to come out of a
conference. None of the responsible men ever tried to
respect the right of self-determination of peoples, a
principle previously so much praised.
. . . the notorious Article 231 . . . made our people
wage-slaves for decades and almost hurled the world
into a bolshevistic dissolution. There are no terms suf-
ficiently strong with which to brand this crime to our
people and to all the dead of the World War.[31]

[30] *Die Neueste Zeit*, p. 358.
[31] M. Edelmann, *Volkwerden der Deutschen: Die Entscheidungsjahre
seit dem Weltkrieg* (1936), pp. 10–11 (a supplement to Wilmanns,
Deutsche Geschichte).

More pithy but not less damning is the statement of Gruenberg:

> German disarmament was intended to be only the first step, which was to have been followed by the disarmament of the other powers. Germany had disarmed only on this assumption. The Entente nevertheless did not fulfill this presupposition. Thus arose the picture of a defenseless Germany in the middle of Europe surrounded by highly prepared, stiffly armed neighbors.[32]

And that of Edelmann:

> No great human traits called the work of Versailles into being. Hate and revenge, to which were devoted the policies of French statesmen who saw France's salvation in the weakness of Central Europe, a commercial spirit, and greed brought this bungled job to the light of day.[33]

While such vituperation is nourishing a will to revision and revenge among the German schoolboys, American scholars are reading that it was the statesmen of America's allies, and not Wilson, who were chiefly responsible for whatever harshness there might have been in the terms of peace.

Guitteau, for example, writes:

> Wilson approached the problem of peace in the spirit of Lincoln, seeking to heal the wounds of war; but the Allies were determined to punish Germany and compel her to make reparation for the havoc of war.[34]

And Barker, Dodd, and Commager rise to defend Wilson:

> Though President Wilson was still committed in his own mind to a "peace without victory" — one which

[32] L. Gruenberg, *Zusammenbruch und Wiederaufbau: 1918–1936* (1936), p. 20 (a supplement to Schnabel, *Geschichte der Neuesten Zeit*).
[33] *Volkwerden der Deutschen*, p. 13.
[34] *History of the United States*, p. 629.

would not impose unnecessary hardship and humiliation upon Germany — his colleagues were of a different intention. . . . Knowing the President's mind, the European diplomats drove a hard bargain. As the price of their agreement to the creation of the League of Nations, they compelled him to accept provisions of the treaty which he knew to be profoundly unwise. No doubt he consoled himself with the thought that the League, when formed, would remedy injustices growing out of the treaty as well as other injustices.[35]

*   *   *   *   *

It is plain, then, that in chronicling the most recent of our wars, our historians, as well as those of Germany, have fallen into prejudices similar to those that have directed their accounts of other wars. This being the case, it is not strange that German youths succumb to Nazi anti-democratic propaganda; nor will it be surprising if American citizens are graduated from the secondary school with an anti-German prejudice similar in kind, if not in intensity, to the Anglophobia that some of our forebears have nourished for a century and a half.

[35] *Our Nation's Development*, p. 515.

BIBLIOGRAPHY

In 1934 the ratio of students in institutions of higher learning to students in secondary schools in the United States was 1 to 5.8.[1] Most of the students in both types of institution take a course in United States history before graduation. Carl A. Jessen, Senior Specialist in Secondary Education at the United States Office of Education, writes: "it is fair to conclude that approximately 14 of every 20 eligible to take the subject [American history in the secondary school] were pursuing it in 1934." [2] Therefore, even though we were to assume that all students in institutions of higher learning studied the history of the United States, it is obvious that far more young people are taking their final course in their country's history in the secondary school than in a higher institution. The enrollment figures for 1934 of the United States Office of Education indicate that between 50 and 60 per cent of the pupils graduated from the elementary school complete the secondary school course. Since almost all study American history in grade seven or grade eight and since about three-tenths do not study this subject in the secondary school, the number of those who take leave of the subject in the elementary school is probably slightly greater than the number of those who get their last impressions in the secondary school. But the former are probably less influential in shaping public opinion.

Because it is probable that they exert a greater influence upon public opinion, the history books used in the

[1] Carl A. Jessen, *Statistics of Higher Education, 1933–1934.* Bulletin 1935, No. 2, of the United States Office of Education (Washington, D. C., 1937), p. 11.
[2] "Registrations in History," *School Life*, XXII, No. 8 (1937), 243.

secondary school have been chosen for this study, rather than the more scholarly college books or the less detailed elementary books.

Since this study is concerned with the present influence of secondary-school histories on public opinion, the sole criterion applied in the choice of titles for analysis has been the extent of their actual use in secondary schools. This criterion has been applied in choosing the books from each country.

Older textbooks in American history, both elementary and secondary, have been drawn upon in preparing the outlines of contemporary superpatriotic adult opinion with which each chapter is introduced.

Histories of the United States

An unpublished survey made in 1936 by an educational publisher indicates that the nine American textbooks listed below are those used in the course in American history in the high schools in eleven of the twelve states that are under statewide adoptions, and also in more than 90 per cent of those adopting units over 10,000 in population that are free to choose their own textbooks. It seems safe to assume, therefore, that at least nine of every ten secondary-school students in American history study one or more of these nine books.

Passages from these books have been reprinted by permission of the respective publishers.

In the case of each of the American histories, the latest copyright date is given. Many of these books appeared in earlier editions.

Adams, James Truslow, and VanNest, Charles Garrett, *The Record of America* (New York: Charles Scribner's Sons, 1935).

Barker, Eugene C., Dodd, William E., and Commager,

Henry Steele, *Our Nation's Development* (Evanston, Illinois: Row, Peterson & Company, 1934).

Beard, Charles A., and Mary A., *The Making of American Civilization* (New York: The Macmillan Company, 1937).

Faulkner, Harold Underwood, and Kepner, Tyler, *America: Its History and People* (New York and London: Harper and Brothers, 1934).

Guitteau, William Backus, *History of the United States* (Boston: Houghton Mifflin Company, 1937).

Latané, John Holliday, *History of the American People* (Boston: Allyn and Bacon, 1930).

Muzzey, David Saville, *History of the American People* (Boston: Ginn and Company, 1936). The first Muzzey history for the secondary school was published in 1911. It is probably fair to estimate that one of the editions of this book is still used by about one-half of the students in American history in the secondary school.

Wertenbaker, Thomas Jefferson, and Smith, Donald E., *The United States of America* (New York: Charles Scribner's Sons, 1931).

Wirth, Fremont P., *The Development of America* (New York: American Book Company, 1936).

CHAPTERS I AND II

CANADIAN HISTORIES

Bingay, James, *A History of Canada for High Schools* (Toronto: Thomas Nelson and Sons Ltd., 1934). Authorized for use in the province of Nova Scotia.

Burt, A. L., *The Romance of Canada* (Toronto: W. J. Gage & Co. Ltd., 1937). Authorized for use in the Protestant high schools of the province of Quebec.

McArthur, Duncan, *History of Canada for High Schools* (Toronto: W. J. Gage & Co. Ltd., 1931). Authorized for use in the provinces of British Columbia, Manitoba, and Saskatchewan. Recommended for use in the province of Alberta.

Wallace, William Stewart, *A History of the Canadian People* (Toronto: The Copp Clark Co. Ltd., 1930). Authorized for use in the province of Ontario.

ENGLISH HISTORIES

Brett, S. Reed, *British History, A School Certificate Course, 1688–1815* (London: John Murray, 1936).

Carrington, C. E., and Jackson, J. Hampden, *A History of England* (Part III, 1714–1935) (Cambridge: The University Press, 1936; New York: The Macmillan Company, 1936).

Mowat, R. B., *A New History of Great Britain*, Section III (London, New York, Toronto, etc.: Oxford University Press, 1931).

Muir, Ramsay, *British History* (Part III: 1688–1815) (London: George Philip and Son Ltd., 1929).

Rayner, Robert M., *A Concise History of Britain, 1688–1815* (London, New York, and Toronto: Longmans, Green, 1934).

Trevelyan, George Macaulay, *History of England* (London and New York: Longmans, Green, 1937). Though somewhat fuller than the other English texts studied, this standard history is used in English "public schools" at the secondary level.

Warner, G. T., and Marten, C. H. K., *The Groundwork of British History*, Section III, 1714–1921 (London and Glasgow: Blackie & Sons Ltd., 1931).

CHAPTER III

MEXICAN HISTORIES

(In accord with a resolution adopted at the Pan-American Conference at Buenos Aires in 1933, the Department of Education in Mexico has announced this program: ". . . no textbook to contain unfriendly criticisms of other countries; attenuate the bellicose spirit of most histories; eliminate all references to victories over other countries which reflect upon the moral spirit of the vanquished; eliminate all unfair comparisons between national heroes and those of other countries." Quoted in *The Elementary School Journal*, January 1937.)

Toro, Alfonso, *Compendio de Historia de México*: vol. III: *La Revolución de Independencia y México Independiente* (México: Sociedad de Edición y Librería Franco-Americana, 1926).

Pérez Verdía, Luis, *Compendio de la Historia de México* (7th ed.; Guardalajara: Librería y Casa Editorial Font, 1935).

CHAPTER IV

SPANISH HISTORIES

Ballester, Rafael, *Curso de Historia de España* (6th ed.; Barcelona: Talleres Gráficos de la S.G. de P., S.A., 1933).

Bleye, Pedro Aguado, *Compendio de Historia de España* (4th ed.; Madrid: Espasa-Calpe, S.A., 1933), vol. II.

Espinosa, Alfonso Moreno, *Compendio de Historia de España*: recently corrected by F. Morán (Barcelona: Editorial Atlante).

CHAPTER V

GERMAN HISTORIES

Breiherr, Max, *Die Neueste Zeit von 1789 bis zur Gegenwart für obere Klassen* (Munich and Berlin: R. Oldenbourg, 1935).

Ebner's *Geschichte der Neuzeit*. Revised by Dr. Josef Habisreutinger (Bamberg: C. C. Buchners, 1936).

Edelmann, M., *Volkwerden der Deutschen: Die Entscheidungsjahre seit dem Weltkrieg* (Leipzig and Berlin: B. C. Teubner, 1936). Supplement to Wilmanns. (See explanation below.)

Gruenberg, L., *Zusammenbruch und Wiederaufbau: 1918–1936* (Leipzig and Berlin: B. C. Teubner, 1936). Supplement to Schnabel. (See explanation below.)

Schnabel, Franz, *Geschichte der Neuesten Zeit von der Französischen Revolution bis zur Gegenwart*. Siebente

Auflage des Buches: 1789–1919 (Leipzig and Berlin: B. C. Teubner, 1936).

Suchenwirth, Richard, *Deutsche Geschichte* (Leipzig: Georg Dollheimer, 1937).

Wilmanns, E., *Deutsche Geschichte vom Wiener Kongress bis 1918* (Leipzig and Berlin: B. C. Teubner, 1935).

It is interesting to observe that in the latest printing of the Schnabel text, a note appears on page 186 to explain that pages 186–208 have been omitted by special order. These pages dealt with the post-war period. To replace them, the publishers have issued a supplement by Gruenberg which criticizes the predecessors of the Nazi régime at every opportunity.

Similarly, the pages that dealt with the post-war period have been removed from the Wilmanns history and have been replaced by a pro-Nazi supplement by Edelmann.

DATE DUE

NOV 24 1976		
NOV 30 1976 B R		
NOV 30 1976		
JAN 26 1977		
JAN 27 1977 B R		
JAN 27 1977		
APR 13 1977		
MAY 4 1977		
APR 29 1977 B R		
APR 29 1977		
NOV 2 1977		
FEB 7 1978		
OCT 29 1980		
NOV 4 D U		
NOV 4 1980		
JAN 31 1986		

2-49

Pediatric
Physical
Diagnosis
for Nurses

Pediatric
Physical
Diagnosis
for Nurses

Mary M. Alexander, R.N., M.S.

Assistant Professor of Nursing
Pediatric Nurse Practitioner Program
University of Colorado, Denver

Marie Scott Brown, R.N., Ph.D.

Assistant Professor of Nursing
Pediatric Nurse Practitioner Program
University of Colorado, Denver

McGRAW-HILL
BOOK COMPANY

A Blakiston Publication

New York   St. Louis   San Francisco
Düsseldorf   Johannesburg   Kuala Lumpur
London   Mexico   Montreal   New Delhi   Panama
Paris   São Paulo   Singapore   Sydney   Tokyo   Toronto

R J 50
. A 4

Pediatric Physical
Diagnosis for Nurses

34567890KPKP7987654

This book was set in Times Roman by Black Dot, Inc. The editors were Cathy Dilworth and Renée E. Beach; the designer was Joseph Gillians; and the production supervisor was Sally Ellyson.
Kingsport Press, Inc., was printer and binder.
The line drawings were done by Dorothy Merkel Alexander, B.S.J., M.A.

Portions of this book were adapted for publication in *Nursing '73* and *Nursing '74*.

Library of Congress Cataloging in Publication Data
Alexander, Mary.
    Pediatric physical diagnosis for nurses.
    "A Blakiston publication."
    1. Pediatrics. 2. Physical diagnosis.
I. Brown, Marie, joint author. II. Title.
[DNLM: 1. Pediatrics—Nursing texts. 2. Physical examination—Nursing texts. WY159 A377p 1974]
RJ50.A4   618.9'2'00754   73-12740
ISBN 0-07-001016-1
ISBN 0-07-001017-X (pbk.)

To the two pediatricians
who have most influenced my
well child care
Dr. Henry K. Silver
and
Dr. Burris Duncan

Mary

To Jim

Marie

Contents

Preface

At first glance, the idea of teaching nurses the essentials of physical diagnosis may seem new and perhaps controversial. In 1965, when the authors were students in one of the first Pediatric Nurse Practitioner programs at the University of Colorado, the idea of nurses using stethoscopes, otoscopes, and other instruments traditionally assigned to the physician was heralded with a great deal of skepticism. Many nursing educators feared that, rather than becoming better nurses, these students were rejecting their nursing role in order to be second-rate physicians. It was soon evident that such was not the case, and the term "expanded role of the nurse" began to be accepted for what it really implied—a more thoroughly prepared, more expert nurse-clinician. Nursing had always taught and felt itself responsible for an accurate physical assessment of the patient. Changing from physical assessment to physical diagnosis merely meant increasing the depth of nurses' observational skill by giving them a more thorough conceptual framework for observation and by adding certain technical skills such as the use of the stethoscope and otoscope. This type of expansion in nursing is not so unusual. When nurses first began taking temperatures and later blood pressure readings (skills which had previously been considered the exclusive prerogative of the physician), these new skills were met with the same ambivalence that we find today as nurses learn the skills of physical diagnosis.

This book, then, provides a detailed guide for the nurse learning the skills of physical diagnosis. It is designed to help any nurse interested in improving her skills of physical assessment. It should be utilized by nurses in hospital settings, public health settings, private clinics, and rural settings, as well as by nurses enrolled in formal education settings such as undergraduate programs, graduate courses, and continuing education programs.

Physical assessment does not begin with inspection. The nurse must have some background knowledge of anatomy and physiology to better understand what she is examining within each section of the body. For this reason, each chapter of the book is divided into a discussion of why an examination of a portion of the body is important, a review of the anatomy, a description of the method to be used in the examination, a description of the instruments to be used, and some discussion of conditions of which the nurse should be aware when examining that particular portion of the body. For easy referral the chapters are listed according to the usual sequence of systems as they occur in a normal physical examination write-up. The student should be able to use the book as a basic text on physical diagnosis with additional reading in each area for more depth.

It is impossible to individually acknowledge the many people who have influenced the formation of ideas and thoughts for this book. However, the authors do wish to thank our past students who motivated us and prodded us to become more organized and knowledgeable in various aspects of physical diagnosis; our artist, Dorothy Alexander, who faithfully attempted to fulfill our conceptions of how the pictures should look; and our editors at McGraw-Hill, who gently and firmly pushed us to keep moving.

Mary M. Alexander
Marie Scott Brown

General Approach to the Physical Examination

The physical examination is a tool consisting of certain skills with which the nurse will become proficient by practice. It is a tool that should be used wisely and appropriately. Although the same basic skills and techniques are always used, the system may vary according to the age of the child. For example, the newborn infant does not protest when all his clothing is removed or when he is laid down on the examining table. The examiner can coo at him and make "nonsense" talk in order to watch his responses. The physical examination will usually begin with the feet and finish with the head; then the infant can be returned to his mother's arms for comfort. A 6- to 8-month-old still may not object to having all his clothes taken off, but he will probably protest on being placed on the isolated examining table. The mother's lap usually works best for him, and the examiner may want to begin the examination by listening to the child's chest while he is quiet and then start with the feet, systematically working up to the head. Again, the examiner should not be all business, but should include time for play, for talking to the child, and for getting acquainted. Most 2-year-olds can be very difficult; they do not like to have their clothing removed and usually do not want to be touched by the

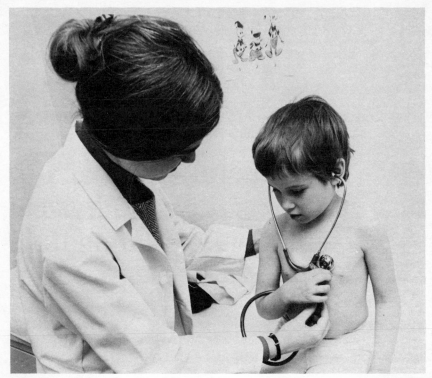

Figure 1-1 Child listening to her own heart.

examiner nor want to play. A 2-year-old is frightened and no one, including his mother, seems able to comfort him. The examiner must decide what has to be accomplished, help the child get through the situation as best he can (kicking and biting are not allowed, but crying is), and finish the examination as quickly as possible. The 4- and 5-year-olds are usually delightful to work with. They will gladly remove all clothing (underpants are usually left on for comfort), stand before the examiner, and sit on the examining table or the mother's lap. Whereas the infant is examined while he is lying down, the older child is examined while he is standing or sitting, with little done when he is lying down. (Usually only inspecting the genitalia, palpating the abdomen, and listening to the chest are done in the supine position). A preschooler likes to help, be talked to, listen to his own heart, and usually does not find any of the examination, including ears and mouth, objectionable. In examining the adolescent, however, it is probably best to examine the genitalia last. It is also important to assure the adolescent that all is well (if that is the case) during each part of the examination, especially because bodily concerns are usual in adolescents.

Not only does the physical examination vary with the age of the child, but it varies with the type of physical examination to be performed. A complete physical examination includes using all basic skills and a review of every part of the body, including a complete neurologic examination. The examiner must learn when this is appropriate and when modifications should be used. Certainly any child coming for a well-child visit should have a complete, thorough physical examination. The child who is ill may need a complete physical or just an examination relevant to the complaint. However, the examiner must be careful not to miss important physical findings by taking care of nothing but the presenting complaint. If the child is too ill for the complete examination when the nurse sees him, it is important to make some arrangements for a return visit when this can be done. However, the child who has been in very recently for a complete physical examination does not need another when he comes in with a specific complaint. The nurse must be thorough and methodical in doing the complete physical examination, but she must also know how to adjust the method for the situation and age of the child.

Physical examinations can be done under many conditions, but it is preferable to secure some privacy, the proper equipment, and some time for the nurse and the child to become comfortable in the setting. The atmosphere should be warm, friendly, and unhurried—this may take real effort when the nurse knows she has a full waiting room. The physical examination really begins the minute the child enters the room. The nurse should notice many things while she introduces herself, makes everyone in the room comfortable, and greets the child by name. If the child already appears frightened he should be encouraged to sit on his mother's lap or given his own chair. The child should be allowed to play quietly with some toys while the nurse interviews the mother, thus letting the child adjust gradually to the situation. As the nurse gains confidence in herself, she will become very proficient at completing the history and physical quite rapidly, even though she gives the impression of having plenty of time for both mother and child.

There are certain skills that are important in physical diagnosis, some of which will be new for many nurses, but the cornerstone of physical diagnosis is not a group of esoteric and complex skills; by far the most important thing in physical diagnosis is thoroughness. Every single part of the body must be examined with every applicable method of examination. By the end of the examination, there should be no accessible part of the body which has not been directly inspected and felt by the examiner. Nor should listening, or percussion, be omitted at any point of the examination where it would be helpful. Certainly, the best insurance for thoroughness is a system. Every examiner should adopt a systematic, logical approach to physical examinations. Once the nurse develops such a system, she should adhere to it as rigidly as possible. The examination always begins with an observation period concerned with the total child—his appearance, his behavior, and his activity. Does he appear to be happy, frightened, ill? Does he seem small or large? Does he have features or characteristics that are particularly striking? What is the general, overall impression the examiner gets from the child?

During the general observation period the nurse must come to a decision on where she will do the examination and if she will have to restrain the child. According to the age, condition of the child, and equipment available, the child may be examined on the examining table, the laps of the nurse and mother, or while standing up. An older child and a young infant can easily be examined on the examining table. The 8- to 15-month-old may be most comfortable on his mother's lap. This can easily be done if the nurse will move her chair in front of the mother's until their knees touch, then the child's buttocks can be supported on the nurse's lap and his head and shoulders on his mother's lap. This provides quite a satisfactory examining table. The nurse may decide during her initial observation that she could use some aid to help during the examinations. Infants will frequently lie quietly if someone will hold a bottle or pacifier in their mouths. Older children may respond to a story or questions about their day, as the nurse begins the physical examination. Some children will hold a doll or stuffed toy or squeeze a toy during the examination. The apprehensive child may quiet down if the nurse does a physical examination on a doll while he watches and helps. If looking in the ears or mouth is particularly upsetting, the nurse may start by examining the mother's ears or mouth while the child watches.

A mirror over the examining table (so long as it is securely fastened) will often quiet the child under 1 year of age, as he watches himself in the mirror. It is much nicer to have a cooperative child and avoid all restraints. But if this is impossible, the nurse must decide how she will restrain the child and if she and the mother can manage or if a third person is needed. Specific ways of restraining will be discussed later.

When doing the physical examination, it is usually best to begin either with the head or the feet and proceed to examine methodically each adjacent part, gradually working up or down to the other end of the child. In this way, one is sure that absolutely nothing has been forgotten. There is an important exception to this rule when working with young children: It is wisest to do those parts of the examination that require a happy cooperative child at the first opportunity; so that if a young baby, for instance, is quiet at the beginning of the examination, the opportunity should be taken to listen to his heart and lungs and to feel his abdomen. The examiner should then return to his usual routine and follow the rest of his system meticulously. A personal preference that seems to the authors to have some usefulness is that a system beginning with the feet and going to the head is most useful in infants and young children, since examination of the ears and throat often results in angry, crying protest,

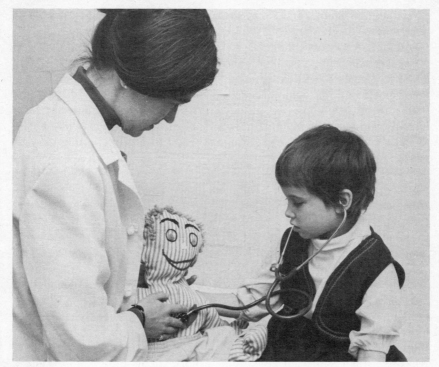

Figure 1-2 A child doing a physical examination on her doll.

making the rest of the examination difficult. If the examination ends with these items, the mother can quickly comfort the child, and the examiner has already gathered all the important data from the physical examination.

For the older child, however, the more traumatic part of the examination is frequently getting undressed, particularly removing the underpants. In this case, it is often wise to begin with certain tests for neurologic functions, since these resemble games and can be used as rapport-gaining devices. The examination is then begun at the head, since with a good explanation, the ear and throat examination is seldom threatening to a child of 3 years or older. If items of clothing are removed one at a time, the child's confidence will hopefully be gained, and by the time the pants are removed, his fears should be largely resolved. If this procedure is still traumatic, the child should be assured that his pants will be off for a very short time, and that the whole examination will then be finished. Another very helpful device in examining children of this age is to enlist their help in the examination whenever possible. It can make a 4-year-old feel very important if he is allowed to hold the stethoscope for you. He will also be interested in listening to his own heart through it. You can effectively use his own hand to palpate his abdomen (a procedure which greatly reduces the amount of voluntary guarding, as well as ticklishness encountered in children of this age). Showing him the "flashlight" (otoscope) that you will use and how it turns on and off will often fascinate him, as will a chance to thoroughly investigate the reflex hammer. If the child is exceptionally fearful, it will be wise to take more time in winning his confidence. When there are several children in the family to be examined on one day, it often pays to examine the least fearful child first, giving the others a chance to see just what will happen to them and that it will not be traumatic, and meanwhile letting the first patient feel important by being "first."

Traditionally, there are considered to be four basic methods of physical examination: inspection, palpation, auscultation, and percussion. Other methods of evaluation, such as using the sense of smell and taking specific types of measurement, are also important in certain parts of the examination. Inspection is certainly the most useful of the methods, although it is often the most difficult to learn. This is probably because we are so used to inspecting in everyday life in a rather haphazard manner. The nurse must be constantly on her guard in a physical examination to use her eyes not only for general inspection as we do in everyday life (although the gestalt we receive in this way is important), but also in a more detailed and meticulous fashion, seeing both the whole and each of the minute parts and their relationships. Her background knowledge of what is normal and what constitutes a normal condition is important to her. She must have sufficient knowledge to judge which things are significant and which are not. The vast majority of information will be gained from inspection with the naked eye. For certain parts of the body, however, special instruments, such as the otoscope or ophthalmoscope, will enhance vision.

Palpation generally follows inspection and is, perhaps, less familiar to the nurse. One usually thinks of palpation as meaning the act of touching and feeling, but it must not be forgotten that touch also includes the sense of temperature, vibration, position, and kinesthesia. Different parts of the hands are used for these different sensations. While the fingertips seem to be most discriminating in the area of fine tactile details, the back of the fingers are most sensitive to temperature, and the flat of the palm and fingers perceive vibrations such as cardiac thrills most accurately. All accessible parts of the body should be palpated thoroughly, using both light and deep palpation. Such different qualities as moisture, pulsatility, crepitus, and texture should all be appreciated wherever they are encountered. Information about bones, muscles, glands, masses, organs, vessels, hair, skin, and mucosa can be gained through palpation. Special types of palpation, such as ballottement, will be discussed under the appropriate parts of the examination.

The third method of physical examination is percussion. Basically, percussion is the method of determining the density of various parts of the body by the sound emitted by these parts when they are struck with the examiner's fingers. They can either be struck directly with the examiner's fingers (direct or immediate percussion), or the examiner may lay the middle finger of one hand flush against the body part to be percussed and then strike this finger with the index or middle finger of his other hand (bimanual, indirect, or mediate percussion). Different densities occur normally in different parts of the body. The terms usually used for these densities from least to most dense are tympany, hyperresonance, resonance, impaired resonance, dullness, and flatness. The sound emitted from gas-filled organs like the intestines or stomach is called tympany, while the sound produced by percussing a bone is said to be flat. Percussion is helpful in discovering unexpected densities, such as a solid mass where there should not be one. Mapping out the borders of certain organs like the heart can also be done by percussion. This is done by gradually comparing the differing densities of the organ one is mapping and the surrounding body tissues.

Auscultation theoretically refers only to sounds transmitted through the stethoscope. This is too narrow a meaning for its use in physical diagnosis, however, since listening with the unaided ear is often equally or even more important. The sound of the child's voice or the pitch of the infant's cry can be of critical importance. Although one first thinks of using the stethoscope to listen to breath and heart sounds, it must not be forgotten that it is equally useful in listening for bruits in the skull or thyroid, or for murmurs in the neck or abdomen.

Smelling, although not traditionally classed with the four methods of physical examination, can be, at times, of great help in evaluating a patient's physical status. Odors from the breath, sputum, vomitus, feces, pus, or urine can be extremely helpful.

Clinical measurements, such as height, weight, head circumference, temperature, pulse, respirations, etc., are quite familiar to the nurse, but their importance must not be overlooked. While the nurse actually may not have to perform the procedures, she is responsible for checking that they have been done and that they are accurate and she must decide whether or not the results are within normal range. Clinical measurements have been universally incorporated into routines because they are extremely important in assessing physical health or illness.

All these techniques are incorporated into a complete, thorough, systematic physical examination. To avoid loss of interest, chilliness, and fatigue in the child, most examinations should be completed within 5 to 10 minutes. The nurse should make positive statements to the child and not allow a choice if there is no choice. The child can be told "Jane, now it is time to take off your clothes," rather than "Jane, will you take off your clothes?" Ideally, all clothing should be removed, but for the uncooperative child, one piece at a time may be removed. An older child may want to have a drape or hospital gown for modesty. The child should be positioned either on the examining table or the mother's lap, and the nurse must make herself comfortable, either standing beside the table or sitting in front of the mother and child.

Anyone can do one examination in an awkward position, but doing a day full of examinations that way leaves the examiner fatigued and sore. Before beginning, the nurse must get all her equipment ready for use. Depending on the age of the child, she may want to lay out otoscope, stethoscope, reflex hammer, tongue blade, etc., within easy reach or introduce one instrument at a time, showing the child what it is and how it is going to be used. The examiner should begin the examination by moving slowly and avoiding sudden, jerky movements. Be gentle but firm in handling the child and proceed as quickly as possible.

In using all the methods of physical diagnosis, the nurse will gradually become more and more proficient. At the University of Colorado, we teach our students that the most important thing is to be familiar with the normal, and it is the normal which is stressed in this book. However, in order to appreciate the normal, it is frequently necessary to be familiar with the abnormals if only in order to compare. For this reason, some discussion of common abnormalities is also included. The nurse must remember, however, that her basic responsibility is not one of differential diagnosis. Once she is certain that a condition is abnormal and abnormal to a greater extent than what she can handle then her responsibility is to refer the patient to the physician. Although it may be fun for her to diagnose the exact type of abnormality, this is not necessary and she should not feel it to be her responsibility. For purposes of clarity, the examination is broken down into sections of the body, and under each section where it is appropriate, there will be discussed six basic aspects of the examination: (1) why the child is examined; (2) what to examine: anatomy of area; (3) how to examine; (4) where to examine; (5) what to examine with; and (6) what to examine for.

BIBLIOGRAPHY

Barness, Lewis A.: *Manual of Pediatric Physical Diagnosis,* Chicago: Year Book Medical Publishers, Inc., 1968, pp. 13–18.
Blum, R. H.: *The Management of the Doctor-Patient Relationship,* New York: McGraw-Hill Book Company, 1960.
Deisher, R., et al.: "Mothers' Opinions of Their Pediatric Care," *Pediatrics,* pp. 35–82, 1965.
Golden, Phyllis, and Barbara Russell: "Therapeutic Communication," *American Journal of Nursing,* vol. 69, no. 9, 1969, pp. 1928–1930.
Green, Morris, and Robert Haggerty: *Ambulatory Pediatrics,* Philadelphia: W. B. Saunders Company, 1968, pp. 118–121.
Green, Morris, and Julius Richmond: *Pediatric Diagnosis,* Philadelphia: W. B. Saunders Company, 1962, pp. 15–20.

SUGGESTED RESOURCES

1 Pamphlets

"Diagnostic Challenges in Pediatrics," Smith Kline and French Laboratories. (Free)
"Recommendations for Human Blood Pressure Determination by Sphygmomanometers," American Heart Association. (Free)*
"Record of Vital Signs," Meade Johnson and Co. (Free)
"Roche Handbook of Differential Diagnosis," Roche. (Free)
"Vital Signs Wheel," Meade Johnson and Co. (Free)

2 Films

"Examination of the Adolescent" (videotape)
   Black and White, 16 minutes
   Cost: Free
   Ross Laboratories
   Local Detailman
"Examination of the Uncooperative Child" (videotape)
   Black and white, 9 minutes
   Cost: Free
   Ross Laboratories
   Local Detailman
"Measurement of Physical Growth" (videotape)
   Black and white, 10 minutes
   Cost: Free
   Ross Laboratories
   Local Detailman
"Physical Examination of the Newborn"
   Color, 33 minutes
   Cost: Free
   The Pfizer Laboratories Film Library
   267 West 25th Street
   New York, New York 10001
"Physical Examination of the Small Child" (videotape)
   Black and white, 12 minutes
   Cost: Free
   Ross Laboratories
   Local Detailman
"Technique of an Effective Examination"
   Color, 20 minutes
   Cost: Free
   Pediatric Basic Film Series
   Audio-Visual Utilization Center
   Wayne State University
   Detroit, Michigan 48202

* Every city has a local chapter.

The Skin

WHY THE CHILD IS EXAMINED

The skin comprises the greatest amount of body tissue that is directly accessible to the examiner. For this reason evaluation of the skin constitutes a major portion of the physical examination. It is important not only because its own health is essential to the proper functioning of the body, but also because it frequently mirrors the health of other systems in the body and can often be the only clue to disease elsewhere.

WHAT TO EXAMINE: ANATOMY OF THE AREA

The skin covers the entire body and has several functions: (1) It protects the deeper tissues from injury, drying, and foreign matter invasion. (2) It regulates the body temperature. (3) It helps in sensation, i.e., touch, heat, or cold. (4) It provides an avenue for excretion. (5) It participates in the production of vitamin D.

The skin varies greatly in different areas of the body. In thickness, for instance, it may vary from 0.5 to 1.5 mm, being thinnest over the earlobes and thick and horny on the palms and soles of the feet. It may be soft, smooth, and pliable as in babies or thick, wrinkled, and loose as in the elderly. It may contain few hair follicles, as on the palms of the hands, or many hair follicles, as on the scalp. Skin may also become extremely hard and form nails, or become elongated and form hair.

The skin is composed of two layers: epidermis and dermis. The epidermis is nonvascular stratified epithelium which varies in thickness. It contains five layers:

1 The stratum corneum (or horny layer) is the topmost surface and contains the remains of deeper cells. This layer continually desquamates, or sloughs off. It also contains keratin, an important fibrous protein.

2 Next is the stratum lucidum, a thin translucent layer.

3 The stratum granulosum underlies the stratum lucidum and contains several layers of flattened cells with large granules of keratohyalin, an early stage in the formation of keratin.

4 The stratum spinosum (or prickle-cell layer) contains polygonal cells that flatten as they move toward the surface.

5 The stratum basale (or basal layer) is the deepest layer which anchors the epidermis to the dermis. Within this layer lies melanin, the pigment that accounts for the black, brown, and tawny colors of the different races. Melanin consists of dark, very small closely packed

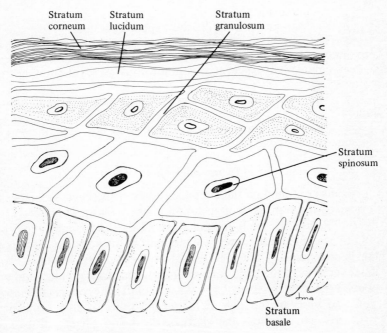

Figure 2-1 The layers of the skin.

granules. Most skin contains some melanin except for albinos whose skin contains little or no melanin.

The dermis is tough, elastic, flexible, and highly vascular. It contains lymphatics and nerves and is composed of two layers: papillary and reticular. The papillary (or superficial) layer contains collagenous, elastic reticular fibers intertwined with superficial capillaries and covered by ground substances. The collagenous fibers are made up of a gluey white substance, forming the matrix for the elastic fibers which provide the flexibility and movement of the dermis. The reticular fibers are important in wound healing and are interspersed irregularly throughout the ground substance, a nonvisible, semiliquid material which fills the spaces and bathes the cells.

The reticular layer is made up of fibroelastic connective tissue, including yellow elastic fibers. The deep layer of the reticular layer contains the sweat glands, sebaceous glands, hair follicles, and small fat cells and is attached to the adipose tissue of the subcutaneous fascia.

The skin contains two specialized forms: (1) nails and hair as well as several upper layers, including the sudoriferous (sweat) glands and ducts; and (2) sebaceous (oil) glands and ducts.

Nails are flattened hard keratin cells. The outer surface is convex and contains:

1 An outer edge.
2 The nail plate, which is the exposed portion.
3 The lunula which is the white moon-shaped section near the proximal end of the exposed nail. The nail is not firmly attached to the deeper connective tissue at this point, thus giving the lunula the white color.
4 The eponychium which is a thin cuticular fold lying over the lunula.
5 The cuticle which is part of the stratum corneum (the first layer of the epidermis) of the finger.
6 The nail root (or fold).
7 The nail matrix from which the nail is produced.

Nails are found on the dorsal surfaces of the fingers and toes and are formed by the 14th week of gestation. Fingernails are completely replaced every $5^1/_2$ months, while toenails take $1^1/_2$ years for total replacement.

Types of hair are found on every part of the body except the palms of the hands, soles of the feet, dorsal surfaces of the terminal phalanges, inner surfaces of the labia, and inner surfaces of the prepuce and the glans penis. Each hair consists of a root and a shaft. The root is implanted in the skin and ends in the hair bulb, which splits to engulf the papilla, a structure that produces the shaft of the hair follicle. The hair shaft is composed of an outer layer (the cuticle), a middle layer (the cortex) and

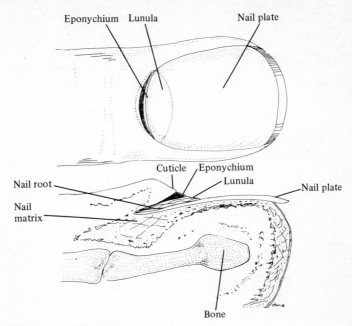

Figure 2-2   The nail.

the inner layer (the medulla); it may be round, oval, or flat and varies in thickness, length, and color. The hair lies in a deep cavity of epidermal cells called the *hair follicle*. Each follicle contains a sebaceous gland and a bundle of smooth muscle fibers (arrectores pilorum muscles). When stimulated these muscles cause the sebaceous gland to secrete sebum and the hair shaft to stand erect.

There are several specialized types of hair. Lanugo is the first, fine hair to cover the body during fetal life; this hair generally disappears before or shortly after birth. Parts of the body contain hair (vellus) that is not apparent, it is fine and nonpigmented. Terminal hair, on the other hand, is coarse, long, and pigmented and covers all ordinarily hairy parts of the body.

Hair growth is cyclic. The active growth stage of the hair is called the *anagen stage*. The *catagen stage* is a transition from activity to nonactivity, and the *telogen stage* is the resting period. Rates of hair growth differ on different parts of the body. A normal scalp usually contains 80 to 85 percent of growing hairs, which grow at a rate of about 1 mm every 3 days or 2.5 mm a week. Adults lose between 20 to 100 hairs daily from their scalp. Body hair has a 3- to 4-month growing period, while facial hair (beard) has a 3- to 4-year growing period.

With the exception of the lips and certain parts of the genitalia, every part of the body has sweat or sudoriferous glands. An average body

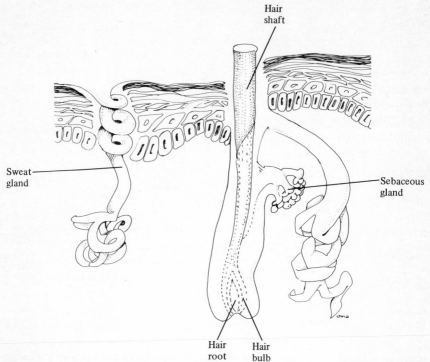

Figure 2–3 The sweat glands.

contains 2 to 5 million such glands, all of which are present at birth. These sudoriferous glands consist of a single duct, opening on the surface of the epidermis and are coiled and twisted deep in the dermis. As the sweat glands open onto the surface of the skin on the palms, fingers, soles, and toes, they form ridges. These ridges fall into normal and abnormal patterns; the tracings of these patterns are called *dermatoglyphics*.

Perspiration is the important function of these glands, and there are two types of perspiration. Sensible perspiration is visible and produced by an emotional or thermal stimulus; insensible perspiration is microscopic and evaporates as it reaches the surface. Perspiration is composed of water, sodium, potassium, chloride, glucose, urea, and lactate. On an average day, a sedentary (inactive) individual will produce 1.5 liters of perspiration in 24 hours; but with dry, hot conditions this can rise to 6 liters in 24 hours.

Sebaceous glands are also excretory glands. They are combined with hair follicles and secrete sebum through the opening for these follicles. Sebaceous glands are found throughout the body, but are particularly abundant and active in the scalp and face. Their activity is controlled by hormones, testosterone increasing the activity and estrogen suppressing it.

HOW TO EXAMINE

Skin is both inspected and palpated. It is checked first for color. Normal skin is whitish pink to light brown, depending on race. Cyanosis is not normal, except in a newborn when he is chilled. Cyanosis develops when the hemoglobin is reduced 5 Gm/100 ml and can be caused by pulmonary disease, congenital heart disease, central nervous system disorders, or hypoglycemia. Normally, by 4 hours postnatally, an infant that was cyanotic at birth will show less cyanosis of the hands than of the feet. Infants with coarctation of the aorta, however, may show an even more striking difference, with the lower extremities distinctly more blue than the upper.

Jaundice is best seen in true sunlight by looking at the sclera, mucous membranes, or skin. Sometimes direct pressure to the skin blanches the blood and leaves only the yellow color. When the total serum bilirubin reaches 5 mg/100 ml in the newborn he is visibly jaundiced. Older children become visibly jaundiced at 2 mg/100 ml. A pale yellow-orange tint seen on the palms, soles, and nasolabial folds may be caused by carotenemia—too much carotene in the blood. Children with this condition have white sclera, rather than yellow. Certain drugs may cause this, as may excessive dietary intake of carrots or other yellow vegetables. Often, physiologic jaundice appears about 24 hours after birth and disappears by the second week. This is usually normal, but may also be due to an abnormal condition such as erythroblastosis, ABO incompatibility, sepsis, viral hepatitis, or bile duct obstruction. Erythroblastosis fetalis, on the other hand, causes jaundice at birth or within the first 12 hours.

Paleness of the face, conjunctiva, mucous membranes, and nail beds may be indicative of anemia; however, this is a subjective sign and should always be checked with laboratory studies. Pallor in the newborn may indicate shock or circulatory failure.

The infant with a beefy-red color over his entire body may be suffering from hypoglycemia. Sometimes one half of a newborn's body is red and the other half pale (harlequin sign); this usually is transitory, and not a pathologic condition. The examiner should also inspect the skin for pigmentation. Pigmentation over exposed areas may be from sun and wind. This may cover large areas of skin or may present as many small pigmented areas called *freckles.* Small, light brown patches are called *café-au-lait spots* and may be indicative of fibromas or neurofibromatosis. Usually one or two patches are within normal range; seven or more are suspect. Absence of pigment (vitiligo) may appear as irregular splotches of white in an otherwise melanotic skin.

The skin is also tested for turgor. This is best done by taking a large pinch of skin on the lower abdomen. Normal, hydrated skin rises with the pinch but quickly falls when released. Dry, dehydrated skin will remain in the pinched position. Turgor is also tested by feeling the calf of the leg. It should feel firm. Newborns, premature infants, and dehydrated infants have loose, extra skin at the calf. Localized edema may be pitting or nonpitting. If a finger is pressed firmly against the skin and the impression remains, the child has pitting edema. This is due to an increased, abnormal amount of extracellular fluid. Pitting edema is frequently seen first over the ankles and sacral region. Children with long-term heart disease, malnutrition, kidney disorders, and certain parasitic diseases, will display pitting edema. Some children have a puffy appearance but finger pressure leaves no mark. This is referred to as *nonpitting edema* and is seen in children who are cretins as well as in some with other conditions. Localized edema may also be caused by allergies, hives, insect bites, or contact dermatitis. Children with a contagious childhood disease also frequently display puffy faces and eyelids.

Texture of the skin is very important. It should be smooth, soft, and flexible. Skin that is rough and dry may be caused by frequent bathing, cold weather, vitamin A deficiency, or hypothyroidism. Scaliness may occur on several parts of the body. Scaliness between the toes and fingers may be due to ringworm. Profuse scaling of the soles and palms is usually caused by *scarlet fever.* Infants with scaliness of the diaper area may be recovering from a diaper rash. Eczema also causes scaliness over the cheeks, behind the ears, behind the knees, and at the elbows. This usually begins when the infant is about 2 months old and may last until he is 2 years old.

Scaliness over the scalp (especially the anterior fontanel) and spreading to a red macular rash over the forehead, cheeks, neck, and chest can be seborrhea and usually clears with washing.

Scaliness and desquamation is seen in many normal newborns. It can be quite pronounced over the feet and ankle creases and usually clears with no special attention. Babies with a lot of desquamation are thought to be postmature.

A crackling sensation when the skin is pressed may be subcutaneous emphysema associated with some bone fractures and lung disorders.

Some newborns have an abundant amount of vernix caseosa, a cheesy white material covering the entire body. Formerly this was vigorously scrubbed off, but the present trend is to leave it on in order to protect the skin.

Very obese children may present striae over the abdomen and thighs. These are pale white or pink stripes. They may fade with age, but generally they will not disappear.

Observation of the skin must also include a look at the dermatoglyphics of the palms and fingers. A good light and magnifying glass (such as the otoscope) are essential. A more detailed description of the patterning is given in other books, but generally, a normal person's ridges fall into arches, loops, and whorls on the fingers; the palm displays a triradius (3 palmar lines meeting) at the wrist area. These patterns will vary

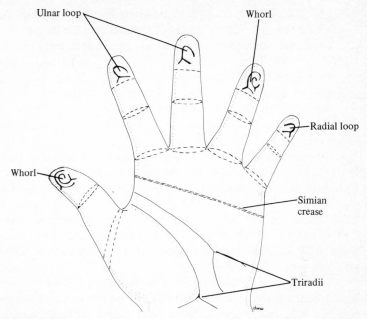

Figure 2-4   Dermatoglyphics of the palm with a simian line.

in children with such specific diseases as Down's syndrome, Trisomy 18 syndrome, and XO syndrome. Children with Down's syndrome frequently display the prominant simian line straight across the palm; however, this can also be seen in some normal children.

It is difficult to evaluate skin sensitivity. A child who reacts to skin touch may be just irritable or may be suffering from systemic disease, central nervous system disease, or skin problems; further investigation is needed.

Inspection and palpation may uncover a variety of skin lesions, some within normal range and some needing referral. Xanthomas are small yellow plaques across the nose of many newborns. They are local accumulations of fatty material and usually dissolve in a few weeks. Miliaria are tiny red, irritated lesions found in prickly heat. Keeping the baby cool, with less restrictive bedding and clothing, will generally clear up this condition. Mongolian spots are bluish discoloration of the skin, usually seen over the coccygeal area most often in Black and Chicano babies. The spots sometimes disappear with time. Erythema toxicum neonatorum is a condition in which a rash of pinpoint, red-based macule may appear on the cheeks or trunk during the first 3 days of life. They sometimes appear and disappear within an 8-hour period and should not be a matter of concern.

Hemangiomas are vascular lesions present at birth. They should be noted for size and shape. Superficial infantile hemangiomas are frequently seen as irregular blotchy pink patches over the eyelid or bridge of the nose of a newborn. They gradually fade and are usually gone by 2 years of age. Port wine stain (nevus flammeus) is present at birth as a flat, reddish capillary lesion. It is most common around the scalp and face and may be superficially or deeply involved in the dermis. It may be associated with convulsions as part of the Sturge-Weber syndrome. It will not disappear. Hemangioma simplex (strawberry mark) is a soft, red, raised lesion present at birth. It may occur anywhere on the skin and sometimes enlarges during the first 6 to 10 months of life before spontaneously shrinking and disappearing. Treatment is not generally suggested, since it usually leaves a scar. A cavernous hemangioma is a reddish, soft, rounded lesion found on any portion of the skin; it usually disappears spontaneously.

Other abnormalities of the skin may also be noted. A nontender, fluid-filled mass felt in the superficial layers of the skin may be a cyst. Cysts found on the hand or wrist may be ganglions; cysts found in other parts may be tumors. Both types of cyst need attention and further referral.

Trauma to the skin produces ecchymoses (bruises), a collection of blood beneath the skin causing the top layers to turn bluish purple and become firm and tender to the touch. Active, normal children can have many ecchymoses, usually below the knees and elbows. Children with such diseases as hemophilia, the purpuras, or leukemia display many bruises all over their bodies and have a history of decreased play and activity. Children who are battered or abused often display bruises, but in peculiar places, and have a history of odd and unusual falls or accidents.

Erythema means a *reddened area.* Erythema nodosum causes painful, tender nodules 2 to 4 cm across, along the fibula of the leg. These are often produced in connection with some systemic disease, such as streptococcicosis, rheumatoid arthritis, or drug reaction. Erythema marginatum is seen in children with rheumatic fever. The lesion is a flat 1- to 2-cm circular reddened area with a definite border. These areas may change from hour to hour. Erysipelas produces erythema that is localized, tender, and firm, with areas of raised borders. Early diaper rash also produces erythematous eruptions.

In describing some lesions of the skin it is wise to know several terms. Primary lesions are those originally produced by trauma or some other stimulation. The nurse-practitioner should be familiar with the seven basic types of primary lesions:

1   A macule is a flat, small (no larger than 1 cm) lesion which shows a color change. Macules are seen in rubeola, rubella, scarlet fever, and roseola infantum.

2   A papule is elevated, sharply circumscribed, small (1 cm), and colored. It may be any color—pink, tan, ted, or several variation of these colors. Papules are seen in ringworm, pityriasis rosea, and psoriasis.

3 A vesicle (or blister) is a small (under 1 cm) sharply defined lesion filled with clean, free fluid. Vesicles are seen in herpes simplex, varicella, poison ivy contact dermatitis, and herpes zoster.

4 Bullae are large vesicles—any vesicle over 1 cm—often seen on the soles and palms in scarlet fever and in connection with sunburn.

5 A pustule is an elevated, sharply circumscribed lesion filled with pus—measuring less than 1 cm—seen in impetigo, acne, and staphylococcal infections.

6 A wheal is an elevated, white-to-pink, edematous lesion that is unstable and associated with pruritis. Wheals are evanescent; that is, they appear and disappear quickly. Wheals are seen in mosquito bites, hives, urticaria.

7 Petechiae are tiny, reddish purple, sharply circumscribed lesions in the superficial layers of epidermis. They can be a sign of severe systemic disease, such as meningococcemia, bacterial endocarditis, and nonthrombocytopenic purpura, and must be reported immediately.

Secondary lesions result from some alteration—usually traumatic—to the primary lesion.

1 Scales are the dried fragments of the sloughed dead epidermis, usually seen in seborrhea and tinea capitis.

2 Crusts are dried blood, scales, pus, and serum from corrosive lesions, usually seen in infectious dermatitis.

3 Excoriation is the mechanical removal (as a scratch or scrape) of the epidermis, leaving the dermis exposed.

4 Erosion is the loss of the superficial portions of the epidermis.

5 Ulcers are sores resulting from destruction and loss of epidermis, dermis, and possibly the subcutaneous layers.

6 Fissures are vertical linear cracks through the epidermis and dermis.

7 Scars are formations of dense connective tissue resulting from destruction and healing of skin.

8 Lichenification is an increase and thickening of the epidermis and dermis due to chronic scratching or rubbing.

Sweating is an important function of skin. It is necessary both for excretory purposes and for heat regulation. Normal newborns begin to sweat when they are about 1 month old. It is usually not seen sooner unless the infant has brain irritation, a sympathetic nervous system disorder, or a mother who is a chronic morphine user. Sweating may be normally produced by exercise, crying, excessively hot environment, or eating, but excessive sweating may be an indication of fear, fever, hypoglycemia, hyperthyroidism, or heart disease.

While checking the skin, it is important to observe the nails. Normally the nail beds should be pink, the nails convex, and the edges should cover the edge of the fingers. Nail color should be noted. Cyanosis is easily seen in nail beds. Postmature infants may show yellow nail beds, while children with porphyria display darkened nail beds. A hemorrhage under the nail (from trauma) causes darkening of the nail. Fungal infections may also be evident, since they cause the nails to become pitted. Paronychia, which is an infection around the nail, is frequently seen in children.

Another important aspect of evaluating the skin is examination of the hair. Normal head hair should be clean and shiny, should cover the entire head, and should be of generally the same color. Hair distribution is important to note. Hair covers the entire body, but is normally easily detected on the head, eyebrows, and eyelashes. Newborns may have lanugo over the shoulders, back, and sacral area. Long eyelashes may be familial or a sign of a possible chronic disease. Hairiness over the arms, legs, and other parts of the body may be familial or a sign of excessive vitamin A, hypothyroidism, or Cushing's syndrome. Tufts of hair over the spine and sacral area may mark spina bifida or spina bifida occulta. Hair on other parts of the body begins to develop with puberty. Pubic hair appears between ages 8 and 12 years, followed by axillary hair about 6 months later. Boys usually develop facial hair 6 months after the appearance of pubic and axillary hair. Curling of the pubic hair is thought to signify the onset of sperm formation.

Hairiness should be noted. Normally the scalp hair begins high over the eyebrows and extends midway down the back of the neck; infants of Spanish or Mexican descent, however, may have hairlines that normally begin at the middle of the forehead. Infants with some types of chronic debilitating syndromes have hair very low on the back of the neck.

Hair texture should also be evaluated. Normally, hair may be thick and coarse, thin and fine, straight, or curly. Very brittle dry, coarse hair is often associated with hypothyroidism. Some nutritional disturbances also effect hair texture.

Hair may be yellow, brown, black, or red or various shades and combinations; normally hair displays slight variations in shades and colors due to different growth patterns and exposure to sun. Infants or children displaying a single patch of white hair (called a "white forelock") may have a disease known as *Waardenburg's syndrome*. Of these children 20 percent may be deaf bilaterally. Children showing hair tipped with a reddish rust color may have had severe nutritional deprivation, usually a lack of protein. At present, children who are undergoing severe protein malnutrition display such hair.

WHERE TO EXAMINE

It is of utmost importance, that at some time during the examination, the nurse carefully inspect and palpate every square inch of skin, hair, mucous membranes, and nails. It will be necessary to smooth out creases carefully and to open folds wherever appropriate. Although each section of skin is usually inspected and palpated while the examiner is evaluating the relevant area of the body, it is also important to inspect the skin as a whole either at the beginning or the end of the examination. In this way, the examiner will be more likely to pick up changes, such as color or texture, between areas of skin.

WHAT TO EXAMINE WITH

For the most part, the skin is examined without specialized equipment. The nurse must rely heavily on her techniques of inspection and palpation. Good lighting, preferably natural lighting, is by far the most essential equipment. Other minor equipment is sometimes also used. A microscope slide, for instance, is often pressed flush against the skin to better evaluate jaundice; a Wood's lamp is sometimes used for inspection of fungus. Other specialized tests, such as smears, cultures, and patch and intradermal tests, might also be considered here.

WHAT TO EXAMINE FOR

One of the most common problems a nurse-examiner is sure to face will be skin conditions. Children are always coming in with a rash, a cut, or an abrasion, and the nurse must decide if it is a normal developmental occurrence, a condition that needs some remedy which she may administer, or a condition that needs medical attention. Sometimes the skin gives very important signs that disease is about to appear and the observant, knowledgeable nurse may make the condition less severe by her prompt action.

Only minor skin problems will be discussed in this section. The nurse is referred to a good book on dermatology for more complex skin problems.

Miliaria, or prickly heat, is a common complaint. New mothers often feel that their babies must be securely clothed, even in the summer, so that the nurse often sees newborns with layers of blankets and clothing, displaying a red, irritated, macular rash under his chin. The most important treatment is reduction of clothing. If the mother is comfortable in short sleeves and sandals, the infant will be comfortable in a cotton shirt or nightie and diaper. Wool should never be used directly over the skin. Adjustment of room temperature to 70°F should also be suggested. During very hot weather, cooling baths can be very refreshing, especially if the excess skin folds are rinsed and carefully dried.

Seborrheic dermatitis is another common problem. This is the "cradle cap" that most babies show at some time during infancy. It is encouraged by the mother's reluctance to scrub the "soft spot" over the anterior fontanel, so that she just rinses that area or never even touches it. The mother may complain that the infant has a rash—usually a red, macular, diffuse rash—over the forehead, then on the cheeks, neck, and chest. Looking at the scalp, the examiner will see dry, scaly, sometimes greasy flakes. Running the fingernail firmly across the fontanel will loosen the flakes. The rash is usually not at the elbows, or behind the knees as it is in eczema. The nurse should advise the mother to wash the scalp daily, using soap and firm pressure, even over the fontanel. Thorough rinsing is important. Assurance should be given that the fontanel is well protected and will not be damaged, even by very firm pressure. If washing is done faithfully for a week, the scalp will clear up as will the forehead, cheeks, neck, and chest. Nothing need be done directly to the forehead, cheeks, neck and chest. These will clear spontaneously when the scalp clears. If the mother feels she must do more, she can be advised to apply a small amount of oil to the scalp, massage it in, and comb the hair with a fine baby comb *before* the shampoo. No oil should be applied *after* the shampoo, since this only pastes the scales down and creates the illusion that the dermatitis is disappearing.

Diaper rash is probably the most common of all skin problems in the very young child. Most babies have diaper rash at some time during their infancy. There are considered to be three degrees of rash. Mild diaper rash is similar to chafing—mild erythematous nonraised areas over the genital and buttock area. Ammoniacal diaper rash is more severe. It presents as bright red, raised papules which erupt and weep and then form craterlike ulcers over the genital and buttock area. This rash is produced by the interaction of the urea, which contains ammonia, and bacteria on the skin or diaper. Diapers that are tight fitting and covered with plastic pants provide an ideal warm, wet environment for multiplication of bacteria. Infected diaper rash is the most severe form. A mild diaper rash can progress to ammoniacal diaper rash and the skin may then become infected with microorganisms of *Candida albican,* staphylococci, or intestinal bacteria. The entire diaper area may be inflamed, bright red, indurated, and tender. Any diaper rash treatment has four aims:

1 To remove the source of irritation
2 To reduce the immediate skin reaction
3 To relieve discomfort of the area
4 To prevent secondary infection

Treatment for mild diaper rash is simple but very effective if applied meticulously. With the young infant, encourage the mother to leave the diaper off during nap time. Turn the infant on his abdomen, place the diaper under his buttock area, and leave the buttocks exposed. The greater the length of time the buttocks are exposed to the air, the more rapidly healing will take place. There are many ointments and creams available for diaper rash. A thin layer of petroleum jelly applied after each diaper change and vigorously removed with each cleaning is the simplest treatment. A thin layer of some commercial product, such as Desitin or A and D Ointment, will also suffice, although it is more expensive. With all ointments it should be stressed that a small amount goes a long way and it must be cleaned off at changes to prevent further complications. Thick, white, sticky zinc oxide ointment can be applied as long as the skin is intact and the mother will take care to wash the area thoroughly at diaper changes. Most important, encourage the mother to change the diapers as soon as they become wet. The treatment for ammoniacal diaper rash is a little more complex but is again usually quite effective if adhered to scrupulously. Treatment is the same as for mild diaper rash plus the exposing of the buttock area to heat. While the infant is sleeping, have his buttock area exposed to a household lamp which should be placed 2 feet above the crib to help dry out the area. If the mother complains also of the ammonia smell, have her offer the infant extra water to drink. This will sometimes dilute the urine and avoid the strong odor. Treatment for infected diaper rash is important, both to keep mother and baby happy and to prevent spread of the infection, particularly to the urinary tract. A diaper rash that is infected needs to be cultured in a laboratory in order to discover the causative agent and to administer proper therapy. The nurse may have to obtain medical advice and specific medication. Infection caused by *Candida albicans* requires keeping the area dry, except for moist soaks of aluminum acetate solution (Burow's solution) and applications of Vioform or Mycostatin creams three times daily.

Prevention of diaper rash is, of course, most important. Prevention really comes in two ways—care of the diaper and care of the baby. Care of the diapers will be discussed first. Soiled diapers should be soaked in a solution of borax ($^1/_2$ cup to 1 gallon of water) while awaiting washing. Diapers should be washed with a mild soap such as Ivory. Avoid using commercial presoaks, harsh detergents, and water softeners. Some mothers insist on these because of increased whiteness of the diapers, which is fine if the baby's skin tolerates them; if not, it is better to have a happy baby and less-than-white diapers. Diapers should be thoroughly rinsed—at least two times and preferably three or four times; if possible, hang these in the sun to dry. In rare cases boiling diapers will remove the ammonia and urea-splitting bacteria, but this is a chore and usually unnecessary.

Care of the baby is the other half of preventing diaper rash. Encourage mothers to change the diaper as frequently as possible. Leaving a wet diaper on for several hours increases the chances of rash. When changing the diaper, the area should be thoroughly cleansed with water (soap will be necessary after soiling), dried, and some lubrication or powder applied. Some mothers like oils (mineral, baby, or cottonseed), some like ointments (A & D, Vasoline, Desitin), and some like powders (talc, baby). Whatever is preferred, however, should be used sparingly, with a little spread on the mother's fingers and patted on the baby's bottom. Shaking powder from the container may cause the baby to inhale and possibly to aspirate it. Plastic or rubber panties worn over the diapers are very handy for visiting or visitors, but mothers should be encouraged to use them only for the above reasons or for outings and to leave the diaper exposed to air the remainder of the time. A wet diaper exposed to air will dry with time, while a wet diaper protected with a layer of plastic stays warm, wet, and a good medium for bacterial growth. Disposable diapers are very fashionable now; many babies can tolerate them exclusively, and they are handy for travel and visiting. However, many babies cannot tolerate them, since they work on the same principle as the rubber pants by protecting the mother's lap while holding the warm, wet urine close to the baby's skin. If a mother wishes to use them, she should buy one box and try it. If a rash develops, she can try another brand, but if the rash continues, she will be forced to use cloth diapers. Disposable diapers are expensive, but there is a dispute over cost of disposable diapers versus cost of cloth diapers, labor, washing, etc. It is something best discussed with each mother.

A common skin condition found in older children is acne. Acne begins as a mild, slightly disturbing skin condition which may progress to a severe, inflammatory skin problem called *acne vulgaris*. This book will discuss only the mild form of acne which the nurse can deal with, since the severe form requires referral of the child to the pediatrician or dermatologist.

Acne is thought to be caused when the androgenic hormones become increasingly active in preparation for puberty and adolescence. The increased hormone levels cause the sebaceous glands of the skin to secrete large amounts of sebum. With the excessive sebum, the hair follicle opening becomes enlarged and plugged. Slowly, the sebaceous gland is destroyed and releases fatty acids into the surrounding tissues, which cause an inflammatory reaction resulting in an acne nodule.

Acne generally begins appearing around puberty, but may be seen in some children as early as one to two years prior to puberty and lasting until their early twenties. Symptoms usually begin with an enlargement of the skin follicles and increased oiliness of the skin. Next, the child may be bothered by the appearance of comedones (blackheads) as the sebum plugs cover the sebaceous gland ducts. This may result in formation of papules, then pustules, and finally cysts. The areas most susceptible are the face (forehead and cheeks) and the upper trunk (back and shoulders). Some children are lucky and their acne is controlled at the papular or pustular level; other children are less fortunate and the acne progresses to the painful, disfiguring stages of cystic acne vulgaris.

A nurse can manage many children with mild or beginning acne, but she must know her limits and must be aware of the time at which the child should be referred to the pediatrician. Control of acne is long (usually several months or years) and tedious. The goal of all treatment is regulation of the oiliness of the skin, suppression of acne lesions and sebaceous gland activity, and the prevention of severe acne (nodules and cysts). Treatment varies from specific instructions concerning cleanliness to antibiotic treatment, steroid injections, x-ray treatment, and surgery. There is much controversy over acne treatment and the nurse would be wise to treat each child as an individual, knowing that some advise will help one child, but not another. Cleanliness is a large part of the management. The child should be encouraged to wash the area with soap and warm water several times a day. Using a fresh washcloth every day is important because bacteria can multiply overnight on a damp cloth. Some nurses also recommend soaps that are slightly abrasive. The hair should be shampooed at least once weekly and maybe more frequently. The hair style should not include bangs and locks of hair over the face, since this seems to encourage the spread of oil from the hair to the face. The skin can be further dried with the topical application of alcohol or lotions that cause peeling. However, both of these measures should be done with caution, since they can dry the skin so severely as to cause further irritation. The child should be encouraged not to pick at his face or attempt to open the blackheads or pimples, since this may increase the inflammation and pain. Exposure to wind and sun also helps some facial problems, but this exposure should be moderate, since severe sunburn, particularly with a sunlamp, may be very damaging. Diet is a large part of the management and there is a great deal of controversy over what helps and what hurts. Generally the child should be helped to discover if there are foods which seem to activate his facial problems and, if so, he should be helped to avoid them. The foods listed as suspect are chocolate, dairy products (milk, cheese, ice cream), fried foods (fried fish, french fried potatoes), potato chips, pork, nuts, salt, and spices. Many dermatologists feel, however, that none of these foods influences acne. Even those who do believe that they aggravate acne realize that these particular foods are often very important to the young person's social life and avoidance of all of them could be very difficult. Thus, a small search to discover which specific foods are most harmful, and counseling with the adolescent about how best to avoid them will usually be the best approach. The discussion of food substitutions in certain situations may help avoid feelings of ostracism and the fear of peer rejection. With these measures the nurse can successfully manage many children with acne; at the same time, she must be aware of the children who are not improving and refer them for further treatment.[1]

[1]Bibliography and Glossary for this chapter are at the end of Chapter 3.

Chapter 3

Lymphatic System

WHY THE CHILD IS EXAMINED

Because the lymphatic system acts as a drainage system for wastes from the entire body, it is often a very sensitive indicator of health or illness. It is most frequently useful as an indicator of either localized or generalized infection, but it can also give the examiner clues concerning certain hypersensitivities and metabolic and lymphoid diseases.

WHAT TO EXAMINE: ANATOMY OF THE AREA

The lymphatic system is almost as extensive as the vascular system and consists of:

1 A network of capillaries which collect lymph from the organs and tissues
2 A system of collecting vessels which carry the lymph from the lymphatic capillaries to the bloodstream via openings in the neck
3 A series of lymph nodes which are filters for the collecting vessels
4 Certain lymphatic organs such as the tonsils, spleen, and thymus

Lymph is a clear, watery fluid which flows within its own system of vessels, and mixes with blood only at the jugular and subclavian veins within the neck, the point at which the lymph is emptied into the bloodstream.

Although the lymph nodes are scattered throughout the lymphatic system, the examiner is interested in those lymph nodes found in four main areas: the head and neck, the axillae, the arms, and the groin (inguinal region).

The greatest number of palpable nodes are concentrated in the area of the head. The nodes to be palpated in this area are: posterior auricular (postauricular), occipital (preoccipital), superficial cervical, submental, submandibular, mandibular, parotid (preauricular), and inferior deep cervical. Nodes up to 3 mm in diameter are normal in all areas, but nodes in the cervical and inguinal areas may normally be as large as 1 cm. Normal nodes can be easily moved under the fingers during palpation. The examiner should be concerned about nodes which feel as though they are attached to underlying tissue. This type of node is said to be "fixed" or "immobile." Normal nodes are nontender and cool. In acute infections, nodes will frequently present as tender, warm, and large.

Knowledge of the drainage system will often be helpful in locating the source of infection. Foot and leg infections cause the inguinal nodes to enlarge, as does the common diaper rash. Finger and arm infections cause the epitrochlear and axillary nodes to enlarge; scalp infections, rubella, pediculosis, and tick bites can cause occipital nodes to swell; and mouth and throat infections usually cause cervical gland swelling. Generalized glandular disease (adenopathy) is often a symptom of systemic disease.

The upper limbs contain the axillary and epitrochlear nodes. Five to six small groups of nodes lying at the lateral edge of the pectoralis major muscle are called the axillary nodes; they drain the arm, thoracic wall, and breast. The epitrochlear nodes are on the medial aspect of the arm, slightly above humerus and ulnar junction at the elbow. They drain the lymph vessels of the fingers and forearm.

The inguinal nodes lie along the inguinal ligament and the saphenous vein and are easily palpated along the crease separating the thigh from the abdomen. These inguinal nodes drain the entire lower limb, gluteal area, perineal area, and all the skin from the lower abdominal wall.

HOW TO EXAMINE

The lymphatic system is examined by both inspection and palpation. Auscultation and percussion are not used in this area. It is best to examine that part of the lymphatic system in each body area as you examine that body area. Thus, the nurse should incorporate the four main areas of lymph nodes into her general system of examination. It is important, however, that she not forget to evaluate the general status of the entire lymphatic system when she is finished with the examination, since a generalized lymphadenopathy has implications which may be different from localized lymphadenopathy.

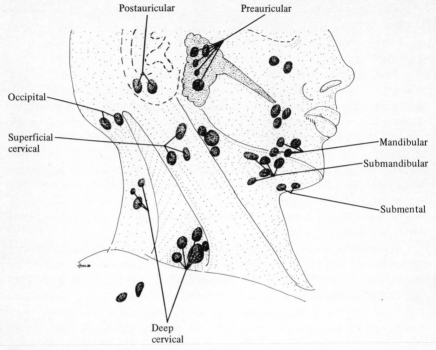

Figure 3–1 Lymph nodes of the face and neck.

WHERE TO EXAMINE

Although the lymphatic system permeates the entire body in both a deep and superficial level, not all areas of it are accessible to the examiner. That part of the system which is accessible, and should be examined during every physical, consists primarily of four groups of nodes: those located around the head and neck areas, the axillary nodes, the arm nodes, and the inguinal nodes.

WHAT TO EXAMINE WITH

For this part of the examination, no specialized instruments are necessary. The nurse's observational skills are crucial and she must depend on them entirely.

WHAT TO EXAMINE FOR

When examining the lymphatic system, the nurse is primarily concerned with evaluating any lymphadenopathy. Lymph nodes are often palpable in normal infants and children, but they should always be evaluated carefully. Small firm nodes are called "shotty," and are generally normal in moderate amounts. These are signs of past infections and are often found in the inguinal area from past diaper infections and in the cervical area from past respiratory infections. If lymph nodes are enlarged, warm, tender, or perhaps even red, however, it is a sign of current infection and the source of the infection should be found. Lymphadenopathy may be caused by an infection of any type—bacterial, viral, or fungal. If the examination reveals localized lymphadenopathy, the anatomy of the drainage system must be reviewed to locate the infection. Tonsillitis and pharyngitis, for instance, usually cause cervical adenitis, but stomatitis may result in submaxillary adenopathy. Swelling of the occipital and postauricular nodes indicates some infection of the scalp, usually seborrheic dermatitis or pediculosis. Infections occurring along the arms will result in swelling of the epitrochlear and axillary lymph nodes, while those along the legs will result in lymphadenopathy of the inguinal and femoral areas.

Certain infectious diseases have characteristic distributions of lymphadenopathy. Rubella, for instance, is accompanied by inflamed nodes in the occipital, posterior cervical, and posterior auricular chains; cervical, suboccipital, and postauricular lymphadenopathy is also found in infectious mononucleosis, although generalized lymphadenopathy may also be found. In this disease, the nodes are felt to be discrete and firm; usually they are not tender and may be anywhere from $1/2$ to 3 inches in diameter. Scarlet fever is characterized by cervical adenitis. Mumps, chickenpox, and measles may result in generalized superficial inflammation of lymph node chains.

Vaccinations may also be the cause of symptoms relating to the lymphatic system. Smallpox and other vaccinations injected into the arm may cause axillary node enlargement, while generalized adenopathy may be found after typhoid inoculation. Vaccination given in any area may cause palpable nodes in nearby localized areas.

Generalized lymphadenopathy may be found in *Salmonella* infections, eczema, histoplasmosis, sarcoidosis, or bacteremia.

Conditions other than infections may also result in adenopathy. Drugs such as Dilantin may cause adenopathy, as may diseases such as lupus erythematosus, rheumatic fever, and juvenile rheumatoid arthritis.

Cancerous illnesses, such as leukemia, Hodgkin's disease, several types of sarcoma, neuroblastoma, and cancer of the thyroid, may be accompanied by lymphadenopathy. Sickle cell anemia, Cooley's anemia, and hemolytic anemia may also be typified by this symptom, as may certain metabolic diseases such as cystinosis and Gaucher's disease.

BIBLIOGRAPHY

Barness, Lewis A.: *Manual of Pediatric Physical Diagnosis*, Chicago: Year Book Medical Publishers, Inc., 1968, pp. 32–47.

Brown, Claude P., and Frederic H. Wilson: "Diaper Region Irritations: Pertinent Facts and Methods of Prevention," *Clinical Pediatrics*, vol. 3, no. 7, 1964, pp. 409–413.

DeGowin, Elmer L., and Richard L. DeGowin: *Bedside Diagnostic Examination*, New York: The Macmillan Company, 1971, pp. 39–52.

Gellis, Sydney S., and Benjamin M. Kagan: *Current Pediatric Therapy*, Philadelphia: W. B. Saunders Company, 1971, pp. 293–304, 454–502.

Montagna, William: *The Structure and Function of Skin*, New York: Academic Press Inc., 1962.

Pack, George T., and Theodore R. Miller: "Hemangiomas," *Angiology: The Journal of Vascular Disease*, vol. 1, no. 5, 1950, pp. 405–425.

Roach, Lora B.: "Skin Changes in Dark Skins," *Nursing '72*, vol. 2, no. 11, 1972, pp. 19–22.

Silver, Henry K., C. Henry Kempe, and Henry B. Bruyn: *Handbook of Pediatrics*, Los Altos, Calif.: Lange Medical Publications, 1969, p. 6.

Smith, David W.: *Recognizable Patterns of Human Malformation*, Philadelphia: W. B. Saunders Company, 1970, pp. 340–342, 345.

Stewart, William D., Julius L. Danto, and Stuart Maddin: *Synopsis of Dermatology*, St. Louis: The C. V. Mosby Company, 1970.

Stough, Thomas R., and J. Rodman Seely: "Dermatoglyphics in Medicine," *Clinical Pediatrics*, vol. 8, no. 1, 1969, pp. 32–41.

Written, Victor H., and Marion B. Sulzberger: "Acne Vulgaris and Seborrhea Capitis," *Pediatric Clinics of North America*, August 1956, pp. 719–739.

SUGGESTED RESOURCES

1 Pamphlets

"Birthmarks," Meade Johnson and Co. (Free)
"Common Skin Diseases: An Atlas," Abbott Laboratories. (Free)
"The Skin," Meade Johnson and Co. (Free)

2 Films

"Allergy"
    Color, 20 minutes
    Cost: $5.00
    Pediatric Basic Film Series
    Audio-Visual Utilization Center
    Wayne State University
    Detroit, Michigan 48202
"Communicable Diseases"
    Color, 32 minutes
    Cost: $5.00
    Ciba Pharmaceutical Company
    P.O. Box 1340
    Newark, New Jersey 07101

"Identification of Early Syphillis"
   Color, 30 minutes
   Cost: Free
   Colorado State Health Department
   4210 East 11th Avenue
   Denver, Colo. 80220
"Physical Diagnosis: Abnormalities in Color; General Diseases with Skin
   Manifestations"
   Color, 30 minutes
   Cost: $5.00
   American Medical Association
   535 North Dearborn Street
   Chicago, Illinois 60610

GLOSSARY SKIN AND LYMPH

bullae vesicles over 1 cm in diameter
café-au-lait spots small light-brown patches on the skin
cavernous hemangiomas soft, reddish rounded lesions present at birth
comedones blockages of a skin excretory duct by dried sebum; blackheads
crust a collection of dried blood, scales, pus, and serum produced by a corrosive
   lesion
cyst a nontender fluid-filled mass felt in the superficial layers of the epidermis
   and dermis
ecchymoses a collection of blood beneath the skin, causing the top layers to turn
   bluish purple and become firm and tender to the touch; a bruise
erosion the loss of the superficial portions of the epidermis
erythema toxicum neonatorum a pinpoint red-based macule on cheeks and trunks
   of newborns
evanescent pertaining to a skin lesion that appears and disappears quickly, as a
   wheal
excoriation the mechanical removal of the epidermis, leaving the dermis exposed; a scratch or scrape
fissure a vertical linear crack through the epidermis and dermis
furuncle a bacterial infection causing the formation of a painful nodule around a
   hair follicle or sweat gland
hemangioma a collection of blood vessels, forming a benign tumor
induration a firm, hard area felt in the skin
inflammation a reaction to trauma, including the signs of heat, pain, redness, and
   edema
lanugo the first, fine hairs to cover the body during fetal life
macule a flat small (no larger than 1 cm) lesion which shows a color change
miliaria prickly heat
papule an elevated sharply circumscribed small (1 cm) lesion which may be a
   variety of colors
petechia a tiny reddish purple, sharply circumscribed lesion in the superficial
   layers of epidermis

port wine stain (nevus flammeus)   a flat reddish hemangioma present at birth, usually found around the scalp and face, with the dermis superficially or deeply involved

pruritis   an itching condition

pustule   an elevated, sharply circumscribed (less than 1 cm) lesion filled with pus

scales   dried fragments of the sloughed dead epidermis

scar   a formation of dense connective tissue as a result of destruction of skin

seborrhea (or cradle cap)   an overproduction of sebum from the sebaceous glands producing whitish yellow, greasy scales over scalp

strawberry mark (or hemangioma simplex)   a soft red, raised lesion present at birth

striae   pale white or pink stripes seen in obese children

sudoriferous glands   sweat glands

superficial infantile hemangiomas   irregular blotchy pink patches covering the eyelid or bridge of the nose of a newborn

telangiectasis   a tiny dot formed on the skin surface by a capillary that becomes dilated

turgor   the normal fullness and resistance seen in healthy skin

ulcer   destruction and loss of epidermis, dermis and subcutaneous layers

vernix caseosa   a cheesy, white material covering the entire body of some newborns

vesicle (or blister)   a small (under 1 cm.) sharply defined lesion filled with clean, free fluid

vitiligo   absence of pigment in the skin

wheal   an elevated, white to pink, edematous lesion which is unstable and associated with pruritis

xanthomas   small yellow plaques seen across the nose of many newborns

adenopathy   any disease of the glands and involving the lymph nodes

axillary lymph nodes   the five to six small groups of lymph nodes lying at the lateral edge of the pectoralis major muscle

epitrochlear nodes   lymph nodes on the medial aspect of the arm, slightly above the humerus and the ulnar junction at the elbow

lymph   a clear, watery fluid flowing through the lymphatic system

lymphadenopathy   disease within the lymph nodes

occipital lymph nodes   two distinct lymph nodes felt over the occipital bone during some diseases

posterior (postauricular) auricular lymph nodes   several small lymph nodes lying behind the ear

"shotty" lymph nodes   small, firm lymph nodes

submandibular lymph nodes   small lymph nodes felt below the jaw

submental lymph nodes   small lymph nodes felt along the posterior border of the jaw

superficial cervical lymph nodes   shallow lymph nodes felt in the cervical regions of the neck

Head, Face, and Neck

WHY TO EXAMINE

The head, face, and neck are vital areas of the physical examination. The brain and the organs of vision, hearing, and speaking are all located here; it is obvious how important their adequate functioning is to the future happiness of the child. Parents also are very concerned with these areas, especially in regard to cosmetic questions. Particularly in the newborn period, some of the most important parts of the physical examination, such as taking careful serial head circumferences, are a part of the examination.

WHAT TO EXAMINE

The skull and face comprise a vault designed to protect the brain and certain other vital centers of the central nervous system. The skull is divided into two sections: (1) the cranium and (2) the facial skeleton. The first of these, the cranium, is composed of 8 bones, joined together by immoveable sutures; these are 2 frontal bones, 2 parietal bones, 2

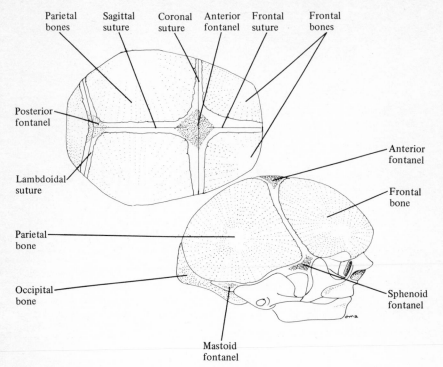

Figure 4–1   The infant skull bones showing fontanels and sutures.

occipital bones, and 2 temporal bones. These bones are soft and separated at birth; the fontanels, unossified membranous spaces, are found at the junctions between the frontal and parietal bones and the parietal and occipital bones.

Most infants are born with 6 fontanels, but the most prominent are the anterior and the posterior. However, some infants have an additional or third fontanel usually along the sagittal suture between the anterior and the posterior. This is present in some children with Down's syndrome, but can also be present in normal infants. The spaces between the skull bones are called sutures and are frequently palpable at birth. The coronal suture goes from ear to ear across the top of the skull, while the sagittal suture divides the parietal bone, running at a right angle to the sagittal suture. The lambdoidal suture separates the parietal bones from the occipital bones. The facial bones number 14 and are immovable except for the mandible. These include the mandible, the maxilla, 2 nasal bones, 2 zygomatic bones, 2 sphenoid bones, 2 ethmoid bones, 2 lacrimal bones, and 2 vomer bones. All these bones are present at birth, but the mandible and maxilla are very small, giving the head a flat, squashed shape.

The vertebral column is considered as a whole elsewhere, but the bones of the neck will be considered separately here; these are the first 2 vertebrae. The cranium rests directly on the atlas, or first cervical vertebra, a small vertebra with no body. The atlas, in turn, rests on the second vertebra called the axis. The two form a pivot for rotation of the head.

Vertebrae 3 through 6 are not distinct, but the seventh vertebra has a long spinous process and is used for identification when palpating the spinal column.

The muscles considered in this area are skull muscles, facial muscles, and neck muscles.

The cranium is covered with tough and thick, subcutaneous fascia, and it is below this fascia that the broad, muscular layer called *epicranius* is found. Contraction and relaxation of these muscles controls wrinkling of the forehead, raising of the eyebrows, and some facial expressions.

The muscles of the face are many and varied. They are generally described in connection with certain orifices, that is, the muscles of the ear, of the eye, of the mouth, and of the nose.

The muscles of the neck may be divided into six categories, beginning with the superficial and going deeper and in several directions. The subcutaneous fascia varies from thin on the anterior neck to thick and tough on the posterior areas. The superficial cervical muscle is the

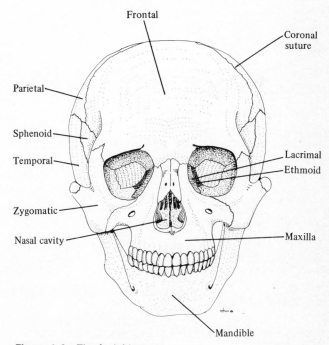

Figure 4–2   The facial bones.

platysma which attaches below the clavicle and runs upward to the edge of the mandible. It assists in opening of jaws. The lateral cervical muscles are the trapezius and sternocleidomastoid. The trapezius is a neck and back muscle arising from the XIIth thoracic vertebra, spreading toward the lateral border of the clavicle and to the edge of the occipital bone, giving it a triangular shape. It acts to turn the head and raise the shoulders. The sternocleidomastoid is a thick, tough muscle running from the mastoid area behind the ear to the sternum and clavicle regions. It is instrumental in turning the head to either side. The suprahyoid, infrahoid, anterior vertebral and lateral vertebral muscles are the deep muscles of the neck and contribute to the sideways movement.

The skin covering the subcutaneous fascia and muscle on the skull is thicker than on any other part of the body. It contains abundant, tightly spaced hair follicles, sebaceous glands, and subcutaneous fat. Thus the scalp has five tightly packed layers: the skin, subcutaneous tissue, epicranius, connective tissue, and pericranium. The face and neck are covered with a layer of skin containing hair follicles and sebaceous and sweat glands.

Circulation for the entire head and neck is supplied through the two

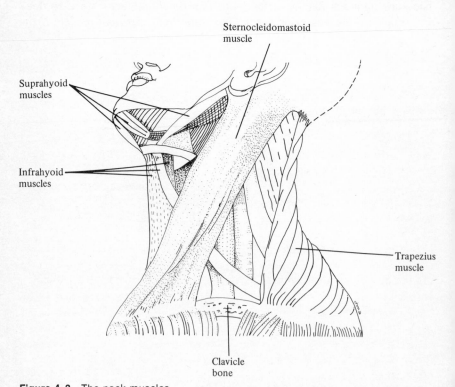

Figure 4-3 The neck muscles.

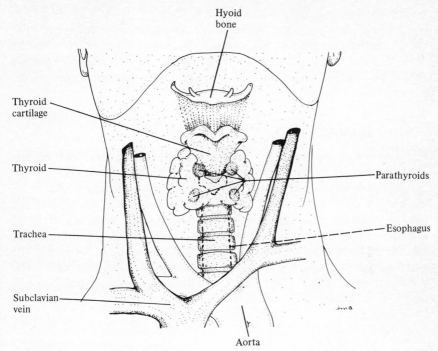

Hyoid
bone

Thyroid
cartilage

Thyroid

Parathyroids

Trachea

Esophagus

Subclavian
vein

Aorta

Figure 4-4 The neck structures.

common carotid arteries: the external and the internal. The external carotid artery carries blood to the head, face, and neck, while the internal supplies the structures within the cranium. Blood is drained from the head, neck, and face through 2 deep and superficial veins of the face, 4 veins from the cranium, and 3 large veins in the neck. The neck contains the external and internal jugular veins.

The face and head form a highly sensitive, highly coordinated area with many nerve innervations. The most important nerves in this area are the cranial nerves. There are 12 pairs, which are discussed in the chapter on the nervous system.

There are also some additional structures within the neck to be considered. The trachea (windpipe) is a cartilaginous, membranous tube extending from the larynx to the bronchi. Posteriorly it lies against the esophagus and anteriorly the isthmus of the thyroid gland covers it. Males have larger tracheas than females; in children the trachea is deeply buried in the neck and is more moveable.

The thyroid gland is an extremely vascular endocrine gland located at the fifth or sixth tracheal ring. Like all endocrine glands, the thyroid has no ducts and secretes hormones directly into the bloodstream. It contains a right and left lobe connected by a neck called the *isthmus* and secretes thyroxine which is essential for normal body growth. The diet must contain adequate amounts of iodine for thyroxine to be produced. The parathyroid glands are flat, oval disks, averaging 6 by 4 mm located on the thyroid gland along the dorsal borders of the lateral lobes. These are endocrine glands which secrete parathyroid, a hormone needed for calcium metabolism.

HOW TO EXAMINE

Examination of the head, face, and neck, including the ears, nose, mouth, and eyes may be uncomfortable; therefore, it might be best to do this part of the examination last on the young child and then return him to his mother for comforting. Much of the examination of the head, face, and neck consists of observation and can be done while watching the child play on his mother's lap. Palpation can be accomplished by gently running the fingers over most of the head in general sweeping movements. The examiner should touch every part of the head, face, and neck. The examiner should remember to start with the general and go to the specific detail in the examination. Thus the head is looked at as a whole before focusing on the fontanels and other specifics.

WHERE TO EXAMINE

All parts of the head, face, and neck must be included in this part of the examination. Most of these areas will be accessible to direct inspection and palpation, but in certain areas, some manipulation of parts may be necessary. This is particularly true of the hair in older children. Although the hair may be long and thick, the examiner must remember to inspect the scalp carefully.

The examiner will first want to observe the head and face for symmetry, paralysis, weaknesses, head shape, and movement. Often this can be done when the child cries, laughs, or wrinkles his forehead. Symmetry is usually regained by the end of the first week. Small rounded depression in the frontal and parietal bones are a normal result of the birth process and should disappear soon after birth. Any prominent bulges or swelling should be observed and felt for size, location, and density. Frontal bulges are known as *bossing* in infants. This may be the first indication of rickets or syphilis. Facial swellings, cephalohematoma (bleeding below the periosteum of the skull bones is normally restricted to one bone; when it crosses a suture line, it may indicate a skull fracture), and caput succedaneum (edema of the scalp which generally crosses suture lines) are noted on infants. Prominent foreheads sometimes seen in children may be a sign of Hurler's syndrome or rickets. The shape of the head may be long or broad, or may assume a squashed appearance. Some races are noted for specific head shapes, for example, members of the

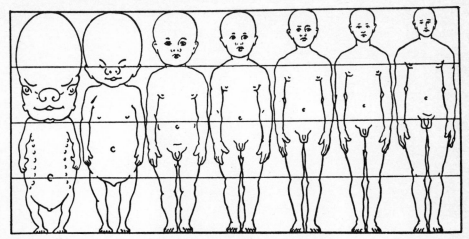

Figure 4-5 The Stratz chart of proportional size. *(From Stratz, modified by Robbins, et al., Growth, Yale University Press, 1928. Original source, C. M. Jackson in Morris' Human Anatomy, 5th ed., P. Blakiston's Son and Co., Philadelphia, 1914.)*

Nordic race are characterized by long heads. The head shape must be observed from all angles. The examiner must look at it from the front, the sides, and the top; otherwise, a flat occiput may be missed. Prematurity will sometimes be the cause of long, narrow heads in children. Premature closing of the suture lines may cause many abnormal shapes, depending on which sutures close. The child may present with oxycephaly, scaphocephaly, plagiocephaly or trigonocephaly. Any indication of premature closure of the sutures must be thoroughly investigated, since the first 2 years of a child's life are vital for brain growth. The size of the head is extremely important in infancy and childhood and should be a routine part of every examination. Head size changes proportionally throughout life as shown in the Stratz chart. The normal head size, as shown by Nellhaus, is between 32 and 38 cm at birth, the average being around 34 cm.[1] In the infant the head is generally 2 cm larger than the chest. However, during childhood the head is generally 5 to 7 cm smaller than the chest. The head is measured with a metal or paper tape measure (cloth has a tendency to stretch and give an inaccurate reading). The measurement is taken around the greatest circumference, thus the tape runs over the occipital protuberance and ends midforehead. As can be seen from the previous chart, a single measurement can be meaningless. It is important to obtain a series of measurements to ascertain that growth is occurring at the proper rate.

Heads are generally measured at every visit until the child is 2 years old. Any sudden increase or failure to increase at the rate predicted by the

[1]Gerhard Nellhaus, "Head Circumference from Birth to Eighteen Years," *Pediatrics*, vol. 41, no. 1, pt. 1, 1968, pp. 106–133.

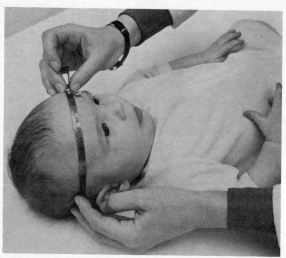

Figure 4–6 Placement of measuring tape when measuring the head circumference.

graph should be explored immediately. Some terms in describing head size are: normocephalic (normal-size head), microcephalic (small-size head for body size and age), macrocephalic (large-size head for body size and age), and hydrocephalic (indicating excessive fluid in the cranial cavity). The examiner must observe and feel the fontanels in infants. Infants are born with six fontanels, but generally only two are easily palpated: the anterior and the posterior. A third fontanel may be normal, but should be reported; it may occur along the sagittal suture between the anterior and posterior fontanels. The anterior fontanel may be small or absent at birth and then enlarges to an average of 2.5 by 2.5 cm. Ninety-seven percent will close between 9 to 19 months of age. Early closure is not a reason for concern so long as head growth is proceeding normally. Late closure may be due to cretinism, rickets, syphilis, Down's syndrome, osteogenesis imperfecta, or hydrocephalus, and these possibilities must be investigated. The posterior fontanel, which is often not palpable at birth averages 1 by 1 cm. It will close by 1 to 2 months of life. Fontanels are observed for their number and position and for their bulging, flattened, or sunken appearance. They are palpated for size, pulsations, and tenseness. Always write the size to give both dimensions, not just "anterior fontanel 2 cm," but "anterior fontanel 2 by 3 cm." Pictures may be helpful. Slight pulsation of the fontanels is within normal range, but definite, great pulsations may be an indication of intracranial pressure and should be reported immediately.

The scalp is observed and palpated for sutures, scaliness, infections, and hair. Sutures may be prominent ridges at birth from the overriding of the edges during the birth process. These usually flatten by 6 months. Some infants have wide spaces along the suture lines, giving the impression of very large fontanels. Cranial margins adjacent to these sutures can be appreciably depressed by palpation in many normal infants. An osseous ridge may be palpable along the sagittal and metopic suture lines. Although they do not actually close until adult life, suture lines should not be palpable after 5 or 6 months of age. The coronal, sagittal, and lambdoidal sutures are normal breaks in the skull, any other ridges or breaks are fractures and should be reported. In American Indian children however, there is one additional horizontal suture in the occipital bone.

The scalp should not be dry or flaky. On an infant this is usually an indication of cradle cap. As the examiner's fingers palpate each area of scalp, they should feel for the two occipital lymph nodes. These are never present except in infection of the scalp, roseola infantum, or rubella. The hair is observed for color, texture, distribution, amount, and presence of nits or pediculi. Hair can be any one of a number of colors, but the color should be fairly even throughout the hair strand. Children with a white streak of hair running from their forehead towards the crown of their head may have Waardenburg's syndrome and should be suspect for deafness. Children with kwashiorkor (protein deficiency disease) display patches of reddish, coarse hair throughout their regular hair color. Generalized malnutrition may result in dry, gray hair. There is little or no pigment in children with albinism. Hair should have a smooth, fine texture. If it is brittle and chopped looking, hypothyroidism or ringworm may be present. It should be evenly distributed over the entire scalp, beginning with a hairline at the forehead and going to the nape of the neck. Normal children of certain racial backgrounds and some with such syndromes as Hurler's syndrome or cretinism have hairlines beginning mid-forehead and excessive hair at the nape of the neck. Bald spots (alopecia) may be familial or due to ringworm. It may also be a sign of hair pulling, an indication of serious emotional problems. All of an infant's hair is often replaced by 3 months of age, usually of a darker color and sometimes with bald spots over the occiput if they have been lying in the crib, face up, for extended periods of time.

The head is observed for control, position, and movement. Control comes with age; most infants have some head lag as they are pulled to a sitting position until about 3 months. Control is attained gradually, but should be almost complete by 3 months. If much head lag remains at this age, the nurse should be suspicious of some abnormality. This may be the first sign of cerebral palsy or other neuromuscular deficit. Children should be observed for the position they hold their head in while in a resting position. If it is constantly held at an angle, torticollis or hearing or vision difficulties should be suspected. Movement is also important. Passive range of motion must be done for the infant, but the older child can follow a toy or bright light so that the examiner can evaluate the full movement. The head should move easily and smoothly from left to right and towards the ceiling and floor. Any jerking, tremors, or inability to move in one direction must be investigated.

The face is observed for the spacing of the features, symmetry, paralysis, skin color, and skin texture. Looking at the child, face to face, the examiner should be able to note eyes set at the same level, nostrils of the same size, lips equal on both sides of the midline, and ears set at the same level on both sides of the head. There will normally be slight differences in each side, but any major differences are important to note. Eyes that are at the same level but very wide set, giving the nose a wide bridge, is indicative of a condition called *hypertelorism*. Hypotelorism is the condition in which the eyes are set unusually close together. Any clefts or dimples are noted at this time.

The skin should be a good color and smooth over the entire face; there should be no pallor, cyanosis, or jaundice. Infants may display slight circumoral cyanosis when crying or cold during the first few days of life, but such a sign in an older child is suspect. The examiner must also turn the child's head to each side to inspect hemispherical symmetry and spacing. Normally the top of the pinna of the ears crosses an imaginary line drawn from the lateral corner of the eye to the most prominent protuberance of the occiput. The pinna should touch or cross this eye-occiput line. Ears that do not cross the line are said to be low set and must be reported, since this is most often associated with mental retardation or kidney abnormalities. From the side, the child's chin can also be checked. Infants normally have very little chin; however, a marked decrease in chin, called *micrognathia*, is abnormal and must be reported promptly, since the child may have breathing difficulties due to the tongue falling backward and blocking the nasopharynx. The cheeks should be palpated for tone and muscle pressure. Infants normally have very fat, well-developed cheeks for sucking. If hyperirritability, tetanus, or hyperventilation are suspected, Chvostek's sign can be elicited by tapping the cheek just below the zygomatic bone. The sign is positive if that side of the face shows a grimace. It is present in children normally under 1 month of age and over 5 years.

As the examiner finishes the head and face, she should move on to the neck. The neck is also observed for symmetry, size, shape, control of movement, and pulsation; it is palpated for pulsations, strength, and position of the trachea and thyroid. The neck should be symmetrical from all angles. It is normally short in infants and difficult to see, but if the shoulders are supported, the head may be tilted back and forth for a look at its symmetry and size. Posteriorly the neck should be checked for webbing—the presence of loose, extra folds of skin. These are often associated with certain syndromes and should be investigated further.

Movement and control may be checked by rotating the head in all directions. As the head turns to the right, it is important to palpate along the left sternocleidomastoid muscle for strength, tone, and presence of any hematomas. By turning the head to the left, the procedure is repeated along the right sternocleidomastoid. Strength in the neck can be tested in older children by having the child look over his right shoulder while the examiner attempts to force the face to rotate forward. This is repeated with the child looking over his left shoulder.

Excessive pulsations observed and palpated in the neck may be signs of cardiac problems. The neck is also palpated for the location of the trachea, which should be felt as series of cartilaginous rings. It should be midline, descending towards the sternum. In the infant this can be done only by supporting the shoulders and tilting the head back to expose the short neck area. The thyroid can be palpated as a firm, smooth mass which moves upward with swallowing. It is difficult to palpate in infants and is often not felt in normal adults. It may be palpated with the examiner in front of or behind the child. From the front the examiner has the child flex his head forward and uses one hand to palpate along both sides of the trachea. From behind, the examiner places two or three fingers of both hands on either side of the trachea below the thyroid cartilage. The child flexes the head slightly forward and swallows. A light, rotary motion may help to locate nodules or any irregularities. Each side can be palpated individually by asking the child to flex his neck and head to the side being examined. In rare instances the thyroid can be auscultated for bruit.

The above are procedures normally done in examining the head, face, and neck. There are several procedures, also, that can be done if the examiner suspects certain conditions. They are not normally done at each examination. Craniotabes is the softening of the outer layer of the skull. Premature infants or children suspected of rickets, syphilis, hypervitaminosis A, and hydrocephaly will display craniotabes, that is, a ping-pong snapping sensation if the scalp is firmly pressed behind and above the ears in the temporoparietal region and along the suture. This can also be present in normal children up to 3 months of age.

Children with increased intracranial pressure will demonstrate Macewen's sign—a resonant, cracked-pot sound heard when the finger is used to percuss the skull. In an infant with an open fontanel, this sound is normal, but once the fontanels are closed the sound is indicative of a pathologic condition.

Children suspected of having intracranial lesions, hydrocephalus, or decreased brain tissue should have their skulls transilluminated. A special rubber ring is fitted to a flashlight for the procedure. The room must be completely darkened as the rubber ring of the flashlight is pressed firmly against the skull. A small ring of light is normal, but any increased area of light around the edges denotes abnormality. Infants with anencephaly will transmit the light placed at the occiput through the eyes. The flashlight must be moved over the skull covering both sides, front and back.

WHAT TO EXAMINE WITH

Not much in the way of special instruments is needed for the examination of the head, face, and neck. Of course, this area does include the eyes, ears, and other special features, but instruments for their examination will be discussed separately. A stethoscope will sometimes be used for auscultating bruits; a Wood's lamp may be needed for evaluating the scalp; a flashlight with a rubber cuff attachment for the glass end will be used at times for transillumination; and a tape measure will be most important in keeping track of head circumference.

WHAT TO EXAMINE FOR

In examining the head, face, and neck there is one condition the examiner may find that can be handled easily. As the examiner rotates the infant's head and checks for shape, she may discover that either side of the occipital area is decidedly flat. A few questions to the mother may reveal that the crib is placed against a certain wall, the child is always placed in the crib in the same way and the child always prefers to lie on that side. Since the skull bones are soft and pliable in the infant, this condition is easily corrected by placing the crib against a different wall, putting the child's head where his feet used to be in the crib, and helping him to sit up more so that he is not left lying in the crib for long periods of time. If nothing is done, the skull will remain flattened in this area.

BIBLIOGRAPHY

Aisenson, Milton R.: "Closing of the Anterior Fontanelle," *Pediatrics*, vol. 6, no. 2, 1950, pp. 223–225.

Barness, Lewis A.: *Manual of Pediatric Physical Diagnosis*, Chicago: Year Book Medical Publishers, Inc., 1968, pp. 48–56, 93–97.

Boyd, Julian D.: "Clinical Appraisal of Infants' Head Size," *American Journal of Diseases of Children*, vol. 69, no. 2, 1945, pp. 71–82.

———: "Graphic Portrayal of Infants' Growth with Consideration of Head Size," *American Journal of Diseases of Children*, vol. 76, no. 7, 1948, pp. 53–59.

DeGowin, Elmer, and Richard DeGowin: *Bedside Diagnostic Examination*, London: Macmillan & Co., Ltd., 1971, pp. 53–64, 188–210.

Jolly, Hugh: *Diseases of Children*, Philadelphia: F. A. Davis Company, 1968, pp. 155–156.

Judge, Richard D., and George D. Zuidema: *Physical Diagnosis*, Boston: Little, Brown and Company, 1963, pp. 46–59.

Kempe, C. Henry, Henry K. Silver, and Donough O'Brien: *Current Pediatric Diagnosis and Treatment*, Los Altos, Calif.: Lange Medical Publications, 1970, pp. 1–37.

Nellhaus, Gerhard: "Head Circumference from Birth to Eighteen Years," *Pediatrics*, vol. 41, no. 1, pt. 1, 1968, pp. 106–113.

Silver, Henry K., C. Henry Kempe, and Henry B. Bruyn: *Handbook of Pediatrics*, Los Altos, Calif.: Lange Medical Publications, 1969, pp. 7–8.

SUGGESTED RESOURCES

1 Pamphlets

"The Head," Meade Johnson and Co., Evansville, Indiana 47721. (Free)

2 Films

"Physical Diagnosis: The Face—Part I"
  Color, 21 minutes
  Cost: $5.00
  Ciba Pharmaceutical Co.
  P.O. Box 1340
  Newark, New Jersey 07101
"Physical Diagnosis: The Face—Part II"
  Color, 33 minutes
  Cost: $5.00
  Ciba Pharmaceutical Co.
  P.O. Box 1340
  Newark, New Jersey 07101
"Physical Diagnosis: The Neck"
  Color, 30 minutes
  Cost: $5.00
  Ciba Pharmaceutical Co.
  P.O. Box 1340
  Newark, New Jersey 07101
"Physical Diagnosis: The Larynx"
  Color, 15 minutes
  Cost: $5.00
  Ciba Pharmaceutical Co.
  P.O. Box 1340
  Newark, New Jersey 07101

GLOSSARY

alopecia lack of hair in spots that normally have hair
anterior vertebral muscle a deep muscle of the neck that aids in sidewise movement
atlas the first cervical vertebra supporting the cranium
axis the second cervical vertebra forming a pivot for the atlas and cranium
bossing the rounded bulges, as of the frontal bones of the cranium
bruits abnormal sounds heard during auscultation of certain parts of the body, for example, the thyroid or cranium

caput succedaneum the clear fluid trapped under the scalp, but on top of the pericranium and not confined to one bone

cephalhematoma a soft, fluctuating mass of blood trapped beneath the pericranium and confined to one bone

Chvostek's sign a facial grimace elicited when the zygomatic bone is taped.

coronal suture the space separating the frontal from the parietal bones of the skull and interrupted by the anterior fontanel

craniotabes a softening of the outer layer of the skull

epicranium the skin, muscles, and fasciae of the scalp

ethmoid bone one of the 14 facial bones

fontanels unossified membranous intervals of the infant skull

hydrocephalic excessive fluid in the cranial cavity

hypertelorism wide-set eyes, with a broad flat nasal bridge

hypotelorism close-set eyes,with a small nasal bridge

infrahyoid muscle one of the deep muscles of neck controlling sideway movements

lacrimal bone one of the 14 facial bones

lambdoidal suture the suture separating the parietal bones from the occipital bones and interrupted by the posterior fontanel

lateral vertebral muscle one of the deep muscles of the neck aiding in sideway movements

Macewen's sign a resonant, cracked-pot sound heard when the finger is used to percuss the skull of a child with increased intracranial pressure

macrocephalic designating a large-sized head for body size and age

mandible the one moveable facial bone which forms the lower portion of the oral cavity

maxilla the bone forming the upper portion of the oral cavity

microcephalic designating a small-sized head for body size and age

micrognathia an abnormally tiny mandibular bone

normocephalic designating a normal-sized head

oxycephaly a dome-shaped head caused by the coronal sutures closing prematurely

parathyroid hormone a hormone secreted by the parathyroid glands and needed for calcium metabolism

parathyroid glands flat, oval endocrine glands located on the dorsal borders of the thyroid gland

pericranium the periosteum covering the cranium

plagiocephaly a deformity of the skull due to irregular sutures which cause the cranium to assume a twisted, asymmetrical shape

platysma muscle the superficial cervical muscle attaching below the clavicle and running towards the mandible, necessary for opening the jaws

sagittal suture the suture dividing the right from the left parietal bone with the anterior fontanel on the anterior end and the posterior fontanel at the posterior end

scaphocephaly a narrow, long cranium due to early closure of the sagittal suture

sphenoid bone one of the 14 facial bones

suprahyoid muscle one of the deep muscles of the neck aiding in sideway movement

suture   a closure or juncture between bones, as of the head or skull
torticollis   asymmetry of the neck muscles causing the head to be tilted to one
   side
trigonocephaly   a flattened frontal skull bone giving the head a flat anterior shape
vomer bone   one of the 14 facial bones
webbing   the loose, extra folds of skin seen in the posterior neck area
zygomatic bone   one of the 14 facial bones forming the upper cheek area

The Eyes

WHY THE CHILD IS EXAMINED

A careful eye examination is an important part of every physical. The eye is obviously a vital part of the human person and the practitioner will discover that every parent shows particular concern over the health of their child's eyes. Many parental questions will focus on this area for both cosmetic and health reasons. Will my baby's eyes stay this shade of blue? Will these folds over my baby's eyes go away? Can my child see well? Are my child's eyes healthy? All are common questions which the nurse will frequently encounter. The eye examination is also important because the eyes will frequently give the nurse clues as to the general and systemic health of the child. The color of the sclera may be the tip-off that makes the nurse further investigate the possibility of liver disease, osteogenesis imperfecta or certain other diseases. The shininess of the child's eyes can also be important to a general assessment of his or her health. A very careful and thorough ocular examination, then, is a necessary part of the health evaluation of every child the nurse sees.

WHAT TO EXAMINE: ANATOMY OF THE AREA

For purposes of study, the eye can be divided into the eye proper and its surrounding structures: the ocular orbit, muscles controlling movement, eyebrows, eyelids, eyelashes, tarsal glands, conjunctiva, and lacrimal apparatus.

The eye is situated in the orbit which is a bony cavity formed by the bones of the upper face (palatine, lacrimal, zygomatic, sphenoid, ethmoid, maxillary, and frontal bones); it is cushioned with fat for extra protection. There are 7 ocular muscles to control the movement of the eye. The levator palpebrae superior is a thick, long muscle attaching behind the eyeball and running anteriorly to the eyelid, which helps the upper eyelid rise. The rectus superior, rectus inferior, rectus medialis, and rectus lateralis surround the eyeball on all four sides joining at the posterior portion of the eye. They act singly to move the corneal surface in different directions. The obliquus superior runs parallel to the levator palpebrae and acts as a pulley as it attaches to the bulb of the eye. The obliquus inferior is small and thin, attaches near the sclera, and runs across the other muscles. Both the obliquus superior and obliquus inferior work in refining the movements of the recti muscles.

The eyebrows are arched prominences placed above the eye orbit,

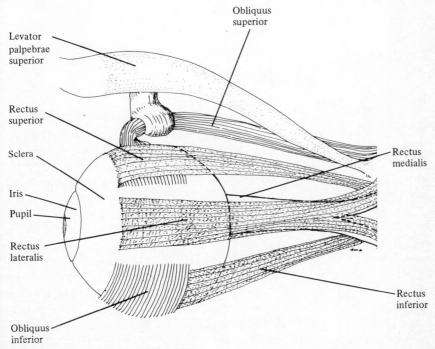

Figure 5–1   The muscles of the eye.

which consist of thickened skin and many thick short hairs. The skin attaches to the orbicularis oculi, corrugator, and frontalis muscles for various movements.

The eye gains additional protection from the two eyelids which are narrow, moveable layers of skin, areolar tissue, glandular fibers, conjunctiva, and muscle. The lower lid is smaller, contains no muscle layer and is less mobile than the upper lid; the upper lid is large and contains the levator palpebrae superioris muscle for upward movement. The elliptical space left by the open eyelids is called the palpebral fissure.

Eyelashes are thick, curved hairs connected to the moveable edges of the eyelids, which add further protection for the surface of the eye. The hairs may be long or short and arranged in double or triple rows; they are surrounded by modified sudoriferous glands called *ciliary glands*.

Between the skin and the conjunctiva of the eyelids lie strings of modified sebaceous glands called *tarsal glands* which become visible when the eyelids are everted, and form a hardened area called the *tarsal plate*.

Conjunctiva is formed by mucous membrane lining the eyelids and anterior surface of the sclera. It is composed of two parts: the palpebral

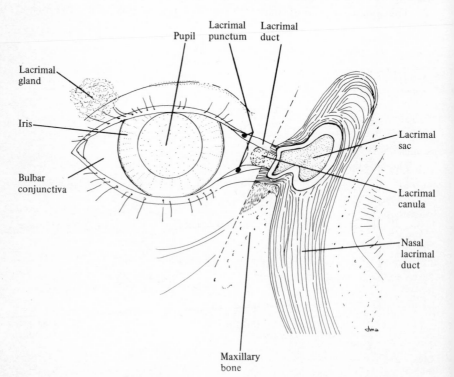

Figure 5–2 The lacrimal system.

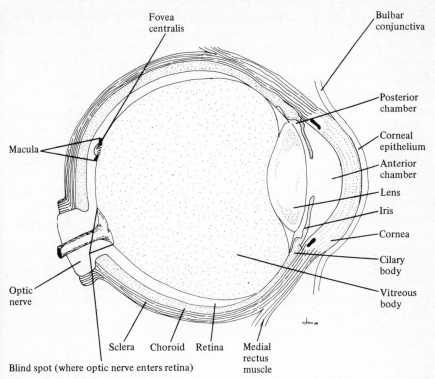

Figure 5-3 A cross section of the eye.

portion and the bulbar portion. The palpebral portion lines the eyelids and is thick, opaque, vascular, and covered by many papillae; the bulbar portion lies loosely over the sclera and is thin and clear, containing no papillae and very few blood vessels.

The lacrimal apparatus consists of the lacrimal glands, lacrimal ducts, lacrimal sac, and nasolacrimal duct. The lacrimal gland is the size of a large peanut and similar in structure to the serous salivary glands; it is lodged in the lacrimal fossa of the frontal bone where its function is to secrete tears. Each eyelid also contains one lacrimal duct, which opens on the margin of the eyelid, and one nasolacrimal duct, which opens into the lacrimal sac buried in the frontal process of the maxilla bone.

The eye proper sometimes called the *eye bulb*, is composed of three layers: (1) the outer, fibrous layer containing the anterior cornea and the posterior sclera; (2) the vascular, pigmented tunic containing the choroid, ciliary body, and iris; and (3) the inner nervous tunic containing the retina. The outer layer makes up a large part of the eye proper. Its cornea is thin, transparent, and convex; it forms the anterior one-sixth of the covering, and is a five-layered membrane. The thick, tough, opaque, inelastic membrane covering the remaining five-sixths of the eye is the sclera.

Muscles are inserted into the scleral surface. The vascular layer is composed of choroid, ciliary body, and iris. The choroid lies in the posterior five-sixths of the eye with the optic nerve penetrating it. It is a deep chocolate color, thin, and highly vascular. The ciliary body is a thick, vascular surface extending from the posterior optic nerve opening to the sclerocorneal junction. The ciliaris muscle attaches to the ciliary body and is the major muscle in accommodation. The iris is the colored, round, contractile disk floating in the aqueous humor between the cornea and the lens. It contains four layers and the center is perforated to form the pupil. The color of the iris is determined by the amount of pigment present and its distribution within the layered membrane.

The inner layer of the eye is divided into a posterior portion containing many nerves and an anterior portion containing no nerves. The retina proper is the most important structure of the posterior inner layer. It forms the optic nerve which receives the images from external objects. It is soft, semitransparent, made up of ten layers and contains rhodopsin (or visual purple) which gives it a lavendar color. The macula is an oval yellowish area at the exact center of the posterior retina. The fovea centralis is the central depression in the macula, the area where vision is most perfect. The optic nerve exits through the optic disk, which is located 3 mm to the medial side of the macula; the blind spot of the retina is the depressed center of this optic disk.

The anterior, nonnervous portions are called the *pars ciliaris retinae* and the *pars iridica retinae*.

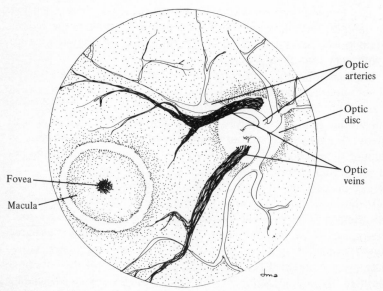

Optic
arteries

Optic
disc

Optic
veins

Fovea

Macula

Figure 5–4 The retina.

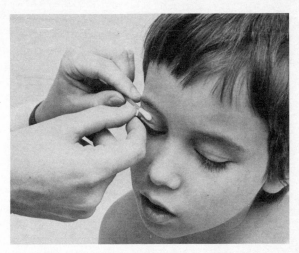

Figure 5–5 The lid being everted for inspection.

There are five structures for refraction within the eye proper: the cornea, aqueous humor, vitreous body, zonula ciliaris, and crystalline lens. The cornea has already been discussed. The aqueous humor is an alkaline watery fluid secreted by the ciliary process which fills the anterior and posterior chambers of the eyeball. The vitreous body is a transparent semigelatinous substance filling the main cavity of the eye; the retina and ciliary processes maintain its nutritional balance. The zonula ciliaris (or suspensory ligament of the lens) attaches the ciliary body to the lens by several straight fibers, which helps to position the lens and change its shape. The crystalline lens is a transparent, soft cortical body, biconvex in shape, which is suspended between the suspensory ligaments; it is contained within a thick, transparent elastic membrane called the capsule.

HOW TO EXAMINE AND WHAT TO EXAMINE FOR

The primary method used in evaluating the eye is inspection. In both the external and internal parts of the eye, the nurse's observational skills are the single most valuable tool. Palpation of the eye is also important and may reveal certain conditions of the eye more readily than will inspection. Auscultation is not used frequently, but may be important for detecting bruits. Percussion is not generally used in examining the eye. Some specific methods of examination, such as the cover test and ophthalmoscopic examination, will be described in more detail later in this chapter.

There should be a definite system in examining the eye. The nurse may well choose to begin with the lids. The eyelids are carefully inspected and palpated. They are examined for ptosis or drooping of the lid. There are two types of ptosis: congenital and acquired. Congenital ptosis is often inherited, and a family history should be taken. Some babies are born with ptosis; frequently this type of ptosis disappears with maturation, but any infant with ptosis should be examined for the jaw-winking reflex or Marcus Gunn phenomenon. In this reflex, moving the jaw to one side results in the child raising the opposite eyelid. In infants, sucking may cause this same response. This type of ptosis may be due to paralysis of the superior rectus muscle or to oculomotor nerve damage. Acquired ptosis may be due to several causes, such as polio, encephalitis, meningitis, pineal tumors, Horner's syndrome, or myasthenia gravis. Whatever the cause, it is important for the nurse to assure herself that the ptosis does not obstruct the child's vision in one eye (it should not cover the pupil), since this can cause amblyopia (loss of vision in the covered eye) in the same way that strabismus does. Pseudoptosis is a type of ptosis caused by the weight of the upper lid, usually due to edema.

The upper lid should also be examined for retraction. If the nurse finds that the upper lid does not cover the usual area of the globe (or eyeball), she must discover why. It may be that the globe is protruding, as in exopthalmus or advanced hydrocephalus, where the sclera is exposed above the iris and there is a downward displacement of the iris and pupil. Hyperthyroidism may also be accompanied by a widened palpebral fissure due to retraction of the lids. This results in a wide-eyed staring expression. The examiner must also ascertain that the lids are long enough to cover the eye. Lagophthalmos (lids which do not close entirely) may result from facial nerve paralysis or from a congenitally shortened muscle. Whatever the cause, if the cornea or bulbar conjunctiva remains exposed, a consultation should be sought, since this may result in damage to the exposed portion of the eye due to dust or other environmental irritants.

Blepharospasm (excessive blinking) is another situation which may be encountered in the examination of the eye. This may be due to a tic or habit or may be a sign of eyestrain or irritation.

Squinting should be noted, and where it occurs, a thorough visual examination is imperative.

Upward slanting of the eyes may be indicative of Down's syndrome, while the opposite (downward) kind of slanting may be indicative of Treacher Collins syndrome. (This may also be accompanied by a notched lower lid called a *coloboma*).

The "setting sun" expression in which sclera is exposed above the iris may be elicited by rapidly lowering the infant from a sitting to a supine position. This sign may be present in some normal full-term infants and in many premature infants. Children with hydrocephalus and brainstem lesions may also exhibit this sign.

Many types of infections may be discovered while examining the eyelids. Styes, or hordeola, are inflammations of the sebaceous glands near the lashes. They are painful, red, tender and swollen. The immediate

Mongolian slant

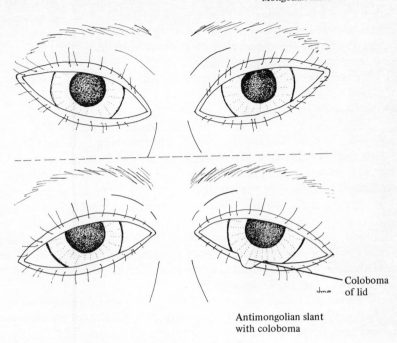

Coloboma
of lid

Antimongolian slant
with coloboma

Figure 5–6   Mongolian and antimongolian slants.

cause is almost always staphylococcal infection; however, when they recur frequently, the clinician should look for an underlying reason, such as poor general health or poor vision which causes the child to irritate the lids by rubbing his eyes constantly.

Internal styes are acute inflammations of the Meibomian glands, which cause pain in the upper lid. They are also usually caused by infection with staphylococci. If chronic they can result in a sensation of sandiness under the lid, and if the upper lid is everted, a vertical yellow line across the tarsus can be seen.

Chalazions, or Meibomian cysts, are another frequent finding of the lids. They are granulomas of the internal sebaceous glands and tarsus. They consist of localized, nontender, firm, discrete swellings. These small, hard, slow-growing nodules are covered with freely movable skin and are usually located on the bulbar part of the lid next to the tarsal plate. They produce no subjective symptoms, but they can often be palpated through the lid and can be seen as enlarged erythematous glands if the lid is everted.

Furuncles, or boils, are staphylococcal infections of the hair follicles while carbuncles are large loculated furuncles. Both are relatively common findings in this area of eyelids, eyelashes and eyebrows.

Marginal blepharitis is another fairly common finding on the eyelids.

It consists of red, scaly crusted lid edges. If this is caused by staphylococci, the scales will cling and leave open lesions if removed; pustules may form around the base of the lashes and the Meibomian glands may contain pus. If the blepharitis is part of a seborrheic dermatitis, the scars are waxy, greasy, and come off easily.

Eyelids must also be inspected for nits or lice. This condition, called *phthiriasis*, is usually caused by head lice, although pubic lice may occasionally be involved.

The lids must be examined for positional faults. There are two possible malpositions of the eyelids: (1) ectropion, or a rolling out of the lids, and (2) entropion, or a rolling in of the lids. Ectropion may be a result of scar tissue formation or of spastic or paralytic muscles. Whatever the cause, it usually requires surgical correction. The everted part of the lid develops a velvety red appearance and is accompanied by an epiphora (excess amount of tears) which frequently causes an eczematous reaction of the lower lid. Entropion, or turning in of the lid, can also be caused by scars or muscle spasticity (usually from inflammation). It is present normally in many Oriental children. It is harmless unless the lids scrape the cornea and cause abrasion.

Epicanthal folds are vertical folds of skin covering the inner canthus. They may be present in Oriental infants, and 20 percent of Caucasian newborns have them also. In 97 percent of these, the folds will disappear

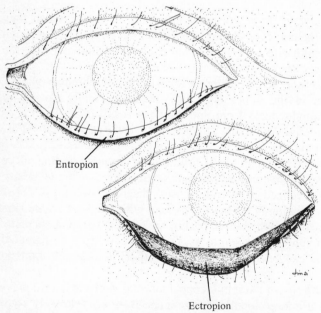

Entropion

Ectropion

Figure 5-7   The eye with ectropion and entropion.

by 10 years of age. If they fail to disappear, surgery may be performed for cosmetic reasons. Epicanthal folds can also be a sign of Down's syndrome, hypercalcemia, glycogen storage disease, or renal agenesis. This type of fold is quite different from a Mongolian fold, or epiblepharon, which is a horizontal fold in the upper lid, overhanging the superior tarsus. This fold is normal in Asiatic children, but wherever it occurs, it will generally disappear by the end of the first year. The nurse must be sure, however, that it does not rub the cornea.

Edema of the lids must also be noted; it may indicate hyperthyroidism, ethmoid sinusitis, measles, infectious mononucleosis, nephritis, nephrosis, chronic upper respiratory infections, sinusitis, or allergies.

The eyelashes of the child must be examined. A lack of pigment may indicate albinism. Lashes which are absent on the inner two-thirds of the lid may be seen in children with Treacher Collins disease. They may be particularly bushy in Hurler's syndrome or absent in premature infants.

The lacrimal apparatus, including glands and ducts, must also be assessed. Enough lacrimal fluid for tearing is not usually present until the third month of life or later, but if the lacrimal duct is not patent, the minimal lacrimal fluid present in the young infant may overflow into tears. For this reason, excess tearing before the age of 3 months must be further investigated. Such a blockage can be caused from an accumulation of debris or from a thin congenital membrane covering the punctum. The mother of such an infant should be taught to massage the infant with each feeding, exerting pressure with her index finger directly under the punctum and then sweeping the finger down and out of the general area of the gland. If no results are obtained by 6 months, the punctum is probably covered by a thin membrane and will need to be probed. If the blockage was caused by an accumulation of debris, the massage will usually unplug the duct. The clinician must be very careful in this situation, however, since a clogged lacrimal duct predisposes a child to infection of the lacrimal sac (dacryocystitis). This will be manifested by swelling and redness below the inner canthus; by local conjunctivitis; by a turbid, yellow secretion; and at times by a palpable mass. In this situation, massage is contraindicated since it may spread the infection.

Other conditions that may be encountered in the lacrimal apparatus are disorders of tearing. Dysautonomia is a condition in which tears are produced in inadequate amounts. Epiphora, or excessive tearing, may result from an allergy or inflammation, a foreign body, a plugged lacrimal duct, or exophthalmos.

Dacryoadenitis or inflammation of the lacrimal gland may also be found. Usually, this is accompanied by pain within the temporal edge of the orbit, although it may be painless if it is chronic.

Next, the conjunctiva is examined. Both the palpebral and bulbar parts must be evaluated carefully. Chemosis, or edema of the conjunctiva, is encountered at times and is usually an indication of infection. Infections of the conjunctiva can be of many types, and a more thorough description of them will be found in a book on ophthalmology. Suffice it to say here that there are many different types of physical findings that may indicate conjunctivitis. The so-called "cobblestone" or "ground glass" appearance consists of enlarged follicles in the palpebral conjunctiva, which impart a bumpy appearance to the membrane. This can indicate allergic conjunctivitis. Conjunctivitis may also be suspected with highly erythematous palpebral and bulbar conjunctiva. Mucoid secretions or plaques on the bulbar conjunctiva may indicate similar problems.

The pallor of anemia can be reflected in the palpebral conjunctiva; and vitamin A deficiency may result in dryness and hyperemia of this area, sometimes accompanied by Bitot's spots (irregular yellow patches).

The pinguecula, if irritated from wind, sand, and irritation, may darken and begin to encroach on the iris and even into the pupil. This is called pterygium.

Next, the orbit of the eye must be assessed. Sunken, blank eyes are a matter of concern. They may be an indication of a malnourished or dehydrated baby or a baby severely ill from any reason. Microphthalmia or very small orbits are another condition the nurse must be alert for. They may be a sign of encephaloophthalmic dysplasia, toxoplasmosis, or retrolental fibroplasia.

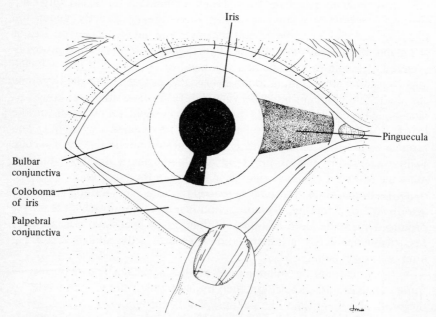

Figure 5–8 The front of the eye displaying a coloboma of the iris and a pinguecula.

There are also rare occasions when a careful examination of the orbit will reveal a small meningocele.

Spacing of the orbits should also be evaluated. Hypertelorism, or abnormally widely spaced eyes, may be present in normal children, but is frequently associated with various syndromes of mental retardation or Waardenburg's syndrome. Hypotelorism, or eyes that are abnormally closely spaced may indicate an absence of the nasal bridge or trigonocephaly.

Prominent supraorbital ridges should also alert the nurse to the possibility of ectodermal dysplasia, gargoylism, or Marfan's disease.

Condition of the ocular muscles is a very important part of the eye examination. Full range of motion must always be checked; it is particularly important to remember to include the movement of the eyes toward the upper outer, upper inner, lower outer, and lower inner quadrants. Noncomitant, or paralytic strabismus, occurs as a result of a paralyzed extraocular muscle; this type will frequently not be evident when a child stares straight ahead, but will become apparent only at some point in a complete range of motion. Usually this type of strabismus is posttraumatic and will probably not disappear at all if it is not gone by 1 or 2 months after the trauma. The other type of strabismus is called concomitant strabismus and will appear no matter in which direction the eyes are gazing. However, the examiner must frequently be quite astute to discern mild degrees of this type of strabismus. It is very important that this be picked up as early as possible, since amblyopia or loss of vision can occur if it persists for any length of time; this loss may not be reversible. Many infants exhibit concomitant strabismus in early life. This can be a normal condition in a very young infant. However, any child who is still exhibiting this type of strabismus by 6 months of age (some ophthalmologists say by 3 months of age) should be referred. Any infant younger than this should be followed closely and referred only if the strabismus is constant rather than intermittent, if it is getting worse or showing no improvement, or if there is any sign of vertical rather than horizontal strabismus. These conditions should be referred very early. Some children will exhibit not a tropia (overt strabismus), but only a phoria (tendency toward strabismus), particularly when tired or sick. Mothers must be questioned regarding this situation since it will frequently not be present when the child is being examined.

There are two very important screening tests which should be performed on every child over 6 months of age to rule out subtle strabismus. The first is a light reflex (or Hirschberg's) test in which the room is darkened and a penlight is shone into the child's eyes. The reflection of the light should be in exactly the same position on each pupil. If there is even a slight difference, strabismus is present. This test is particularly useful in children with pseudostrabismus. Usually pseudo-

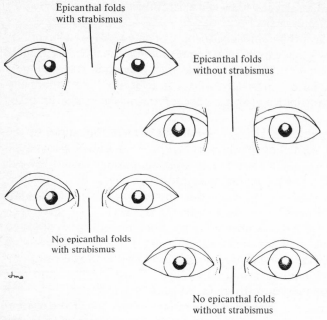

Epicanthal folds
with strabismus

Epicanthal folds
without strabismus

No epicanthal folds
with strabismus

No epicanthal folds
without strabismus

Figure 5–9 Strabismus.

strabismus results from an epicanthal fold which makes the eyes appear crossed even when they are not. In this situation, two types of mistakes can occur. The nurse may be unaware that this will make the child appear cross-eyed and will refer him with no further evaluation. This will result in overreferral. The other possible mistake is that a nurse who is familiar with the fact that epicanthal folds will result in this appearance may dismiss the child without further study. This mistake is far worse. It must be remembered that even though a child has epicanthal folds, it is also possible for him to show true strabismus. Here is where the light reflex test is so useful.

The second screening test that should be done on all children over 6 months of age is a cover test. In this test, the child is asked to focus on an object about 12 inches from his eyes. He must be encouraged to hold his eyes perfectly still or the test cannot be performed. The examiner then holds his hand or a small card in such a way that it occludes the vision of one eye but does not touch it. Both eyes must remain open, however. The card is held there several seconds and then quickly removed. The covered eye is observed closely as the card is withdrawn. There should be no movement of this eye. A slight jerking movement of the previously covered eye indicates that some amount of strabismus is present. The same procedure should then be followed with the opposite eye. Finally, the test should be repeated with the child focusing on a distant object. Again, both eyes must be tested.

Finally, the eye proper is examined. This consists of the cornea, sclera, iris, pupil, and lens. The cornea is examined for any enlargement or clouding. These signs, along with dilatation of the pupil, epiphora, and a thin, bluish white sclera, may indicate infantile glaucoma. Clouding or opacities may also indicate Hurler's syndrome or cystinosis.

The cornea should further be inspected for any ulceration. Most often such ulcers are a result of a herpes infection and may begin with a gray or yellowish cornea, accompanied usually be a reddened conjunctiva, intense pain, photophobia, and lacrimation. Ciliary flush is usually a good indication that an infection of the deeper structures exists, and it appears as congested, hyperemic vessels forming a partial or complete reddened circle around the limbic area of the eye.

The cornea should further be examined for any dermoids or any evidence of abrasion or irritation.

The sclera may also provide important information. It should be inspected for any irregularities or local manifestations such as staphyloma (small area of outpouching where parts of the sclera seem to be pushed forward and may take on a slightly bluish tinge). The color is important. Jaundice may be best detected in the sclera, particularly in the fornices where the yellow may appear darker. Some sclera may appear slightly brownish. This can be normal in all races although it is more frequent in Blacks. In alkaptonuria, large pie-shaped patches of brown pigment pointing toward the limbus may be found. The sclera of newborns will usually be slightly bluish, but a darker blue may indicate osteogenesis imperfecta or glaucoma.

The iris and pupil are examined as a unit. An irregular iris may be due to adjacent adhesions from previous inflammation and should be carefully investigated. Dulling of the color of the iris, ciliary flush, a small pupil, and an eye soft and tender to palpation, particularly when accompanied by pain and throbbing in the ocular area, may indicate iritis.

Anisocoria (difference in pupil size) can be normal, and 5 percent of the normal population manifests this condition. However, it should make the nurse highly suspicious concerning the possibility of central nervous damage, and a complete and thorough neurological examination should be performed on any child with anisocoria.

Pupil size is quite important. Dilatation of the pupil may be a clue to retinoblastoma, intracranial damage, glaucoma, or poisoning from atropine or barbiturates. A constricted pupil, on the other hand may indicate morphine poisoning or intracranial damage. Pupils should always be checked for their equality in size and reaction to light. The reaction to light should be checked both consensually and directly. A pupil reacts to light directly if the pupil into which the light is shone constricts; it reacts consensually if it constricts when the light is shone in the opposite eye. Accommodative constriction is also important. To test this, the nurse should have the child look far off into the distance (to be effective, the authors have found that this must be a distance of some miles through a window); then the child is asked quickly to focus on something within 12 or 14 inches of his eyes. The pupils should dilate when looking into the distance and constrict when focusing on a nearby object. Obviously this test cannot be done on an infant or very young child.

The color of the iris should also be evaluated. The permanent color of the iris will be manifested in 50 percent of children by 6 months of age and in all children by 12 months. A pinkish or blue iris color may appear in albinism.

Brushfield's spots (a light or white speckling of the outer two-thirds of the iris) may occur in normal children, but particularly in its more striking appearance, may be an indication of Down's syndrome or other syndromes associated with mental retardation.

Heterochromia, or irises of different colors bilaterally, can be normal or can be associated with Waardenburg's syndrome or with chronic low-grade infection of the iris. Even in normal children, heterochromia is associated with a higher incidence of cataracts as they grow into adulthood.

Coloboma can occur on many structures. Earlier in this chapter, coloboma of the eyelid was discussed. A coloboma of the iris is also sometimes found. The notch may include only the iris or may extend through the choroid and retina. If it involves only the iris, there is usually no problem, but vision may be impaired if the retina is involved.

A Kayser-Fleisher ring is another possible finding in this area. It consists of a brown or grayish green circle at the limbus and can be a sign of Wilson's disease. It may be unilateral or bilateral and can be partial or complete.

Nystagmus, another important condition of the pupil, can be horizontal, vertical, or rotary, and can be a result of vestibular, neurologic, or ocular causes. The ocular causes include cataracts, astigmatism, muscle weakness, poor vision, albinism, and retrolental fibroplasia. Short periods of nystagmus in an infant who is not yet focusing can be normal, but any continuous nystagmus, even in infants, should be referred. Children of all ages may demonstrate slight nystagmus when gazing from the far corners of their eyes; this should be considered normal.

Finally, in the external examination of the eye proper, the lens should be considered. The primary defects that may be revealed on physical examination in this area are cataracts and dislocated lenses. Cataracts are opacities of the lens. Some can be seen by flashing a light into the eye; this is particularly useful if done at an angle. Some, however, need an ophthalmoscopic examination, at times even with a slit lamp and with dilatation for peripheral opacities. When a flashlight or otoscope light is shone directly into the pupil, it should produce a red reflex in much the same way that the headlights of a car will shine directly into a cat's eyes and they will appear bright red or orange. If, rather than a circular red reflex, an opaque density surrounded by the red reflex appears, this may be an indication of a cataract. For the most part, however, if there is any reason to suspect a cataract, the child should be seen by an ophthalmologist. Causes of cataracts include maternal rubella or toxoplasmosis, galactosemia, hypoparathyroidism, Lowe's syndrome, or trauma.

A dislocated lens may be seen on ophthalmoscopic examination, but should be suspected with a trembling iris that moves in quick horizontal movements. Trauma, Marfan's syndrome, or homocystinuria can all cause dislocated lenses.

The final part of the ocular examination to be discussed in this chapter is the use of the ophthalmoscope. Only a very brief description of it will be given here. It should be stressed again that the authors do not feel this should be the nurse's responsibility, except as a part of a neonatal physical examination where she merely is looking for the red reflex or in unusual situations where she has occasion to use this skill extensively and constantly. Even then, it will probably take her a long time to feel very confident in her findings.

When using a ophthalmoscope, the examiner must be sure that the child will hold his eyes still. He should be asked to focus on a specific

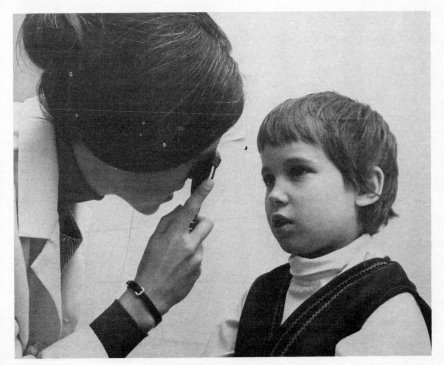

Figure 5–10 Proper usage of the opthalmoscope.

object in the room and told to try to keep his eyes on that object during the entire examination. It should be explained that the examiner may step in front of the child's eyes, and in that case, the child should pretend that he can still see the object and continue to hold his eyes still. The room should be darkened, admitting perhaps a small amount of light from a door left slightly ajar. The examiner holds the ophthalmoscope in his right hand and looks through her own right eye into the child's right eye. The reverse is true for the examination of the left eye. The ophthalmoscope should be held firmly against the examiner's own forehead and the dial should be turned to the black plus numbers, beginning at about +8 to +10. With the ophthalmoscope at this setting, the examiner begins her evaluation at a distance of about 12 inches from the patient. At this point, the red reflex should be visible and opacities in it should be noted. The nurse must then approach to within about 3 inches of the patient and turn the ophthalmoscope dial to successively smaller plus numbers and then through the red minus numbers to about −5 for an optimal look at the retina. The exact number at which the view is optimal depends on the refractory ability of both the examiner's eyes and the patient's eyes. As the nurse dials to smaller and smaller numbers, she should also be approaching closer to the patient's forehead, and by the time she finds the optimal view of the retina, she should be touching foreheads with the child.

Five parts of the internal examination will be discussed: the red reflex, the optic disc, the macula, the fundus and vessels, and the vitreous and aqueous humors.

The red reflex has been discussed previously in this chapter, and it should be obtained on all newborn examinations by looking directly into the eye with a flashlight or the ophthalmoscope. It should be orange-red and the color should be fairly uniform; no dark or opaque spots should be seen.

The optic disc should be evaluated as to size, shape, color, margins, and physiologic depression. The practitioner must learn the normal size by experience. The important thing to remember is that everything else found on the fundus is measured in "disc diameters," abbreviated "DD's." The size indicated by one disc diameter is the size of the optic disc in that eye. The optic disc is usually round but sometimes vertically oval. Any irregularities may indicate adjacent disease. The color should be creamy pink and lighter than the surrounding fundus. In the center of the optic disc should be an indented area called the physiologic depression. This depression should be grayish in color and slightly temporal of center. It should never extend all the way to the disc margin. The disc margins should be smooth and may be slightly darker in color than the rest of the disc. They may be surrounded by a white, clearly demarcated ring called the *scleral ring* which sometimes has a pigmented crescent adjacent to it on the temporal side. These are normal findings, although they are also frequently absent in normal eyes.

Some conditions that may be encountered in evaluating the optic disc should be mentioned. A small optic disc associated with a pallid color may indicate atrophy, while blurred margins accompanied by an obliterated depression and a reddened disc covered with large tortuous vessels may indicate papilledema.

The macula is a small circular landmark, 1-disc diameter in size with a tiny gleaming light near its center, the fovea centralis. It is located 2-disc diameters temporal to the disc; if you do not see it, ask the patient to look directly into your light; this will center it. However, this is a light-sensitive area and the patient will not be able to gaze directly into a light for any length of time.

The fundus is usually an orange-red color, although it is lighter in albinos and darker in blacks and some other individuals. There is a wide range of individual variation even within a race. Whatever color is present, however, should be fairly uniform throughout the fundus although the outside periphery may be slightly lighter. White blotches scattered throughout the area may indicate scarring.

There are both arteries and veins in the area. The arteries are one-fourth narrower than the veins and reflect a light reflex from their center. The veins are slightly wider, have no light reflex and manifest slight pulsations.

Abnormalities should be suspected if these vessels are notched at the crossings, if they are abnormally tortuous, if they manifest hemorrhages or exudates, or if the veins show no pulse.

When the examiner finishes inspecting the most posterior surfaces, she should gradually turn the dial on the ophthalmoscope to the black, or plus numbers, going from zero to each higher number in turn. She will then be able to see in succession the posterior vitreous, the anterior vitreous, the lens, and finally, when she is at about the +15 or +20, she will be focusing on the iris and cornea. No opacities or irregularities should be seen in any of these structures.

WHERE TO EXAMINE

The entire external eye, orbit, and surrounding tissue must be thoroughly evaluated. The internal eye may also be evaluated ophthalmoscopically. We do not feel, however, that nurses should generally accept the responsibility of the ophthalmoscopic examination. This examination is quite difficult and requires a great deal of practice. The nurse working primarily with young children will not usually have occasions enough to keep up her skill in this area. For this reason, this chapter has discussed only the basic elements of the ophthalmoscopic examination.

WHAT TO EXAMINE WITH

The external eye, for the most part, is examined by gross inspection. A penlight or some other good source of light such as an otoscope head is needed to test the strabismus. A cover card may be used for the cover test although many clinicians use their hand in place of such a card. An ophthalmoscope is necessary only if an internal examination is to be done. This is not generally part of a routine physical examination.

BIBLIOGRAPHY

Abbas, L., et al.: "Functional Results in Alternating Esotropia," *Bulletin of the Ophthalmological Society of Egypt*, 1962, pp. 175–186.

Abboud, I.: "Eye Manifestation in Nutritional Deficiencies," *Bulletin of the Ophthalmological Society of Egypt*, 1967, pp. 223–230.

(Editorials), "Nystagmus: Recent Studies," *Journal of the American Medical Association*, March 10, 1969, pp. 1906–1907.

(Editorials), "The Red Eye," *Lancet*, July 29, 1972, p. 221.

Azar, R. F.: "The Squinting Child," *Journal of the Louisiana State Medical Society*, March 1969, pp. 81–86.

Barness, Lewis A.: *Manual of Pediatric Physical Diagnosis*, Chicago: Year Book Medical Publishers, Inc., 1968, pp. 56–69.

Barnett, Henry L.: *Pediatrics*, New York: Appleton Century Crofts, 1968, pp. 1627–1646.

Beard, C.: "Blepharoptosis: Clinical Evaluation and Therapeutic Rationale," *International Ophthalmology Clinics*, Spring, 1970, pp. 97–115.

Cullen, J. F.: "Diagnostic Index for Diseases of the Eye," *British Journal of Ophthalmology*, May 1970, pp. 348–355.

Davis, D. G., and J. L. Smith: "Periodic Alternating Nystagmus: A Report of Eight Cases," *American Journal of Ophthalmology*, October 1971, pp. 757–762.

DeGowin, Elmer L., and Richard L. DeGowin: *Bedside Diagnostic Examination*, New York: The Macmillan Company, 1970, pp. 65–118.

Delp, Mahlon H., and Robert T. Manning: *Major's Physical Diagnosis*, Philadelphia: W. B. Saunders Company, 1968, pp. 62–74.

Emarah, M. H.: "The Diagnosis and Management of Abnormal Retinal Correspondence," *Bulletin of the Ophthalmological Society of Egypt*, 1969, pp. 398–401.

——— "The Diagnosis and Management of Fixation Disparity," *Bulletin of the Ophthalmological Society of Egypt*, 1969, pp. 399–402.

Feingold, M., and S. S. Gellis: "Ocular Abnormalities Associated with First and Second Arch Syndromes," *Survey of Ophthalmology*, July, 1969, pp. 30–42.

Forster, R. K., N. J. Schatz, and J. L. Smith: "A Subtle Eyelid Sign in Aberrant Regeneration of the Third Nerve," *American Journal of Ophthalmology*, May 1969, pp. 696–698.

Gardiner, P. A.: "Infantile Nystagmus," *Developmental Medicine and Child Neurology*, April 1971, pp. 244–245.

Green, Morris, and Julius B. Richmond: *Pediatric Diagnosis*, Philadelphia: W. B. Saunders Company, 1962, pp. 30–49.

Gundersen, T.: "Early Diagnosis and Treatment of Strabismus," *Sight-Saving Review*, Fall, 1970, pp. 129–136.

Johnston, G., and F. Roy: "Strabismus: Early Diagnosis and Treatment," *Journal of the Arkansas Medical Society*, November 1970, pp. 190–192.

Judge, Richard D., and George D. Zuidema: *Physical Diagnosis: A Physiology Approach*, Boston: Little, Brown and Company, 1963, pp. 57–81.

Kempe, C. Henry, Henry K. Silver, and Donough O'Brien: *Current Pediatric Diagnosis and Treatment*, Los Altos, Calif.: Lange Medical Publications, 1970, pp. 125–141.

Kesby, B.: "Amblyopia in Concomitant Esotropia," *Transactions of the Ophthalmological Societies of the United Kingdom*, vol. 87, 713–714.

Laibson, P. R.: "Diagnosing Corneal Disease," *Pennsylvania Medicine*, December 1968, pp. 41–43.

Leone, C. R., Jr.: "Congenital Blepharoptosis: Varieties, Differential Diagnosis, Treatment," *Clinical Pediatrics*, March 1972, pp. 171–173.

————"Entropion: Diagnosis and Treatment," *Texas Medicine*, January 1969, pp. 44–47.

Lerman, Sidney: *Basic Ophthalmology*, New York: McGraw-Hill Book Company, 1966.

Liebman, Sumner D., and Sydney S. Gellis (eds.): *The Pediatrician's Ophthalmology*, St. Louis: The C. V. Mosby Company, 1966.

Luke, J. L., "Conjunctival Petechiae," *New England Journal of Medicine*, May 13, 1971, p. 1101.

Macmillan, D. W.: "Differential Diagnosis of the 'Red Eye,'" *Virginia Medical Monthly*, January 1972, pp. 35–40.

Malbran, E., and R. Dodds: "Different Types of Holes and Their Significance," *Bibliotheca Ophthalmologica* (Basel), 1967, pp. 170–86.

Nelson, Waldo: *Textbook of Pediatrics*, Philadelphia: W. B. Saunders Company, 1964, pp. 1482–1499.

Ophthalmologic Staff of the Hospital for Sick Children, Toronto: *The Eye in Childhood*, Chicago: Year Book Medical Publishers, Inc., 1967.

Prior, John, and Jack Solberstein: *Physical Diagnosis*, St. Louis: The C. V. Mosby Company, 1969, pp. 71–115.

Putterman, A. M.: "Evaluation of the Lacrimal System," *Eye, Ear, Nose and Throat Monthly*, June 1972, pp. 212–216.

Raab, E., "Useful Extensions of Common Strabismus Tests: The Combined Worth 4-Dot Flashlight," *American Orthoptic Journal*, 1972, pp. 47–58.

Robb, R. M.: "Observations on a Child's Eyes," *Sight-Saving Review*, Summer, 1970, pp. 67–70.

Romano, P., and G. K. Von Noorden: "Limitations of Cover Test in Detecting Strabismus," *American Journal of Ophthalmology*, July 1971, pp. 10–12.

Schaeffer, Alexander J., and Mary Ellen Avery: *Disease of the Newborn*, Philadelphia: W. B. Saunders Company, 1971, pp. 798–815.

Shanholtz, M.: "Amblyopis Ex Anopsia," *Virginia Medical Monthly*, May 1969, pp. 275–276.

Silver, Henry K., C. Henry Kempe, and Henry B. Bruyn: *Handbook of Pediatrics*, Los Altos, Calif.: Lange Medical Publications, 1965, pp. 352–367.

Stafford, T. J.: "The Normal and the Abnormal Pupil," *Postgraduate Medical Journal*, May 1969, pp. 75–79.

Staton, Y.' "Responsibility of the Pediatrician and the Family Physician for Prevention of Blindness in the Preschool Child," *Journal of the Florida Medical Association*, October 1968, pp. 926–928.

Stein, Harold A., and Bernard J. Slatt: *The Ophthalmic Assistant*, St. Louis: The C. V. Mosby Company, 1971.

Von Nooden, G. K.: "Diagnosis and Management of Eye Muscle Problems in Childhood," *Surgical Clinics of North America*, August 1970, pp. 885–894.

Watson, P. G.: "Diseases of the Cornea," *Practitioner*, June 1969, pp. 759–768.

Weinstein, G. W.: "Signs and Symptoms of Ocular Disease," *Occupational Health Nurse* (Auckland), May 1971, pp. 7–12.

Wirtschafter, J. D., and I. P. Stapp: "Strabismus Cover Test Demonstrator," *American Journal of Ophthalmology*, March 1971, pp. 760–762.

Ziai, Mohsen: *Pediatrics*, Boston: Little, Brown and Company, 1969, pp. 699–710.

SUGGESTED RESOURCES

1 Pamphlets

"The Eyes," Meade Johnson and Co. (Free)

"Some Pathological Conditions of the Eye, Ear, and Throat: An Atlas," Abbott Laboratories. (Free)

2 Films

"Errors of Refraction"
   Color, 21 minutes
   Cost: Free
   Abbott Laboratories
   Abbott Park
   North Chicago, Illinois 60064

GLOSSARY

amblyopia loss of vision caused from constant disuse of the eye

anisocoria the condition in which one pupil is larger than the other

aqueous humor a clear watery secretion that fills the anterior and posterior chambers of the eye

Bitot's spots irregular yellow patches on the palpebral conjunctiva, caused by vitamin A deficiency

blepharospasm excessive blinking

cataract a clouding of the lens

chalazion a cyst of the Meibomian glands

chemosis edema of the conjunctiva

ciliary glands the modified sweat glands found throughout the eyelashes

coloboma a notch; especially a notch of the lid or the iris of the eye

conjunctiva a thin layer of mucous membrane lining the inner portion of the eyelids and part of the sclera

conjunctivis inflammation of the conjunctiva

cornea the transparent, anterior portion of the fibrous layer of the eye which is contiguous with the sclera

dacryoadenitis inflammation of the lacrimal gland

dacryocystitis infection of the lacrimal system

dysautonomia production of an inadequate amount of tears

ectropion a condition in which the borders of the eyelids turn out

entropion a condition in which the borders of the eyelids turn in

epiblepharon (Mongolian fold) a horizontal fold in the upper lid, overhanging the superior tarsus

epicanthal folds vertical folds of skin covering the inner canthus of the eye

epiphora excessive tearing

exopthalmos the condition in which the globe of the eye protrudes from the socket

eye bulb the eye proper, consisting of the outer layer with its cornea and sclera, the middle layer with its choroid, ciliary body and iris, and its inner layer with its retina

fovea centralis the central depression of the macula

heterochromia the condition in which an individual has irises of different color

hordeola (styes) inflammations of the sebaceous glands near the lashes

internal hordeola (styes) inflammation of the Meibomian glands

iris the colored, round, contractile disc surrounding the pupil

Kayser-Fleisher ring a brown or grayish green circle at the limbus, may be a sign of Wilson's disease

lagophthalmos a condition in which the upper and lower eyelids do not completely meet, causing incomplete closure

lens the transparent biconvex structure immediately behind the pupil whose function is to focus light rays on the retina

macula an oval yellowish area at the exact center of the posterior retina where vision is most perfect

Marcus Gunn phenomenon (jaw-winking reflex) the phenomenon in which movement of the jaw to one side causes the child to raise the opposite eyelid

marginal blepharitis red, scaling, crusted lid edges often caused by *Staphlococcus* infection.

Meibomian glands a sebaceous gland between the tarsal plate and the conjunctiva

microphthalmia small orbits

nasolacrimal duct the duct that leads from the lacrimal gland to the lacrimal sac

noncomitant (paralytic) strabismus strabismus that occurs as a result of a paralyzed extraocular muscle

nystagmus a continuous jerky movement of the iris and pupil

papilledema swelling of the optic nerve where it enters the retina

phoria a latent tendency toward strabismus

pinguecula a yellowish triangular thickening of the bulbar conjunctiva, extending from the outer canthus to the limbic area

pseudoptosis ptosis caused by the weight of the upper lid, usually due to edema

pterygium an increase in growth of the pinguecula due to irritation, usually from wind

ptosis drooping of the upper eyelid

retina the inner layer of the eye whose function is to receive images focused upon it by the lens

retinoblastoma a malignant glioma of the retina

rhodopsin (visual purple) a lavendar pigment found in the retinal rods

strabismus (squint) a disorder of the eye in which both eyes are unable to fixate on the same object at the same time due to lack of coordination of the optic axes

tarsal glands modified sebaceous (fat-producing) glands located between the skin and the conjunctiva of the eyelid in the area of the tarsal plate

tarsal plate the supporting plate of the upper eyelid

tropia overt strabismus

vitreous body a clear semigelatinous mass which fills the cavity of the eyeball

zonula ciliaris the suspensory ligament that attaches the ciliary body to the lens and helps to position the lens and change its shape

The Ears

WHY THE CHILD IS EXAMINED

A thorough examination of the ears is an important part of every physical examination. Certainly ear infections are one of the most common of the early childhood infectious diseases. Ear disease can present with classic textbook symptoms: painful ears, fever, upper respiratory infection, etc., but they can also present, particularly in young children, with symptoms that seem totally unrelated, such as nausea and vomiting or generalized symptoms like lethargy. For this reason, the ears of every sick child, no matter what the presenting complaint, must be carefully examined. Likewise, the ears of every well child must be examined, since ear infections, particularly in infants, are frequently found with no symptoms at all.

WHAT TO EXAMINE: ANATOMY OF THE AREA

The ear is divided into three parts: external, middle, and internal ear. The portion of the ear protruding from the head is called the auricle, or pinna, and is composed of a thin sheet of cartilage covered with skin. It is sometimes useful to know the specific names of the areas of the auricle in order to be able to describe the findings of the examination more accurately. The prominent, outer rim of the auricle is called the *helix*, while the antihelix is the area parallel and anterior to it. *Concha* is the term given to the deep cavity at the middle of the pinna, the entrance to the meatus. Lying anteriorly is the protuberance called the *tragus* and opposite it is the *antitragus*. The bottom, elastic portion of the pinna is called the lobe.

The position of the pinna is important. The tip of it should cross the eye-occiput line (an imaginary line drawn from the lateral aspect of the eye to the most prominent protuberance of the occiput). The angle should be almost vertical; if it is more than 10° from vertical, the examiner should make specific notation of it and look closely for further abnormalities.

The external meatus is a canal approximately 2.5-cm long, leading from the concha to the tympanic membrane. This canal follows an S-shaped curve; first inward, forward, and downward. This is important to remember when attempting to straighten the canal for vision. The curvature is slightly different in infants and young children, and this must be remembered when examining each age group. The canal is formed of cartilage and membranes at the outer opening and of bone, and is lined

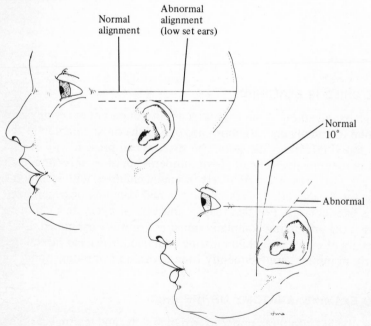

Figure 6–1 Normal and abnormal ear alignment.

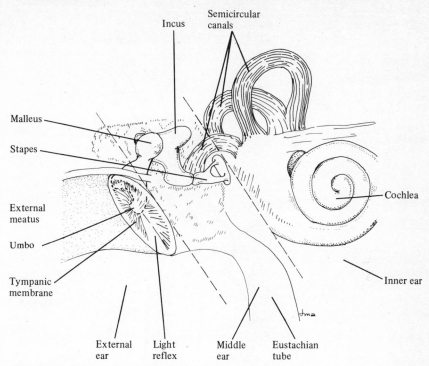

Figure 6–2 Ear canal and ossicles.

with skin towards the inner end. This skin lining is very thin and easily broken.

The middle ear is an air-filled space within the temporal bone, consisting of the tympanic membrane, the malleus, incus, and stapes. The tympanic membrane, or eardrum, is a thin, almost transparent membrane, angled inferiorly and medially so as to join the floor of the meatus at an angle of about 55°. This vertical and horizontal inclination is greatly exaggerated in the infant and young child. This is an important fact for the examiner to bear in mind, since the inexperienced will often interpret this normal angle as a bulging of the pars flaccida. Remember, the posterosuperior quadrant will be closest as you look down the canal; the anteroinferior quadrant will be farthest from you. The tympanic membrane may be divided into four portions for easy reference: anteroinferior quadrant, anterosuperior quadrant, posteroinferior quadrant, posterosuperior quadrant. Due to looseness of the top quadrants, this area is designated the *pars flaccida*, while the lower, more taut area is called the *pars tensa*. The white dense fibrous ring surrounding the tympanic membrane is called the tympanic ring or annulus. It completely surrounds the tympanic membrane with the exception of the anterior and posterior malleolar folds.

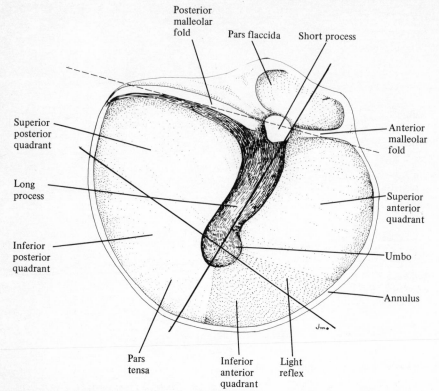

Posterior
malleolar
fold Pars flaccida Short process

Superior
posterior
quadrant

Anterior
malleolar
fold

Long
process

Superior
anterior
quadrant

Inferior
posterior
quadrant

Umbo

Annulus

Pars
tensa

Inferior
anterior
quadrant

Light
reflex

Figure 6–3 Tympanic membrane and landmarks.

Directly behind the tympanic membrane lie three moveable ossicles: the malleus, incus, and stapes. The malleus is a small, inverted T-shaped bone often compared to a hammer. The long end of the malleus is attached to the inner surface of the tympanic membrane extending as far as the center of the membrane. This attachment causes the tympanic membrane to be drawn inward, creating a concavity called the *umbo*. The incus is the middle bone and serves to connect the other two ossicles. The short end is attached to the malleus, leaving the long end for the stapes.

The innermost of the three bones is called the *stapes* and resembles a stirrup in shape. The head of the stapes connects to the incus and the flat base attaches to the fenestra vestibuli which leads to the inner ear.

The inner ear contains some of the essential organs of hearing which distribute the sound waves entering the canal. The main parts of the inner ear are the vestibule, semicircular canals, and cochlea. The detailed description of these organs is not the subject of this book, and the interested reader is referred to a good anatomy book.

Throughout the external, middle, and internal ear are blood vessels and nerves, often very near the surface. This means the nurse must be very careful, since the examination of these parts can often be painful or draw blood very easily.

HOW TO EXAMINE

The examination of the ears can be virtually painless if the child will cooperate or can be helped to cooperate. It is most important that he remain absolutely still during the examination. The older, cooperative child may be willing to stand in front of the examiner or to sit on the examining table or the mother's lap. The younger child (1 to 3 years old) may do better held on mother's lap or on the examining table. If the lap is chosen, turn the child to mother's side. Have the mother hold his head firmly against her chest with one hand and use the other hand to restrain the child's arms and chest. The child's legs can be secured between the mother's knees. If using the table, the child should be placed on his back with his head turned to one side and his arms held straight over his head. The mother may stand at the head of the table and firmly hold the child's

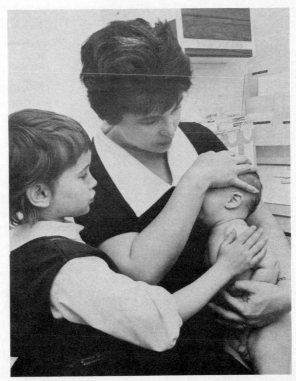

Figure 6-4 Child being restrained in the upright position.

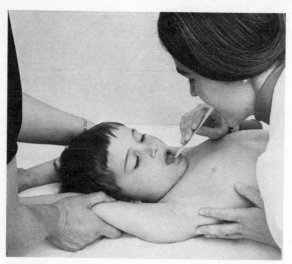

Figure 6-5 Child being restrained on the examining table.

arms at his elbows. The examiner leans her upper body on the child's chest and can then use both arms for examining the ear. The infant from birth to 1 year of age is best examined on the table in this fashion.

The child should be told he is going to have his ears looked at and should be given a chance to become accustomed to the otoscope. The nurse may show the child that it is a funny-looking flashlight and let him watch the light hit his palm. Once the initial introduction is made, the child is positioned. Place the speculum of the otoscope at the edge of the meatus, turning the child's head back and forth so he may become accustomed to the feel of something at his ear. If the child is sitting, remember that the tympanic membrane is at a 55° angle and that the child's head should be tilted away from the examiner in order to bring the membrane into an upright position. Because the canal is curved, the auricle must be firmly gripped and pulled to straighten the canal for a view. Since the canal curves upward in infants, the ear is pulled down; in the older child, the canal has a downward and forward position, and the ear must be pulled up and back. As the child becomes accustomed to the feel, tell him you are going to take a longer look in this ear; and slowly insert the speculum and take a look. Then go on to the other ear. Even though there is no pain connected with the examination, most children dislike the feeling of being restrained and will cry. Often babies will cry until the speculum is inserted and then stop while the actual visualization is taking place. Considering this, it is probably best to examine the ears last and then let the child recover from the ordeal in his mother's arms.

As with other parts of the body, the most important part of the examination is observation. With the exception of palpation of the outer auricle and the mastoid, the entire ear examination is done by observation—first with no instrument and then deeper with the otoscope. Observation of the outer ear should include several points. Location of the ears on the head is important. Are they low set? Are both ears at the same level? Are they flat against the head or protruding? Size of the ears should also be evaluated. Are they bigger or smaller than normal? Do they have large hanging ear lobes? The nurse must inspect the shape of the ears as well. The helix should be checked for normal amount of curvature and presence of the tragus. Color must be considered as must any discharges. Observation of the canal includes looking at the amount and texture of the cerumen and checking for any furuncles. Inspection of the inner canal requires the use of the otoscope. The otoscope consists of:

1   A handle, often containing the batteries.
2   The neck.
3   The head, containing the lens, the rim for attaching the speculum, a bulb, and often a small spigot for a pneumonic device.
4   Speculums are sized 2, 3, 4, and 5 mm and 9 mm for the nose. For the ears, most examiners do not use the 2-mm ones, because they are too small and could easily go too far into the canal.

Two batteries fit into the handle of the otoscope. It is extremely important to check the batteries to make certain they are still fresh.

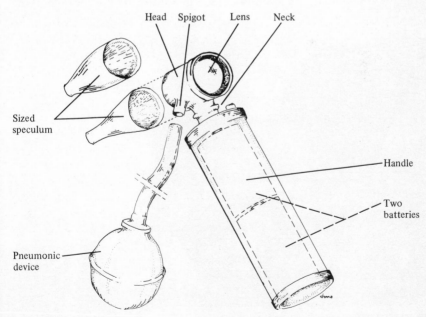

Figure 6-6   Otoscope parts.

Regular batteries may last between 1 and 2 weeks, depending on the amount of use. Long-life batteries will last considerably longer and may be worth the added expense. The batteries should not be used when they give off a yellow rather than white light. If the otoscope is going to be unused for several weeks, remove the batteries so they do not corrode the inside of the handle. Learn to turn the otoscope on just as the speculum enters the ear and to turn it off immediately after withdrawal. This will save the batteries. Always carry an extra bulb in case one burns out during an examination. Bulbs do not burn out gradually and you generally have no warning of when you will need a replacement.

The speculum should be cleaned with an alcohol sponge after each use. Always use the largest possible speculum to fit the child's ear and be certain to fix the speculum firmly to the head rim. It is embarrassing to remove the otoscope from the ear and have the speculum remain in the canal.

It is important to hold your otoscope correctly from the first time you begin to use it. Hold it securely like a pencil with the head down and the heavy handle resting between your thumb and forefinger. This will seem awkward in the beginning. Rest your hand securely on the child's head. This is especially important with younger children who may suddenly draw away. The bracing allows the speculum to move with the child's head and prevents the examiner from jamming the speculum through the tympanic membrane. The free hand can be used to pull the ear to straighten the canal. It should be pulled in a direction appropriate to the

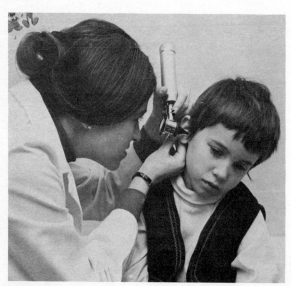

Figure 6-7   The correct way to hold the otoscope for the examination of the ear.

age of the child. Slowly insert the speculum $1/4$ to $1/2$ inch into the canal, looking at the canal as the speculum passes.

When examining the tympanic membrane, the nurse is looking for five main characteristics: color of the membrane, light reflex, umbo, long process, and short process.

The color of the tympanic membrane is normally a light, pearly gray translucent color. The light reflex is a small cone of light reflected from the otoscope light. It should be a rather sharply demarcated triangular shape pointing posteriorly (away from the nose). A diffuse or spotty light reflex is not normal and needs further investigation. At the top point of the light reflex is the umbo. This is the long end of the malleus and is so firmly attached that it causes an indentation of the tympanic membrane. It is viewed as a small, round, white opaque spot. Looking anteriorly and superiorly to the umbo the examiner can see the long process of the malleus. This often appears as a whitish line extending from the umbo to the end of the tympanic membrane, consisting of several folds of membrane. At the upper end of the long process is the short process of the malleus. This appears as a sharp protuberance through the tympanic. The annulus is another important landmark; it is the fibrous ring surrounding the periphery of the tympanic membrane. It must be inspected carefully, since this is a very likely spot to find perforations. The examiner should locate this landmark and follow it completely around the drum; it will appear whiter and denser than the rest of the membrane. It should form a circle which is complete except for a small missing portion between the anterior and posterior malleolar folds. There are three other landmarks: the anterior and posterior malleolar folds, the long process of the incus, and the chorda tympani nerve. These landmarks are not so constant as the previously discussed ones, but the nurse should know their location. They are included in the diagram for that reason. Frequently the view in the speculum shows only a portion of the tympanic membrane, and the otoscope must be adjusted to see the remainder. While learning, remove the entire speculum to do this adjusting. With practice, the head of the otoscope can be moved slightly without disturbing the tip. Since the tip of the speculum is fit snuggly against the walls of the canal, any large movement will cause discomfort. Also remember to retract the speculum fully before releasing the ear. As the ear pinna is released the canal returns to its curved position and the speculum remains straight causing pressure in the canal.

The examiner should always test for mobility of the eardrum. A normal tympanic membrane covering only air in the middle ear will move smoothly if slight pressure is applied. If the middle ear contains fluid, the tympanic will not move or will move in a sticky or jerky fashion. A small puff of air can be applied by attaching a small tube to the head of the otoscope with the pneumonic bulb (or probably more effectively, by

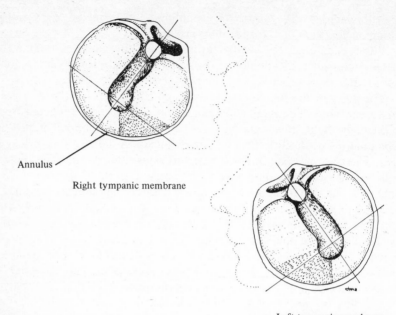

Annulus

Right tympanic membrane

Left tympanic membrane

Figure 6–8   The right and left tympanic membrane with landmarks.

placing the end in the examiner's mouth) and gently blowing small puffs of air in and out while watching the tympanic. The speculum must fit the head and the canal snugly for this procedure to be effective.

No examination of the ear is complete without examining the child for hearing. Tests for hearing are not discussed in this book.

WHERE TO EXAMINE

The entire ear, both inside and outside, must be examined carefully. The mastoid process directly behind the pinna must also be included. This is particularly important when ear infection exists, since mastoiditis is sometimes associated with this condition. An edematous tender area is usually the presenting symptom. If this condition does exist it must be drawn to the attention of the physician, since, not only should it be treated for its own sake, but the infection can spread directly from the mastoid area to the brain.

WHAT TO EXAMINE WITH

An otoscope is the usual instrument utilized in the examination of the ear. This can be either the type that plugs into an electrical outlet in the wall or the battery type. The fiberoptic light is now used most commonly with both types. The speculum end is generally one of two types. The first has a space between the magnifying glass and the speculum. This type is the best for curetting ears. However, it is impossible to use a pneumonic tube with it—a device which is indispensible in pediatrics. Therefore, the other type of speculum attachment is recommended. This is the one in which the magnifying glass is directly attached to the speculum; it also has an attachment for a pneumonic tube. This is somewhat more difficult to handle when curetting, but it is possible, and the directions given in this chapter assume the use of this type of otoscope.

Specialists in ear, nose, and throat almost always use and strongly recommend a head mirror. The light source with a head mirror is far superior to that of an otoscope; however, few clinics are set up to utilize this type of equipment since it requires a gooseneck lamp. Also, the examiner does not have the aid of magnification. If the nurse is practicing where a gooseneck lamp is available, it is certainly recommended that she learn to use a head mirror. She will find it excellent equipment for examination not only of the ear, but of the nose and throat as well.

WHAT TO EXAMINE FOR

As with other parts of the body, if the examiner knows what normal looks like, the abnormal will be easily recognized when it appears. It is not as important to specify the exact abnormality as it is to say that the ear is definitely not normal and that the child needs to be seen by a physician. The following are some minor conditions nurses need to be aware of when examining ears. For a discussion of more serious ear conditions the reader is referred to a good pathology book.

The external ear should be examined for malformations, nodules, cysts, or any type of lesions.

The middle ear should be examined for any abnormalities, such as furuncles, foreign bodies including insects (a common problem in the young child), polyps, and swelling of the walls of the canal.

An important aspect of the middle ear which deserves careful evaluation is cerumen. Cerumen (ear wax) is a mixture of sebum from sebaceous glands and from apocrine sweat glands produced in the ear canal. Reports indicate that there may be racial differences; i.e., the Japanese[1] and Chinese[2] apparently have no or very little ear wax.[3] Patients with acne vulgaris often have excessive ear wax. Some patients complain of external otitis have been found to have no ear wax.[4] The cerumen may be of several consistencies. Yellow cerumen tends to be

[1]H. S. Muckleston, "Keratosis Obturans," *Eye, Ear, Nose and Throat Monthly* vol. 8, 1929, p. 65.
[2]John Gunther, *Inside Asia*, New York: Harper & Brothers, 1939, p. 285.
[3]C. Keating, "Diagnosis and Treatment of Inflammation of the External Acoustic Meatus," *Journal of the Royal Naval Medical Service*, vol. 18, 1932, p. 281.
[4]Branca, H. E. "External Otitis," *Archives of Otolaryngology*, vol. 57, 1953, p. 310.

soft and wet, while black and brown cerumen is often drier and harder. No one has been able to report the purpose of cerumen. The best hypothesis is that it is produced to carry foreign matter away from the tympanic membrane and avoid damage to that area.

A small amount of cerumen causes no problem, since the examiner can look past it for a view of the tympanic membrane and it does not harm the ear itself. Mothers should be instructed on how to clean the ears and should be told not to worry about the cerumen. Ears are best cleaned with a wash cloth during the regular bath. If wax has been a problem before, the mother may use a medicine dropper to put a few drops of liquid soap into the canal at the beginning of the bath which should be rinsed out at the end. The nurse must be sure an intact tympanic exists before advising this procedure. Discourage the use of cotton-tipped applicators for digging out wax. It only pushes the wax further toward the tympanic and makes it very difficult to remove. It can also be potentially dangerous. Certainly the use of bobby pins or other pointed objects should be discouraged. If there is excessive wax in the ears and the tympanic membrane cannot be visualized, the wax must be removed. There are two methods available and they depend on the type of wax present (dry, scaly, wet, sticky, etc.) and the condition of tympanic membrane. If the wet sticky type is present, it is best to dig it out with a curette (No. 0-1 with blunt ends). This can be a painful and often bloody procedure. No matter what the age of the child, he must be restrained. It may take the examiner, the mother, and an additional person. The child should lie on the table with his head to one side. The otoscope is held in one hand, the lens slid to the halfway point, and the curette inserted through the head rim into the ear. The closeness of the blood vessels and nerves to the surface make it very easy to draw blood and cause pain. With practice, the nurse will learn to avoid pain and blood, in most cases. Curettes come in several sizes, usually Nos. 0 and 00 are used on children.

If the wax is dry, hard, and scaly, irrigation may be the only way to remove it. However, the examiner first must be certain that the tympanic membrane is intact, otherwise water is forced straight into the inner ear. This is a messy procedure and cannot be done on a child who will not cooperate. The equipment needed will be a large water syringe, a large basin of warm water (not hot), a small ear or kidney basin, and 4 to 6 towels. The child sits and is draped with towels. The syringe is filled with warm water and squirted with force at the superoposterior canal wall. If the water is not warm enough, the child will become dizzy. It will take several pans of water and about 20 minutes to remove the wax from each ear. As pieces of wax float out, the procedure can be stopped for a look through the otoscope to see if the tympanic membrane is in view. The child who comes in complaining of ear pain and who has an ear full of dry scaly wax, should have his ears curetted rather than irrigated. The examiner cannot take the chance that the tympanic membrane is broken.

The tympanic membrane is, of course, of utmost importance in an evaluation of the ear. As previously mentioned, the examiner must search meticulously, both centrally and peripherally, for perforations. Further disorders of the eardrum will not be considered in this book. The reader is referred to a good pathology book.

The inner ear is not immediately accessible for physical examination and the tests used to determine its functioning are rather complex and not routinely done. The nurse need not concern herself with these tests. If she is worried about the functioning of the inner ear, the child should be referred to a physician.

BIBLIOGRAPHY

Barness, Lewis A.: *Manual of Pediatric Physical Diagnosis*, Chicago: Yearbook Medical Publishers, Inc., 1968, pp. 70–76.

DeGowin, Elmer, and Richard DeGowin: *Bedside Diagnostic Examination*, London: Macmillan & Co., Ltd., 1971, pp. 173–188.

Delp, Mahlon H., and Robert Manning: *Major's Physical Diagnosis*, Philadelphia: W. B. Saunders Company, 1968, pp. 56–60.

DeWeese, David D., and William H. Saunders: *The Textbook of Otolaryngology*, St. Louis: The C. V. Mosby Company, 1964.

Ferguson, Charles F.: "Changing Concepts in Otolaryngology for the Pediatrician," *Pediatrics*, vol. 25, no. 6, 1960, pp. 1043–1066.

Gellis, Sydney S.: *Current Pediatric Therapy*, Philadelphia: W. B. Saunders Company, 1971, pp. 522–534.

Green, Morris, and Julius Richmond: *Pediatric Diagnosis*, Philadelphia: W. B. Saunders Company, 1962, pp. 54–55.

Gunther, John: *Inside Asia*, New York: Harper & Brothers, 1939, p. 285.

Judge, Richard D., and George D. Zuidema: *Physical Diagnosis*, Boston: Little, Brown and Company, 1963, pp. 117–118, 124–125.

Keating, C.: "Diagnosis and Treatment of Inflammation of the External Acoustic Meatus," *Journal of the Royal Naval Medical Service*, vol. 18, 1932, p. 281.

Longnecker, Charles G., Robert F. Ryan, and Richard W. Vincent: "Malformations of the Ear as a Clue to Urogenital Anomalies," *Plastic and Reconstructive Surgery*, vol. 35, no. 3, 1965, pp. 303–309.

Muckleston, H. S.: "Keratosis Obturans," *Eye, Ear, Nose and Throat Monthly*, vol. 8, 1929, p. 65.

Perry, Eldon T.: *The Human Ear Canal*, Springfield, Ill.: Charles C Thomas, Publisher, 1957.

Smith, David W.: *Recognizable Patterns of Human Malformation*, Philadelphia: W. B. Saunders Company, 1970, p. 339.

SUGGESTED RESOURCES

1 Pamphlets

"The External Ear," Meade Johnson. (Free)

"Some Pathological Conditions of the Eye, Ear and Throat: An Atlas," Abbott
Laboratories. (Free)

2 Films

"The Ear and Hearing"
Color, 28 minutes
Cost: $5.00
Ciba Pharmaceutical Co.
P.O. Box 1340
Newark, New Jersey 09101

3 Ear Model:

Cost: $100.00
Denoyer-Geppert
5235 Ravenswood Avenue
Chicago, Illinois 60640

GLOSSARY

annulus   the white dense, fibrous ring surrounding the tympanic membrane
antihelix   the area parallel and anterior to the helix of the auricle
antitragus   the protuberance lying in the deep cavity at the midauricle
auricle (pinna)   portion of the ear protruding from the head
cerumen (ear wax)   a combination of sebum and apocrine sweat produced within
    the ear canal
concha   the deep cavity lying at the midauricle
eye-occiput line   the imaginary line drawn from the outer corner of the eye to the
    most protruding part of the occiput for lining up the top edge of the auricle
helix   the prominent, outer rim of the auricle
incus   the middle bone connecting the malleus and stapes within the middle ear
light reflex   a small cone of light reflected from the otoscope light
long process   the whitish line extending from the umbo to the end of the tympanic
    membrane when looking in the ear. It is the long end of the malleus.
malleus   a small, inverted T-shaped bone attached to the inner surface of the
    tympanic membrane in the middle ear
pars flaccida   the top, loose area of the tympanic membrane
pars tensa   the lower, tightly stretched area of the tympanic membrane
pneumonic tube   the rubber tubing and bulb that can be attached to many
    otoscope heads for gently blowing on the tympanic membrane when testing
    mobility
polyps   growths arising from mucous membrane tissue
short process   a sharp protuberance seen through the tympanic membrane. It is
    the superior process of the malleus.
stapes   the innermost of the three ossicle bones. It is attached to the incus and
    fenestra vestibuli of the inner ear

temporal bone   the cranial bone that contains the middle ear
tragus   the anterior protuberance of the concha
tympanic membrane   the thin, transparent membrane covering the ossicles and
dividing the outer and middle ear
umbo   an indentation of the tympanic seen at the top point of the reflex. It is the
long end of the malleus firmly attached to the inner surface of the tympanic
membrane

The Nose

WHY THE CHILD IS EXAMINED

The nose is the beginning of the respiratory system and may give several clues as to how the rest of the system is functioning. It is also important in its own right since it can be the site of several disease processes, particularly those of an allergic nature.

WHAT TO EXAMINE: ANATOMY OF THE AREA

The respiratory system is composed of the nose, nasal passages, naso-pharynx, larynx, trachea, bronchi, and lungs. This chapter shall be concerned with those structures accessible to physical examination, that is the nose, nasal passages, and paranasal sinuses.

The nose is divided into the external nose and internal nose, or nasal cavity. The external nose is shaped like a triangle with the angle distal to the face being the apex. The base of the nose contains orifices called *nares* (*nostrils*) and is separated by a cartilaginous membrane called the *median septum.* The upper third of the nose is bone—nasal bones and the frontal processes of the maxilla; the remainder of the nose is cartilaginous. Fibroadipose tissue gives some of the shape to the medial portion.

There are three muscles connected with the nose: procerus, nasalis, and depressor septi. The procerus inserts between the eyebrows and runs towards the apex of the nose; it is the muscle used to wrinkle the nose. The nasalis runs along the side of the nose and helps keep the nares open during normal breathing. The depressor septi runs from the maxillary area towards the upper portion of the nose. It is the antagonist to the other two muscles.

The blood supply of the external nose comes from the external and internal carotid arteries; the nasal lymphatic system drains into the submandibular nodes in the area directly below the angle of the mandible. Nasal nerve supply originates from the Vth and VIIth cranial nerves.

The internal nose is divided into two symmetrical, equal chambers separated by the nasal septum; the front portion of the nasal septum is cartilaginous, and the posterior section is bony. At birth, the septum is straight, but becomes deviated and deformed by adulthood causing the two cavities to be unequal in size. The cavities have two openings: (1) the anterior cavity is the vestibule where the nares are located, and it is thickly lined with small hairs; and (2) the posterior cavity or choana leads to the throat. The lateral walls of the cavities are divided into the superior, middle, and inferior nasal conchae (sometimes referred to as *turbinate bones*) and the superior, middle, and inferior meatuses. The superior turbinate is part of the ethmoid bone, and the smallest and most difficult to visualize. The middle turbinate is also part of the ethmoid bone and is intermediate in size. The inferior turbinate is a separate bone with a mucous membrane very rich in blood vessels. It is most easily visualized and most strongly affected by vasoconstrictors. Occasionally people have a fourth turbinate named the *supreme turbinate*, located high above the superior.

The meatuses are openings and drainage tubes that correspond to the turbinates lying directly above them. The superior meatus is short and drains from the sphenoethmoid recess, or pocket, above the superior turbinate. The middle meatus lies under the middle turbinate and drains the maxillary, frontal, and anterior ethmoid sinuses. The inferior meatus lies below the inferior turbinate and may change from large to small, depending on the amount of drainage. The nasolacrimal duct empties here. If there is a supreme turbinate there is a supreme meatus to drain from that area.

The olfactory region of the nose is located high on the superior turbinate and may be disturbed or absent if nasal obstruction becomes so great that air currents cannot reach the olfactory mucosa.

The nasal cavity is lined with a mucous membrane which is thick and

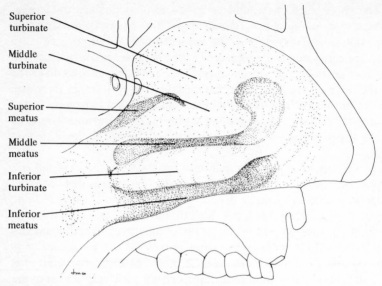

Superior turbinate

Middle turbinate

Superior meatus

Middle meatus

Inferior turbinate

Inferior meatus

Figure 7-1 A side view of the internal nasal cavity.

vascular over the turbinates and septum, and is thin over the meatuses, the floor of the cavity, and the sinuses. The blood supply for the internal nose is similar to that for the external nose; it comes from the external and internal carotid arteries. Through branching, the arterial blood flows into the anterior ethmoid artery and the sphenopalatine artery which form a fine network of small vessels towards the tip of the nose. These are called Kiesselbach's triangle and frequently are the site of bleeding in epitaxis.

The lymphatic system of the internal nose drains into three areas: the submandibular nodes, the retropharyngeal nodes (deep in the neck), and the superior deep cervical nodes.

The nerve supply for the internal nose is more complex than that of the external. The main source is the Vth cranial nerve, but the nasal mucosa has a distribution of parasympathic and sympathic fibers as well.

The paranasal sinuses are air-filled spaces lined with mucous membrane. There are eight all together—four on each side. These sinuses are the ethmoid, the maxillary, the frontal, and the sphenoid. The ethmoid sinus is made up of many small cavities and lies behind the frontal sinus and near the anterior part of the nasal cavities. It is composed of the frontal, lacrimal, sphenoid, and palatine bones and the maxilla. The maxillary sinus is the largest of the sinuses (sometimes called the *antrum of Highmore*) and lies along the lateral wall of the nasal cavity. Most of it is carved out of the maxilla. The average adult sinus will hold 9 to 20 ml of fluid. The frontal sinuses are located behind the superciliary arches of the frontal bone. They are separated by a septum and usually the two cavities are not symmetrical. The sphenoid sinus lies deep within the skull behind the ethmoid sinus. It lies within the sphenoid bone and is divided by a septum into two unequal portions. The ethmoid and maxillary sinuses are present at birth, while the sphenoid is a minute cavity at birth and is fully developed after puberty; the frontal sinus is absent at birth and develops around 7 to 8 years of age. All sinuses are lined with ciliated mucous membrane which is continuous from the nasal cavity; they drain into the nasal cavity and out through the various nasal meatuses.

The nose must be able to perform a variety of functions. Since it provides the entry of air into the respiratory system, it must temper the air, humidify, and filter it. By the time the air hits the trachea, bronchi, and lungs, it must be between 96.8 to 98.6°F. The nose accomplishes this by passing the air over the turbinates. This large surface area, rich in blood supply, warms the air as it passes. Cold air stimulates swelling of the turbinates with more warm blood for the warming effect. Air must also be humidified and conditioned by the time it arrives at the inner system. The nasal mucosa can add or remove moisture from the air to give a constant relative humidity of 75 to 80 percent by the time the air arrives in the

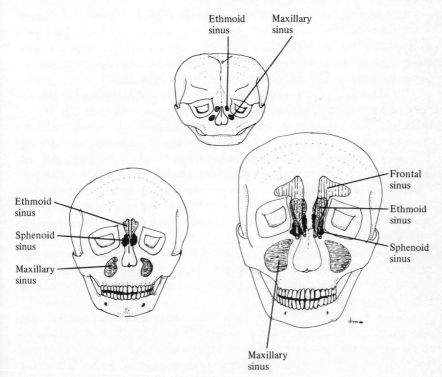

Figure 7-2 The sinuses in the infant, child, and adult.

nasopharynx. It is estimated that 1,000 ml of moisture is evaporated during the breathing that takes place in one day. A blanket of moisture covers the nasal cavity, sinuses, eustachian tube, and trachea. Bacteria and foreign matter are deposited on this blanket and must be removed. A constant ciliary action moves this material to the nasopharynx and pharynx for swallowing and exiting through the stomach.

The nose is also used for olfaction. Although the sense of olfaction (smell) may not be needed for survival by the human being, it makes life much more pleasant. When the ability to smell is reduced, most people find a reduction in the taste of food.

HOW TO EXAMINE

As with other parts of the body, the examiner must observe, palpate, and percuss to gather adequate data about the nose. Auscultation is sometimes used as well.

The child is best approached when he is sitting—either on the table or on the mother's lap. For a very young infant, the examination can be done with the child lying on his back on the table. This part of the examination is usually done as part of the head.

Before touching the child the examiner should observe the external nose. Consider its shape. Is it straight? Examine the nares. Are they symmetrical? Do they flare? Is there anything significant about the skin? Does it have milia, freckles, or acne? Is there any discharge? If so, is it purulent, watery, bloody, or crusty? How much is there?

To observe the inner nose most examiners use an otoscope with the very short broad speculum which is gently inserted into the rim of the nares. Here the nurse should carefully examine the septum and the mucosa. Are there any polyps or tumors on the septum? Is it perforated? The easiest way to check for perforation is to shine the flashlight into one side of the nose while looking at the other side. Is the bright white light visible through to that side? If so, a perforation exists. Examine the color of the mucosa. Inflammation and erythema indicate infection; pale, boggy mucosa is typical of allergy, while swollen, gray mucosa usually results from chronic rhinitis.

When looking through the otoscope the examiner should also be able to visualize the vestibule, the septum, the turbinates and the meatuses. The middle turbinate and meatus are most easily visualized because of their location.

Some examiners prefer using a head mirror and long-handled nasal speculum. To be useful, the mirror must be used regularly. It is attached to the examiner's head with a leather strap and is positioned over one eye, with both eyes remaining open for binocular vision. The focal length is usually 14 inches from the patient's face. In addition to the mirror, the examiner must obtain a good source of light, usually a moveable, gooseneck lamp that can be repositioned for the reflection.

The nose should be palpated along the ridge for the presence of bone and cartilage. The maxillary sinus may be palpated by holding the head steady with one hand while pressing on both cheeks simultaneously with the other hand. The frontal sinus can be palpated by placing two fingers below the eyebrows and pressing upward from the eye socket.

Percussion is usually reserved for the sinuses; both the maxillary and frontal sinuses may be lightly tapped with a forefinger to ascertain if the patient feels pain. The sinuses may also be transilluminated. However, this procedure has its limitations. Only the maxillary and frontal sinuses can be transilluminated and the procedure is not highly successful in children. The examiner is looking for asymmetry of the illumination, but sometimes even normal sinuses will show different degrees of light. In transilluminating the frontal sinuses, a small light is placed firmly against the upper eye socket in a totally darkened room; for the maxillary sinuses a light is placed in the patient's mouth and the lips closed. In a darkened room the red pupillary reflexes will show with cresents of light under them.

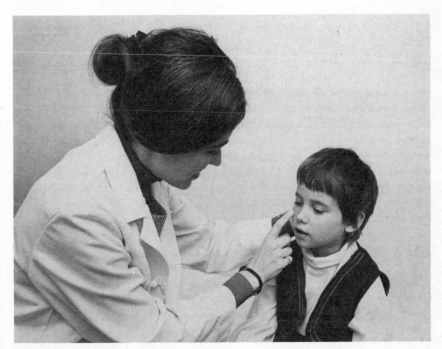

Figure 7-3   Palpation of the maxillary sinus.

WHERE TO EXAMINE

A complete examination of the nose includes the entire exterior nose and sinus areas and as much of the internal nose as can be seen with a nasal speculum.

WHAT TO EXAMINE WITH

Either the otoscope with the nasal speculum attachment or the head mirror with the long-handled nasal speculum and gooseneck lamp are used in the examination of the nose. Their use has been discussed previously in this chapter. A flashlight to examine for perforated septum has also been explained. A stethoscope is sometimes used to be sure that each side of an infant's nose is patent. The diaphragm is held over the naris (nostril) in question while the other naris is occluded by the examiner's finger. Breath sounds should be audible if the tested naris is open. Some condensation will also appear on the diaphragm.

WHAT TO EXAMINE FOR

Knowing what is normal, the examiner will be able to recognize conditions that need remedy.

Of the conditions that the examiner may deal with, nosebleeds are by far the most common. The largest percentage of nosebleeds (or epistaxis) are caused by trauma to the nose, usually by falling or being hit. Excessive picking of the nose can also cause nosebleeds, as can excessive sneezing or violent nose blowing. A high dry altitude, such as that found in Colorado, may cause frequent, unexpected nosebleeds. A foreign body stuffed up the nose may cause bleeding. Hypertension, as well as more exotic causes like tuberculosis, kidney disease, or syphilis, are sometimes indicated as causes. Exposure to certain chemical fumes, such as chromic, sulfuric, and nitric acids, can have the same result.

Ninety percent of all nosebleeds, whatever the cause, come from a rupture of the vessels in Kiesselbach's triangle. The remaining 10 percent come from the posterior portion of the nose. Treatment of the nosebleed which comes from Kiesselbach's triangle is usually not difficult. Have the child remain in a seated position; if he lies down and swallows large quantities of the blood, he will vomit. Compress both nostrils between the fingers for no less than 10 minutes; do not release intermittently to check on blood stoppage. An ice pack may be placed over the bridge of the nose or against the nape of the neck. Slight retroflexion of the neck is sometimes helpful. Cotton plugs may be inserted into the nose and left for several hours after the bleeding has stopped. If the bleeding does not stop within 10 to 15 minutes, or if the child is reporting frequent or several nosebleeds daily, he should be referred. Treatment of the cause is important. Some may need referral for further work-up, particularly if there is reason to suspect hypertension. If the nosebleed is caused by trauma, some advice on accident prevention may be helpful. If it is a result of constant nose picking, helping the child to do something else with his hands may decrease the frequency of the nosebleeds.

Another common complaint concerning the nasal area is that infants, as well as older children, have dry noses, causing them to itch and the child to pick. This is particularly true during the winter months when the air in most houses is dry due to heating, and the mucosa has a tendency to dry out. If after a normal history and examination the nurse can find nothing else wrong, she can suggest that the mother use a small amount of petroleum jelly at the *tip* of the nose, but not to stick large globs of the jelly up the nostrils, since it can be aspirated. A humidifier near an infant's crib or a young child's bed also helps. Be sure, however, that it is not the type a child can burn himself on.

Red irritated nostrils from constant drainage can also be painful. Colds and allergies will not be discussed in this book but something must be said for the discomfort these conditions cause. Often it helps to apply mentholatum or petroleum jelly to the base of the nose to soothe the area and waterproof it long enough to let some healing take place. Again, mothers must be warned against applying an excess amount of any jelly medication for fear that it might be aspirated.

BIBLIOGRAPHY

Barness, Lewis A.: *Manual of Pediatric Physical Diagnosis*, Chicago: Year Book Medical Publishers, Inc., 1968, pp. 76–79.

Barnett, Henry L., and Arnold H. Einhorn: *Pediatrics*, New York: Appleton Century Crofts, 1968, p. 1673.

DeGowin, Elmer, and Richard DeGowin: *Bedside Diagnostic Examination*, London: Macmillan & Co., Ltd., 1971, pp. 118–132.

DeWeese, David D., and William H. Saunders: *The Textbook of Otolaryngology*, St. Louis: The C. V. Mosby Company, 1964.

Flake, Carlyle G., and Charles F. Ferguson: "Congenital Choanal Atresia in Infants and Children," *Annals of Otology, Rhinology and Laryngology*, vol. 73, no. 2, 1964, pp. 458–473.

Green, Morris, and Julius Richmond: *Pediatric Diagnosis*, Philadelphia: W. B. Saunders Company, 1962, pp. 55–58.

Judge, Richard D., and George D. Zuidema: *Physical Diagnosis*, Boston: Little, Brown and Company, 1963, pp. 114–117.

Nelson, Waldo E., *Textbook of Pediatrics*, Philadelphia: W. B. Saunders Company, 1964, pp. 801–803.

Shulman, Irving I.: "The Significance of Epitaxis in Childhood," *Pediatrics*, vol. 24, no. 2, 1959, pp. 489–492.

SUGGESTED RESOURCES

1 Pamphlets

"Upper Respiratory Tract," A Pediatric Aid in Anatomical Illustrations. Carnation Company, Los Angeles, Calif. 90036. (Free) (Also available as slides)

GLOSSARY

antrum of Highmore   the maxillary sinus
conchae (turbinates)   the shell-shaped bones forming the lateral walls of the nasal cavities
depressor septi   the antagonist of the three muscles attached to the nose
epistaxis   bleeding from the nose
ethmoid sinuses   paranasal sinuses located behind the frontal sinus and near the anterior part of the nasal cavities
frontal sinuses   paranasal sinuses located behind the superciliary arches of the frontal bone
Kiesselbach's triangle   a fine network of small blood vessels located near the tip of the nose
maxillary sinuses   the largest of the paranasal sinuses located along the lateral wall of the nasal cavity
meatus   an anatomic opening or passage
nares   orifices at the base of the nose; nostrils
nasalis muscle   one of the three muscles attached to the nose and that aids in keeping the nares open
nasopharynx   the area where the nasal cavity enters the pharynx
procerus muscle   one of the three muscles attached to the nose and that aids in wrinkling the nose

The Mouth and Throat

WHY THE CHILD IS EXAMINED

Exploration of the mouth and throat is an extremely important part of the physical examination of a child. A large majority of ambulatory illnesses in the pediatric age group focalizes in the mouth and throat. (Indeed, one of the major health problems of our civilization—dental disease—is found in this area.) These areas are equally important as focal points in identifying certain systemic disease, for example, the Koplik spots of measles or the enlarged Stensen's duct in mumps.

WHAT TO EXAMINE: ANATOMY OF THE AREA

Anatomically, the mouth and throat can be seen simply as the beginning of a long tube, the digestive tube, which continues throughout most of the body to terminate in the rectum and anus. Each part of this tube is highly specialized to perform some function in the utilization of food, but in this section, only the mouth and throat and their structure and function will be considered.

The mouth is composed of a vestibule, the cavity proper, the lips, cheeks, labial glands, buccal glands, gums, and hard and soft palate; it contains the teeth, tongue, and salivary glands. The encasement of the mouth is a combination of hard and soft areas—the floor and roof consisting of hard bone, and the lateral walls formed by soft, elastic muscles. The floor, although formed by the hard mandibular bone that supplies the needed firmness for tooth attachment, is covered by extremely loose and mobile tissue. The roof of the oral cavity is formed by the maxilla and divided into two parts: the hard and soft palate. The hard palate is anterior and separates the nasal and oral cavities. The soft palate is posterior continuing this separation between the nasal and oral cavities.

When in a relaxed position, the soft palate is concave as it leaves the hard palate and convex at the posterior edge, where the uvula hangs loosely from the midposterior border. The soft palate is a fold of muscular fibers; the hard and soft palates both are covered with mucous membranes. The lateral walls of the oral cavity are soft, mobile and composed of layers of muscles.

The muscles involved in the oral area are complex. Ten of them are intricately involved in controlling the lips and allowing motion in all directions. One large muscle, the orbicularis oris, surrounds the entire lip area and controls closure of the lips. The buccinator is the deep muscle of the cheek and forms the lateral wall of the oral cavity. Because it controls contraction and pressure of the teeth, this muscle is important for mastication. (Trumpet players rely heavily on this muscle in forcing air out through the mouth.) Four major muscles are concerned with mastication; as a unit they control the opening and closing of the jaws. One of the most powerful muscles in the body is the masseter. The masseter muscle in an adult female can exert pressure up to 150 lbs/sq inch, and the adult male can double that—a good reason for keeping fingers out of hostile mouths!

The gingivae (gums) are a dense fibrous tissue attached directly to the bony alveolar surface and covered with smooth, vascular mucous membranes, as are all the internal surfaces of the oral cavity.

The primary blood supply is the external carotid artery which supplies blood to the mouth through three main branches: (1) the facial branch which supplies the oral cavity itself, (2) the lingual branch which supplies the tongue, and (3) the maxillary branch which supplies the teeth and gum areas.

The lymphatic system in the oral cavity is profuse and drains into the lymph nodes along the neck. The gums drain into the submandibular nodes; the hard and soft palates drain into the deep cervical and subparotid nodes; and the floor of the oral cavity drains into the submandibular, superior deep cervical, or submental nodes. Knowledge of this drainage system is very useful when evaluating enlarged lymph nodes in the neck, a common finding in the pediatric patients.

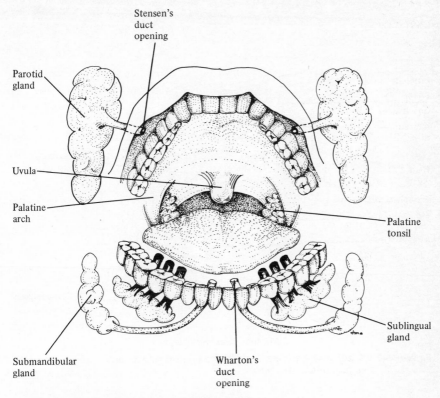

Stensen's
duct
opening

Parotid
gland

Uvula

Palatine
arch

Palatine
tonsil

Sublingual
gland

Submandibular
gland

Wharton's
duct
opening

Figure 8–1   The internal structures of the mouth.

Innervation of the oral cavity is supplied by two main nerves: the Vth cranial nerve (the trigeminal) and the VIIth cranial nerve (the facial).

There are two important sets of nonsalivary glands located in the mouth. The labial glands are small, pea-sized glands situated in the orbicularis oris muscles, and their ducts open into the mucous membranes. The second group, the buccal glands, are smaller and located between the buccinator and masseter muscles, with the ducts opening opposite the last molar tooth.

The posterior portions of mouth and nose join to form the throat or pharynx. The pharynx is a musculomembranous tube divided into three sections: the nasopharynx, the oropharynx, and the laryngopharynx. The nasopharynx is posterior to the nasal cavity and above the soft palate; it always remains open. The posterior wall of this cavity contains the pharyngeal tonsil which, when enlarged during childhood, is called the *adenoid tissue*. The opening for the eustachian tubes is also found in this cavity.

The oral pharynx is posterior to the oral cavity. Along both lateral walls of this pharynx are two palatine arches and between them are lymph

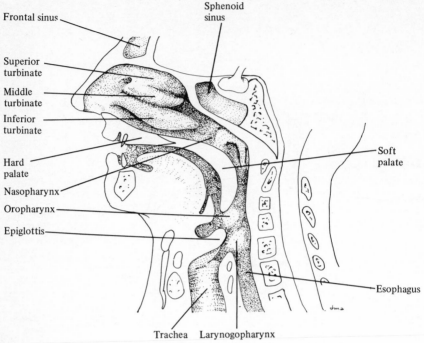

Figure 8–2 A side view of the nasopharynx, oropharynx, and laryngophargynx.

nodules called *palatine tonsils*. This tonsillar tissue enlarges until puberty and then shrinks back into the folds of the palatine arches.

The last section of the throat is the laryngopharynx which lies between the oropharynx and the cricoid cartilage and esophagus. It is in this section that the epiglottis is contained.

There are three related structures found within the mouth which are important to have in mind during the examination: the salivary glands, the tongue, and the teeth. The salivary glands are exocrine glands which perform excretory and secretory functions in the first stages of digestion.

Secretions from three salivary glands—the parotid, submandibular, and sublingual—pour into the oral cavity. The largest of these is the parotid which lies in front of and below the external ear. The parotid (Stensen's) duct opens into the oral mucosa opposite the second upper molar tooth, and is an important landmark for certain diagnoses. The submandibular gland is the size of a walnut and lies below and in front of the parotid and deep within the lower cheek. Its duct, Wharton's duct, runs upward from the gland and opens at the side of the frenulum linguae which lies on the undersurface of the tongue. The sublingual gland is the size of an almond and lies on the floor of the mouth near the center of the

underside of the tongue. Its ducts join with the openings from the submandibular ducts. These three glands produce saliva for the oral
cavity. Depending upon the age, diet, and exercise, they can produce an
average of 1,500 ml/day. The glands are sensitive to touch, smell, sight,
and thought. Saliva is a clear, colorless fluid that contains water, proteins,
minerals, and certain enzymes. Salivation begins at 3 months of age and
infants usually drool for several months until they learn how to swallow
the saliva. This has nothing to do with teething, although many mothers
will expect their baby to get his first teeth soon after this drooling begins.

The tongue's function in taste, speech, and mastication makes it an
extremely important organ in physical diagnosis. It is composed of a mass
of muscles crossing each other at various angles. Posteriorly the tongue is
attached by the hyoid bone near the epiglottis, and anteriorly it swings
loose and lies against the inner surfaces of the lower teeth. The crisscross
effect of the muscles allows the tongue to alter its position, shape, and
contour. The inferior surface of the tongue is also attached to the floor of
the oral cavity by a central mucous membrane called the *frenulum
linguae*. The dorsum or superior surface of the tongue is convex and
covered with papillae. The four types of papillae, papillae vallatae,
papillae fungiformes, papillae filiformes and papillae simplices (conical),
give the tongue a rough appearance. Looking like 8 to 12 large mush-
rooms, the papillae vallatae form the letter V across the posterior surface
of the tongue. Each of them contains many taste buds. The papillae
fungiformes are large, deep red, and rounded. They are more numerous in
number than the papillae vallatae and scattered over the sides and tip of

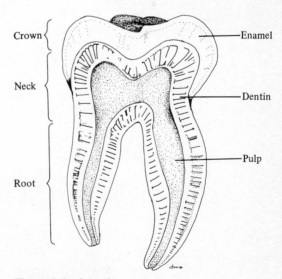

Crown — Enamel
Neck — Dentin
Root — Pulp

Figure 8-3 A tooth.

the tongue. They contain fewer taste buds. The papillae filiformes are tiny, fringed, and cover the anterior two-thirds of the tongue, while the papillae simplices cover the entire surface of the tongue.

The teeth are extremely important in the physical examination. During life, two sets of teeth appear: the deciduous, or baby teeth, and the permanent teeth. Each tooth is divided into three parts: the crown, the neck, and the root. The crown is the exposed portion of the tooth and composed of enamel. The neck of the tooth is the constricted connecting portion of the tooth between the crown and root. The root of each tooth is implanted in the alveoli of the mandibular and maxillary bones.

By the 6th week of fetal life, deciduous teeth are beginning to form. Each tooth is allowed to erupt through the gums when calcification is sufficient to allow the pressure it must endure for chewing. Every child gets 20 deciduous teeth, each jaw containing 4 incisors, 2 canines, and 4 molars. Generally the lower incisors are the first to erupt, usually around 6 months of age; however, the first teeth may not erupt until 12 months and still be considered within normal limits. All the 20 teeth should be present by $2^1/_2$ years of age.

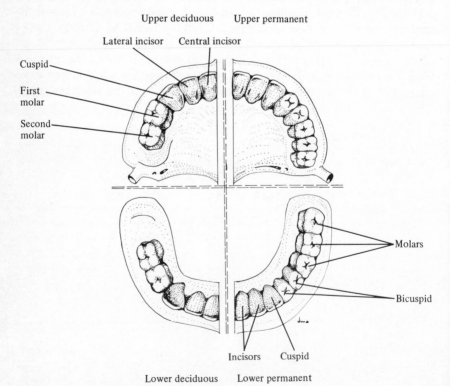

Figure 8-4 The deciduous and permanent teeth.

The permanent teeth begin developing within the jaw during the first 6 months of life. A person normally has 32 permanent teeth: 4 incisors, 2 canines, 4 premolars, and 6 molars in each jaw. Usually the lower incisors are shed around the end of the sixth year as the first molars begin erupting. The two central incisors erupt by the seventh year and the teeth are shed and erupt in an orderly fashion until the seventeenth to twenty-fifth year, when the third molars appear.

HOW TO EXAMINE

Because the mouth and throat can be a touchy area to examine, it may be wise to leave it for last. The position and the degree of difficulty depend on the age of the child. Since the infant does not need an explanation and will not open his mouth on command, it is best to examine his mouth and throat while he is lying on his back on the examining table. The mother can hold his arms firmly over his head, and the examiner can use her body and arms to stabilize the rest of the child.

The older child might be shown the equipment, watch the examination of his mother's mouth, and probably be held in position on her lap. With his legs caught between the mother's knees, the child should be facing the examiner. The mother can place one arm around the child's chest to restrain his arms, and her other hand can hold the child's head firmly against her chest. A school-age child is generally happy to show off his teeth and tongue if the examiner takes time to show him the light and the stick. This child can sit on the examining table in front of the examiner.

The only way to see all areas of the mouth and throat adequately is with a light. A small pencil-sized flashlight or an otoscope (minus the speculum) works well. The tongue blade is also helpful in pushing aside the tongue or gums for a better look. In infants, the tongue blade is essential for testing the gag reflex. In the older child, it may be needed for a better look at the uvula and tonsils. To avoid the feeling of gagging that children dislike, they should be instructed to pant like a puppy, and the tongue blade can be placed on the lateral portions of the tongue. Some children can easily stick their tongues out far enough for the examiner to get a good look at it, and the stick will be unnecessary. If it is necessary to test for Xth cranial nerve function, an applicator stick should be brushed lightly along the lateral walls of the uvula. The uvula should respond by moving upward toward the stimulated side.

To examine the mouth the examiner uses the techniques of inspection and palpation. Percussion and auscultation are not used in this area. Following the rule of moving from front to back, the examiner begins with the lips. The lips should be inspected for symmetry (any twisting, drooping, or clefts), for fissures, for color, and for edema. The lips may be

Table 8-1   Chronology of the Human Dentition

Tooth	Hard tissue formation begins	Amount of enamel formed at birth	Enamel completed	Eruption	Root completed
Primary Dentition					
Maxillary					
Central incisor	4 mo in utero	Five sixths	1¹/₂ mo	7¹/₂ mo	1¹/₂ yr
Lateral incisor	4¹/₂ mo in utero	Two thirds	2¹/₂ mo	9 mo	2 yr
Cuspid	5 mo in utero	One third	9 mo	18 mo	3¹/₄ yr
First molar	5 mo in utero	Cusps united	6 mo	14 mo	2¹/₂ yr
Second molar	6 mo in utero	Cusp tips still isolated	11 mo	24 mo	3 yr
Mandibular					
Central incisor	4¹/₂ mo in utero	Three fifths	2¹/₂ mo	6 mo	1¹/₂ yr
Lateral incisor	4¹/₂ mo in utero	Three fifths	3 mo	7 mo	1¹/₂ yr
Cuspid	5 mo in utero	One third	9 mo	16 mo	3¹/₄ yr
First molar	5 mo in utero	Cusps united	5¹/₂ mo	12 mo	2¹/₄ yr
Second molar	6 mo in utero	Cusp tips still isolated	10 mo	20 mo	3 yr
Permanent Dentition					
Maxillary					
Central incisor	3–4 mo		4–5 yr	7–8 yr	10 yr
Lateral incisor	10–12 mo		4–5 yr	8–9 yr	11 yr
Cuspid	4–5 mo		6–7 yr	11–12 yr	13–15 yr
First bicuspid	1¹/₂–1³/₄ yr		5–6 yr	10–11 yr	12–13 yr
Second bicuspid	2–2¹/₄ yr		6–7 yr	10–12 yr	12–14 yr
First molar	At birth	Sometimes a trace	2¹/₂–3 yr	6–7 yr	9–10 yr
Second molar	2¹/₂–3 yr		7–8 yr	12–13 yr	14–16 yr
Mandibular					
Central incisor	3–4 mo		4–5 yr	6–7 yr	9 yr
Lateral incisor	3–4 mo		4–5 yr	7–8 yr	10 yr
Cuspid	4–5 mo		6–7 yr	9–10 yr	12–14 yr
First bicuspid	1³/₄–2 yr		5–6 yr	10–12 yr	12–13 yr
Second bicuspid	2¹/₄–2¹/₂ yr		6–7 yr	11–12	13–14 yr
First molar	At birth	Sometimes a trace	2¹/₂–3 yr	6–7 yr	9–10 yr
Second molar	2¹/₂–3 yr		7–8 yr	11–13 yr	14–15 yr

Source: After Logan and Kronfeld (slightly modified by McCall and Schour). From Finn, *Clinical Pedodontics*, W. B. Saunders Co., 1962.

palpated for muscle tone. The orifice of the mouth is observed for the child's ability to open his mouth; the examiner should note any odors coming from the area and should observe the amount of moisture and salivation. The teeth are inspected for number, location (missing or extra spaces), bite, caries, and color, and the child should be asked to close his mouth so that occlusion can be checked. The gums should be inspected for color, swellings, and texture; healthy gums are smooth and pink.

The floor of the mouth should be palpated bimanually for possible neoplasms or calculi formation in the submaxillary glands. The buccal mucosa is inspected for color, Koplik spots, and any swelling around Stensen's duct.

The tongue is observed for movement in all directions, for any coating, and for the size of the papillae and the frenulum. An infant is not tongue-tied (tight frenulum) if he can advance the tip of his tongue to his lips. Inspection of the hard palate should show its color and shape, the presence or absence of jaundice or petechiae, and any cleft. The palate should have a gentle slope to it and not a high arched cavity. The soft palate is watched for movement. By eliciting a gag reflex, or by saying "ah," the palate should move upward, allowing the examiner to see the palate and the uvula. The uvula should be midline and move upward in a straight line. Its length should be noted and if bifid, a finger should be inserted (with care) into the child's mouth to palpate the soft palate. If the palate is intact, the bifid uvula is noted on the chart. If the soft palate is incomplete and a notch is felt at the hard and soft junction, the child needs further evaluation. If a submucous cleft exists, it may lead to speech difficulties later.

The tonsils are checked for color, edema, size, symmetry, coating, and crypts. It is easiest to indicate the size of tonsils as plus (+) 1, 2, 3, or 4, each examiner estimating the size in her own mind. Thus + 1 might mean that only the edges are seen; + 2, that they are larger; + 3, that they are touching the uvula; and + 4, that they are meeting at the midline. The last area to be checked is the posterior pharynx for color, discharge, and edema.

WHERE TO EXAMINE

The entire mouth must be examined thoroughly. Inside and outside of the cavity itself, as well as all surfaces of the relevant structures, must be inspected carefully and where indicated, palpated.

WHAT TO EXAMINE WITH

The equipment needed to examine the mouth adequately is simple and inexpensive. A tongue blade and good light are essential. The batteries in the light, whether flashlight or otoscope light, must be new. It is easy to grow accustomed to a gradually fading light, but without realizing it, the examiner will greatly decrease her observational powers in this way. The nurse should make it a habit to change these batteries at least once a week (less often for the "long life" batteries). An applicator may be used to test the function of the Xth cranial nerve. Although it is not generally used, a postnasal mirror is recommended by many authors, as is a retractor to pull back the tonsillar pillar to view the complete tonsil behind it. Although helpful at times, these items are probably not absolutely necessary. A nasopharyngoscope, although used in certain types of specialized examinations of the nasopharynx, is not used in a routine examination, and the nurse-examiner need not concern herself with it.

WHAT TO EXAMINE FOR

The following is a discussion of some of the physical findings the nurse should be on the alert for when examining the mouth or throat. Other diseases of the mouth and throat are discussed in greater detail in a book on oral pathology.

The normal lips of infants are moist and pink-tinged, and the skin is fairly smooth. A sucking tubercle may be found in the middle of the upper lip of bottle- or breast-fed infants; this is normal, and mother should be assured that it will disappear within a few weeks after weaning. Cracked, bleeding lips (cheilitis) may be due to wind and sun; protection from the elements will allow healing and the application of an ointment or cream may speed the process. Children with upper respiratory infections or any febrile illness may also exhibit cheilitis. Again, the application of a cream may help, but of course, the mother must always be warned to apply only a thin covering, since there is a possibility that an excess amount might be aspirated. Some children have a habit of licking their lips until they are red, sore, and chapped. Usually, a coating of cream will help the child to remember not to lick and will also help to heal the chapping. Children with dry, scaly patches at the corners of the lips should be examined for nutritional deficiencies, and a careful history should be taken. The color of the lips is important. A gray cyanosis may mean the child has a congenital heart lesion, while a deep purple hue may indicate severe congenital heart disease. A child with pale lips and gums may be anemic. Bright cherry-red lips may be indicative of acidosis from aspirin poisoning, diabetes, or carbon monoxide poisoning. A glance at the child's lips may give many clues as to what questions to ask in the history taking, what else to look for in the physical examination, and whether this child needs to see the doctor.

A cold sore (herpes simplex infection) may present as an inflamed base with burning and itching. The child presents with a fever of 100 to 104°F, malaise, sore throat, red bleeding gums, and small vesicles on the tongue, palate, and gums. Eating is painful. Treatment consists of mouth hygiene and specifically stated dosages of aspirin. The symptoms may persist for 1 to 2 weeks. If the infection spreads to generalized skin areas, the physician must be contacted for additional sedation and systemic antibiotic treatment.

The oral cavity itself must be examined thoroughly. The mouth is inspected for odor. Halitosis may be due to poor hygiene, a local or systemic infection, sinusitis, mouth breathing, or a foreign body (as a pea or bean) in the nose. The child who is brought in with a specific complaint or illness frequently has halitosis which clears up when he regains his health and begins to eat and drink normally.

The child with many caries and red tender gums probably needs some instruction on tooth brushing and oral hygiene and should be referred to a dentist or doctor.

A mother will sometimes bring her child in, complaining that in the last few days there is a dreadful stench about him. The child should have his nose examined. Often the examination will show that the child has stuffed a bean up his nose, and as the bean became moist, swelled, and rotted, a very bad odor resulted. Treatment is removal of the foreign body. The nurse may attempt the procedure if the bean is easily visible and can be plucked out with long tweezers. However, if the child has already moved the bean higher in the nasal cavity by sniffing, it is best to refer him to the doctor.

Children with dehydration, malnourishment, or diabetic acidosis give off a sweet smell like acetone and need prompt referral.

Some diseases give off distinct odors. For example, diphtheria causes a mouse-like odor; typhoid fever smells like decaying tissue; and uremic patients have ammoniacal breath.

The buccal mucosa may display several important physical signs: An enlarged Stensen's duct, often puffy and red, should lead one to think of mumps or other infections of the parotid gland, while Koplik spots should tell the examiner that the child is in the prodromal stage of measles. These spots are grayish in the center and are surrounded by a red, irregular areola. They first appear on the buccal mucosa opposite the lower molars, although they may later become much more widespread. Traumatic aphthae produces a white raised line directly adjacent to the biting surface of the molars and is caused by sucking or biting on the cheek and is harmless unless very severe and painful. Brownish or blackish blue areas on the buccal mucosa may be a sign of Addison's disease or may appear in children suffering from intestinal polyposis. Blue translucent cysts that may block any mucous gland in the mouth are usually benign.

Tonsillar tissue, of course, must be examined for enlargement, erythema, and white or yellowish follicles filling the crypts. These signs, as well as general erythema of the posterior pharynx, will usually be present in varying degrees in pharyngitis.

The hard and soft palates should be inspected and palpated. Epstein's pearls (or Bohn's nodules) are frequently found along the alveolar ridge or bilaterally along the median raphe in the newborn. These represent an accumulation of epithelial cells and appear as white glistening circular patches a few millimeters in diameter.

Bednar's aphthae are reddish or yellow-gray patches of eroded tissue found posteriorly on each side of the midline of the hard palate. They are usually due to vigorous aspiration at birth or to trauma from sucking on a very hard nipple. The height of the palatal arch should also be evaluated. High palatal arches are normal in the newborn, but very high narrow arches appear with several syndromes, such as Marfan's, Treacher Collins, Ehlers-Danlos, and Turner's, and are often present in children who constantly breathe through their mouths.

During examination of the mouth and throat, the size of the lower jaw should be considered. The mandible is excessively small in the birdface (vogelgesicht) syndrome and in juvenile rheumatoid arthritis; on the other hand, it is quite large in chondrodystrophy and in Crouzon's disease.

The teeth can easily give clues of health or illness. The delayed appearance of teeth after the first 12 months may be normal, due to genetic factors, but it should not be assumed to be normal until the child has been checked for signs of cretinism, rickets, and congenital syphilis, which may also cause the delay.

Bruxism is the grinding of the teeth. Infants often develop this habit as they acquire a few teeth, and older children will sometimes grind their teeth in sleep, sometimes resulting in teeth with flattened edges. The cause is usually attributed to nervousness and tension, and the history taking should be directed along those lines. In older children, treatment seems to be the removal of tensions; infants frequently outgrow the habit as more teeth develop. Checking for malocclusion can often be a discouraging finding, especially if the family cannot afford repair or the area in which the family lives offers no resources for orthodontics. Generally, teeth are not classified as malocclusive unless there is an interference with the ability to chew properly, or the condition presents a severe cosmetic problem. Children who continue to suck their thumbs after the age of 6 years are likely to push their jaws and teeth out of alignment, sometimes causing malocclusion.

Caries are a very common health problem and should be checked for at every visit.

Discoloration of the teeth can be due to several factors. Green and black teeth usually come from iron ingestion and will disappear as soon as the child's diet contains less iron. It is important to tell mothers this so that they do not become upset when the teeth turn green. Children who have had jaundice at birth will also occasionally display green teeth. Mottled and pitted teeth are seen in children who have been exposed to excess fluoride in the drinking water or to tetracycline treatment.

Just as important as evaluation of the teeth is an evaluation of the gums. The alveolar frenulum, a septum extending downward from the central upper gum line and causing a separation between the central incisors, is a common occurrence in children, and mothers should be assured that this will correct itself. Children who are taking Dilantin will frequently have gingival hypertrophy; however, meticulous attention to dental hygiene and digital pressure to the gums several times a day will usually help or completely eliminate the problem. A black line along the margin of the gums may be a sign of metal poisoning, but this should not be confused with the melanotic line along the gums normally seen in the Black child. Purple, bleeding gums are seen with scurvy; leukemia and poor oral hygiene also cause bleeding gums. Children with hypertrophy around each tooth crown are usually mouth breathers or are taking Dilantin or are vitamin deficient. Normal infants have retention cysts in or near the midline of the gums. When on the gums, they are called *Epstein's pearls,* when on the midpalate, they are called Bohn's nodules or Epstein's pearls. However, both types usually disappear in 2 to 3 months.

Variations in the condition of the tongue can be very significant. A white, cheesy coating on the tongue and often extending to the buccal mucosa is most likely to be thrush, caused by infection with *Candida albicans.* It is usually easy to identify macroscopically, but if there is any doubt, a smear of the coating should be mixed with 10 percent potassium hydroxide. The hyphae of the organism will show up clearly under the microscope. The tongues of babies who have just taken a formula may have a coating similar to thrush, but the white patches can be brushed off easily with a tongue blade. Thrush patches, on the other hand, leave a red, bleeding spot when they are scraped off. A doctor will usually prescribe an antifungal agent such as Mycostatin drops in the mouth or, sometimes, the less expensive but messier form of gentian violet.

Geographic tongue is sometimes seen in children. In this condition, the tongue has irregular areas of differently textured papillae, which change from day to day, and usually cause no problems. Macroglossia, or large tongue, is a sign of cretinism, Down's syndrome, Hurler's syndrome, and many other syndromes. These children should be referred for further evaluation.

If a child presents with unexplained dysphagia and stridor, palpation of the base of the tongue is indicated. In rare situations there will be duplication of the alimentary canal, beginning at the level of the tongue.

Glossoptosis refers to a tongue whose attachment is more forward than usual. It is frequently accompanied by a small mandible which may create problems in feeding, as well as cause episodes of hypoxia, cyanosis, and dyspnea. Also, glossoptosis may be associated with cleft palate.

Protrusion of the tongue is frequently seen in children suffering from mental retardation. Rhythmic protrusion, however, has been implicated in intracranial hemorrhage and edema of the brain.

A *white strawberry tongue* consists of erythematous, swollen fungiform papillae intermingled with smaller white filiform papillae. This is the classic sign of scarlet fever, occurring on the second to third day of the illness, but it sometimes occurs in measles or other febrile diseases. *Raspberry tongue* refers to a condition in which the filiform papillae desquamate and take on a beefy-red appearance; the fungiform papillae appear quite large and erythematous. This occurs on the sixth to seventh day of scarlet fever and sometimes in other febrile conditions.

A beefy-red, swollen tongue may also be an indication of pellagra and a careful history should be taken.

Tremor of the tongue may be a sign of thyrotoxicosis.

Deviation of the tongue to one side may indicate an impairment of the XIIth cranial nerve or a neoplasm on one side of the tongue.

Fissures of the tongue should be inspected carefully. If the tongue has fissures that extend transversely, it is called *scrotal tongue* which is a normal variant. Longitudinal fissures, however, are more worrisome and may indicate syphilitic glossitis.

Glossitis in general may be from any type of infection, usually one extending from a pharyngitis. Atrophic glossitis appears as a smooth, glistening, erythematous tongue. The papillae are small and appear as tiny pinpoints here and there on the glistening surface.

Evaluation of the salivary glands is accomplished by means of inspection and palpation. Inflammation of the parotid gland is the most common finding. To be sure that the swelling is indeed due to the parotid gland, one must be familiar with the distribution of this gland. Swelling due to its inflammation usually will be found beginning in front of the tragus, extending downward to the angle of the jaw, and then up and behind the pinna, frequently pushing it outward to form an acute angle with the skull. Painful swellings with this distribution will be found in mumps. Similar but painless swellings can be found in several conditions.

Purulent parotitis is sometimes encountered in the child. In this condition, the parotid gland is enlarged, often erythematous, and warm to the touch. Pus can be expressed through Stensen's duct. In infants, this problem seems to be associated with a general failure to thrive.

Calculi can at times be lodged in the ducts leading to the salivary glands. The most frequent site is the submaxillary gland. Swelling will often occur only with meals and will subside within an hour or two after eating.

BIBLIOGRAPHY

Barness, Lewis A.: *Manual of Pediatric Physical Diagnosis*, Chicago: Year Book Medical Publishers, Inc., 1968, pp. 79–93.

Brem, Jacob: "Koplik Spots for the Record," *Clinical Pediatrics*, vol. 11, no. 3, 1972, pp. 161–163.
Calnan, James: "Submucous Cleft Palate," *British Journal of Plastic Surgery*, vol. 6, 1953–1954, pp. 264–282.
DeGowin, Elmer, and Richard DeGowin: *Bedside Diagnostic Examination*, London: Macmillan & Company, Ltd., 1971, pp. 132–172.
Graber, T. M.: "Orthodontic Problems in Pediatric Practice," *Pediatrics*, vol. 9, no. 6 1952, pp. 709–719.
Judge, Richard D., and George D. Zuidema: *Physical Diagnosis*, Boston: Little, Brown and Company, 1963, pp. 101–111, 125–126.
Roth, John B., Annemarie Sommer, and Craig Strafford: "Microglossia–Micrognathia," *Clinical Pediatrics*, vol. 11, no. 6, 1972, pp. 357–359.

SUGGESTED RESOURCES

1 Pamphlets

"The Care of Children's Teeth," American Dental Association. (Free)
"The Mouth," Meade Johnson and Co. (Free)
"Some Pathological Conditions of the Eye, Ear, and Throat: An Atlas," Abbott Laboratories. (Free)

2 Films

"Oral Cancer"
  Color, 22 minutes
  Cost: Free
  American Cancer Society
  1764 Gilpin Street
  Denver, Colorado 80220
"Oral Lesions in Children and Adults"
  Color, 28 minutes
  Cost: Free
  Abbott Laboratories
  Abbott Park
  North Chicago, Illinois 60064

GLOSSARY

atrophic glossitis   a smooth, glistening, erythematous tongue
bednar's aphthae   reddish or yellow-gray patches of eroded tissue found posteriorly on each side of the midline of the hard palate
bruxism   tooth grinding
buccal glands   nonsalivary glands located between the buccinator and masseter muscles of the mouth
caries   tooth decay leading to destruction of the tooth
cheilitis   cracked, bleeding lips

dysphagia   inability to swallow
epiglottis   the flap covering the superior opening of the larynx
Epstein's pearls   retention cysts found on the gums of newborns
frenulum   mucous membrane attaching the inferior surface of the tongue to the floor of the oral cavity
geographic tongue   irregular areas of differently textured papillae on the tongue
gingivae   the gums
glossitis   infection of the tongue
glossoptosis   a tongue whose attachment is more forward than usual
halitosis   foul breath
hard palate   the anterior portion of the maxilla bone dividing the nasal and oral cavities
herpes simplex (cold sore)   a viral infection causing inflamed, burning, itching vesicles on the lips, gums, palate, and tongue
Koplik spots   red, irregular spots with a grayish center seen on the buccal mucosa of children with measles
labial glands   small, pea-sized glands located in the orbicularis oris muscles
laryngopharynx   the lower end of the pharynx which opens into the larynx
occlusion   the normal relationship of the upper and lower teeth when the jaws are closed or when masticating
oropharynx   the junction between the oral cavity and the pharynx
papillae filiformes   tiny, fringed bumps covering the anterior two-thirds of the tongue
papillae fungiformes   large, deep-red, rounded bumps scattered over the sides and tip of the tongue
papillae simplices   small, rounded bumps covering the entire surface of the tongue
papillae vallatae   large, mushroom-like bumps forming a large V across the posterior surface of the tongue
parotid gland   a salivary gland located in front of and below the external ear on each side of the face
pharynx   the throat
raspberry tongue   a beefy-red tongue due to the desquamation of papillae filiformes
salivary glands   exocrine glands which perform excretory and secretory functions in the first stages of digestion
soft palate   the soft posterior roof of the mouth, separating the nasal and oral cavities
Stensen's duct   the opening for the parotid gland which is located in the oral mucosa opposite the second upper molar tooth
strawberry tongue   a tongue covered with erythematous, swollen fungiform papillae intermingled with smaller white filiform papillae
sublingual glands   a salivary gland the size of an almond, located on the floor of the mouth near the center of the underside of the tongue
submandibular gland   a salivary gland the size of a walnut, located below and in front of the parotid and deep within the lower cheek
sucking tubercle   a small, firm, rounded pad of skin seen in the middle of the upper lip in bottle- or breast-fed infants

thrush a fungal infection caused by *Candida albicans*

tonsils the small, oval-shaped, lymphoid tissue seen dividing the two palatine arches in the oropharynx

uvula a small tag of tissue hanging from the posterior edge of the soft palate

Wharton's duct the opening for the submandibular gland at the side of the frenulum linguae on the undersurface of the tongue

The Chest and Lungs

WHY THE CHILD IS EXAMINED

The condition of the chest and lungs in children are of vital importance. The cartilage and bones of the chest may give an early indication of nutritional problems, as well as clues to pathologic disturbances in the organs below or adjacent to them. The lungs are certainly the seat of one of the most common of childhood ailments, the upper respiratory infection, but also of many more serious problems, including respiratory distress syndrome, cystic fibrosis, asthma, and many others.

WHAT TO EXAMINE: ANATOMY OF THE AREA

The chest, or thorax, is the large cavity occupying the upper portions of the trunk, which contains the heart and lungs. It is enclosed in a bony, cartilaginous cage made up of 12 thoracic vertebrae, 12 ribs, the costal cartilages, and the sternum. The vertebrae are described in more detail in the chapter, "The Skeletal System: Spine and Extremities."

The majority of the bony thorax is composed of ribs. Each rib is a highly vascular structure covered with a small layer of dense bone. There are 12 ribs on each side. The 7 true, or vertebrocostal, ribs are attached posteriorly to the vertebrae and anteriorly through the costal cartilages to the sternum. Of the 5 false, or vertebrochondral, ribs the first 3 have cartilages that attach to the rib above them, while the remaining 2 are called *floating ribs*, because they do not attach to either the upper rib or the sternum. The anterior portion of all the ribs attaches to cartilage. These costal cartilages frequently become enlarged in rickets, causing the condition known as *rachitic rosary* which can be palpated as a series of small lumps running down each side of the sternum.

The sternum is a flat, narrow bone composed of highly vascular cancellous tissue enclosed by dense bone. The superior portion attaches to the first 7 ribs. It is composed of three parts: the manubrium, the body, and the xiphoid process. The manubrium is roughly triangular and attaches to the first and second ribs and provides a place of attachment for the pectoralis major and sternocleidomastoid muscles. The body of the sternum consists of four segments which become fused throughout life. The xiphoid process is the small, thin, long cartilaginous end of the sternum. It may remain cartilaginous throughout life or it may ossify around 30 to 40 years of age. There are great variations in the xiphoid: some are flat, some bifid, some curved, and some one-sided.

The chest can assume several'different shapes. Many of these are associated with disease. The normal shape is generally conical and slightly kidney-shaped. Various abnormalities will be discussed under the section "What To Examine For."

The thorax contains many muscles used in the movement of the upper extremities (which are further described in the section on extremities), as well as 8 thoracic muscles: the intercostales externi, intercostales interni, subcostales, transversus thoracis, levatores costarum, serratus posterior superior, serratus posterior inferior, and diaphragm. There are 11 intercostales externi muscles which extend from the dorsal sections of the ribs to the ventrocostal cartilages. These help in increasing the volume within the thoracic cage. The intercostales interni also number 11 and extend from the sternum to the vertebrae. They help to decrease the thoracic cavity volume. The subcostales attach the upper to the lower ribs and help in decreasing the thoracic volume. The transversus thoracis is a thin sheet of muscle and tendon fibers extending from the sternum to the costal cartilages. It also helps to decrease the chest volume. The 12 levatores costarum muscles extend from the cervical and thoracic vertebrae to the outer surfaces of the ribs. The thoracic volume is decreased and the vertebral column laterally curved by these muscles. The thin serratus posterior superior muscles extend from the spinous processes of the cervical and thoracic vertebrae to the upper borders of the second,

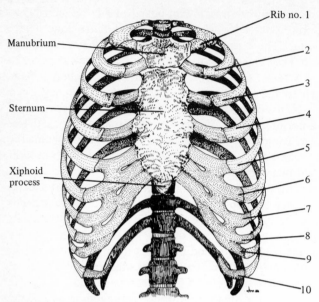

Figure 9–1 The rib cage and sternum.

third, fourth, and fifth ribs. The thoracic cage is increased in volume by this muscle. The broad serratus posterior inferior runs from the spinous processes of the thoracic and lumbar vertebrae to the lower edges of the last 4 ribs. It works as the antagonist to the diaphragm. The diaphragm is a large, musculofibrous membrane dividing the abdominal cavity from the thoracic cavity; its cranial surface is convex, while its caudal surface is concave. There are three parts to the diaphragm: the sternal portion, costal portion, and lumbar portion. The sternal portion lies near the posterior xiphoid process; the costal portion is near the rib cartilages, and the lumbar portion rests near the lumbar vertebrae. There are three large openings in the diaphragm which allow certain structures to pass from one cavity to the other. The aortic hiatus lies in a dorsal and lateral position and allows the aorta, azygos vein, and thoracic duct to pass. To the left of the aortic hiatus lies the esophageal hiatus. The esophagus, vagus nerves, and some esophageal blood vessels travel through this opening. The inferior vena cava and several branches of the right phrenic nerve pass through the third opening—the foramen venae cavae.

In examining the chest, the nurse must also be familiar with the anatomy of the mammary glands, or breast. These structures are situated on the anterior chest wall between the second and seventh ribs midway between the sternum and axilla. In adulthood the average female breast weighs between 150 to 200 Gm and the left is usually slightly larger than the right. It is composed of glandular tissue, adipose tissue, and suspensory ligaments, which are situated within the subcutaneous fascia, as well as a nipple and areola on the cutaneous level. Between 15 to 20 lobes make up the glandular tissue which encircles the nipple. Adipose tissue is found interspersed among these lobes and between them and the skin. The suspensory ligaments (Cooper's ligaments) are fibrous bands which run vertically throughout the breast and attach the deep subcutaneous tissue to the skin. The nipple (or mammary papilla) is the rough, wrinkled, pigmented projection slightly below the center of the breast and at the fourth intercostal space. From 15 to 20 lactiferous ducts open into the tip of the nipple. The rough, pigmented area surrounding the nipple is called the *areola*. The areolar, or Montgomery's, glands are large sebaceous glands distributed throughout the areola. These glands secrete a substance for lubrication and protection during lactation. The areola also contains smooth muscle fibers which can cause the nipple to become erect with stimulation. At birth the lactiferous ducts within the nipples may be the only breast structures that are present. At puberty the glandular tissue increases as the ducts and the amount of adipose tissue increases.

Basically the thorax is innervated by the intercostal, thoracic, phrenic, and cervical nerves.

Blood supply to the chest comes from the thoracic branch of the descending aorta. The thoracic aorta has 7 branches (pericardial, bronchial, esophageal, mediastinal, posterior intercostal, subcostal, and superior phrenic) to carry blood to the thorax. Blood is carried from the thorax via the azygos veins and tributaries which pour into the superior vena cava.

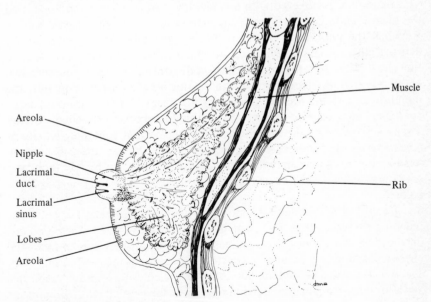

Areola

Nipple

Lacrimal duct

Lacrimal sinus

Lobes

Areola

Muscle

Rib

Figure 9-2 The mature breast.

The chest is a cavity which contains several important organs: the heart and great vessels, as well as the organs of the lower respiratory tract. (The heart will be described elsewhere.)

The chest cavity is divided into halves, with a middle portion known as the *mediastinum*. The superior portion of the mediastinum is divided into the anterior mediastinum, middle mediastinum, and posterior mediastinum.

The lower respiratory tract consists of the trachea, the bronchi, the pleura, the mediastinum, and the lungs. The trachea, or windpipe, is a 2-cm, almost cylindrical cartilaginous tube that connects the larynx and the bronchi. In children it is quite mobile and lies deep within the neck musculature. The trachea contains between 16 and 20 cartilages, some of which form the larynx, or voice box. As the trachea extends downward towards the bronchi, its ventral surface passes behind the isthmus of the thyroid, several neck muscles, cervical fascia, the manubrium of the sternum, the thymus, the left brachiocephalic vein, the aortic arch, and the common carotid arteries. The dorsal side of the trachea lies against the esophagus.

The trachea bifurcates at the fifth thoracic vertebra to form the right and left bronchi. The right bronchus is broad and short and curves gently to the right. It subdivides into three smaller bronchi, each one entering one lobe of the lung. These again divide into smaller and smaller bronchi within the lung. The left bronchus is narrower but longer than the right. It divides into two smaller bronchi, going to the lung lobes.

Each lung is covered with a single layer of serous membrane called the *pleura*. Different portions of the membrane are given different names. Between the pulmonary pleura (which covers the surface of the lungs) and the parietal pleura (which covers the diaphragm and inner surface of the chest wall) lies the pleural cavity. In health, these are simply two membranes lying together. In illness, air or fluid may separate the membranes and the area of the cavity increases.

The lungs are two spongy sacs placed in the lateral aspects of the thorax separated by the heart and other mediastinal contents. The lungs are made up of serous tissue, subserous areolar tissue, and parenchyma (small lobules). An infant's lungs are pink and white, but by adulthood the carbon granules deposited on the areolar tissue give the lungs a gray-black color.

Each lung is divided into an apex, which is the rounded, blunt top reaching the first rib, a base, which is the wide, concave bottom that lies on the diaphragm; and two surfaces: the costal surface which faces the chest walls, and the mediastinal surface which faces the mediastinal area. The lungs can also be divided into lobes. The right lung is heavier, shorter, has a larger total capacity and contains three lobes, while the left lung has only two lobes. Entering the lungs are many subdivisions of the bronchi.

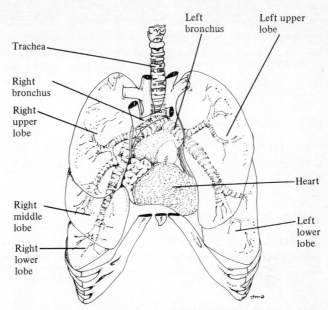

Figure 9–3 The structures within the chest.

After the trachea bifurcates to form two bronchi, each bronchus divides to form secondary multiple bronchi which enter the lobes of the lung. These multiple bronchi continue to divide into smaller branches called *bronchioles* and finally become microscopic tubules called *respiratory bronchioles*. Well within the lung, the respiratory bronchioles divide into many alveolar ducts, which connect to the atria, and contain alveolar sacs. The alveoli are tiny areas 0.25 mm in diameter, lined with pulmonary alveolar epithelium. Its walls contain blood capillaries and collagenous, reticular, and elastic connective tissue fibers. In this area the exchange of gases from the air to the blood takes place.

Respiration is the exchange of gases from the air into the blood-stream and vice versa. This is performed by coordinated efforts of the chest muscles to expand and decrease the volume of the chest cavity.

After the deepest inspiration, the largest amount of air that can be exhaled (vital capacity) is about 3,700 ml for an adult man and less for a growing child. An adult male can exchange about 500 ml of air during quiet, normal respiration while the infant exchanges around 20 ml. This is called *tidal air*. Normal respiration may be diaphragmatic (abdominal) or costal (thoracic). Costal breathing is more predominant in the prone position and in women. Respiration consists of two processes: inspiration and expiration. During inspiration the diaphragm contracts and pulls away from the thoracic cage into the abdominal cavity. This decreases the pressure within the thorax and draws air into the lungs. It also increases the pressure within the abdominal cavity. During expiration the diaphragm relaxes and rises to its original position. This increases the pressure in the thoracic cage and forces the gases into the bloodstream or out through the upper respiratory tract. The relaxed diaphragm decreases the pressure in the abdominal cavity.

HOW TO EXAMINE

For examination of the chest and lungs, all four basic methods of assessment are utilized: inspection, palpation, percussion, and auscultation.

WHERE TO EXAMINE

The entire chest from neck to abdomen and from front to back must be thoroughly examined. The sides under the arms must not be ignored in the examination.

WHAT TO EXAMINE WITH

Besides inspection, palpation, and percussion, for which no specialized instruments are needed, examination of the lungs entails thorough auscultation. For this a stethoscope is necessary; the details of stethoscopes are discussed in the chapter "The Heart."

WHAT TO EXAMINE FOR

In examining the chest, all the anatomical structures must be considered and assessed. The skin in this area is examined in much the same way as skin on any other part of the body. There are a few skin manifestations, however, which are peculiar to this area. The spider nevi of liver disease, for instance, will frequently occur only on the chest and shoulders. The nipples are a cutaneous structure which deserve special attention. Supernumerary (extra) nipples will occasionally be found and should be considered normal. If found, they are most commonly 5 to 6 cm below the normal nipple; however, they can be located anywhere on the milk line which extends on a diagonal from the upper outer shoulders, cutting through the true nipples and continuing to the medial pubic bone. Supernumerary nipples which are located at a lateral, superior position on this line are more likely to be large and to lactate during pregnancy. Extra nipples are more common in black women. Nipple color must also be checked; particularly dark nipples may indicate adrenocorticosteroid problems. Spacing is also important. Wide-set nipples (the condition in which the distance from the outside areolar edges is more than $1/4$ of the chest circumference) can be a sign of Turner's syndrome.

Nipples should further be checked for fissures, inversions, secretions, scaling (as in Paget's disease), and lumps. These conditions are uncommon in younger children and a good pathology book will give more detail.

The muscles of the chest must be assessed next. Atrophy or agenesis of the pectoralis major muscle is an infrequent finding as is pseudohypertrophy of the chest muscles.

The cartilage must be carefully inspected and palpated. Rachitic rosary at the costochondrial junction may be an indication of vitamin C deficiency. These sharp, angular bumps in this area give the examiner a clue to search for further signs of scurvy, although hypophosphatase and chondrodystrophy may also cause these bumps. Painful swellings of the first 4 costochondral junctions may be an indication of the Tietze syndrome. In this case, the nodules are firm but tender on palpation; this tenderness and at times actual pain may radiate the length of the rib. Usually, it subsides spontaneously in 4 to 5 months. It is uncommon in children this age.

The bones are another chest structure which must be evaluated. Shape of the individual bones and the general bony configuration must be assessed through inspection and palpation. Pigeon chest is the condition in which the sternum protrudes from the chest wall and a series of vertical depressions along the costochondral junction appear. This can accompany rickets, Marfan's syndrome, Morquio's disease, and any type of chronic upper respiratory obstruction.

Funnel breast is a condition most obvious on inspiration. It begins with a mild oval pit at the sternal notch and progresses to form an indentation in the sternal area. It can be seen in rickets and Marfan's syndrome.

Barrel chest refers to the condition in which the ribs form perfect circles. This is usually accompanied by kyphosis and may be an indication of pulmonary emphysema or such chronic lung problems as asthma and cystic fibrosis.

Localized bulges may also occur from underlying pressure. Cardiac enlargement and aneurysms are two examples of such conditions.

Spinal deformities, such as kyphosis (humpback), gibbus (angular humpback), and scoliosis should also be evaluated. Scoliosis is considered functional if there is only one curve present. In this situation the curve of the back resembles the letter C. If a compensatory curve has appeared forming an S shape, it is considered organic. The best test for scoliosis is to have the child bend over to touch his toes. A functional scoliosis will disappear with this maneuver.

Harrison's groove is a horizontal groove at the level of the diaphragm, with some flaring of the rib cage below the groove. This sign may indicate rickets or congenital syphilis. A very mild degree is present in newborn infants and should be considered normal.

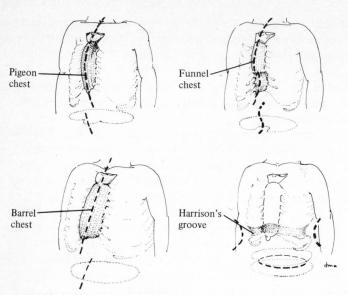

Pigeon
chest

Funnel
chest

Barrel
chest

Harrison's
groove

Figure 9–4   Different chest shapes.

The nurse-examiner should be familiar with accepted anatomic landmarks in this area of the body in order to be able to coherently convey her findings to other clinicians. The nipple is usually considered inadequate as a landmark because its placement is so inconsistent. The anterior landmarks most commonly used are the midsternal line (a line bisecting the sternum) and the right and left midclavicular lines (a line drawn from the middle of the clavicle straight down). Laterally there is considered to be an anterior axillary line which originates at the anterior axillary fold (the fold formed when the arm is abducted to a 90° angle), the posterior axillary line (the line drawn from the posterior axillary fold downward) and the midaxillary line, beginning at the apex of the axilla and proceeding downwards.

There are three landmarks posteriorly. The first is the midspinal or vertebral line, which is down the center of the vertebral column. The other two are not often used because they are somewhat less exact. They are the right and left scapular lines which begin at the inferior angle of the scapula, as the patient stands erect with his arms at his sides, and proceed straight downward.

The next structure in the chest to be evaluated are the lungs. The lungs must be evaluated by all four means of examination: observation, palpation, percussion, and auscultation.

In observing the lungs the nurse must first evaluate their expansion. This is best observed if the nurse holds the palms of her hands flush against the patient's chest and with her fingers spread out. Hands should be held in symmetrical areas of the chest. As the chest expands, it will push the fingers further apart; in this way the nurse can easily observe whether both sides are expanding to the same degree.

Retractions of the chest are also important. Any intracostal, subcostal, or suprasternal retractions indicate abnormally labored breathing; these cases should be referred. They usually occur in pneumonia and other abnormal conditions.

Respiration must be assessed in regard to its rate, quality, and depth. Normal rates vary, of course, with the age of the individual, and a chart, such as the following, should always be easily accessible to the nurse-examiner.

Age	Respiration rate
Newborn	30–50
6 months	20–30
2 years	20–30
Adolescent	12–20

Bradypnea, or a slow rate of breathing, is a cause for concern, since this may be due to brain tumors or opiate poisoning. Tachypnea, or a very fast

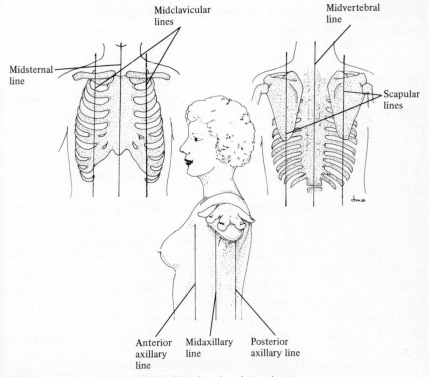

Figure 9–5 Accepted anatomical landmarks of the chest.

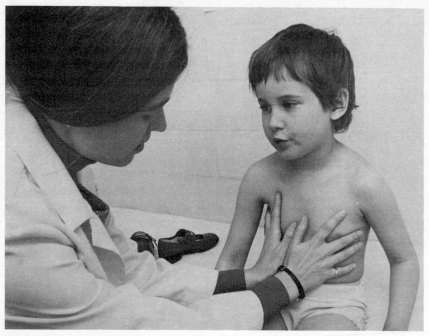

Figure 9-6 Proper placement of hands for ease in observing chest expansion.

rate of breathing can be equally alarming and may indicate pneumonia, fever, heart failure, meningitis, shock, anxiety, salicylate poisoning, alkalosis, or pleurisy. The ratio of respiration to pulse should be 1:4, and the ratio of respiration to temperature should be 4:1 (4 respirations for every 1°F of fever over normal). Apnea, or temporary cessation of breathing, is also a cause for concern if it continues for extended periods of time. Very short periods of apnea may occasionally be normal in the neonatal period.

The quality of respiration is also important. Respiration is basically abdominal in infancy, and the transition to costal respiration is gradual until about 7 years of age, at which time it should be predominantly costal. A very young child who breathes costally or an older child who primarily breathes abdominally should be watched for dyspnea. There is probably some truth to the fact that males tend to breathe more abdominally than females. All accessory muscles should be checked to see if the child is using them to help in the breathing process. A child who is actively using his neck or shoulder muscles to help him breathe is in respiratory difficulty, and should be referred.

Expiratory grunts are another respiratory quality which is worrisome; this occurs in pneumonitis, respiratory distress syndrome, and left-sided heart failure. Two rather serious patterns of respiration are Biot's breathing, which is a rapid, irregular breathing, first shallow and then deep, and Cheyne-Stokes respiration, which is a regular predictable pattern of several breaths followed by a pause and again by several breaths.

Depth of respiration, or hyperpnea, must also be assessed. Hyperpnea is a deep, gasping kind type of breathing such as occurs in metabolic acidosis, when it is called *Kussmaul breathing*. Alkalotic breathing is diminished in depth; it is slow and shallow. Shallow breathing may also be present in pleuritis or pleural effusion, in a child with broken ribs, or in any condition in which breathing causes pain.

The nurse must be familiar with such signs of dyspnea as restlessness, apprehension, retractions, nasal flaring, cyanosis, and clubbing. If these signs occur primarily on inspiration there is usually an obstruction of the larger tubes, such as the trachea and mainstem bronchi, a tumor or foreign body. If these signs occur primarily on expiration, there may be an obstruction of the small bronchi or bronchioles, often causing asthma, bronchitis, or emphysema.

After a thorough inspection, the examiner proceeds to palpate the thorax. Palpation will reveal only those abnormalities that are within 4 to 5 cm below the surface; consequently the nurse should expect to pick up only gross or superficial pathologic conditions.

Fremitus is the procedure by which the examiner palpates the conduction of voice sounds through the thorax. She does this by placing her hands in much the same way as she did for testing expansion, palm down on the chest in symmetrical bilateral positions. She begins at the top of the chest and slowly inches her way down, first in front and then in back. Each time she moves her hands further down, she instructs the patients to say "99" or "blue moon"; the vibrations of the vocalization should be felt.

The vibrations should be felt by the fingertips in areas such as the trachea and bronchi, where the tubes are bigger and closer to the surface. They will be absent or decreased in situations of bronchial blockage, emphysema, asthma, pneumothorax, pleural effusion, or pleural thickening. The sensation will be increased in conditions where a solid mass is present, such as pneumonia, atelectasis, or other types of consolidation.

The chest should also be palpated for pleural friction rubs and crepitation caused by the escape of air into the subcutaneous fat.

Percussion is the third method of examination utilized in evaluation of the chest. The basic method of percussion has been explained in the introductory section and only the specifics which refer to the thoracic region will be discussed here.

At the fifth interspace on the right in the midclavicular line, percussion can be expected to turn dull; this is where the liver begins. A few

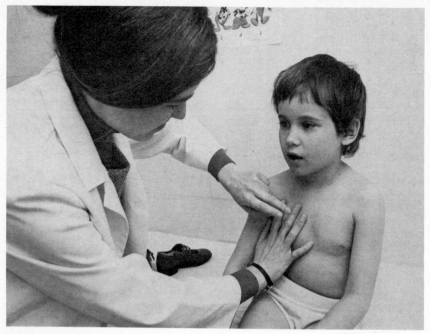

Figure 9–7 Percussion of the chest.

inches further down, where the lung ends and the liver alone remains, the percussion note should become flat.

Tympany can be expected at the sixth interspace and below on the left side; this is due to the air-filled stomach and bowel.

The following is a description of the other areas of the chest and where the nurse can expect to find various percussion notes.

Dullness encountered in areas where it would not normally be expected may be a sign of lobar pneumonia during the consolidation phase, atelectasis, pleural effusion, empyema, pleural thickening, intrathoracic neoplasms, or a diaphragmatic hernia.

Hyperresonance in unexpected areas may indicate pneumothorax, lobar emphysema, asthma, or pneumonia.

Auscultation is the final method of evaluation utilized in the physical examination of the chest. Most textbooks suggest using the diaphragm rather than the bell since most of the important sounds will be of high frequency. The nurse should begin at the top, inching the stethoscope from side to side, covering all areas of the lung, including the region under the arms. Gradually she should work her way down, listening to three things: breath sounds, voice sounds, and adventitious sounds.

Breath sounds should always be evaluated as to pitch, intensity, quality, and duration. Although they are expected to be louder in infants and very young children (under about 6 years of age), the nurse will find three basic categories of breath sounds in children of all ages. The first category is vesicular breath sounds. These breath sounds are characterized by having a louder, longer, and higher-pitched inspiration and a shorter, softer, and lower-pitched expiration. The ratio of the length of inspiration to expiration is about 5:2. Visceral sounds should normally be found all over the chest except in the areas of the manubrium and the upper interscapular area. They may be exaggerated in tuberculosis, emphysema, and late stages of pneumonia, but diminished during the early stages of pneumonia.

Bronchial or tubular breath sounds have a shorter inspiratory phase and a longer expiratory phase; they are usually louder than other types of breath sounds. They should never be considered normal except over the tracheal area; if they are found elsewhere, they may indicate atelectasis or consolidation.

Bronchovesicular breath sounds are a combination of both bronchial and vesicular breath sounds; they can be recognized by the fact that inspiration is louder and higher in pitch than vesicular breath sounds, and inspiration and expiration are equal in quality, intensity, pitch, and duration. These sounds are normal at the manubrium and upper intrascapular area; if found in other areas they should be suspect, since they may indicate an abnormality such as consolidation.

There are also several types of abnormal or unusual types of breathing. Amphoric breathing produces a hollow, low-pitched sound which resembles that produced by blowing over a bottle. The expiratory phase is lower in pitch than the inspiratory phase. Amphoric breathing may indicate pneumothorax, pleural effusion, or a bronchopleural fistula.

Cogwheel breath sounds are an unusual, but not abnormal, type of breathing that may be encountered sometimes. They are very similar to vesicular breath sounds, except that the inspiratory phase is quite jerky, being broken by short pauses.

The nurse-examiner must also pay attention to absent or decreased breath sounds. These may indicate a diaphragmatic hernia, fluid or air in the pleura, a thickened pleura, bronchial obstruction, or any condition that might cause shallow breathing, such as painful pleurisy.

After breath sounds, the nurse must evaluate voice sounds. Three types of voice sounds will be discussed here. The first is whispered pectoriloquy. This refers to the procedure in which the child is asked to whisper several words while the nurse listens to the chest through the stethoscope. She should not be able to understand the syllables. If the syllables are clearly distinguishable, an abnormality should be suspected.

Bronchophony is similar to whispered pectoriloquy. In bronchophony, however, the child is asked to speak rather than whisper. The intensity of the sounds should be increased to the nurse as she listens through the stethoscope, but again, the syllables should not be understood.

Egophony is a type of bronchophony in which a particularly nasal quality is heard through the stethoscope. When the child makes the sound "eeee," it is heard through the stethoscope as a nasal "aaaa."

Adventitious sounds must also be evaluated. Basically, these sounds can be classified into the categories of rales, rhonchi, and pleural friction rub. There is great disagreement among clinicians as to exactly what constitutes a rale or a rhonchi. There is also quite a bit of controversy concerning the best way of subdividing these categories. For purposes of clarity, the authors have chosen the categorization explained here, but the nurse must remember that this is only one method of classifying the possible sounds; if there is any doubt in her mind, probably the best solution is simply to describe what she hears as clearly as possible on the chart. Accurate description is far more important than categorization.

Rales are discrete sounds best heard during forced respiration, primarily at the end of inspiration. They are not cleared by coughing. For our purposes we will discuss two divisions of rales. The first is the division of wet and dry rales. Wet rales are caused by air rushing through mucus or some type of exudate. This occurs in bronchitis, pneumonia, atelectasis, bronchietasis, pulmonary edema, or cardiac failure. Dry rales are caused by air rushing through tubes which are narrowed because of edema, a foreign body, or bronchospasm. They are heard best during expiration and can indicate asthma, bronchitis, or sometimes pneumonia. They are usually inconstant and changing.

Rales can also be divided into fine, medium, or coarse. The sound of a fine rale can be simulated by rubbing a lock of hair between the thumb and forefinger right directly in front of the ear. Fine rales originate in the alveoli and are indicative of serious difficulty, such as pneumonia or pulmonary congestion.

Medium rales sound much like the fizz of a carbonated drink or the sound made by rolling a dry cigar between the fingertips. These rales originate in the bronchioles and occur later in respiration; they may be cleared by coughing.

Coarse rales have a bubbling, gurgling character. They are much louder than fine or medium rales and originate in the trachea or bronchi. Except in moribund individuals, coarse rales can be cleared by coughing. Coarse rales are one of the divisions of lung sounds on which clinicians frequently differ. Many clinicians will refer to these as rhonchi.

Rhonchi are loud gurgling noises transmitted from secretions in the pharynx; they are continuous sounds, usually more prominent during expiration, which are cleared with coughing. One category of rhonchi divides them into sibilant and sonorous rales. The sibilant rales are high pitched and musical. They emanate from the smaller bronchi and bronchioles. The wheezing type of sibilant rhonchi is usually worse with forced expiration.

Sonorous rhonchi are lower pitched and are recognized by their moaning, snoring characteristics; they originate in the larger bronchi and trachea.

The final adventitious sound to be discussed in this chapter is the pleural friction rub. It is caused by the lung wall scraping against the pleura. Its sound can be simulated by cupping the hand to the ear and rubbing a finger of the other hand on the cupped one. Although pleural friction rub can occur during both phases, it is usually loudest at the end of inspiration. To differentiate it from cardiac friction rub, the examiner should ask the child to hold his breath. A pleural friction rub will disappear, but a cardiac friction rub will continue.

BIBLIOGRAPHY

Barness Lewis A.: *Manual of Pediatric Physical Diagnosis*, Chicago: Year Book Medical Publishers, Inc., 1968, pp. 100–110.
Barnett, Henry L.: *Pediatrics*, New York: Appleton Century Crofts, 1968, pp. 1422–1489.
DeGowin, Elmer L., and Richard L. DeGowin: *Bedside Diagnostic Examination*, New York: The Macmillan Company, 1970, pp. 219–315.
Delp, Mahlon H., and Robert T. Manning: *Major's Physical Diagnosis*, Philadelphia: W. B. Saunders Company, 1968, pp. 202–220.
Green, Morris, and Julius B. Richmond: *Pediatric Diagnosis*, Philadelphia: W. B. Saunders Company, 1962, pp. 81–88.
Judge, Richard D., and George D. Zuidema: *Physical Diagnosis: A Physiological Approach*, Boston: Little, Brown and Company, 1963, pp. 107–139.
Kempe, C. Henry, Henry K. Silver, and Donough O'Brien: *Current Pediatric Diagnosis and Treatment*, Los Altos, Calif.: Lange Medical Publications, 1970, pp. 166–184.
Nelson, Waldo: *Textbook of Pediatrics*, Philadelphia: W. B. Saunders Company, 1964, pp. 693–786.
Prior, John, and Jack Silberstein: *Physical Diagnosis*, St. Louis: The C. V. Mosby Company, 1969, pp. 156–196.
Schaeffer, Alexander J., and Mary Ellen Avery: *Diseases of the Newborn*, Philadelphia: W. B. Saunders Company, 1971, pp. 52–177.
Silver, Henry K., C. Henry Kempe, and Henry B. Bruyn: *Handbook of Pediatrics*, Los Altos, Calif.: Lange Medical Publications, 1965, pp. 253–273.
Ziai, Mohsen: *Pediatrics*, Boston: Little, Brown and Company, 1969, pp. 253–281.

SUGGESTED RESOURCES

1 Pamphlets

"Upper Respiratory Tract," Carnation Co. (Free)

2 Films

"The Asthmatic in the Family Album"
    Color, 24 minutes
    Cost: $5.00
    Ciba Pharmaceutical Co.
    P.O. Box 1340
    Newark, New Jersey 07101
"Bronchitis and Bronchiectasis"
    Color, 29 minutes
    Cost: Free
    The Pfizer Laboratories Division Film Library
    267 West 25th Street
    New York, New York 10001
"Bronchitis in Childhood and its Therapy"
    Black and White, 25 minutes
    Cost: Free
    Lederle Laboratories, Film Library
    American Cyanamid Co.
    1 Casper Street
    Danbury, Connecticut
"Differential Diagnosis of Chest Pain"
    Color, 25 minutes
    Cost: Free
    American Heart Association Film Library
    44 East 23rd Street
    New York, New York 10010

GLOSSARY

alkalotic breathing   slow, shallow breathing heard in systemic alkalosis
amphoric breathing   a hollow, low-pitched type of breathing resembling the noise
    produced by blowing over a bottle, the expiratory phase being lower pitched
    than the inspiratory phase
anterior axillary line   a thoracic landmark consisting of an imaginary line which
    originates at the anterior axillary fold and proceeds downward
aortic hiatus   an opening in the dorsal lateral portion of the diaphragm, allowing
    the aorta, azygos vein, and thoracic duct to pass through
areola   the circular pigmented area surrounding the nipple
barrel chest   a condition in which the ribs form perfect circles rather than the
    usual ellipse
Biot's breathing   rapid irregular breathing, first shallow and then deep
bradypnea   slow breathing
bronchial (tubular) breathing sounds   breath sounds which have a shorter in-
    spiratory than expiratory phase and are loud compared to other types of
    breath sounds; considered normal only over the trachea
bronchophony   the phenomenon in which an examiner, listening through a
    stethoscope to the lungs, will hear an increase in the intensity of words, but
    will be unable to identify syllables

bronchovesicular breath sounds a combination of both bronchial and vesicular breath sounds in which inspiration and expiration are equal in quality, intensity, pitch, and duration; considered normal at the manubrium and upper intrascapular area

Cheyne-Stokes respiration a regular, predictable pattern of several breaths followed by a pause and again by several breaths

cogwheel breath sounds an unusual, but normal breath sound with inspiratory phase quite jerky and broken by short pauses

Cooper's ligaments suspensory ligaments formed from fibrous bands running vertically throughout the breast which attach the deep subcutaneous tissue to the skin

costochondral junction the cartilaginous juncture between the ribs and the sternum

crepitation the crackling sound caused by the escape of air into the subcutaneous fat

diaphragm a large, musculofibrous membrane dividing the abdominal cavity from the thoracic cavity

dyspnea difficult breathing

egophony a type of bronchophony in which a particularly nasal quality is heard through the stethoscope as the patient speaks

esophageal hiatus an opening in the diaphragm lying to the left of the aortic hiatus which allows the esophagus, vagus nerves, and several blood vessels to pass between the thoracic and abdominal cavity

foramen venae cavae an opening in the diaphragm through which pass the inferior vena cave and several branches of the right phrenic nerve.

fremitus the conduction of voice sound through the thorax in such a way that a vibration is palpable when the examiner places his hands flush against the child's chest

funnel breast an abnormal structure of the thoracic cage in which there is an indentation of the sternal area

gibbus angular humpback

Harrison's groove a horizontal depression formed around the chest at the level of the diaphragm

hyperpnea increased depth of respiration

intercostales externi the 11 muscles extending from the dorsal section of the ribs to the ventral costal cartilages which help in increasing the volume of the thoracic cavity

intercostales interni the 11 chest muscles extending from the sternum to the vertebrae which help to decrease the volume of the thoracic cavity

Kussmaul breathing the deep breathing characteristic of metabolic acidosis

kyphosis humpback

levatores costarum the 12 chest muscles extending from the cervical and thoracic vertebrae to the outer surfaces of the ribs which help decrease the thoracic volume and bend the vertebral column laterally

manubrium the uppermost triangular portion of the sternum which attaches to the first and second ribs and provides a place of attachment for the pectoralis major and sternocleidomastoid muscles

midaxillary line an anatomical landmark beginning at the apex of the axillary line and proceeding directly downward

Montgomery's glands   large sebaceous glands distributed throughout the areola which secrete a substance for lubrication and protection during lactation

pectoralis major   the large triangular muscle of the upper chest which raises and lowers the humerus

pigeon chest   the condition in which the sternum protrudes from the chest wall and a series of vertical depressions along the costochondral junction appear

posterior axillary line   a thoracic landmark consisting of an imaginary line from the posterior axillary fold downward

pleural friction rub   a grating sound caused by the lung wall scraping against the pleura

rachitic rosary   an inflammation of the costochondral junction, forming a series of palpable bumps similar to rosary beads; usually an indication of vitamin C deficiency

rales   discrete abnormal sounds (usually classified as fine, medium, or coarse) best heard during forced respiration, primarily at the end of inspiration

rhonchi   loud gurgling noises transmitted from secretions in the pharynx

scapular line   an anatomic landmark consisting of an imaginary line beginning at the inferior angle of the scapula and proceeding directly downward

scoliosis   a lateral curvature of the spine

serratus posterior inferior   a chest muscle which runs from the spinous processes of the thoracic and lumbar vertebrae to the lower edges of the last 4 ribs and acts as an antagonist to the diaphragm

serratus posterior superior   a group of muscles extending from the spinous processes of the cervical and thoracic vertebrae to the upper borders of the second, third, fourth and fifth ribs which increase the chest volume

sonorous rhonchi   low-pitched rhonchi originating in the larger bronchi and trachea, characterized by their moaning snoring quality

sternocleidomastoid muscle   one of the major muscles of the neck, used to rotate and lower the head

subcostales   chest muscles which attach the upper to the lower ribs and help in decreasing the thoracic volume

tachypnea   rapid breathing

thymus   a small organ found in the mediastinal cavity anterior and superior to the heart, important in the immune response in infants and young children

tidal air   the amount of air exchanged during a normal respiratory cycle

Tietze syndrome   painful swellings of the first 4 costochondral junctions

transversus thoracis   a thin sheet of muscle and tendon fibers which extends from the sternum to the costal cartilages and helps to decrease the chest volume

tympany   a clear, hollow note obtained by percussion

vital capacity   the total amount of air that can be expelled after a full inspiration

whispered pectoriloquy   the normal phenomenon in which the examiner is unable to distinguish the syllables whispered by the patient when listening to the chest with a stethoscope

The Heart

WHY THE CHILD IS EXAMINED

Careful examination of the heart and circulatory system is essential; it will assure the clinician that her patient is not endangered from the two most common cardiac problems of childhood: congenital heart problems and rheumatic fever. Congenital heart defects have their highest incidence of morbidity and mortality in infancy. Five of every thousand infants are born with a congenital heart defect (the incidence is two to three times higher in premature infants). Most of the deaths from congenital heart defects occur within the first week of life, and of these about half would have been eligible for surgery if the defect had been recognized early. Transposition of the great vessels, coarctation of the aorta, aortic atresia, and pulmonary atresia are the most common causes of these early deaths.

Rheumatic fever and its sequelae are the second largest causes of cardiac problems in the pediatric age group, and one reason a careful heart evaluation should always be done on the 2-week follow-up visit after streptococcal infection. The peak age of incidence for this disease is from 5 to 15 years.

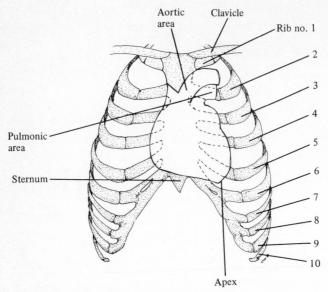

Figure 10–1   Position of the heart within the chest cavity.

WHAT TO EXAMINE: ANATOMY OF THE AREA

The heart is a muscular, four-chambered organ located between the lungs and above the diaphragm. It is shaped like a blunt, inverted cone with the apex pointed caudalward and posteriorly. By the eighth year of life, the tip of the apex reaches the left fifth intercostal space, and the broad base is directed cranially and anteriorly. The size of the heart approximates an individual's doubled fist. Its walls are constructed of outer epicardium, middle myocardium, and inner endocardium, and it is covered by a membranous sac called the *pericardium*. There are four chambers divided into two strongly muscular chambers called *ventricles* and two smaller chambers called *atria*. The right atrium contains the openings for the superior vena cava, inferior vena cava, coronary sinus, and smaller minor vessels. The right ventricle is larger and lies beneath the right atrium; it contains the opening for the pulmonary artery. The left atrium is smaller than the right atrium, but its walls are much thicker. It contains openings for the four pulmonary veins and the remnant of the closing of the foramen ovale which fuses at birth. The left ventricle lies below the left atrium and has the thickest walls of the heart. This chamber empties into the aorta.

The heart is fitted with a system of valves to control the flow of blood from chamber to chamber. The opening between the right atrium and ventricle is called the *tricuspid valve*. The three flaps (or cusps) of the valve are held in place by the chordae tendineae. The opening for the pulmonary artery in the right ventricle is guarded by the pulmonary valve. The left atrium and ventricle are separated by the bicuspid (mitral) valve which contains only two cusps, and the pulmonary veins leaving the left atrium contain no valves. The aortic opening from the left ventricle is regulated by the aortic semilunar valves composed of three strong cusps.

The conduction system of the heart is complex, and only a brief description of it will be given here. The interested reader is referred to a good physiology book for a more complete discussion. The heart muscle has an innate ability to produce spontaneous contractility as well as a conduction system which controls the rhythm of this contractility. The system consists of a sinoatrial node ("the pacemaker") located in the right atrium; an atrioventricular node in the septal wall of the right atrium; an atrioventricular bundle (bundle of His) which begins at the atrioventricular node and travels toward the apex and ventricles; and a terminal conducting fiber (Purkinje fibers) which runs throughout the musculature of both ventricles.

One of the most important things the nurse-examiner must remember when she is evaluating the heart and cardiovascular system of a child is that she must examine a great deal more than just the heart itself. There are some measures with which the nurse has long been familiar and which are extremely important in this evaluation. It is easy to slight a pulse and blood pressure just because they are such common measurements, but the fact is that the reason these measures are so commonly taken is because they are so useful. Pulse rates are very helpful in determining the health of the child in general and the cardiovascular system in particular. It is very important to know, or at least be able to find, the normal rates

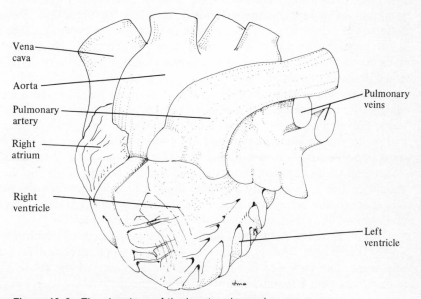

Figure 10-2   The chambers of the heart and vessels.

for particular ages. The following chart should be easily accessible during every examination.

Age	Pulse rates
Newborn	70–170
11 months	80–160
2 years	80–130
4 years	80–120
6 years	75–115
8 years	70–110
10 years	70–110

An increase in rate may indicate many things. Excitement, hyperthyroidism, heart disease, severe anemia, or fever are all manifested in increased pulse rates. Tachypnea is particularly significant if it persists during sleep. In fever there is usually an increase of 8 to 10 pulse beats for every degree of fever. An increase higher than this ratio needs an explanation and may indicate rheumatic fever. A child who has a fever accompanied by a slow pulse may have a *Salmonella* infection. Rhythm of the pulse is also important and usually corresponds to the rhythm heard while auscultating the heart. This will be discussed further under the discussion of auscultation. The character of the pulse is also important. There are several characteristic types which are common enough to be given names. Pulsus alternans is one that consists of one strong beat followed by a weak one. This can be a sign of myocardial weakness. A water-hammer, or Corrigan's, pulse is a very forceful bounding pulse felt best at the radial and femoral areas and accompanied by an increase in pulse pressure. This is often accompanied by capillary pulsations of the fingernail. This usually indicates some kind of insufficiency and can be a symptom of patent ductus arteriosus or aortic regurgitation. Pulsus bisferiens, or dicrotic pulse, is a double radial pulse for every apical beat. It can be auscultated over the brachial artery or felt with light palpation over the carotid. It can be a sign of aortic stenosis, hyperthyroidism, or other diseases. A plateau pulse, or pulsus torlus, is characterized by a normal upstroke and downstroke, but with an elongated peak, forming a plateau. Pulsus bigeminus is a coupled rhythm in which the beat is felt in pairs. Pulsus paradoxus is a pulse characterized by exaggerated waxing and waning. It is sometimes found in children with asthma. One of the most important parts of evaluating the pulses and the cardiac status of a young child is to compare the radial and femoral pulses. Normally these should be felt at essentially the same time. A time lag between the beat felt at the radial artery and that at the femoral artery may be a sign of coarctation, and a blood pressure reading should be obtained.

Blood pressure reading is another common procedure which many nurses underrate. The technique of taking a blood pressure is very important. The cuff size is essential to the accuracy of the reading. It should be not more than two-thirds nor less than one-half the length of the upper arm. In a pediatric facility where many ages of children are seen, standard cuff sizes of 2.5 inches, 5 inches, 8 inches, and 12 inches should be available. The child should be sitting, and the arm should be at heart level. There are actually five sounds in a blood pressure reading, but most clinicians cannot accurately hear them all. At least three should be noted and recorded; these include the point at which the sounds are first heard, the point at which these sounds become muffled, and the point at which they disappear. The American Heart Association says that the muffling should actually be considered the diastolic in children; there is still some controversy over whether it is the muffling or the disappearance of sound which should be considered the diastolic in adults.

Thigh blood pressures can also be important. In a child under 1 year of age, the systolic pressure in the thighs should be equal to that in the arms. After that age it may be 10 to 40 mm Hg higher; the diastolic, however, should always be the same. If it is lower, the nurse-examiner should suspect coarctation. In children under 1 year of age, the blood pressure is inaudible, and the flush technique should be used. The nurse elevates the arm, draining the blood from it. Wrapping it in an Ace bandage may help drain it. The blood-pressure cuff is then applied and inflated, and the arm is lowered. The cuff is then gradually deflated, while the examiner observes the point at which the arm distal to the cuff flushes with color. This point is considered the median between the systolic and diastolic readings. Again, it is important that the nurse have easy access to a chart of normal blood pressure readings for different ages. The following is such a table:

Table 10–1   Normal Blood Pressure for Various Ages

Ages	Mean systolic ± 2 S.D.	Mean diastolic ± 2 S.D.
Newborn	80 ± 16	46 ± 16
6 months–1 year	89 ± 29	60 ± 10*
1 year	96 ± 30	66 ± 25*
2 years	99 ± 25	64 ± 25*
3 years	100 ± 25	67 ± 23*
4 years	99 ± 20	65 ± 20*
5–6 years	94 ± 14	55 ± 9
6–7 years	100 ± 15	56 ± 8
8–9 years	105 ± 16	57 ± 9
9–10 years	107 ± 16	57 ± 9
10–11 years	111 ± 17	58 ± 10
11–12 years	113 ± 18	59 ± 10
12–13 years	115 ± 19	59 ± 10
13–14 years	118 ± 19	60 ± 10

*In this study the point of muffling was taken as the diastolic pressure.
Adapted from data in the literature. Figures have been rounded off to nearest decimal place.
Source: R. J. Haggerty, M. W. Maroney, and A. S. Nadas, "Essential Hypertension in Infancy and Childhood," A.M.A.J. Dis. Child. 92:536, 1956. Copyright 1973, American Medical Association.

A very important part of the blood pressure that is sometimes ignored by examiners is the pulse pressure or difference between systolic and diastolic readings. Normally this is about 20 to 50 mm Hg throughout childhood. An unusually wide pulse pressure may be due to an abnormally high systolic reading or an abnormally low diastolic reading. Of these two, the diastolic reading is usually the more important. If a widened pulse pressure is due to an unusually high systolic reading, it may indicate exercise, excitement, or fever. If, however, it is due to an abnormally low diastolic reading, the probability of patent ductus arteriosus, aortic regurgitation, or other serious heart disease should be raised. An abnormally narrow pulse pressure may indicate aortic stenosis.

The skin and mucous membranes can be another sensitive indicator of the health of the cardiovascular system. Pallor can be a sign of anemia in the older child or severe heart problems in the infant. Cyanosis will usually appear first in the lips, nail beds, or earlobes; it is often associated with polycythemia (usually considered when a hematocrit is over 70). Any persistent cyanosis is a matter of concern. Minor cyanosis in a neonate can be normal, but even then it must be evaluated carefully. Cyanosis should not be excessive or persistent; it should not cover the entire body, and it should not be darker in the upper extremities than in the lower. Any child with these conditions should be referred to the physician. They can be a symptom of either cardiovascular or respiratory difficulties. Edema of any part of the body, but particularly of the eyelids in the neonate, can be another cutaneous manifestation of cardiovascular problems.

Respiratory symptoms, while sometimes a sign of respiratory difficulties, can also reflect cardiovascular insufficiency. Symptoms like dyspnea, orthopnea, and frequent upper respiratory infections should be evaluated with this fact in mind. Other miscellaneous symptoms should also alert the practitioner to cardiovascular origins. Continuous squatting and sleeping in the knee-chest position is almost diagnostic of cardiac difficulty. An older child who is easily fatigued or an infant who takes only 2 to 2½ ounces of milk and falls asleep immediately or who manifests excessively labored breathing during defecation may be suffering from heart disease. Anorexia, vomiting, profuse sweating, or delays in growth and development, especially in infants, may be symptoms of heart problems. Enlarged liver, clubbing of the digits, enlarged heart, pulsating neck vessels, and tachypnea without retractions can be further symptoms.

HOW TO EXAMINE

Most of the cardiovascular examination depends not on instruments, but on the acute powers of observation of the clinician. However, some specialized equipment is used in this part of the examination. The blood pressure cuff and its requirements have already been discussed. The stethoscope is also important. There are many types available. When choosing one, the nurse should remember a few important points. The earpieces should fit comfortably; this means both the size and angle must be correct. The American Heart Association recommends that the tubing be as short as possible and that the diameter of the tubing be $^1/_8$ inch. Both the bell and diaphragm types should be available, since the bell is constructed to pick up low-frequency sounds and the diaphragm, high frequencies. In using the bell, however, the examiner must be careful that the entire circumference of it touches the skin very lightly. If too much pressure is exerted, the surrounding skin will be flattened and will act like a diaphragm, blocking out low-frequency sounds.

WHERE TO EXAMINE

There are seven areas which the clinician must examine when evaluating heart function. Each has a specific name, and that name should be used when recording any abnormal sounds, murmurs, or thrills found in that location. The first is the sternoclavicular area, which extends to the right side, left side, and directly over the sternoclavicular junction. The second, or aortic, area is located at the second right intercostal space immediately adjacent to the sternum. Next is the pulmonic area which is found in the second and third left intercostal space near the sternum. The anterior precordial area consists of the third, fourth, and fifth intercostal space to

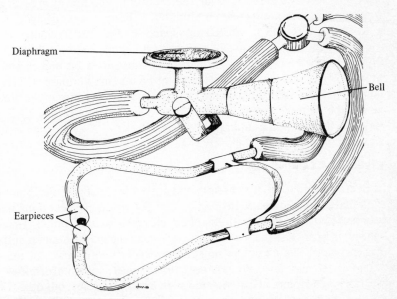

Figure 10–3 The stethoscope.

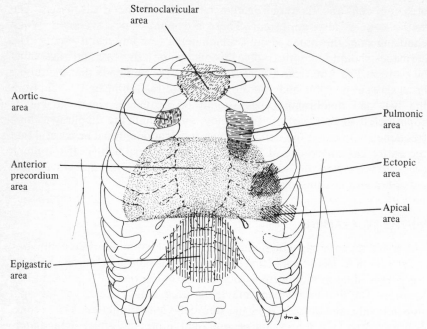

Figure 10-4 The seven areas to be examined when listening to the heart.

the right, left and directly over the sternum. The apical area is a very important one. In adults and children over about 8 years of age, this area is located at the fifth intercostal space in the midclavicular line. In younger children, it is usually higher and more medial. Pregnancy or anything causing a high diaphragm may cause it to be higher and more lateral. This is not necessarily the point of maximal impulse (PMI) but it usually is. The sixth area is the epigastric area, and any other areas are called the ectopic areas; usually the ectopic area refers to a space between the pulmonic and apical areas.

WHAT TO EXAMINE

Inspection, palpation, percussion, and auscultation are all important in the examination of the heart. Inspection and palpation are best done with the patient flat on his back with his chest elevated to a 45° angle. Tangential lighting is best. The most accurate assessments can be obtained at the end of expiration. The examiner must be aware that deformities of the shape of the chest may alter the position of the heart; some deformities, as in Marfan's syndrome, are associated with heart problems, but others which are not may give the appearance of heart problems just because of the alteration in position of the heart. The process of auscultation is very important. The nurse must develop her own system and "inch" the stethoscope around all seven areas of the heart, first with the bell and then with the diaphragm. This should be done with the child standing, sitting straight, sitting with the chest bent forward, lying flat on his back, and lying on his left side. Percussion is the least useful, but can be performed to outline the border of the heart. The important findings from percussion would be enlargement or displacement of the heart.

WHAT TO EXAMINE FOR

Basically the nurse is examining for visible, palpable, and auscultatory indications of normal or abnormal heart functioning. The first evaluation should be to determine whether the heart sounds are normal. There are four possible heart sounds. The first is designated S_1 and indicates the systolic part of the cardiac cycle; it is the "lub" of the "lub-dub." Generally it is louder than the second heart sound at the apex and is longer and lower pitched than second in all areas. It is synchronous with the apical pulse or carotid pulse, and when first beginning to auscultate hearts, it often helps to time the heart sounds by simultaneously feeling the carotid pulse. The first heart sound is caused by the closure of the mitral and tricuspid valves.

The second heart sound (S_2) is caused by the closure of the semilunar valves (both the aortic and pulmonary); it is shorter and higher pitched than S_1 and is louder than S_1 at the base. It reflects diastole and is the "dub" of the "lub-dub."

A third heart sound (S_3) is occasionally heard. S_3 is a low-pitched, early diastolic sound due to blood rushing through the mitral valve and hitting an empty ventricle. When heard, it is best heard at the apex. This sound is sometimes normal in a child; but it is almost never normal in an adult.

A fourth heart sound (S_4) is also possible, although almost never normal. It is caused by an audible atrial contraction at the very end of diastole and is heard best at the apex.

In evaluating the normalcy of heart sounds, the practitioner should concentrate on four characteristics: rate, intensity, rhythm, and abnormal or unusual sounds.

The rate should be evaluated in the same manner as the rate of a peripheral pulse (i.e., the pulse palpated in an extremity) as was discussed previously. The apical and radial pulse should be the same, and there should be no significant lag between the two.

Intensity of heart sounds is also important. As mentioned before, the intensity of S_1 is normally greater than that of S_2 at the apex, while that of S_2 is greater than S_1 at the base. An increase in the intensity of S_1 may indicate anemia, fever, exercise, or tachycardia; a decrease in the intensity of S_1 is usually more serious and can accompany an infarction. If the S_1 is increased in the presence of bradycardia (a rate of 60 to 80 beats/minute, for instance), the examiner might consider the possibility of mitral stenosis, heart block, or atrial flutter. If S_1 is constantly changing in intensity and is accompanied by bradycardia, the possibility of heart block should be considered. An increase in S_2 may be normal or may indicate coarctation or arterial hypertension.

The nurse-examiner must evaluate carefully the rhythm of the heart sounds. She must listen for irregularity and then decide if the irregularity follows any pattern. It may be either a disordered arrhythmia or an ordered arrhythmia. There are two types of disordered arrhythmia, both very serious and usually heard only in hospitalized individuals. The first is atrial fibrillation. At first this sounds very fast but regular; but if the examiner listens more carefully, she realizes that a few beats are being dropped. This is always abnormal and can be from organic heart disease, rheumatic fever, thyrotoxicosis, or other serious illnesses. Ventricular fibrillation is the second disordered arrhythmia; it is grossly arrhythmic, always abnormal, and almost always fatal.

There are several types of ordered arrhythmias. The most common is sinus arrhythmia—an arrhythmia in which the heart speeds up with inspiration and slows down with expiration. This arrhythmia is found in normal children and should cause no concern. The problem is differentiating it from abnormal rhythms. In an older child, this can be done by asking him to hold his breath. When he does so the arrhythmia should disappear if it is sinus arrhythmia. In an infant, the examiner must observe very closely to see if the arrhythmia fluctuates with respiration.

There are other types of ordered arrhythmias. Bigeminy or coupled rhythm consists of a normal beat followed by a premature contraction. This can be normal in some children, but can also indicate organic heart disease. Another type of ordered arrhythmia is composed of three normal-sounding beats (some are actually premature contractions) followed by a pause. Again, this can be normal but can also be a sign of organic heart disease. Dropped heart beats constitute another ordered arrhythmia and can be an indication of rheumatic heart fever or organic heart disease. Atrial or ventricular premature beats can be either normal or a result of organic heart disease. Gallop rhythms are combinations of premature beats. An atrial gallop is the addition of an abnormal S_4; a ventricular gallop is the addition of an abnormal S_3; and a summation gallop is a combination of all 4 beats. All persons with gallop rhythms should be referred to a doctor.

The fourth category of things the nurse-examiner is listening for while evaluating the heart sounds is a series of abnormal or unusual sounds. S_3 has already been discussed. It is best heard at the apex in a child. Sometimes in a child and always in an adult, this is not just an S_3, but really a pathologic gallop rhythm. S_4 is also heard best at the apex. It is much more rare than S_3 and is always abnormal. It can be a sign of aortic stenosis, hypertension, anemia, hyperthyroidism or other diseases. Its addition to S_1 and S_2 forms the atrial gallop.

A pericardial friction rub is also always abnormal. It is a scratchy high-pitched, grating sound not affected by changes in respiration (as is the pleural friction rub which has a similar sound). It extends through both systole and diastole and is best heard with the child leaning forward in deep expiration.

A mediastinal crunch (Hamman's sign) is a randomly distributed crunching noise resulting from air in the mediastinum. It is rare, but should always be referred when found.

Clicks and ejection sounds form another group of unusual sounds. A pulmonary ejection click is a click localized at the base which decreases during inspiration. It can be caused by pulmonary stenosis or hypertension. An aortic ejection click occurs in early systole at the base and apex of the heart. It exhibits no change with respiration. It can be caused by aortic valve stenosis, coarctation, or aneurysm.

An opening snap is similar to the click sounds but has a different quality. It occurs soon after S_2 in the third to fourth left intercostal space. Mitral stenosis and atrial tumors may cause this type of snap.

There are two types of splits which may occur. The first is a split of the first heart sound (S_1). The reader will remember that the first heart sound is caused by the closure of the tricuspid and mitral valves. Generally the mitral valve closure precedes the tricuspid closure by a small fraction of a second; however, the timing is usually so close that the two closures seem to produce one sound. There are times, particularly in children, when this double sound will be normally audible over the left lower sternal border. Whenever there is a wide split or the split is heard in other areas, particularly at the apex, it should be considered abnormal and referred. A split of the second sound (S_2) is also possible, and, in fact, more common. S_2 is caused by the closure of the two semilunar valves, the aortic and pulmonary valves. The aortic valve closes slightly ahead of the pulmonic valve, but again, this slight difference in timing is often not detectable. When it is, it is called a split. It is best heard at the pulmonic area (the third left intercostal space) and is normally wider on inspiration than on expiration. If the width of the split does not vary (a "fixed split") with respiration or if it is wider on expiration than on inspiration (paradoxical splitting), the child should again be referred for a further cardiac evaluation.

Another sound the nurse-examiner may occasionally encounter is a venous hum. This is a continuous low-pitched hum heard throughout the cardiac cycle, but loudest during diastole. It is heard most clearly at the supraclavicular fossae, but also in the second to third interspace on both sides of the sternum. It is not usually affected by respiration and may be louder when the child is standing. Its most distinguishing quality is the fact that it can be obliterated by turning the neck of the child or occluding the carotid pulse with your fingers. It is almost always normal, although it sometimes occurs in thyrotoxicosis and anemia.

There is one final classification of abnormal or unusual sounds which may be heard during auscultation. These are murmurs. All murmurs should be evaluated carefully and recorded with regard to their timing, location, radiation, intensity (grade I being the softest possible to grade VI being the loudest possible, i.e., a murmur which can be heard without a stethoscope), pitch, and quality (musical, blowing, rasping, harsh, or rumbling). There are two kinds of murmurs: innocent, or functional, and organic. Unless the nurse-examiner is very sure of her auscultatory skills, she should refer all murmurs to the physician and let him distinguish between innocent and organic types. There are some clues which the examiner should keep in mind regarding this distinction, however. Innocent murmurs are usually systolic, grade I or II, of short duration, have no transmission, do not affect growth and development, and are usually located at the pulmonic area. These clues are not foolproof, however, so that the examiner will probably want to have all murmurs checked. For those who are beginning to learn auscultation, there are several recordings of heart sounds and heart murmurs which may be useful. These are listed at the end of this chapter.

The signs the nurse is examining for by inspection and palpation are similar, though at times slightly different from those she is examining for with auscultation. In the aortic area a thrill (a feeling similar to that felt when you hold your hand on a purring kitten's stomach) that radiates to the right side of the neck may be indicative of aortic stenosis and should be investigated. Vibrations of aortic closure may be felt in individuals with hypertension in this area, as may some pulsations of patent ductus arteriosus.

In the pulmonic area the nurse should note any thrill radiating to the left side of the neck, as this may be a symptom of pulmonary stenosis. A slight, brief pulsation is normal in this area if the child has a thin chest, but it can also be a sign of anemia, fever, exertion, hyperthyroidism, or pregnancy. A stronger pulsation may exist with mitral stenosis or hypertension.

The anterior precordium should also be carefully inspected and palpated. A systolic thrill in this area may indicate ventricular septal defect, and a pulsation may be seen or felt with any condition that causes increased pressure in the right ventricle. Some of these causes could be mitral stenosis, pulmonary stenosis, pulmonary hypertension, atrial septal defect, or ventricular septal defect. A slight retraction in this area will be seen in many children and can be considered normal. Slight outward pulsation may be seen in children with thin chests or may indicate anxiety, anemia, fever, pregnancy, or hyperthyroidism.

In the apical area, the nurse may encounter a systolic thrill from mitral regurgitation or a diastolic thrill from mitral stenosis. Increased amplitude in this area may be due to a thin or flat chest or a depressed sternum. If the apical area is displaced to the left, enlargement of the heart usually exists. If the heart beat is very prominent, it may be associated with a gallop rhythm; sometimes the actual rhythm can be felt.

Pulsations in the epigastric area are often normal, particularly in children with anemia or fever, but can sometimes be abnormal, as in the case of thyrotoxicosis, tricuspid stenosis, or regurgitation; and these possibilities should be investigated.

Pulsations in the ectopic area are rare in children and usually indicate ischemic heart disease.

BIBLIOGRAPHY

Allen, N.: "The Significance of Vascular Murmurs in the Head and Neck," *Geriatrics*, vol. 20, 1965, pp. 525–538.

Aygen, M. M. and Braunwald, E.: "The Splitting of the Second Heart Sound in Normal Subjects and in Patients with Congenital Heart Disease," *Circulation*, vol. 25, 1962, pp. 328–345.

Barness, Lewis A.: *Manual of Pediatric Physical Diagnosis*, Chicago: Year Book Medical Publishers, Inc., 1968, pp. 111–124.

Barnett, Henry L.: *Pediatrics*, New York: Appleton Century Crofts, 1968, pp. 1219–1329.

Buttross, D.: "The Venous Hum: History, Pathogenesis, Incidence, Recognition and Significance," *American Practitioner and Digest of Treatment*, 6: 1955, pp. 342–345.

DeGowin, Elmer L., and Richard L. DeGowin: *Bedside Diagnostic Examination*, New York: The Macmillan Company, 1970, pp. 316–449.

Delp, Mahlon H., and Robert T. Manning: *Major's Physical Diagnosis*, Philadelphia: W. B. Saunders Company, 1968, pp. 120–187.

Durnin, R. E., and D. A. Ehmke: "Clinical Approach to Heart Murmurs Heard during a Pre-football Examination," *Journal of the Iowa Medical Society*, September 1969, pp. 826–832.

Freeman, A. R., and S. A. Levine: "The Clinical Significance of the Systolic Murmur: A Study of 1,000 Consecutive 'Noncardiac' Cases," *Annals of Internal Medicine*, vol. 6, 1933, pp. 1371–1385.

Gilliland, J. C.: "Congenital Heart Disease in the Immediate Neonatal Period: Differential Diagnosis," *Southern Medical Journal*, September 1970, pp. 1015–1020.

Gordon, M. S.: "The Bedside Evaluation of Common Systolic Murmurs: Brief Review of Current Concepts," *Journal of the Florida Medical Association*, November 1969, pp. 839–844.

Green, Morris, and Julius B. Richmond: *Pediatric Diagnosis*, Philadelphia: W. B. Saunders Company, 1962, pp. 89–100.

Groom, D.: "Comparative Efficiency of Stethoscopes," *American Heart Journal*, vol. 68, 1964, pp. 220–226.

Judge, Richard D., and George D. Zuidema: *Physical Diagnosis: A Physiological Approach*, Boston: Little, Brown and Company, 1963, pp. 140–190.

Kempe, C. Henry, Henry K. Silver, and Donough O'Brien: *Current Pediatric Diagnosis and Treatment*, Los Altos, Calif.: Lange Medical Publications, 1970, pp. 285–235.

Leatham, A.: "An Improved Stethoscope," *Lancet*, vol. 1, 1958, p. 463.

———: "Auscultation of the Heart," *Lancet*, vol. 2, 1958, pp. 703–708, 757–765.

———, B. Segal, and H. Shafter: "Auscultatory and Phonocardiographic Findings in Healthy Children with Systolic Murmurs," *British Heart Journal*, vol. 25, 1963, pp. 451–459.

———, et al.: "Discussion on the Significance of Cardiac Murmurs in the First Few Days of Life," *Proceedings of the Royal Society of Medicine*, vol. 52, 1959, pp. 75–78.

Luisada, A. A.: "Bedside Diagnosis of Arrhythmias," *Advances Cardiopulmonary Diseases*, 1966, pp. 230–239.

Moss, A. J.: "The 'Incidental' Systolic Murmur," *Pediatrics*, April 1970, pp. 687–689.

Nelson, Waldo: *Textbook of Pediatrics*, Philadelphia: W. B. Saunders Company, 1964, pp. 877–988.

O'Rourke, R. A.: "Extra Heart Sounds: What Do They Mean," *Medical Times*, August 1971, p. 188.

Perloff, J. K.: "Highlights of Auscultation in Acquired and Congenital Heart Disease: II. The Pulmonary Orifice," *Nebraska State Medical Journal*, August 1971, pp. 350–351.

Prior, John, and Jack Silberstein: *Physical Diagnosis*, St. Louis: The C. V. Mosby Company, 1969, pp. 211–267.

Ravin, A.: "Disorders of the Heart Beat," *Rocky Mountain Medical Journal*, vol. 43, 1959, pp. 468–471.

———, L. D. Craddock, and L. M. de la Fuente: "The Standing-flexion Position for Auscultation of the Heart," *Journal of the American Medical Association*, 1965, pp. 60–61.

Reddy, P. S., J. A. Shaver, and J. J. Leonard: "Cardiac Systolic Murmurs: Pathophysiology and Differential Diagnosis," *Radiobiologia, Radiotherapia* (Berlin), July 1971, pp. 1–37.

Schaeffer, Alexander J., and Mary Ellen Avery: *Diseases of the Newborn*, Philadelphia: W. B. Saunders Company, 1971, pp. 178–267.

Shah, P. M., S. J. Slodki, and A. A. Luisada: "A Revision of the 'Classic' Areas of Auscultation of the Heart: A Physiologic Approach," *American Journal of Medicine*, vol. 36, 1964, pp. 293–300.

Silver, Henry K., C. Henry Kempe, and Henry B. Bruyn: *Handbook of Pediatrics*, Los Altos, Calif.: Lange Medical Publications, 1965, pp. 214–237.

Suckling, P. V.: "The Arterial Pulse in General Paediatric Practice," *South African Medical Journal*, May 23, 1970, pp. 625–628.

Ziai, Mohsen: *Pediatrics*, Boston: Little, Brown and Company, 1969, pp. 285–330.

SUGGESTED RESOURCES

1 Pamphlets

"Diagnostic Challenges in Cardiology," Smith Kline and French Laboratories. (Free)

"Evaluation and Management of Congenital Cardiac Defects," American Heart Association. (Free)

"Examination of the Heart: I. History Taking," American Heart Association. (Free)

"Examination of the Heart: II. Inspection and Palpation of Venous and Arterial Pulses," American Heart Association. (Free)

"Examination of the Heart: III. Inspection and Palpation of the Anterior Chest," American Heart Association. (Free)

"Examination of the Heart: IV. Auscultation," American Heart Association. (Free)

2 Films

"Atrial Septal Secundum Defect"
  Color, 39 minutes
  Cost: Free
  The Pfizer Laboratories Division Film Library
  267 West 25th Street
  New York, New York
"Auscultation of the Heart: Mitral Stenosis"
  Color, 20 minutes
  Cost: Free
  Colorado Heart Association
  1375 Delaware Street
  Denver, Colorado
"Cardiac Failure in Infancy"
  Color, 30 minutes
  Cost: Free
  American Heart Association
  44 East 23rd Street
  New York, New York 10010
"Congenital Malformations of the Heart: II. Acyanotic Congenital Heart Disease"
  Color, 14 minutes
  Cost: Free
  American Heart Association
  44 East 23rd Street
  New York, New York 10010
"Congenital Malformations of the Heart: III. Cyanotic Congenital Heart Disease"
  Color, 30 minutes
  Cost: Free

American Heart Association
44 East 23rd Street
New York, New York 10010
"Diagnosis of Ventricular Septal Defects"
Color, 20 minutes
Cost: Free
Upjohn Professional Film Library
7000 Portage Rd.
Kalamazoo, Michigan 49001
"Disorders of the Heart Beat"
Color, 20 minutes
Cost: Free
American Heart Association
44 East 23rd Street
New York, New York 10010
"Heart Sounds and Innocent Murmurs: Part I"
Color, 25 minutes
Cost: Free
Colorado Heart Association
1375 Delaware Street
Denver, Colo.
"Heart Sounds and Innocent Murmurs: Part II"
Color, 15 minutes
Cost: Free
Colorado Heart Association
1375 Delaware Street
Denver, Colo.
"Heart Sounds and Murmurs"
Color, 15 minutes
Cost: Free
Colorado Heart Association
1375 Delaware Street
Denver, Colorado
"Movements of Cardiac Valves and the Origin of Heart Sounds"
Color, 20 minutes
Cost: Free
American Heart Association
44 East 23rd Street
New York, New York 10010

GLOSSARY

apical area an area of the chest overlying the apex of the heart and one of the classic areas for auscultation of the heart, located at the fifth intercostal space in the midclavicular line in adults and children over 8 years of age, but in younger children, higher and more medial

arrhythmia a variation of the normal heart rhythm

atria (auricles)   the two superior, smaller chambers of the heart

atrial fibrillation   a very irregular rhythm caused by rapid, uncoordinated contractions of the atria

bradycardia   a slow pulse

bundle of His   a bundle of nerve fibers traveling from the atrioventricular node to the apex, which transmits impulses controlling the heartbeat

clicks (ejection sounds)   sharp "clicking" heart sounds considered abnormal

Corrigan's pulse (water-hammer pulse)   a forceful bounding pulse, best felt at the radial and femoral areas and accompanied by an increase in pulse pressure

disordered arrhythmia   a variation of the normal heart rhythm in which no repeated pattern can be discerned

dyspnea   difficult breathing

endocardium   the membrane lining the inside of the myocardium

epicardium   the visceral layer of the pericardium, surrounding and closely covering the myocardium

innocent murmur (functional murmur)   the type of heart murmur that does not indicate a pathologic condition

mediastinal crunch (Hamman's sign)   a randomly distributed crunching heart sound resulting from air in the mediastinum

myocardium   the muscular layer of the heart

opening snap   an abnormal heart sound similar to a click which occurs soon after S_2 in the third to fourth left intercostal space, often due to mitral stenosis

ordered arrhythmia   a variation of the normal heart rhythm in which a repeated pattern can be discerned

organic murmur   a heart murmur indicating an underlying pathologic condition of the heart

orthopnea   difficulty in breathing in any but an upright position

pericardial friction rub   a scratchy, high-pitched grating heart sound caused by the myocardium rubbing against the pericardium during the cardiac cycle

plateau pulse   a pulse consisting of a normal upstroke and a normal downstroke, but which is characterized by an elongated peak forming a plateau

point of maximal impulse (PMI)   the cardiac area at which the strongest beat can be felt; most often at the apex

precordial area   the area of the chest overlying the precordium and one of the classic areas for auscultation of the heart, located at the third, fourth, and fifth intercostal spaces

pulmonic area   an area of the chest that is one of the classic areas for auscultation of the heart, located in the second and third left intercostal space near the sternum

pulsus alternans   a pulse consisting of one strong beat followed by one weak beat; it can be a sign of myocardial weakness

pulsus bigeminus   a coupled pulse in which the beats are felt in pairs

pulsus bisferiens (dicrotic pulse)   a double pulse in which two beats are felt in the radial area for every one beat at the apex

Purkinje fibers   a group of nerve fibers distributed throughout the musculature of both ventricles, which conduct nervous impulses concerned with the action of the heart

S_1 the first heart sound, synchronous with the carotid pulse; systole

S₂   the second heart sound; diastole

semilunar valves   the aortic and pulmonary valves that separate the atria from the vena cava and aorta

sinus arrhythmia   a normal arrhythmia associated with respiration; the heartbeat becomes faster during inspiration and slower during expiration

splits   the double sound caused by the slightly asynchronous closing of two heart valves.

sternoclavicular area   an area of the chest and one of the classic areas for auscultation of the heart, lying directly over and to both sides of the sternoclavicular junction

systole   the S_1 of the cardiac cycle; the "lub" of the "lub-dub"; caused by the contraction of the ventricles

tachycardia   a rapid pulse

thrill   a palpable murmur

venous hum   a continuous low-pitched sound heard in normal children throughout the cardiac cycle, most clearly at the supraclavicular fossae or in the second and third interspaces on both sides of the sternum

The Abdomen

WHY THE CHILD IS EXAMINED

Careful examination of the abdomen can reveal many clues to the health or illness of a child. The abdomen contains many of the vital organs of the body, and careful examination of them is imperative. Organomegaly, tenderness, or masses are all important signs that should be sought for in the examination.

WHAT TO EXAMINE: ANATOMY OF THE AREA

In discussing the anatomy of the abdomen, the skin, fasciae, muscles, nerves, blood supply, and various organs must all be considered. Immediately beneath the skin there are several layers of fascia covering the abdomen. The superficial subcutaneous fascia is soft and moveable and may contain some adipose tissue; in obese persons, this layer may be several centimeters thick. The deep subcutaneous fascia contains yellow elastic fibers and very little adipose tissue; it covers the external areas of the obliquus externus abdominis muscle.

The abdominal muscles are divided into two groups: the anterolateral

149

muscles and the posterior muscles. The anterolateral muscles include the obliquus externus abdominis, the obliquus internus abdominis, the transversus abdominis, the rectus abdominis, and the pyramidalis. The obliquus externus abdominis is a large flat, irregular muscle covering the lateral portions of the abdomen. It aids in urination, defecation, vomiting, and parturition. Covering the entire ventral surface of the abdomen is the aponeurosis of the obliquus externus abdominis, a sheet of muscles which meets at the midline to form the linea alba (a line entering from the infrasternal notch to the pubic symphysis, intersected by the umbilicus). The thick, inferior edge of the aponeurosis of the obliquus externus abdominis forms the inguinal ligament. Superior and lateral to the pubis is an opening in the aponeurosis of the obliquus externus abdominis which is called the superficial inguinal ring. The spermatic cord passes through this opening.

The obliquus internus abdominis is the thin, small layer of muscle lying beneath the obliquus externus, which functions in conjunction with the obliquus externus. The cremaster muscle is attached to the obliquus internus, inguinal ligament, and the rectus abdominis which help to raise the testis into the inguinal ring. The transversus abdominis lies beneath the obliquus internus and has fibers running transversely across the abdomen towards the midline; it aids the other muscles in voiding, defecation, vomiting, and parturition. The rectus abdominis is a broad, thin muscle running parallel to the linea alba which helps to flex the vertebral column. The pyramidalis is a tiny, thin muscle running beside the lower rectus muscle and aiding in tensing the linea alba. Between the anterolateral muscles and the posterior muscles lie several additional layers of fascia. The four posterior muscles are the psoas major, psoas minor, iliacus and quandratus lumborum. The psoas major is a long, thin muscle attached to all the lumbar vertebra and running towards the lesser trochanter of the femur. With contraction it flexes both the thigh and lumbar vertebral column. The psoas minor is a thin, long muscle running parallel to the psoas major and is frequently missing. The iliacus is a thin, flat, broad muscle filling the fossa of the iliac; it is used in flexing the thigh. The quadratus lumborum is a broad, irregularly shaped muscle arising at the iliac crest and inserting on the inferior border of the last rib. It aids in flexion of the rib cage and the lumbar vertebral column.

The abdomen has no bones, but is bordered by bony landmarks. The lower edge of the ribs forms the upper border of the abdomen while the bones of the pelvis form its lower border. The protruding tubercle on the ilium crest can be palpated, and the anterior superior iliac spine can often be felt at the outside end of the inguinal ligament.

Each specific layer of abdominal muscle is innervated by a specific group of nerves, but generally, the spinal nerves involved are the VIIth through the XIIth intercostals, the lower thoracic, lumbar iliohypogastric, and ilioinguinal.

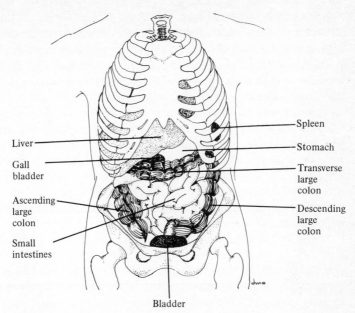

Liver

Gall
bladder

Ascending
large
colon

Small
intestines

Spleen

Stomach

Transverse
large
colon

Descending
large
colon

Bladder

Figure 11–1   Organs contained within the abdomen.

Blood is supplied to the abdomen through the descending aorta which divides into the thoracic and abdominal aorta. The aorta contains three main sets and branches: the visceral with 7 smaller branches; the parietal with 3 smaller branches; and the terminal with 1 branch. Blood returns from the abdominal cavity via the inferior vena cava and its tributaries.

It is important that the nurse practitioner be familiar with the organs contained within the abdomen.

The stomach is situated below the diaphragm and between the spleen and the liver; its shape and position vary according to the contents of the stomach, the digestive process going on, the gastric musculature, and the contents within the intestines. It has two openings: the cardiac and the pyloric orifices. The cardiac sphincter joins the esophagus to the stomach, and the pyloric valve allows the stomach to empty into the duodenum. The stomach has two curvatures: the lesser and the greater. The lesser curvature forms the concave border of the stomach, while the greater curvature produces the ventral, longer curve. The stomach wall is composed of four layers: mucous, submucous, muscular, and serous. The mucous and submucous lie in deep, curving folds called *rugae*. These layers produce two types of muscular activity within the stomach: peristalsis and pressure. Peristalsis moves the food through the stomach into the intestine, and constant pressure forces the food into contact with the stomach wall and gastric juices.

The small intestine is a 7-meter-long tube extending from the pyloric orifice of the stomach to the ileocecal valve. It is divided into the duodenum, the jejunum, and the ileum. The duodenum is the shortest and most immobile portion of the small intestine, and the jejunum is vascular and contains large villi. The jejunum is found in the umbilical and left iliac portions of the abdomen. The ileum is narrow, slightly vascular, and contains lymph nodules; its distal end lies within the pelvis and opens into the large intestine. Both the jejunum and ileum are connected to the abdominal wall by the mesentery (a large fold of peritoneum).

The large intestine or large colon is a 1.5-meter tube extending from the ileum to the anus; it is composed of the cecum, appendix, colon proper, rectum, and anus and forms a large arch around the small intestine. The cecum begins at the ileocecal valve and runs in an upward direction 6.25 cm toward the right colic flexure. At its apex is a 5- to 10-mm projection called the *appendix*. The cecum can display a considerable amount of movement and can become herniated.

The colon proper has four portions: ascending, transverse, descending, and sigmoid. The ascending colon begins at the cecum and runs upward toward the right lobe of the liver. It turns suddenly to the left to form the right colic (hepatic) flexure which can be palpated in the right upper quadrant of the abdomen. The transverse colon runs transversely across the epigastric areas and bends suddenly to the left to form the left colic (splenic) flexure. The descending colon runs downward past the kidney, turns medially toward the psoas muscle, and then descends again to end in the sigmoid colon. The sigmoid colon is an S-shaped loop within the pelvis which ends with the rectum.

The liver is the largest and heaviest gland in the body; it lies beneath the diaphragm and fills most of the right upper quadrant. It weighs from 1.2 to 1.4 kg and is soft and highly vascular. It is divided into four lobes: the right lobe which is large, the left lobe which is smaller, and the caudate and quadrate lobes which are both quite small. The main functions of the liver are the production of bile for fat digestion, metabolism of proteins and carbohydrates, and production of certain substances to aid in the development of red blood cells. The bile ducts, the hepatic artery, and the portal vein lie between the quadrate and caudate lobes on the under-surface of the liver. The two bile ducts join to form the common hepatic duct which meets the cystic duct from the gallbladder; all three then form the common bile duct which empties into the duodenum.

The gallbladder with the hepatic duct, cystic duct, and common bile duct form the excretory structures of the liver. It is a small, pear-shaped sac located under the right lobe of the liver, whose function is to store bile.

The pancreas is an exocrine and endocrine gland lying transversely on the posterior abdominal wall. It weighs between 70 and 106 Gm and is between 12 and 15 cm long. The exocrine portion secretes pancreatic juice into the duodenum for the digestion of proteins, carbohydrates, and fats, and the endocrine portion of the gland, consisting of the island of Langerhans (islet of the pancreas), secretes insulin for the metabolism of sugars.

The spleen is a highly variable organ. It is a soft, highly vascular organ which lies between the stomach and the diaphragm. It grows from 17 Gm at birth to 170 Gm by 20 years of age and decreases to around 122 Gm by 75 years. Its function also seems to change throughout life. For example, during the first year of life it helps with the production of red blood cells, thereafter it aids in the destruction of red blood cells and the formation of hemoglobin.

Also contained within the abdomen are organs of the genitourinary system.

The ovaries and the fallopian tubes are within the lower quadrants of the abdomen; the ovaries can be palpated in a vaginal-abdominal examination. The uterus is midline of the two lower quadrants and can also be palpated in this way. In the male the vas deferens and seminal vesicles are found low in the lower quadrants. The kidneys are two small (125 to 170 Gm, 11 by 7 cm) bean-shaped organs of the urinary system; the right kidney is normally 1 cm lower than the left. Both kidneys are attached to the posterior surface of the abdomen, but can be felt with deep palpation in the upper quadrants.

The urinary bladder is a muscular, membranous sac located at the midline of the lower quadrants. The size and exact position will vary according to the amount of urine being stored in the bladder, the size of the person, and whether the person is male or female. In a child the urinary bladder lies between the symphysis pubis and the umbilicus. It descends lower into the abdomen in the adult, although a distended bladder holding as much as 500 ml of urine will rise into the abdomen even in an adult.

HOW TO EXAMINE

All four methods of physical examination are important in assessing the abdomen. Inspection, palpation, percussion, and auscultation are all utilized, but the order is slightly reversed from that used on other parts of the body, with auscultation rather than percussion following immediately after inspection. This is because percussion and palpation may disturb the normal sounds heard on auscultation.

WHERE TO EXAMINE

The entire abdomen must be carefully examined. There are two accepted methods of subdividing this region. The first is the traditional method and

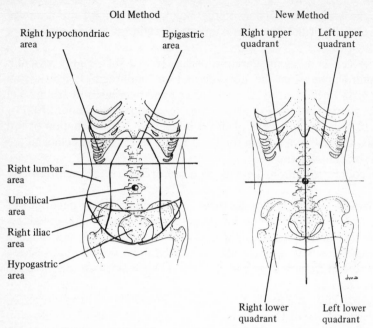

Old Method

New Method

Right hypochondriac area

Epigastric area

Right upper quadrant

Left upper quadrant

Right lumbar area

Umbilical area

Right iliac area

Hypogastric area

Right lower quadrant

Left lower quadrant

Figure 11–2 The two accepted methods of subdividing the abdomen.

is less popular today. This method divides the abdomen into the nine sections shown above.

The current method of division is simpler and consists of only four divisions.

WHAT TO EXAMINE WITH

There is really no specialized equipment for examining the abdomen except the stethoscope which is used for auscultation. This instrument has been discussed more fully in the chapter "The Heart."

WHAT TO EXAMINE FOR

In this section, each method of examination will be considered separately and will specify what the examiner should be looking for in relation to the method discussed. Inspection is the first method of examination utilized when assessing the abdomen. First, the abdomen is observed for movement; normally there should be only respiratory movements visible. As discussed under the chapter "The Chest and Lungs," the child under about 6 or 7 years of age will breathe primarily with his abdominal muscles. A child over this age who is using his abdominal muscles for breathing should be examined carefully for the possibility of thoracic problems. Greatly restricted abdominal movement in a child under 6 years old may indicate peritoneal irritation.

Peristalisis is not normally seen on a child. Visible peristaltic waves usually indicate an obstruction at some point along the gastrointestinal tract. Peristaltic waves which move from left to right are the classic sign of pyloric stenosis, but can also occur in malrotation of the bowel, duodenal ulcer, urinary tract infection, gastrointestinal allergy, or duodenal stenosis.

The contour of the abdomen should also be assessed. The abdomen normally bulges slightly at the beginning of inspiration; with certain central nervous system diseases such as chorea, it may retract rather than bulge; this is called *paradoxical respiration* (Czerny's sign).

Any localized fullness should be noted. Such a fullness found in the right lower quadrant may be an appendiceal abscess.

A potbelly is normal in young children, but should be carefully investigated, for it may conceal organomegaly, ascites, neoplasm, cysts, or defects in the abdominal wall.

Bulging of the flanks may indicate ascites, while a generalized scaphoid abdomen (an abdominal wall with a concave, depressed contour) in which the abdominal organs are unusually palpable may indicate extreme malnutrition.

Abdominal distention should be investigated for the possibility of pregnancy in older children, for feces (in the case of megacolon, palpation will reveal a plastic feel to the mass), organomegaly, or ovarian cysts.

The superficial vessels of the abdomen should also be observed. It is sometimes possible to see a pulsating aorta over the epigastric area in normal children, but excess pulsation in this area may indicate an aortic aneurysm.

Superficial veins are normally present in infancy, but in later childhood their presence may be a sign of abdominal distention or obstruction. Venous return in the abdomen should be checked if there is any question of vascular obstruction. Above the umbilicus the refilling of veins should take place from the bottom up; below the umbilicus the flow should be from the top down. Obstruction of the inferior vena cava may result in a reversed filling below the umbilicus while obstruction of the superior vena cava may result in a reversed filling in the veins above the umbilicus.

The skin of the abdomen should be inspected much as skin anywhere else on the body. For details the reader is referred to the chapter "The Skin." There are, however, a few specifics referring primarily to abdominal skin rather than skin elsewhere in the body. Abdominal skin should be carefully observed for scars, and an explanatory history should be obtained for each scar. Recent scars will appear pink or blue; older ones take on a silvery hue. In certain adrenal problems purple scars associated with fragile, easily broken skin may be seen. Striae should also be noted on the abdomen as well as on the shoulders, thighs, and breasts.

Glistening, thick skin may be a sign of underlying edema or ascites.

Spider nevi may appear with liver disease. These are spider-shaped reddened areas with a central arteriole and several extending rays. Pressure on the central arteriole will cause the entire marking to blanch.

Hair distribution on the abdomen is important. Excess hairiness may be a sign of adrenal corical problems. In older children, the nurse should expect to find a triangular distribution of hair in the pubic area in girls and a diamond-shaped distribution in boys. Alterations of the appropriate hair distribution for each of the sexes may indicate endocrine or liver disorders.

Grey Turner's sign is another possible finding on the abdominal skin. This consists of a massive ecchymosis with no history of trauma, the mark appearing as reddish blue, bluish purple, or greenish brown, and primarily found on the flanks and lower abdomen. It indicates extravasation of blood from some place in the abdomen.

The umbilicus is an important region of the abdomen and should be inspected thoroughly. A bluish umbilicus (Cullen's sign) may occur with intraabdominal hemorrhage, while a nodular umbilicus (Sister Joseph's nodule) may be a sign of abdominal cancer. An everted umbilicus, if it occurs without hernia, may be the result of some kind of increased intraabdominal pressure.

The nurse should check carefully for umbilical fistulas. Drainage from the umbilicus may be urine in a case such as patent urachus, a small amount of feces, if a fistula to the colon exists, or pus, if a urachal cyst or abscess exists.

Sometimes an umbilical calculus will be found; it is not a true stone, but rather a hard mass of debris resulting from poor hygiene.

If serous or serosanguineous discharge continues after the cord has separated, a granuloma may be suspected. This consists of a small red solid button deep in the umbilicus. Most physicians cauterize such granulomas with silver nitrate sticks, although some prefer borax powder.

Particularly in newborn infants, the umbilicus should be carefully inspected for any signs of infection. Foul-smelling discharge, periumbilical redness and induration, or skin warmth should alert the nurse to this possibility. This condition can be quite dangerous in a young infant, since the infection can travel up the open arteries into the peritoneum, causing sepsis which is frequently fatal.

Omphaloceles are unusual defects the umbilical area. In an omphalocele, the peritoneal contents bulge through a muscular defect in the umbilical area; these contents are covered only by a thick transparent membrane. One-third to one-half the number of children with this condition have associated defects, such as malrotation of the bowel, Meckel's diverticulum, cardiovascular problems, or patent vitelline ducts.

Umbilical hernias are a common finding. Their size should always be judged by palpating the actual opening, not by measuring the contents which protrude through the opening. They should be expected to attain their maximum size by about 1 month of age or sometimes later and will generally close by 1 year of age. There is great disagreement as to their treatment. Schaeffer operates on openings of more than 5 cm in early infancy. If the hernia is between 2 and 5 cm, he tapes it and operates if its size has not decreased by age 6 to 8 months (Schaeffer, 1971). Not all physicians will operate this early, and many will not tape an umbilical hernia at all, feeling that this procedure is useless. Whether taping is useful or not remains moot, and the practitioner may decide to follow this practice or not. The one practice that should definitely not be followed, however, is that of taping a coin into the umbilical ring; this can interfere with its closure.

Double or multiple herniations can occur in the region of the umbilicus and above; operations on these are usually not performed unless they are very small, but are usually taped for a year (Schaeffer, 1971).

Finally, the umbilicus should be checked for a single umbilical artery. Realistically this can only be done in the delivery room because within a very short time, the cord is too dried out to discern the vessels clearly. If only a single artery is seen, the clinician must be alerted to search for other abnormalities, particularly abnormalities of the kidneys.

Other muscular defects of the abdominal wall can also occur. Diastasis recti abdominis is the condition in which the two recti muscles do not approximate each other. This is a rather common condition, particularly in Black babies, and should be considered normal as long as no hernia is associated with it. Incisional hernias are a not infrequent occurrence, and any child with an operational scar should be observed while doing a sit-up. An incisional hernia will present as a protuberance adjacent to the scar.

Epigastric hernias are encountered occasionally. Usually, they are accompanied by pain resembling a chronic peptic ulcer. When the child stands, the examiner should run her finger down the midline of the abdomen. A small nodule protruding outward between the fibers of the linea alba will be felt if an epigastric hernia is present.

Inguinal hernias will be discovered in some children. The inguinal ligament runs from the anterior superior iliac spine to the pubic tubercle; the inguinal canal parallels this ligament and is about 3.5 cm long. The internal ring of this canal is located at the midpoint of this line but is not palpable; the external ring lies just lateral to the pubis and can be palpated in males through the scrotum. A direct inguinal hernia bulges through the

Indirect   Direct
hernia   hernia

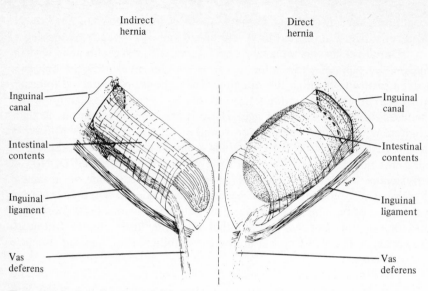

Inguinal   Inguinal
canal   canal

Intestinal   Intestinal
contents   contents

Inguinal   Inguinal
ligament   ligament

Vas   Vas
deferens   deferens

Figure 11-3 The direct and indirect hernia.

posterior wall of this canal in an area called *Hesselbach's triangle,* directly behind the external ring. It seldom causes pain. It is never congenital, but always acquired. It is much more frequent in males than females. An indirect hernia does not bulge through the wall of the canal but actually enters it from the abdomen through the internal ring.

The final type of hernia to be discussed here is the femoral hernia. This hernia will present as a small bulge adjacent and medial to the femoral artery by about 2 fingerbreadths. It is more common in females than males.

As explained before, auscultation should take place immediately after inspection, since percussion and palpation may disturb the bowel sounds.

The first sound the nurse should assess when auscultating the abdomen is peristalsis. The most important point is simply to ascertain that peristalsis exists. The clinician should be careful in concluding that it does not exist, however. Before concluding this, she must listen at least 5 minutes, timed by the clock, since peristaltic sounds can be very irregular. Paralytic ileus is unusual in ambulatory children, and when it exists it is most often due to diffuse peritoneal irritation. Hyperperistalsis occurs with diarrhea or, more severely, with early obstruction in the intestine or pylorus. It presents as a frequent high-pitched tinkling sound accompanied by pain.

The nurse must also listen for vascular sounds. Venous hums similar to those which can occur in the neck may be found in cases of congenital abnormalities of the umbilical vein, vascular problems located in the portal system, or hemangiomas of the liver.

A murmur heard near the umbilical area may indicate a renal artery defect.

Friction rubs can sometimes be heard in the abdomen. They may originate in an inflamed spleen or a liver with a tumor or with generalized peritoneal obstruction. These rubs are often quite soft and can be mistaken for breath sounds.

A bruit is important only if heard consistently with change of position and even with the stethoscope held very lightly against the abdominal wall. In such case it may be a sign of some kind of vascular problem. A bruit may indicate a dilated, tortuous, or constricted vessel. If heard over the aorta, it may be a sign of aneurysm; if heard in other places, it may be a sign of congenital bands of tissue that constrict other places in the vascular system.

Stomach contents can also be heard. To do this, the stethoscope should be held over the upper part of the stomach while the patient's body is rocked back and forth. A splash will be heard if the stomach contains the normal amount of fluid.

After auscultation, percussion is performed. The examiner stands at the patient's right side and begins with the thorax, first going down the midaxillary line. In this line, the nurse should encounter a tympanitic note where the lung overlies the splenic flexure of the colon. Dullness above the ninth interspace in the left midaxillary line may originate with the spleen. Occasionally, a kidney or the left lobe of the liver or even consolidation of the left lower lung will produce the same note in this area.

The procedure should then be repeated on the patient's right side. Liver dullness is expected at the sixth rib or interspace anteriorly and at the ninth rib posteriorly. Relative dullness may occur one or two interspaces above this. The lower border of the liver should be encountered at the costal margin or 2 to 3 cm lower. The liver moves with respiration, so that if it is percussed with held inspiration and expiration, its position should move about 2 fingerbreadths. Sounds in the rest of the abdomen should be tympanitic. This tympany may be more pronounced in children who swallow air extensively or in those with any obstructive lesions of the gastrointestinal tract.

Shifting dullness may indicate ascites. In this condition, dullness will be heard in the midabdomen when the child is standing, but will shift to the flank areas when the child is lying on his back. If the child is rolled from side to side, the area of dullness will shift to the dependent portion.

The final method of examination employed in assessing the abdomen is palpation. In general, a light touch should be employed. The examiner's hands should be warm; cold fingers usually cause muscular contraction to such an extent that the examiner's ability to palpate is severely impaired. Flexion of the knees and a pillow beneath the head may take strain off the abdominal muscles and result in less resistance to palpation. It is sometimes helpful to use the child's own hand to palpate, particularly if he is apprehensive. Distracting a child's attention is frequently a vital part of this examination, especially if the child is ticklish. The nurse should begin with superficial palpation, gradually increasing the pressure. Certain types of masses, such as various cysts and hematomas of the rectus muscles of the abdomen, may be felt in this manner. Rebound tenderness, or Blumberg's sign, may also be encountered on superficial palpation.

The nurse may also wish to test for cutaneous hyperesthesia. This may be done by gently stroking skin in parallel lines with a pin or by pulling the skin gently away from the abdomen. These maneuvers will be painful if hyperesthesia is present. Sometimes only a localized area of hyperesthesia will be found. This may be the case, for instance, in an inflamed appendix, where a small area of skin overlying it may manifest hyperesthesia.

Subcutaneous crepitus may also be discovered on palpation. The examiner will feel freely moveable nontender bubbles directly under the skin. These may indicate subcutaneous emphysema or gas gangrene.

Muscle tone can also be evaluated through palpation. Involuntary muscle rigidity—sometimes unilateral, sometimes bilateral—may be an important sign of peritoneal irritation. Board-like rigidity or spasm may occur in peritonitis, although in very young infants, peritonitis may not have any effect on the muscle tone at all.

Tissue turgor should also be tested in the abdominal area by pinching a small piece of skin and then releasing it. Normally, the skin will quickly revert to its original position, but in dehydration, a peak of skin may remain standing out from the body, and return only very slowly.

After the entire abdomen has been superficially palpated, deep palpation should be performed over the same area. Deep palpation is important for discovering masses, tenderness, deep vessels, and palpable organs. All masses should be evaluated for size, consistency, tenderness, mobility, position, shape, pulsatility, and surface characteristics. If there is any suspicion of a neoplasm, palpation should be limited, since excess manipulation may spread it.

Fecal masses may sometimes be felt on palpation in children with constipation; if this seems excessive, the nurse should check for megacolon.

Wilms' tumor may sometimes be felt by deep palpation; this tumor is usually adjacent to the vertebral column and does not extend across the midline.

A pyloric tumor is palpable in about 95 to 98 percent of infants with pyloric stenosis. This is easiest to palpate immediately after vomiting, since the abdominal muscles are soft at this time. The examiner should stand at the child's left side and palpate with the middle finger held at a flexed right angle. The tumor is usually found deep between the edges of the rectus muscle and the costal margin on the right side; it is about the size and shape of an olive.

Tenderness in the abdominal area is very difficult to assess in a child. It is often very difficult for a child to be able to verbalize location and character of pain. Frequently, if a child is asked if something hurts, he will automatically say yes, thinking that the normal pressure he feels when the examiner palpates his abdomen should be interpreted as pain. It is probably best to avoid direct questions of this nature and to rely more on such nonverbal clues as wincing. Distraction is extremely important because many children will complain of ticklishness. It is probably best not to reinforce this response by paying too much attention to it, since if a child is encouraged to continue this response, it will be almost impossible to examine him. Firm rather than light pressure may help avoid this kind of response.

It is normal to complain of pain or wince during deep palpation of the midepigastrium, since this is the area of the aorta. Other areas of pain should be carefully noted. Many types of pain in the abdomen are referred to other locations. It is sometimes helpful to be aware of these referral pathways. For example, pain originating in the common bile duct may be referred to the midline in the upper abdomen; pain may be referred to the midline anterior wall of the abdomen, from the stomach, liver, gallbladder, pancreas, and intestinal tract; pain in the kidneys, ovaries, fallopian tubes, or ureters may be experienced in the ipsilateral flank; and splenic pain may be referred to the left shoulder.

Rebound pain occurs only if the peritoneum is involved; this occurs even when pressure is exerted far from the diseased area and may occur merely from coughing or straining. In general, visceral pain is dull and difficult to characterize and localize; somatic pain is sharp and well localized. Some types of pain, like that originating in the appendix, will start out poorly localized and then gradually become more well defined, as in the case of appendicitis, to the right lower quadrant. Pain caused by inflammation is generally constant or increases when pressure is applied; visceral pain caused by distention or contraction of an organ decreases when constant pressure is applied.

Some vessels may also be encountered with deep palpation. Femoral pulses may have been encountered with superficial palpation or may be felt better with deep palpation. The aorta can often be palpated and it should be carefully investigated to make sure there is no area where it seems to balloon out in width, indicating the possibility of an aneurysm.

Palpable organs must be examined carefully. In order to palpate the spleen, the examiner should stand at the patient's right side with her left hand behind the child's left costovertebral area and push gently up from behind. Simultaneously with the nurse's right hand, she should work gently under the left anterior costal margin. The child is then asked to take

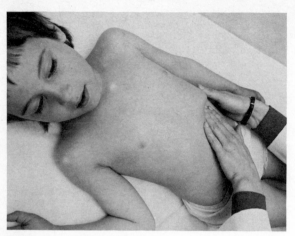

Figure 11–4 Palpation for a spleen.

a deep breath; inspiration will push down on the spleen, causing the tip to strike the examiner's fingers. Some clinicians prefer to palpate the spleen by ballottement. In this case, the nurse's left hand pushes gently in an anterior direction from behind the costovertebral angle, but her right hand pushes the abdominal wall directly below the costal margin in toward the backbone in short, ballottement movements. If the spleen is present, it will be felt bouncing back against the fingers. The spleen may be palpated more easily if the child rolls over onto his right side. Being able to feel the tip of the spleen is normal; it is more frequently felt in premature infants and thin children, but nothing more than the tip should normally be felt. In certain conditions such as erythroblastosis or infectious mononucleosis, in which spleen inflammation is likely, great care should be taken in palpating because it is possible to rupture an inflamed spleen.

Palpation of the liver should always be attempted, although in many normal children, it will not extend below the costal margin and consequently will not be felt. It is also normal, however, if the liver extends 1 to 3 cm below the costal margin in young children. If the examiner palpates with the flat of her fingers, starting at the lower abdomen and working gradually upward, she will hit the liver edge if it does extend below the costal margin. If the liver extends further than 3 cm or so below the costal margin, it should be considered enlarged, and the child should be referred to a physician. In rare instances of a congenital anomaly called *Riedel's lobe,* the liver will extend downward on the right side. At times systolic pulsations may be felt in the liver of a child with certain cardiac problems. Masses on the liver can also be palpated in certain conditions.

Liver tenderness may occur in children suffering from infectious hepatitis, infectious mononucleosis, liver abscesses, or certain other problems.

The nurse-examiner should attempt to palpate the kidneys. Although very few clinicians believe they can routinely feel a normal child's kidneys, the nurse-examiner might try to develop the ability to do so. She should always attempt palpation of the kidneys, however, since this may reveal enlargement. Kidneys are retroperitoneal organs and very deep palpation is necessary to feel them. They lie immediately adjacent to the vertebral column and will descend slightly with inspiration. At most, the lower pole will be felt, particularly of the right kidney which is lower. The kidneys are easier to feel in premature infants and neonates, although even in infants it is very difficult, except immediately after birth.

Hydronephrosis may cause a constant or intermittent cystic enlargement that may be felt as will congenital polycystic disease of the kidneys, Wilms' tumor, or a perinephritic abscess.

The urinary bladder may be palpated, particularly during early infancy and early childhood. It should be checked for distention such as that which can occur with certain types of central nervous system defects or urethral obstruction.

Parts of the intestine can at times be palpated. The cecum will present as a soft, gas-filled object in the right lower quadrant. The sigmoid may be rolled over the pelvic brim in the left lower quadrant; it feels like a freely moveable, sausage-shaped mass which may normally be tender. In chronic ulcerative colitis the ascending, descending, and sigmoid colons may be palpable and tender. At times it is possible to palpate bowel duplication as an extra moveable, nontender, smooth, round mass. The newborn with meconium ileus may have palpable rubbery or hard masses. In intussusception a sausage-shaped tumor is present 85 percent of the time in either the right or left upper quadrant.

BIBLIOGRAPHY

Barness, Lewis A.: *Manual of Pediatric Physical Diagnosis*, Chicago: Year Book Medical Publishers, Inc., 1968, pp. 125–143.

Barnett, Henry L.: *Pediatrics*, New York: Appleton Century Crofts, 1968, pp. 1490–1559.

DeGowin, Elmer L., and Richard L. DeGowin: *Bedside Diagnostic Examination*, New York: The Macmillan Company, 1970, pp. 450–551.

Delp, Mahlon H., and Robert T. Manning: *Major's Physical Diagnosis*, Philadelphia: W. B. Saunders Company, 1968, pp. 202–220.

Green, Morris, and Julius B. Richmond: *Pediatric Diagnosis*, Philadelphia: W. B. Saunders Company, 1962, pp. 103–116.

Judge, Richard D., and George D. Zuidema: *Physical Diagnosis: A Physiologic Approach*, Boston: Little, Brown and Company, 1963, pp. 206–220.

Nelson, Waldo: *Textbook of Pediatrics*, Philadelphia: W. B. Saunders Company, 1964, pp. 704–737.

Schaeffer, Alexander J., and Mary Ellen Avery: *Diseases of the Newborn*, Philadelphia: W. B. Saunders Company, 1971.

Silver, Henry K., C. Henry Kempe, and Henry B. Bruyn: *Handbook of Pediatrics*, Los Altos, Calif.: Lange Medical Publications, 1965, pp. 289–303.
Ziai, Mohsen: *Pediatrics*, Boston: Little, Brown and Company, 1969, pp. 331–384.

SUGGESTED RESOURCES

1 Pamphlets

"Physical Examination of the Abdomen," Parts 1–6, A. H. Robbins Drug Company. (Free)

2 Films

"The Abdomen in Infants and Children"
Color, 32 minutes
Cost: $5.00
Ciba Pharmaceutical Co.
P.O. Box 1340
Newark, New Jersey 07101
"The Abdomen in Adults"
Color, 33 minutes
Cost: $5.00
Ciba Pharmaceutical Co.
P.O. Box 1340
Newark, New Jersey 07101

GLOSSARY

ascites an accumulation of serous fluid in the abdomen
ballottement a maneuver for palpating organs such as the spleen by placing one hand behind the organ and one in front of it, and literally bouncing it between the hands
cardiac valve the sphincter of the stomach through which food passes from the esophagus
cremasteric muscle the muscle attached to the obliquus internus, inguinal ligament, and rectus abdominis which helps to raise the testes into the inguinal ring
Cullen's sign a bluish umbilicus resulting from intraabdominal hemorrhage
Czerny's sign (paradoxical respiration) a sign of certain nervous system diseases such as chorea in which the abdomen retracts rather than bulges at the beginning of inspiration
diastasis recti abdominis the condition in which the two rectus muscles separate, leaving the central area of the abdomen with fascia, but no muscular covering
direct inguinal hernia a herniation through the posterior wall of the inguinal canal directly behind the external ring at Hesselbach's triangle
duodenum the shortest, most immobile portion of the small intestine
Grey Turner's sign a massive ecchymosis, usually on the flanks and lower

abdomen, without a history of trauma, indicating extravasation of blood from within the abdomen

hernia   a muscular defect which allows internal organs to protrude

Hesselbach's triangle   a triangular shape formed by inguinal ligament, the epigastric artery, and the rectus abdominis muscle, located in an area in the posterior wall of the inguinal canal

iliacus   a thin, flat, broad muscle which fills the fossa of the iliac and functions in flexing the thigh

Meckel's diverticulum   a blind pouch sometimes found in the lower ileum, at times forming a cord continuous with the umbilicus evident by a fistulous opening through the umbilicus

megacolon   a very dilated, hypotonic colon usually with very little peristalsis

obliquus externus abdominis   a large, flat, irregular muscle covering the lateral portions of the abdomen, which aids in urination, defecation, vomiting, and parturition

obliquus internus abdominis   a thin small layer of muscle lying beneath the obliquus externus which functions in conjunction with it

omphalocele   a muscular defect in the umbilical area which allows peritoneal contents covered only by a thin, transparent membrane to protrude externally

organomegaly   enlarged palpable organs

paralytic ileus   lack of peristalsis

psoas major   a long, thin muscle attached to all the lumbar vertebra which inserts on the lesser trochanter of the femur, flexing both the thigh and lumbar vertebral column

psoas minor   a thin, long muscle which runs parallel to the psoas major, flexing the thigh and lumbar vertebral column

pyloric valve   the sphincter of the stomach through which food passes as it leaves the stomach to enter the small intestine

pyramidalis   a tiny, thin muscle which runs beside the lower rectus muscle and aids in tensing the linea alba

quadratus lumborum   a broad, irregularly shaped muscle arising at the iliac crest and inserting on the inferior border of the last rib, functioning in flexion of the rib cage and lumbar vertebral column

rectus abdominis   a broad, thin muscle running parallel to the linea alba which helps to flex the vertebral column

Sister Joseph's nodule   a nodular umbilicus which may indicate abdominal cancer

spider nevi   spider-shaped, reddened areas with a central arteriole and several extending rays, pressure on it causing the entire mark to blanch; sometimes a sign of liver disease

splenic flesure   the junction of the transverse and descending colon located near the spleen

striae   bands of tissue differing from the surrounding tissue in color and/or elevation; "stretch marks"

subcutaneous crepitus   palpable, moveable nontender bubbles directly beneath the skin

transversus abdominis   an abdominal muscle lying beneath the obliquus internus, whose fibers run parallel to the linea alba

urachal cyst   a cyst formed in the tract between the umbilicus and the urinary bladder

The Male Genitalia

WHY THE CHILD IS EXAMINED

Every complete examination should include a thorough evaluation of the boy's genitalia. It would seem easier to skip this part of the examination for some boys because they are so upset by it; however, this is not wise. The procedures should be done as quickly and matter-of-factly as possible, but it is important that the examiner is certain that no abnormalities exist. This is particularly true in cases of undescended testicles which may be a problem and should definitely be diagnosed before the prepubertal period. Other conditions, such as hermaphroditism, should be diagnosed even earlier, in fact, during the neonatal period.

Another reason that this part of the examination is so important is because so many parents are concerned with the genitalia and yet do not feel free to voice these concerns.

Because our culture puts great emphasis on the genital area and because many parental and child anxieties are concerned with this area, the physical examination of the genitalia must be done with great care and tact. Many parents and children will hesitate to ask questions concerning this part of the examination, and for that reason, it is important that the examiner verbalize his findings. This is particularly true with the adolescent patient. If the findings are normal, this should be plainly stated. If there are findings which, although normal, may be a possible cause of concern to the parent or child (for instance, vaginal bleeding of the newborn), the nurse should be alert to this and reassure the parent, without waiting for specific questions. By the time a child is 3 years old or even younger, it may well have incorporated many of its parents' feelings about its genitalia. If the child lives in a home where sexuality is a subject surrounded with an air of shamefulness, it will soon learn that its genitals may be regarded by some as shameful, and the child may begin to regard them in this way. If this is the case, a physical examination performed brusquely may indeed be traumatic, and the nurse-examiner must be extremely sensitive to the feelings of her patient. Although reticence on the part of the child is no excuse for skipping this part of the examination, it is reason enough to proceed with it in the least possible traumatic manner. Usually a firm, matter-of-fact and rapid but thorough examination is the best approach. Immediately after it is completed the child should be briefly reassured that the examination showed that all is normal, if such is the case, since many unmentioned fears center around this area in the preschool child. Discussion of other less threatening topics might be useful at this time to reestablish rapport if this has been lost.

WHAT TO EXAMINE: ANATOMY OF THE AREA

For study, we can divide the male genitalia into two parts, the penis and scrotum. The penis consists of a shaft, a retroglandular sulcus meatus, prepuce, glans, and corona. The shaft of the penis is made up of three cylindrical structures: one, called the *corpus spongiosum* (sometimes called the *corpus cavernosum urethrae*) and the two structures called the *corpora cavernosa*. The corpus spongiosum is the medial cylinder of the penis and contains the urethra. The anterior end of the corpus spongiosum forms a rounded balloon called the *glans penis*, the border of which is called the *corona glandis*. The urethra is located within this structure. The retroglandular sulcus is the proximal end of the corona and forms the neck of the penis.

The two corpora cavernosa form the major portion of the shaft of the penis and are composed of strong erectile tissue and many fibrous columns. The skin covering the shaft is thin, darkly pigmented and loosely connected to deeper fascia. The prepuce (foreskin) is the fold of skin at the neck of the penis, while a secondary fold of skin from the meatus to the neck is termed the *frenulum*. The glans skin contains no hairs, but small papillae and glands which secrete an odoriferous sebaceous material that mixes with epithelial cells to form smegma.

This penile shaft is supplied with strong ligaments, muscles, and blood vessels.

The scrotum contains the testes, vas deferens, seminal vesicles, ejaculatory ducts, and the prostate and bulbourethral glands. The left and right side of the scrotum are divided by a raphe (ridge) and are covered by a layer of skin and by the dartos tunica.

The testes are the most palpable structures in the scrotum; they are two smooth olive-shaped masses which produce semen. Prenatally, they develop in the abdominal cavity, but by birth they descend along the inguinal canal into the scrotum.

The spermatic cord extends from the testes to the deep inguinal ring. The right cord is shorter, thus the right testis normally hangs higher than the left. The epididymis can be felt as a long, thin mass along the lateral edge of the posterior border of the testes. It consists of three parts: head, body, and tail. The upper pole is called the head, or globus major; the body is an elongated cone down the posterior axis of the testes; and the tail, or globus minor, forms the tip of this cone. The vas deferens, or minor ductus deferans, is a whiplike cord continuous with the tail of the epididymis.

The seminal vesicles are pouches lying along the side of the vas deferens, and they secrete a liquid into the semen as it passes from the testes. The opening of the seminal vesicles joins the vas deferens to make up the ejaculatory ducts which are 2 cm long, and extend from the prostate base to the borders of the utricle. The prostate gland is a small, round, firm mass, the size of a walnut, lying within the pelvic cavity. The urethra and ejaculatory ducts run through this gland. The bulbourethral glands (Cowper's glands) are two pea-sized masses lying along the urethra. Both the prostate and bulbourethral glands produce secretions that neutralize the acidity of the urethra and vagina, which might cause damage to the semen.

HOW TO EXAMINE

The primary methods for examining the male genitalia are inspection and palpation. Very rarely a clinician will choose to use auscultation to help ascertain whether the bowel has slipped through a hernia, by listening for bowel sounds in the scrotum. Percussion is of no use in this area. In general, the nurse-examiner should exercise great care and tact in this part of the physical examination. Many children are quite sensitive about their genitals by the time they are 4 or 5 years old. A kind, firm, and quick examination is best. It must be remembered that the cremasteric reflex in boys can be activated by cold, touch, or emotion, so that if he is frightened or embarrassed, his testes may ascend into the abdomen before the examiner has palpated the scrotum. It can be very difficult in

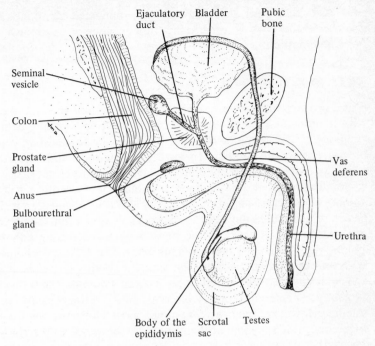

Figure 12-1 The male genitalia.

this case to determine for sure whether the testes had ever descended. This will be discussed at greater length later, but is mentioned here only to remind the nurse that if at all possible, it is helpful to keep this part of the examination as untraumatic as possible, both for psychological well-being of the boy and for the accuracy of physical findings. Also, it is wise to begin by blocking the inguinal canals by applying pressure with the index finger before palpating for testes. If this is done at the beginning of this part of the examination, it will prevent the passage of the testes into the abdomen if the child should later become cold or upset.

WHERE TO EXAMINE

The entire genital and surrounding area must be carefully inspected and palpated. All parts of the penis and scrotum, as well as nearby lymphatic chains, should be included.

WHAT TO EXAMINE WITH

Elaborate equipment is not necessary for this examination. A good light and careful technique are essential. Sometimes an examiner will wish to use a stethoscope for auscultating bowel sounds, as mentioned before. A good penlight with a protruding rubber neck is also necessary for transillumination.

WHAT TO EXAMINE FOR

There are two primary areas of examination, the penis and the scrotum with its contents. All parts of the penis must be carefully evaluated. In newborns and sometimes on older children, the foreskin may be an area of concern to the mother. In an uncircumcised child, the foreskin is normally quite tight for 2 to 3 months and does not retract easily. There is some disagreement on whether it should be forcedly retracted. The authors agree with Schaeffer and Avery (1971) who state that it should not be retracted for cleaning or other purpose, since the thin membrane which connects it to the shaft of the penis may tear, causing adhesions and making retraction even more difficult later. This tightness should be gone in about 2 or 3 months; if after this time the conditions persist it should be considered to be *phimosis*. Starting at about 4 months, the foreskin should be gently retracted at monthly intervals until it retracts easily and without trauma. However, even at that time, most clinicians (e.g., Green and Richmond, 1962) say that nothing should be done unless the phimosis is so severe that urination is impaired.

The question of circumcision is controversial. Basically it is important to remember that this decision belongs to the parents. The nurse-examiner, however, should be aware of the advantages and disadvantages of this procedure and should carefully explain them to the parents. The primary advantage of circumcision is the ease of cleanliness. It eliminates the necessity for cleaning between the foreskin and the penile shaft, an area where smegma can easily accumulate. It is easier not only for the mother to keep this area clean but also for preschooler who is beginning to take care of himself. The second advantage is based on some experimental data that suggest that wives of uncircumcised males have a higher incidence of cervical cancer. These data are not totally conclusive, however. The disadvantage of circumcision seems to be the procedure itself. Not all circumcisions are performed well. There is always the possibility of excessive bleeding, but even more important, of infection. A few cases of gangrene have been reported following a bell clamp circumcision, and there has been a suspicion that some cases of sepsis may have originated with a local infection in this area. Some authors mention the possibility that because the meatus is more exposed to irritation from ammonia from urine breakdown in the diaper area the penis may be more likely to become ulcerated.

During the examination the foreskin must always be carefully retracted in any child over the age of 4 months, if it retracts easily. It must be inspected and palpated carefully. Small white cysts may normally be seen on the distal prepuce in neonates. In older children a condition called *paraphimosis* may be seen. In paraphimosis the foreskin is permanently retracted behind the corona of the glans and cannot be slipped forward; edema of the glans almost always accompanies this condition, since the free flow of blood is constricted by the band of foreskin. This should be brought to the attention of the physician immediately. Balanoposthitis is another condition which may be noticed. Balanoposthitis is the local infection of both prepuce and glans, characterized by redness and tenderness in that area and sometimes accompanied by discharge. Preputial calculus should also be checked for. Rarely these are renal calculi passed into the prepuce, but more often they are actually solidified dirt and smegma caught beneath a phimosis. Preputial adhesions may be another problem found in this area. Most often these are in young infants and are the result of circumcision. They can usually be gently separated and covered with petroleum jelly to keep them from readhering.

Next, the meatus is examined; it should be carefully checked for ulceration, a condition much more common in circumcised children than in uncircumcised ones of diaper age. The ulceration itself is usually not a major problem but may result in stricture which can, if it leads to a small pinpoint meatus, cause urinary obstructive symptoms and will significantly increase the possibility of acute pyelonephritis. The stricture may initially be manifested by frequency, dysuria, and possibly by enuresis. The meatus should also be palpated; a papilloma or benign tumor may at times be found immediately inside it. Urethritis of the meatus results in the edges being erythematous, swollen, and everted. Micturition and erection may be painful, and the nearby lymph nodes will be tender and swollen. If this condition is accompanied by conjunctivitis and arthritis, it forms a triad of symptoms called *Reiter's syndrome*. Morgagni's folliculitis is another condition of this area. These follicles are located just inside the meatal lips, and when infected, the openings will enlarge and a pus-like drainage will be seen.

The position of the meatus is also important; normally the meatus is centered at the tip of the shaft. If the opening is found on the dorsal shaft, it is called *epispadias*. This is a rarer condition than hypospadias and is usually associated with extrophy of the urinary bladder. There are three types of epispadias, depending on the exact position of the meatus; when it is located on the glans, it is called *balanic epispadias*; when on the shaft, it is called *penile epispadias*; and if it is not on the penis at all, but directly below the symphysis, it is called a *penopubic epispadias*. All types should be referred to a physician.

Hypospadias refers to the meatal opening on the ventral surface of the penis. It is often associated with fibrotic chordee which restrict the penis on erection, causing a downward curvature. Again, there are three

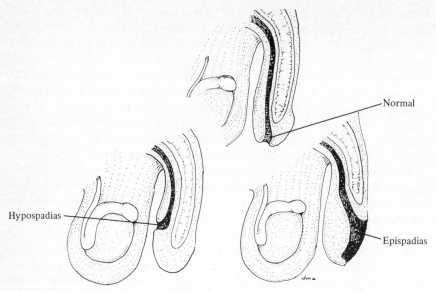

Figure 12-2   Three types of meatal openings: Normal, hypospadias, and epispadias.

types. The balanic or glandular type is located at the base of the glans. It is usually asymptomatic and no treatment is necessary unless the opening is too narrow, in which case a meatotomy is indicated. In the penile type the meatus is found somewhere between the glans and the scrotum. As in epispadias, this type is often associated with chordee, as well as a flattened glans and an absent ventral foreskin. Surgical correction is usually begun at about 4 years of age. A child with this condition should definitely not be circumcised, since the foreskin will be needed in the later operation. The final type is called penoscrotal or perineal. In this type the meatus is located at the penoscrotal junction and often associated with a bifid scrotum. The penis is usually small and the meatus large; the testes are often undescended. A thorough investigation into the possibility of hermaphroditism is indicated. The incidence of hypospadias is 1 in 500.

A thorough inspection of the meatus should also include an evaluation of its size. The difficulty of a pinpoint meatus has been discussed previously. Usually this is due to stricture, but it can be congenital. Actual meatal atresia is usually due to an obstruction caused by a thin membrane. Deeper obstructions may also cause failure to void. All nurses are aware of the importance of observing the neonate for first voiding.

Next in the examination of the genitalia is the glans. Veneral warts (condyloma acuminatum) are a possible finding in this area. They appear as pointed projections, either singly or in groups, often extending to the anus. These are frequently a site of secondary infection. Condyloma latum is a symptom of secondary syphilis and appears flat and wart-like. Erosive balanitis is an infection sometimes found on the glans in which the superficial skin appears eroded where small ulcers form and coalesce. The etiology of this infection is unknown.

The shaft of the penis must also be examined. Acute urethritis may cause palpable, long cords extending the length of the penis; a cord palpable only at one point in the shaft may indicate stricture. Visible swelling associated with a soft midline mass in the penoscrotal juncture may indicate an underlying diverticulum. A periurethral abscess is another condition of the penile shaft. In this situation, pus will accumulate in the middle of the shaft in Littre's follicle and will be palpable. Inflammation of the glans, which spreads and results in a palpable cord about 1 mm in diameter in the midline area of the shaft, may be an indication of dorsal vein thrombosis. The shaft should also be inspected for varicosities as well as for cavernositis, a palpable hard irregular mass in the lateral or ventral shaft. This condition can be from thrombosis, leukemia, septicemia, trauma, or infection. It is accompanied by inflammation and often by priapism and edema. Drainage may appear through the skin or urethra. Priapism is another possible abnormality of the shaft, although again, it is very rarely found in this age group. This is the condition of continuous erection without sexual desire. It is quite painful and may have either a local or central nervous system etiology. If of central nervous system in origin, the cause is usually lesions in the spinal cord or cerebrum. Local causes include neoplasms, inflammation, hemorrhage, and thrombosis. It is often associated with leukemia and sickle-cell anemia. This must not be confused with the transistory erections of infancy, which are completely normal. The size of the penile shaft must also be evaluated. Penile hypoplasia (microphallus) is a possibility. The nonerect length of the infantile penis is about 2 to 3 cm at birth. A penis smaller than this should not be worrisome unless there is a possibility that it is actually an enlarged clitoris rather than a small penis. In any situation of such ambiguity, the possibility of hermaphroditism must be thoroughly explored. A penis which remains infantile in size at adolescence may be an indication of hormonal abnormalities.

Penile hyperplasia (megalopenis) usually does not appear until 1 year of age. Possible causes of this condition are a tumor of the pineal body, a tumor of the hypothalamus, or a tumor of the adrenal glands.

The scrotum and its contents are the second major area of examination. The scrotal wall must be carefully checked for edema such as occurs in nephrosis, local inflammation, or portal vein obstruction and for purpura such as occurs in Schoenlein's disease. Sebaceous cysts will frequently be found in this area and are considered normal. Gangrene is a possibility, particularly when acute urethritis may have resulted in extravasation of urine. This is also a possible site for neoplasms. The color is important. Red, shiny skin may indicate an underlying orchitis. A very dark scrotum, particularly in a child of light-skinned race, may indicate adrenal hyperplasia. It is also important to note rugae. Well-formed rugae usually indicate that the testes have descended at some time even though they may not be palpable at the time of the examination. The normal scrotal contour in the neonate is quite variable. Scrotal skin may be tight and small or loose and hanging. During infancy, the proximal end is widest; the opposite is true after the hormonal influence of adolescence.

Most important of the scrotal contents are the testes. Except in premature infants, the testes should be descended by birth. As previously mentioned, it is wise to palpate for the testes at the very beginning of the genital examination; this lessens the chance of activating the cremasteric reflex by exposing the infant to cold or the older child to embarrassment. Before palpating for them, the inguinal canals should be blocked by the examiner's index finger. It is extremely important to palpate the testes at each visit. This is even more important if there is a question of undescended testes. The term *undescended* refers only to testes which have never descended. Once you are assured that they have been felt at any time in the boy's life, there will no longer be a need to consider surgery. Accurate recording is extremely important because of this. If there is a question of undescended testes, the examiner should attempt to palpate them with the child in a supine and standing position. If neither of these positions is helpful, the child should be asked to sit in a chair with knees flexed against this chest and feet placed on the seat of the chair. This usually forces the testes down. Heat also influences their descent, and an examination in a warm tub of water may be necessary. There is disagreement as to when surgical intervention is indicated, but certainly any boy who has testes that have never been palpated in the scrotum by 11 or 12 years of age should be referred to the physician. Many specialists request that the referral be considerably earlier. If they are not palpable in the scrotum, the examiner should palpate the femoral, inguinal, perineal, and abdominal areas to see if they are palpable in these areas. Scorer says that about one-half the cases of undescended testes at birth will descend by the end of the first month, and one-fourth by the end of the first year. The normal length of the testes at birth is 1.5 to 2.0 cm. The size remains constant until about 11 years of age. Between the ages of 11 and 18, the size increases to about 3.5 to 5.0 cm. Abnormal enlargement may occur in certain precocious boys with neurogenic or idiopathic sexual precocity; it can also occur from a testicular tumor, but in such cases only one testes will enlarge. Testes will be small in Klinefelter's syndrome, in hypopituitarism, or in adrenal hyperplasia. If both are undescended, the examiner should consider the possibility of intersex.

Another important structure in the scrotum is the epididymis. This can be palpated as a vertical ridge of soft nodular tissue from the superior testicular pole to the inferior testicular pole, usually behind the testis, but

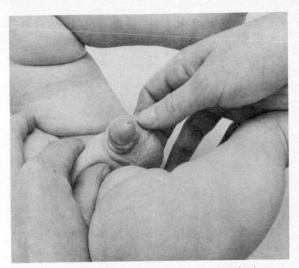

Figure 12-3   Procedure for blocking the inguinal
canal when examining the
scrotal contents.

in front of them in 7 percent of boys (a condition known as anteversion of
the epididymis). The examiner must compare both for size and consistency. A mass may be palpated in some epididymides; this may indicate a
spermatocele or retention cyst. In such a case the mass can be transilluminated. A mass may also fail to transilluminate and appear opaque; the
possibility of neoplasm should always be considered in this situation.
Nodularity of the epididymis may be a result of syphilis and is palpable
though not painful. Hard nodules adherent to the scrotum also may be a
result of tuberculosis. Another possible finding is acute epididymitis,
usually resulting from trauma or an adjacent infection. This condition is
painful and tender and is associated with fever and an increase in the
number of white blood cells.

The spermatic cord should be palpated in the scrotal sac. Both sides
should be felt simultaneously and compared. The vas deferens should be
felt as a hard distinct cord, while the more ambiguous cords are nerves,
arteries, and fibers of the cremasteric muscle. These cords should be
traced with the fingers to their origin in the testes. A thickening of the vas
deferens may be due to inflammation. This may be from syphilis or
tuberculosis or to an extension of any nearby infection. If the inflammation is chronic, nodular formations may be felt. Hydrocele of the cord will
be palpable as a sausage-shaped, smooth bulge above the testes which can
be transilluminated. Hematoma of the cord, on the other hand, is opaque
and feels like a boggy mass in the same area. Usually it is associated with
a history of trauma and often other signs of trauma of the scrotal skin.

Gumma or granuloma is a tertiary sign of syphilis. It also appears as an opaque mass when transilluminated. It is nontender, and if it extends to the testes, they will lose their sensitivity to pain. Neoplasms are indistinguishable from gumma and can be either benign or malignant. Torsion of the cord is a painful emergency occasionally encountered in children. This is the condition in which the spermatic cord becomes twisted, resulting in edema and congestion and a tender, irregular, swollen mass. At times the examiner will actually be able to feel the twist of the cord and will notice that the testis on the affected side is a great deal higher than the other side. The leg on the involved side is often flexed to alleviate the pain. A similar condition is epididymitis which is less of an emergency. Palpation will determine an enlarged epididymis posterior to the testis; it is thickened or nodular and elevation of the scrotum for an hour or so usually relieves it.

Generalized masses in the scrotal sac will also be encountered occasionally. Such a mass may be a scrotal hydrocele. In a scrotal hydrocele, transillumination will show the testes and epididymis as shadows behind the transilluminated mass. (The only situation in which this will not be true is in anteversion.) The external inguinal ring is not usually large, and the mass is seldom communicating. If it is communicating, it will be slightly larger at night after the child has been on his feet all day, and frequently a hernia will be associated with it. Treatment is usually indicated only if a communicating hydrocele contains a hernia or if a noncommunicating one is extremely large and lasts for many months.

Hematoceles are very similar to hydroceles, except that they are filled with blood rather than with clear fluid, and for this reason, do not transilluminate. They are usually associated with a history of trauma as well as traumatic indications of the scrotal skin. Chylocele is a mass very similar to a hydrocele, except that the fluid that fills the sac is lymph. Like a hydrocele it will transilluminate. This condition is unusual in this country and is usually a result of filariasis.

A varicocele is a scrotal sac filled not with fluid but with multiple varicose veins. Palpation reveals a condition usually said to be similar to a bag of worms. Most often this condition is more prominent on the left side and felt only when the patient is standing up. Such a condition should lead the examiner to suspect an obstruction above the scrotal sac.

A malignant condition located in the scrotum may also appear as a mass; in this situation the mass will appear hard, opaque, and usually nontender. Most often this type of malignant mass does not appear until after puberty.

Orchitis is another problem found in this area; usually, it is a sequela of mumps, but sometimes it is a result of other infections. In orchitis there is an acute, tender, painful hydrocele and erythematous scrotal skin.

Hernias are an important finding and can be abdominal or inguinal.

For purposes of clarity both types are considered in the chapter, "The Abdomen."

Regional lymph nodes may be an important manifestation of disease of the genitalia. Both femoral and inguinal nodes must be palpated. Many individuals, however, have chronic, painless nodes in these areas which are usually significant.

GLOSSARY

balanic epispadias   the condition in which the urinary meatus is malpositioned dorsally on the glans penis

balanic hypospadias   the condition in which the urinary meatus is malpositioned ventrally at the base of the glans penis

balanoposthitis   a condition of local infection of the penis

bulbourethral glands (Cowper's glands)   the two pea-sized masses lying along the urethra which produce secretions to neutralize the acidity of the urethra and vagina, which might damage semen

corona glandis   the border of the glans penis

corpora cavernosa   the two cylindrical masses that form the major portion of the shaft of the penis and which are composed of strong erectile tissue and many fibrous columns

corpus spongiosum   the medial cylinder of the penis which contains the urethra

cremasteric reflex   a reflexive withdrawal of the testes into the abdomen when the individual is stimulated by cold, emotion, or stroking of the inner thighs

epididymis   a long, thin mass along the lateral edge of the posterior border of the testes which constitutes the first part of the excretory duct of each testis

frenulum   a fold of skin extending from the meatus to the neck of the penis

glans penis   the anterior end of the corpus spongiosum, which forms a rounded balloon-shaped structure

hematocele   a generalized scrotal mass consisting of blood

meatus   the opening in the corpus spongiosum to allow excretion of urine

megalopenis   hyperplasis of the penis

microphallus   hypoplasia of the penis

Morgagni's folliculitis   the condition in which the follicles located just inside the meatal lips are infected

paraphimosis   the condition in which the foreskin is permanently retracted behind the corona of the glans and cannot be slipped forward

penile epispadias   the condition in which the meatus is malpositioned dorsally on the penile shaft

penile hypospadias   the condition in which the urinary meatus is malpositioned ventrally between the glans and the scrotum

penile shaft   the main body of the penis, composed of one corpus spongiosum and two corpora cavernosa

penopubic epispadias   a condition in which the urinary meatus is malpositioned dorsally directly below the symphysis

penoscrotal (perineal) hypospadias   the condition in which the urinary meatus is malpositioned ventrally at the perineum

phimosis a narrowing of the tip of the foreskin in such a way that it can no longer be slipped back over the shaft of the penis

prepuce (foreskin) the fold of skin at the neck of the penis

preputial calculus hard gritty material found in the prepuce, sometimes passed from the bladder, but more often as solidified dirt and smegma caught beneath a phimosis

priapism a condition of continuous erection without sexual desire

Reiter's syndrome a triad of conjunctivitis, arthritis, and urethritis

retroglandular sulcus the proximal end of the corona glandis which forms the neck of the penis

scrotal hydrocele a generalized scrotal mass consisting of clear fluid

scrotum the pendulous male sac containing the testes and their excretory apparatus

spermatic cord the cord extending from the testes to the deep inguinal ring

testes the two smooth olive-shaped masses that produce semen and are located in the scrotal sac

variocele a generalized scrotal mass filled not with but with multiple varicose veins*

*References for this chapter can be found at the end of the Chapter 13.

Female Genitalia

WHY THE CHILD IS EXAMINED

The genitalia are an important part of the physical examination of girls as well as of boys. In the infant, it is most important that the genitalia be judged to be unambiguous; any question in this regard should be fully investigated before the child is any older. In the toddler and preschool girl, this part of the examination remains an important one, not only in checking for abnormalities, but in providing an excellent opportunity for discussing questions of bodily acceptance and sexuality both for the parents and the child. In the adolescent girl, especially, this part of the examination can be a chance for important counseling in the areas of human sexuality and body image.

WHAT TO EXAMINE: ANATOMY OF THE AREA

For purposes of study the female genitalia can be divided into the internal and external structures. The internal structures include the ovaries, uterine tubes, uterus, and vagina, all of which are contained within the

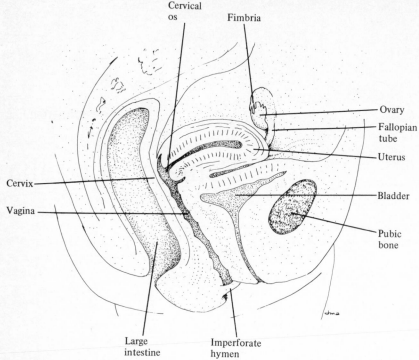

Cervical
os   Fimbria

Ovary

Fallopian
tube

Uterus

Cervix

Bladder

Vagina

Pubic
bone

Large   Imperforate
intestine   hymen

Figure 13–1   Internal female organs.

pelvis; the external structures are the mons pubis, labia majora, labia minora, clitoris, bulbus vestibuli, and Bartholin's and Skene's glands. These are more easily inspected, since they are superficial urogenital structures. In young girls the examiner is concerned mostly with these external structures and the vagina. For a more detailed description of the anatomy of the internal structures the reader is referred to a good text book on obstetrics.

The external genital structures are sometimes referred to as the vulva or pudendum. The first of these, the mons pubis, is a pad of adipose tissue anteriorly surmounting the symphysis pubis. At puberty, the mons becomes covered with hair, the distribution of which forms an inverted triangle in the normal female. If it is diamond-shaped as in males, the examiner should be concerned about possible hormonal abnormalities. The base of this triangle is called *female escutcheon*.

The labia majora are two fatty folds running from the mons pubis posteriorly, containing fat, nerves, and blood vessels. The outer surface is pigmented and covered with thick, curly hairs while the inner surface is smooth, with many sebaceous follicles.

The labia minora are two smaller folds of tissue running parallel to the labia majora; their tissue ends about 4 cm into the vagina, and in the virgin the two labia minora are joined by a fold of skin called the *frenulum* (fourchette). The surface of the labia minora contains many sebaceous follicles.

The clitoris is an organ composed of erectile tissue and joins the labia minora anteriorly. Dense fibrous tissue covers the two corpora cavernosa which are surrounded by folds of the labia minora. These corpora cavernosa are the preputium clitoridis and the frenulum of the clitoris. The clitoris is an erectile homologue of the penis.

The vestibule is the cleft between the labia minora which contains the urethral and vaginal orifices. The urethral meatus is 2.5 cm posterior of the clitoris, and contains Skene's glands which are homologues to the male prostatic gland. The vaginal orifice is immediately posterior to the meatus.

The hymen is a thin membrane covering part of vaginal orifice. Although it is usually a perforated ring with the widest opening posteriorly, sometimes it is cribiform, fringed, or even imperforate. After rupture, only caruncles (small rounded bumps) remain.

The bulb of the vestibule is a 2.5-cm mass of erectile tissue located along both sides of the vaginal orifice.

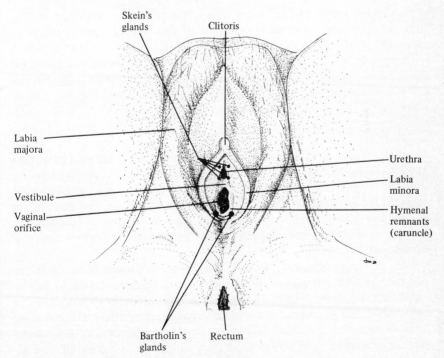

Figure 13–2 External female genitalia structures.

The greater vestibular glands (Bartholin's glands) are small, rounded elevations on both sides of the vaginal orifice. They resemble the bulbourethral glands of the male.

HOW TO EXAMINE

The methods of examination for evaluating the female genitalia are inspection and palpation. Neither auscultation nor percussion has any usefulness in this area.

WHERE TO EXAMINE

Because of the specific age group with which this book is concerned, the examination of the genitalia almost always should be confined to the external genitalia solely. Seldom is an examination of the vagina, cervix, uterus, or adnexa indicated. There are some exceptions to this, particularly in the case of the adolescent girl desiring contraceptives or a confirmation of pregnancy.

WHAT TO EXAMINE WITH

For an examination of the external genitalia of infants and very young girls, no special equipment is required. If for some unusual reason an examination of the internal genitalia is indicated, pediatric speculums and other specialized equipment are useful. In most instances, it will not be the nurse who does this kind of examination; therefore, this book will not be concerned with it.

WHAT TO EXAMINE FOR

All parts of the external genitalia are carefully inspected and palpated. The examination is begun with the mons pubis which in the very young child is inspected for any skin discolorations or abnormalities and palpated for any masses; in the older child, the appearance of hair and its distribution will be used as indicators of adequate hormonal functioning. At this point also, the possibility of pubic lice or crabs must be considered.

Proceeding posteriorly the labia majora are evaluated next. Again the skin is inspected, particularly for its integrity. At times ulcerations will be found. Usually these will be of nonspecific origin, but they should always be cultured. They can be a result of venereal disease, although this finding is more common in older children. Chancres, chancroids, granuloma inguinales, lymphogranuloma venereum and herpes progenitalis are all possible findings. These are discussed more completely in a good book on obstetrical cases.

Vulvitis, another possible finding, is a condition in which the skin will be warm, erythematous, and swollen. The usual cause is an extension of some type of vaginitis with an accompanying irritating discharge. This may result from a trichomonal or gonorrheal infection or, less frequently, from a monilial or nonspecific infection. Vaginitis resulting from a foreign body should also be considered, particularly in preschool-age children.

The vulva should also be palpated and inspected for any masses. Condyloma acuminatum and condyloma latum may be present just as in males. Neoplasms should also be considered.

Swelling of the vulva may be a symptom of lymphedema resulting from an obstruction of the lymphatic system anywhere above the vulva, or, if large, painful, and bluish, may be a hematoma. Usually this will appear within a few hours after trauma. It should always be documented, particularly, of course, if there is any question of sexual molestation. A more localized swelling may result from a labioinguinal hernia, the homologue of a scrotal hernia in the male. Careful palpation will reveal whether this swelling communicates with the abdomen.

The vulva should be further examined for any areas of cellulitis or any suggestion of varicosities. Varicosities in a young child usually suggest a blockage of the circulatory system in any area above the varicosities. Possible causes of such blockage are tumors or enlarged organs which may be obstructing venous return.

Lichen sclerosus et atrophicus is a condition of the vulva in which the skin is white, thin, atrophied, wrinkled, and excoriated. It is usually accompanied by some pruritis. This is quite rare in premenarchal or young adolescent girls, however.

Next Bartholin's glands are inspected and palpated. Normally they are neither visible nor palpable. If they are palpable, enlargement exists and is almost always due to infection, usually gonorrhea.

Skene's glands are likewise not normally seen or felt. Again, Skene's glands which are large enough to be visible or palpable are abnormally enlarged, most often from acute or chronic gonorrhea, although sometimes from other infections.

The labia minora are the next structures to examine. They are normally quite large in the newborn and will frequently be seen protruding from the labia majora. This is even more obvious in premature infants. The edges may show a rather darkly pigmented border; this is to be considered normal in the young infant.

Adhesions are one of the most common difficulties in the infant and young child. Sometimes they are actually present from birth and appear as a transparent membrane which partially or totally occludes the vaginal orifice. Usually there are no symptoms although occasionally complaints of frequency and dysuria will be heard. Adhesions may also follow vulvovaginitis. This must be carefully distinguished from a thick sticky collection of smegma due to lack of hygiene. This frequently appears not because mothers are remiss in caring for their child, but because their own sexual inhibitions prevent them from handling the baby's genitals to any great extent.

Hypertrophy of the labia minor is fairly common and usually has no clinical significance. Some authors feel that it may at times be an indication of excessive masturbation, but this is not usually thought to be the case.

The clitoris also must be inspected closely, although, because of its sensitivity, it is not palpated unless there is definite indication to do so. The clitoris is normally large in newborns, but the examiner must evaluate its size carefully, since hypertrophy of the clitoris is its most common abnormality. When such hypertrophy is associated with labioscrotal fusion and possible pseudohermaphroditism, the clitoris should be thoroughly investigated. This is even more of a possibility if there is an anterior displacement of the urethral meatus associated with the clitoral hypertrophy. Inflammation is uncommon but may present as cellulitis or abscess.

Hypoplasia of the clitoris, on the other hand, is exceedingly rare and has very little clinical significance although some authors have indicated the possibility that this may result later in an individual who has difficulty with sexual arousal. There is some question about this.

The vestibule should be examined next. Although it is the most common site of cancer in the elderly and is a fairly common site of granulomatous and ulcerative venereal lesions in older girls, there are generally very few physical findings in children of this age in this area. The meatus is a very important area for examination in little girls.

Any urethritis, indicated by inflammation, erythema, and discharge, should be cultured. Prolapse of the mucosa should also be sought for, and if found, the mother should be carefully questioned concerning a history of hematuria, dysuria, or other urinary symptoms. Position of the urethra is important in little girls, as well as in little boys. If epispadias is found, accompanied by a complete or partial midline division of mons and clitoris, the possibility of hermaphroditism must be fully investigated. Palpation is also important. Urethral caruncles may appear and be palpated as small red masses, visible just inside the meatus. They are tender and painful on urination and are a complication of urethritis. It is quite unusual to find them in this age group, however.

The final structures to be examined are the vaginal opening and hymen. Congenital absence of a vagina is a possible finding as is an imperforate hymen. In a small infant or young girl, this will not usually be apparent unless there is some type of fluid retained by the hymen. If the fluid is a collection of vaginal secretions, the condition is called *hydrocolpos* and may appear as a small midline lower abdominal mass or a small cystic moveable mass between the labia. This condition may clear spontaneously or surgery may be needed. If the fluid retained by the hymen is blood, the condition is called *hematocolpos* and the mass will usually be suprapubic. The hymen may be bluish and bulging, and there may be associated lower abdominal pain. This condition may occur either in the newborn who has absorbed enough hormones from her mother to set up a small pseudomenstruation or in the adolescent who is actually menstruating. In the newborn, the blood will gradually be reabsorbed if the pressure does not rupture the membrane. In the adolescent, the condition is more serious, mostly because the amount of blood is greater. A back pressure is generated, resulting eventually in cervical dilation. The blood then backs up to the uterus and tubes, making the girl strongly susceptible to infection. Bladder pressure, dysuria, frequency, urinary retention, amenorrhea, and lower abdominal pain are accompanying symptoms in the adolescent. If not corrected, the condition may lead to sterility.

Sarcoma botryoides is another unusual but possible finding. This growth is a grape-like, fleshy group of tissue masses originating beneath the vaginal epithelium.

Vaginal discharge is the final subject to be discussed in the physical examination of the vagina of little girls. A small amount of bloody discharge is normal, though uncommon, in newborns up to 1 month of age. It results from the absorption of hormones from mother during pregnancy. Newborns may also exhibit mucoid discharge which is generally also normal. Foul discharge in older children can be due to foreign body in the vagina, tight pants, pinworms, masturbation, or infection. It should be fully investigated.

BIBLIOGRAPHY

Altchek, A.: "Dermatologic Vulvar Conditions Seen in the Child," *New York State Journal of Medicine*, vol. 69, 1969, pp. 1401–1404.
————: "Valvovaginitis in Children," *General Practice*, vol. 34, 1966, pp. 85–95.
————: "Vulvovaginal Irritation and Discharge in Children," *Surgical Clinics of North America*, vol. 40, 1960, pp. 1071–1083.
Ashby, W. B.: "Torsion of Testis," *British Medical Journal*, vol. 2, April 26, 1969, p. 251.
Barness, Lewis A.: *Manual of Pediatric Physical Diagnosis*, Chicago: Year Book Medical Publishers, Inc, 1968, pp. 135–139.
Bessemer, R.: "Examination for Hernia in Children," *Journal of the American Medical Association*, vol. 210, November 3, 1969, p. 905.
Corriere, J. N., Jr.: "Horizontal Lie of the Testicle: A Diagnostic Sign in Torsion of the Testis," *Journal of Urology*, April 1972, pp. 616–617.
DeGowin, Elmer L., and Richard L. DeGowin: *Bedside Diagnostic Examination*, New York: The Macmillan Company, 1970, pp. 552–604.

Delp, Mahlon H., and Robert T. Manning: *Major's Physical Diagnosis*, Philadelphia: W. B. Saunders Company, 1968, pp. 221–241.

Denis, L.: "Diagnosis of Testicular Torsion," *Acta Urologice Belgica*, 1968, pp. 425–428.

Fodor, P. B., and W. A. Webb: "Indirect Inguinal Hernia in the Female with No Palpable Sac," *Southern Medical Journal*, January 1971, pp. 15–16.

Gardner, H. L., and R. H. Kaufman: *Benign Diseases of the Vulva and Vagina*, St. Louis: The C. V. Mosby Company, 1969.

Ger, R.: "The Scrotal Dimple in Testicular Torsion," *Surgery*, November 1969, pp. 907–908.

Gerlock, A. J.: "Left Testicular Vein Varices Simulating Retroperitoneal Lymphnode Enlargement," *Radiology*, October 1969, pp. 873–874.

Green, Morris, and Julius B. Richmond: *Pediatric Diagnosis*, Philadelphia: W. B. Saunders Company, 1962, pp. 120–124.

Haahr, Jr., and S. Sparrevohn: "Epididymitis in Children: A Brief Review Together with Reports of Six Cases," *Acta Paediatrica Scandinavica*, March 1971, pp. 16–21.

Hardy, J. C., and J. R. Costin: "Femoral Hernias: A 10- Year Review," *Journal of the American Osteopathic Association*, March 1969, pp. 696–704.

Huffman, J. W.: *The Gynecology of Childhood and Adolescence*, Philadelphia: W. B. Saunders Company, 1968.

Hyams, B. B.: "Torsion of the Testis in the Newborn," *Journal of Urology*, February 1969, pp. 192–195.

Immordino, P. A.: "Femoral Hernia in Infancy and Childhood," *Journal of Pediatric Surgery*, February 1972, pp. 40–43.

James, P. M., Jr.: "The Problem of Hernia in Infants and Adolescents," *Surgical Clinics of North America*, December 1971, pp. 1361–1370.

Johnstone, J. M.; and R. F. Rintoul: "Unusual Cause of Inguinal Mass," *British Medical Journal*, April 1970, p. 179.

Judge, Richard D., and George D. Zuidema: *Physical Diagnosis: A Physiologic Approach*, Boston: Little, Brown and Company, 1963, pp. 233–384.

Kaplan, G. W., and L. R. King: "Acute Scrotal Swelling in Children," *Journal of Urology*, July 1970, pp. 219–223.

Karaivanov, M.: "A Case of Atypical Hernia in Infancy," *Folia Medica* (Plovdiv), 1970, pp. 270–272.

Levy, J. L., Jr.: "Evaluation of Transperitoneal Probing for Detection of Contralateral Inguinal Hernias in Infants," *Surgery*, March 1972, pp. 412–413.

Moharib, N. H., and H. P. Krahn: "Acute Scrotum in Children with Emphasis on Torsion of Spermatic Cord," *Journal of Urology*, October 1970, pp. 601–603.

Mohay-Ud-Din, K.: "Torsion of Testis," *British Medical Journal*, February 15, 1969, pp. 445–446.

Nelson, Waldo: *Textbook of Pediatrics*, Philadelphia: W. B. Saunders Company, 1964, pp. 1149–1154.

Prior, John, and Jack Silberstein: *Physical Diagnosis*, St. Louis: The C. V. Mosby Company, 1969, pp. 287–310.

Rowe, M. I., and H. W. Clatworthy, Jr.: "The Other Side of the Pediatric Inguinal Hernia," *Surgical Clinics of North America*, December 1971, pp. 1371–6.

Schaeffer, Alexander J., and Mary Ellen Avery: *Diseases of the Newborn*, Philadelphia: W. B. Saunders Company, 1971, pp. 376–384.

Scorer, C. G.: "A Treatment of Undescended Testicles in Infancy," *Archives of Diseases in Childhood*, vol. 32, 1957, p. 520.

Thambugala, R. L.: "Diagnosis of Hydrocele: A Misleading Physical Sign," *Lancet*, October 31, 1970, p. 936.

SUGGESTED RESOURCES

1 Pamphlets

"Breast Check," American Cancer Society. (Free)

"Diagnosis of Gonorrhea: A Programmed Text," Pfizer Drug Co. (Free)

"Essentials of the Gynecologic History and Examination," Smith Kline and French Laboratories. 19101. (Free)

"The VD Crisis," Pfizer Laboratories Division, Pfizer, Inc., and The American Social Health Association. (Free)

"Treatment of Gonorrhea: A Programmed Text," Pfizer Drug Co. (Free)

"Venereal Disease," Medcom Monograph. (Free)

2 Films

"Inguinal Area and Scrotal Contents"
    Color,
    Cost: $8.00
    National Foundation
    American Films
    Dallas, Texas
"The Menstrual Cycle"
    Color, 12 minutes
    Cost: Free
    Eli Lilly and Company
    P.O. Box 814
    Indianapolis, Indiana 46206
"Treatment of Venereal Disease"
    Color, 30 minutes
    Cost: Free
    The Pfizer Laboratories Film Division
    267 West 25th Street
    New York, New York 10001
"The Urine Examination"
    Color, 20 minutes
    Cost:
    Pediatric Basic Film Series
    Audio-Visual Utilization Center
    Detroit, Michigan 48202

3 Models

"Gynie," a pelvic model, Ortho Company. About $200.00.

GLOSSARY

amenorrhea   absence of menstruation

Bartholin's glands   the two small mucous glands situated on either side of the posterior wall of the vaginal opening

chancre   an ulcer of primary syphilis appearing on mucous membrane, usually in the genital area

chancroid   a highly infectious nonsyphilitic genital ulcer

clitoris   an organ composed of erectile tissue which joins the labia minora anteriorly; considered the erectile homologue of the male penis

condyloma acuminatum   a pointed wart-like nonsyphilitic projection of the genital area

condyloma latum   a flat, wart-like syphilitic lesion of the genital area

dysuria   difficulty or pain on urination

escutcheon   the base of the triangular hair formation on the female pubic area

hematocolpos   the condition in which blood is retained by an imperforate hymen, resulting in distention of the internal genitalia

hematuria   blood in the urine

herpes progenitalis   a herpetic disease of the genital region

hydrocolpos   a condition in which vaginal secretions are retained by an imperforate hymen, resulting in distention of the internal genitalia

hymen   a thin membrane covering part of the vaginal orifice

labia majora   two fatty ridges running from the mons pubis posteriorly

labia minora   the two small folds of tissue running parallel to the labia majora, extending about 4 cm into the vagina

labioinguinal hernia   the abdominal contents into the labioinguinal area, the female homologue of the scrotal hernia a herniation of

lymphogranuloma venereum   a viral venereal disease

pseudohermaphroditism   a condition in which the external genitalia of a member of one sex resembles that of the opposite sex

puberty   period of development when the individual becomes capable of reproduction

sarcoma botryoides   a grape-like fleshy group of tissue masses originating beneath the vaginal epithelium

Skene's glands   tiny glands whose openings are just inside the urinary meatus in the female

urethral caruncles   small red masses visible just inside the meatus

vestibule   the cleft between the labia minora which contains the urethral and vaginal openings

vulvitis   inflammation of the vulva

The Skeletal System: Spine and Extremities

WHY THE CHILD IS EXAMINED

Because of its central function in giving structure to the soft tissues of the body, the health of the skeletal system is extremely important in maintaining the health of the individual. For this reason, a thorough examination of the skeletal system and its functioning is an important part of the examination of every child. Another reason is the fact that the skeletal system is frequently an area of many parental concerns, especially because there are several normal developmental conditions of the skeletal system (for instance, the slight bow-leggedness of the newborn or the knock-knees of the preschooler) which closely resemble pathologic conditions, and parents often worry about them. A third reason for this part of the examination is that there are many minor orthopedic abnormalities (for instance, subluxation of the hip in the newborn) which can be remedied rather easily in the newborn, but which will become major problems if not discovered early.

WHAT TO EXAMINE: ANATOMY OF THE AREA

The skeletal system is a bony structure held together by ligaments, attached to muscles by tendons, and cushioned by cartilage. In this section we will be primarily concerned with the bones themselves. There are 206 bones in the body, and they can be divided roughly into three categories. The first is the axial skeleton which comprises the vertebral column, the skull, the hyoid bone, the ribs, and the sternum—a total of 74 bones. The second major category is the appendicular skeleton which is made up of the 64 bones of the upper limbs and the 62 bones of the lower limbs. (The auditory ossicles total 6 bones and are usually considered separately.) This section will be primarily concerned with the appendicular skeleton, as well as the vertebral column. In discussing the anatomy, the upper extremities, lower extremities, and spine will be considered. In each of these areas the bones, muscles, and blood and nerve supply will be described. First, however, a general introduction to the joint system in all these areas will be given.

Joints are classified as immoveable, slightly moveable, or freely moveable. Immoveable joints are found in the skull at the suture lines. Slightly moveable joints and freely moveable joints include most of the joints in the body and are classified by the kind of motion permitted.

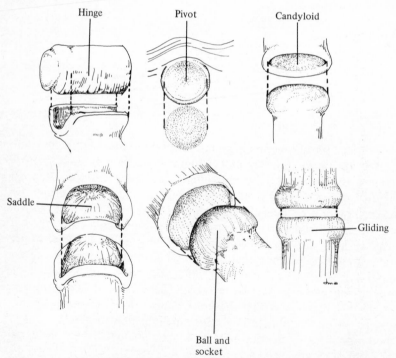

Figure 14–1 Types of skeletal joints.

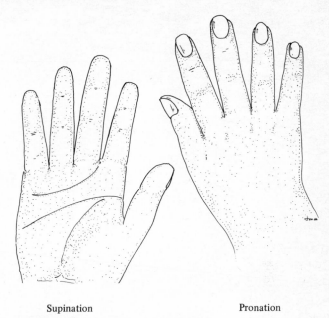

Supination   Pronation

Figure 14–2 Supination and pronation.

Hinge joints permit motion in one plane only; an example is the movement of the humerus and ulna. Pivot joints allow rotation only; examples of pivot joints are the radioulnar articulations and the juncture of the atlas and axis vertebrae. Condyloid joints allow flexion, extension, adduction, abduction, and circumduction, but not axial rotation; the wrist is a joint of this type. Saddle joints are very similar to condyloid joints except that the adjacent surfaces form a concavoconvex fit; the carpometacarpal joint of the thumb is of this type. Ball-and-socket joints have a rounded head fitted into a deep concave cavity which allows motion around many different axes; the hip and shoulder joints are ball-and-socket joints. Finally, the gliding joints allow a gliding motion between two flat surfaces; the vertebral and carpal joints are gliding joints. Types of motion which can be produced by these joints are basically of only four types, but in combination, these movements produce a variety of actions.

Gliding movements, in which two surfaces slide past each other, are the simplest and most common. Angular movements increase or decrease the angle of the two bones. Flexion describes a decrease in the joint's angle; extension increases the joint's angle; hyperextension increases the angle beyond the usual arc. Abduction is movement away from the medial line; adduction is movement towards the medial line. Circumduction movement is a rotation of one bone around a stationary disk. It includes flexion, abduction, extension, and adduction in that order. Rotation movement is motion around a central axis, such as that seen when the radius rotates around the ulna during pronation.

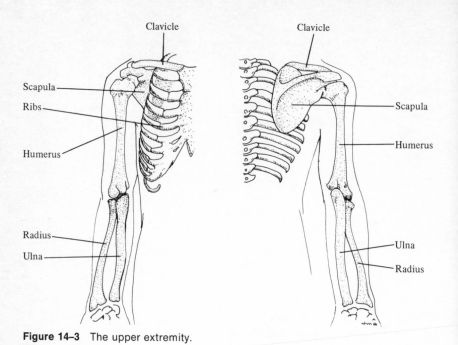

Figure 14–3 The upper extremity.

It is also important for the nurse-examiner to know certain terms used in describing different positions of the extremities. Supination refers to the position of the hand in which the palmar surface faces upward, while pronation describes the position in which the palmar surface faces downward. Inverted refers to a "turning in" position, such as that seen in the feet of pigeon-toed children. Eversion is a term used to describe a situation in which an extremity, or part of an extremity such as the foot, turns outward.

Discussion of the anatomy of the sections of the skeleton will begin with a description of the important bones, muscles, blood and nerve supply of the upper extremity. The bones of the upper extremities form the shoulder girdle and the arm. The shoulder girdle includes two bones, the clavicle and scapula. The clavicle is a long slender bone curved like a shallow S. It is at a horizontal plane directly above the first rib and rotates between the sternum and the superior surface of the scapula. The scapula is a large, flat triangular bone forming the posterior portion of the upper extremity. It contains two surfaces, three borders, and three angles, with the superior, lateral angle containing the articulating capsule for the humerus. Attached to the scapula is the humerus, the first of the arm bones. The humerus is a shaft divided into a head, body, and condyle. The rounded head articulates with the scapula; directly below this head is an indentation called the *anatomical neck* which is not to be confused with the surgical neck at the upper end of the shaft. The body ends at the broad, flattened condyle with its two articulating surfaces. This area is divided into the medial epicondyle and the lateral epicondyle. The ulna is a slender bone on the medial, or little-finger, side of the arm. Its thick, broad proximal end attaches at the articulating surfaces of the humerus; the outer rounded distal surface of the ulna, called the *olecranon*, forms a major portion of the elbow. The distal end is small and articulates with the wrist bones. Along the lateral, or thumb, side of the arm is the radius, the proximal end of which attaches to the humerus at the elbow, while the small distal end forms a large portion of the wrist. The hand contains 14 small bones, 8 carpal bones, 5 metacarpal bones, and 14 phalanges. The carpal bones are arranged in two rows and comprise the wrist; the first row includes the scaphoid, lunate, triangular, and pisiform bones, while the distal row includes the trapezium, trapezoid, capitate, and hamate. At birth many of the carpal bones are cartilaginous. An x-ray of a child's hand at $2^{1}/_{2}$ years of age will show only the capitate and hamate bones ossified, but by 11th year ossification has occurred in all the carpal bones except the pisiform, which develops during the 12th year. The metacarpals are slender bones with the distal ends forming the knuckles of the hand. These articulate with 3 phalanges on each finger and 2 on the thumb.

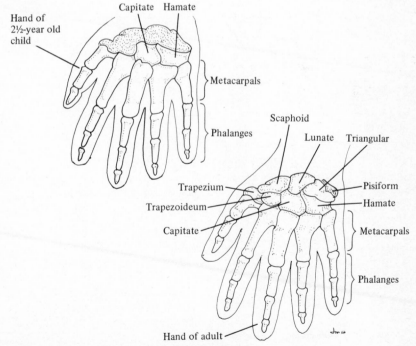

Figure 14-4 The bones of the hand of a child.

   The upper extremity is held in place by large muscles: the pectoralis major, pectoralis minor, subclavius and serratus anterior. These attach at different spots and angles along the vertebral column and are woven into the superior muscles of the upper arm. The shoulder itself contains six big muscles: the deltoid, subscapular, supraspinatus, infraspinatus, teres minor, and teres major; while the upper arm contains four muscles: the coracobrachialis, biceps brachii, brachialis, and triceps brachii. The muscles of the lower arm are smaller and more numerous, allowing for increased dexterity. A good anatomy book will be more descriptive of the muscles in this area.

   Blood is supplied to the upper extremities through the subclavian artery. Although this is one vessel, it has different names at different points; for instance, it is called the *axillary artery* at the axilla, the *brachial artery* coming through the brachial muscles and the *radial* and *ulnar arteries* along the radial and ulnar bones. Blood drains from the upper extremities through both a deep and a superficial set of veins.

   The nerve supply for the upper extremities comes from the cervical and thoracic nerves of the spinal nerves in the vertebral column. These nerves form the brachial plexus which supplies the entire shoulder, arm, and fingers.

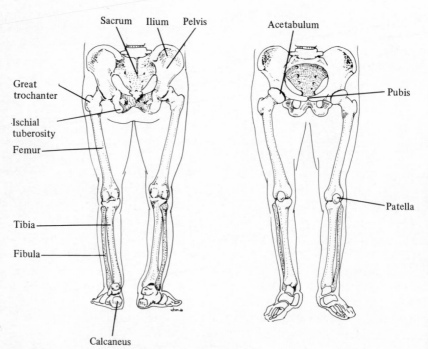

Figure 14-5 The pelvis and the lower extremity.

The lower extremities are attached to the body at the pelvic girdle. The pelvic girdle is a large, rigid, heavy structure made up of four bones: 2 hip bones placed anteriorally and laterally and the sacrum and coccyx placed posteriorly. The pelvis is divided into the greater (or false) pelvis and the lesser (or true) pelvis. The borders of the greater pelvis are formed by the ilium and the base of the sacrum. The lesser pelvis forms a cavity bounded posteriorly by the sacrum and coccyx and anterolaterally by the pubis, the ischium, and a small part of the ilium. It should be remembered that the pelvis of a child is different from an adult's, a man's is different from a woman's; there are also differences of pelvic structure in different races. A more detailed description of the pelvis can be found in a good anatomy or obstetric textbook.

The hipbone contains three distinct parts in childhood, which are fused in adulthood. The ilium is the superior, broad, flat surface of the hipbone; the ischium is the strongest portion of the hipbone and contains a portion of the acetabulum and an opening called *obturator foramen* which carries nerves, muscles, and ligaments; the pubis contains the medial portion of the acetabulum and joins at midline with the opposite pubis to complete the pelvic girdle.

Attached to the hipbone at the acetabulum is the femur, which is the longest and strongest bone of the body. The femur begins ossification during the seventh week of fetal life but does not become completely ossified until the fourteenth year of life. The head of the femur becomes completely ossified sometime during the first year of life. During infancy a major portion of the ends of the long bones are cartilage which gradually ossifies during early and late childhood. Growth in length of the bone will continue as long as the epiphyseal cartilage continues to grow, and bone tissue will gradually replace the cartilage. Epiphyseal cartilage disappears in girls about three years before it disappears in boys. A dense, fibrous tissue called *periosteum* covers the bone shaft and produces layers of bone to widen the shaft. It also produces new bone cells when a fracture occurs. The femur contains five parts: a head (which articulates with the acetabulum), a neck, the greater trochanter (a curved projection), a shaft, and 2 condyles at the distal end. The patella (kneecap) is a small, triangular bone over the junction between the femur and the tibia. The lower leg contains two bones: the larger is the *tibia*, and the smaller is the *fibula*. The tibia consists of a shaft with two enlarged ends; the proximal end articulates with the condyle of the femur, while the distal end forms the medial malleolus at the ankle, which articulates with the tarsal bones. The fibula is smaller and lateral to the tibia. It consists of a shaft with the proximal head resting against the tibia and the distal end spreading to form the lateral malleolus of the ankle.

The foot contains 7 tarsal bones, 5 metatarsal bones, and 14 phalanges. The tarsal bones are arranged and grouped. They include the

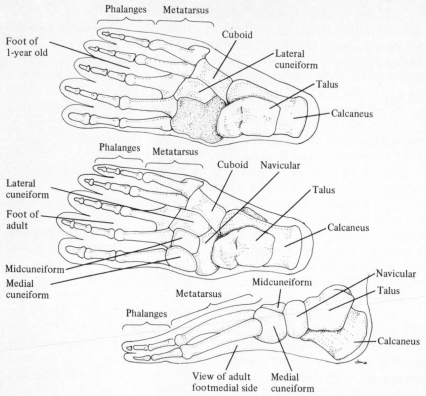

Figure 14–6 A comparison between a child's foot and an adult's foot

talus, calcaneus, cuboid, navicular, and 3 cuneiforms. The calcaneus ossifies at the sixth month of fetal life; the talus is formed by the seventh month of life; the cuboid appears by the ninth month; and the lateral cuneiform is formed during the first year. During the third year the medial cuneiform develops, and by the fourth year the intermediate cuneiform and navicular are formed. The phalanges continue their ossification process until the tenth to eighteenth years.

Four areas of muscles are involved in the lower extremities: muscles of the iliac region, the thigh, the leg, and the foot. The iliac region contains the psoas minor and major and the iliacus which work together to flex the lumbar vertebrae, pelvis, and thigh. There are four large groups of muscles that move the thigh. They are six anterior femoral muscles, including the sartorius, rectus femoris, vastus lateralis, vastus medialis, and vastus intermedius. The five medial femoral muscles include the gracilis, pectineus, adductor longus, adductor brevis, and adductor magnus. There are 10 muscles from the gluteal region, including the gluteus maximus, gluteus medius, and gluteus minimus. The three posterior femoral muscles are the biceps femoris, semitendinosus, and the semi-membranosus. Movement of the leg is produced by 13 muscles divided into three groups: These are the 4 anterior crural muscles, 7 posterior crural muscles, and 2 lateral crural muscles. The foot contains four layers of highly coordinated small muscles.

The lower extremities are supplied blood from the iliac branches of the aorta. This is a single artery with different names applied as it passes different points along the leg. The proximal end is the external iliac artery; the medial portion is the femoral artery; and the distal portion is the popliteal artery. Blood is drained from the lower extremity by the great saphenous vein and its branches. This is the longest vein in the body, starting at the dorsum of the foot and ending at the femoral vein in the pelvic region.

The nerve supply of the lower extremities follows much the same route as the blood supply. The leg is innervated primarily by the tibial and peroneal nerves and their branches.

The vertebral column is a series of 33 connecting bones which support the trunk and protect the spinal cord. These bones are divided into five groups: 7 cervical, 12 thoracic, 5 lumbar, 5 sacral, and 3 to 4 coccygeal; which form four curves. The cervical curve is a ventral, convex line, while the thoracic curve is concave. This is followed by the lumbar curve which is ventrally convex and more pronounced in the

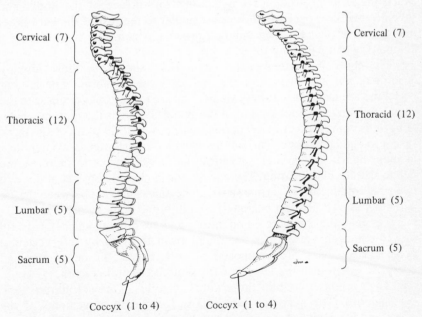

Cervical (7)

Thoracis (12)

Lumbar (5)

Sacrum (5)

Cervical (7)

Thoracid (12)

Lumbar (5)

Sacrum (5)

Coccyx (1 to 4)   Coccyx (1 to 4)

Figure 14-7 Spinal curves of the adult (left) and infant (right)

female. Finally, the pelvic curve is concave, with a caudal and ventral direction. Only the thoracic and pelvic curves are present at birth, thus they are called the primary curves and give the infant a spinal curve shaped like a C rather than the double S of later life. The secondary (or compensatory) curves are the cervical and lumbar because they develop later in life. The cervical is apparent around 3 to 4 months of age when the child begins to hold up his head. The lumbar appears when the child begins to walk, around 12 to 18 months.

The structure of each vertebra is basically the same. The heavy, rough, cylindrical base of the bone is called the *body*. At the posterior of this body two roots (or pedicles) are formed; these roots surround an opening, meeting midline posteriorly to form a bridge called the *lamina*. This opening is the vertebral foramen through which the spinal cord passes. Posteriorly there is a palpable projection from the lamina called the *spinous process*.

The first two cervical vertebrae are known as the *atlas* and *axis* because of their direct support of the cranium and are slightly different in structure from the rest of the vertebrae. The first cervical vertebra (atlas) has no body, only a slight knob for a spinous process and the addition of two transverse processes and two large articulating surfaces to receive the occipital condyles from the skull. The second cervical vertebra (axis) serves as a pivot for the first vertebra and contains a body, 2 roots, 1 spinous process, and 2 articulating surfaces, plus an extra bony projection called the *dens* protruding from the anterior surface of the body. The seventh (and last) cervical vertebra is similar to the rest of the vertebrae, but has an especially long spinous process which can be useful as a landmark when palpating the vertebrae.

The thoracic vertebrae are structurally similar to those already described, but are slightly larger than cervical vertebrae. The lumbar vertebrae are again structurally similar and are the largest vertebrae in the spinal column. The final section of the spinal column is the sacrum which, at birth, is composed of five separate bones; by 18 to 20 years of age these fuse into one large bone. The sacrum is wider and shorter in women than in men, and it has greater curvature and wider angles to increase the pelvic size for childbearing. The coccyx (or tail bone) consists of three to five small rudiments of vertebrae which begin ossification between the 1st and 4th years of life and become fused into one bone by age 25.

To help the spinal column move and to protect against harmful movement each vertebra is separated from the rest by intervertebral disks. These disks are composed of soft, elastic, fibrous tissue and comprise one-fourth the length of the entire vertebral column.

The vertebrae contain three kinds of joints: synovial, fibrous, and cartilaginous. The synovial joints allow for gliding movements of the joints and for flexion, extension, lateral bending, and rotation; the fibrous joints connect the arches and allow flexion and extension to some degree;

and the cartilaginous joints combine with the intervertebral disks to give support as well as some flexion and extension.

The muscles of the spine are difficult to describe because they are usually discussed in connection to other portions of the body. The deep muscles of the back are divided into two groups: the superficial iliocostalis group and the deeper transversospinal group which crosses medially. The iliocostalis group contains three muscles: the splenius capitis, splenius cervicis, and erector spinae; the transversospinal group contains five muscles: semispinalis, multifidus, rotatores, interspinales, and intertransverse. The superficial muscles of the back are also used to connect the upper extremities to the trunk. There are five of these muscles: the trapezius, latissimus dorsi, rhomboideus major, rhomboideus minor, and levator scapulae.

The blood supply to the spinal column originates with the descending aorta. This branches into two posterior intercostal arteries and finally becomes the spinal branch. Blood is drained from the area through the vertebral vein. The spinal column is a primary innervation source for the entire body. Well protected within the vertebral foramen of each vertebra lies the spinal cord. This cord is protected both by the bony framework of the vertebrae and by several layers of protective covering. The first of these layers is a thin membrane called the *pia mater.* Between the pia mater and the next layer, the *arachnoid layer,* are loose spaces called the *subarachnoid spaces.* These allow cerebrospinal fluid to continually bathe the spinal cord. Above the arachnoid layer is the *dura mater,* the outer covering of the cord composed of tough connective tissue. Meninges and fatty connective tissue further cushion the cord from the bony foramen. The internal portion of the spinal cord is composed of ascending and descending tracts from which project 31 pairs of nerves innervating most of the body. The pairs of spinal nerves are divided into sections corresponding to the vertebrae from which they emerge: 8 cervical, 12 thoracic, 5 lumbar, 5 sacral and 1 coccygeal. A good anatomy book will give a more complete description of their locations and functions.

HOW TO EXAMINE

It is difficult to find a child who is motionless. Therefore, much of the musculoskeletal examination can be done while watching or playing with the child before the examination. Some of this examination will depend upon the age of the child. An older child will perform when asked to sit, stand, walk, pick up a ball, or reach. A young infant will have to be helped and supported to be observed for sitting or weight bearing, and much of his range of motion will have to be passive. Some parts of the skeletal examination are fun and an easy way to establish rapport with the child. The child should be fully undressed for the skeletal examination. Older children should be allowed to keep their underpants on, but babies should have their diapers removed. Much of the skeletal system is examined during other parts of the physical examination, but the nurse-examiner must remember to compile all this information at the end of the examination and to record the evaluation of the skeletal system as a whole. Inspection and palpation are the primary methods of examination used in evaluating the musculoskeletal system. Every inch of the body must be thoroughly observed and felt.

The following is a general routine that can be followed for each part of the skeletal system. The individual parts will be described later. Inspection should proceed from the general to the specific. In other words, note how the child walks into the room, how he sits in a chair, etc., before looking at specifics like his legs and spine. This general observation will include symmetry of movement as well as general alignment, position, deformities, shortenings, lengthenings, and unusual postures. Observe the soft tissues and muscles for symmetry, swelling, and muscle wasting. Inspect the skin for color, texture, redness, cyanosis, pigmentation, bruises, and scratches. Scars should be noted and described: linear scars are usually from surgery; irregular scars, from trauma; and puckered scars, from suppuration. Observation should also include the presence or absence of a part, such as polydactyly or syndactyly.

Palpation is the next important part of the examination. The examiner must run her hands over every inch of the spine and extremities to gather all the data needed to make a decision. The bones are palpated for

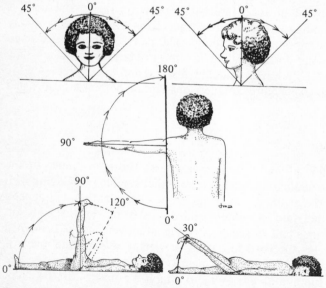

Figure 14–8 Degrees for the range of motion.

general shape and outline. Any thickening, abnormal prominence, or indentations are noted. The skin is palpated for temperature, tenderness, and pain. Erythema, swelling, tenderness, and heat may indicate inflammation. In feeling for temperature it is best to compare sides; the examiner should place her hands on both joints for 30 seconds and then switch hands. Palpation may help to localize tenderness or pain. The examiner must also palpate the soft tissues and muscles for swellings, wastings, and contractures. All joints should be checked for a full range of motion, and this motion should be described in degrees of a circle.

180° _____ 0°

Motion may be active or passive—active if the child will do it himself and passive when the examiner must help him, as is the case with the infant. Unless there is paralysis or damaged muscles or tendons, active and passive motion should be the same. Motion should be checked for extension, flexion, and rotation such as supination and pronation of the palms. Strength and power must be checked. Strength of movement with gravity, against gravity, and against resistance should be tested, and symmetry of strength noted. Different muscle groups can be tested for strength. In testing the upper extremities, the child should be asked to raise both arms over his head, out to both sides, and out in front. He should be able to hold his arms and hands out in front while the examiner applies pressure to force the arms downward. The examiner can also ask the child to squeeze her two index fingers to feel the symmetry of strength in both arms and fingers. Joints that are functioning properly should not exhibit muscle spasms or sudden loss of control. Tests for function include watching the child walk, stand, sit, bend, jump, skip, and run. The child should be able to do these with symmetry, smoothness, and ease.

WHERE TO EXAMINE

The examination of the skeletal system requires both a total examination of the child as a whole and many very specific evaluations of individual parts of the skeletal system, such as the upper extremities, and even smaller parts, such as each finger.

WHAT TO EXAMINE WITH

No specialized equipment is needed for the examination of the skeletal system, although a plastic tape measure will sometimes be useful in evaluating symmetry of parts.

WHAT TO EXAMINE FOR

Some specifics the nurse may encounter during her examination will be discussed under the portion of the skeleton where it is most likely to occur. As in the discussion of the anatomy, the upper extremities, lower extremities, and spinal column will all be considered.

In the upper extremities, the clavicles must be palpated, and full range of motion of the arms must be observed to make sure clavicular fracture does not exist; this is particularly true in the neonate, since a broken clavicle is one of the more common birth injuries.

The long bones of the arm must be examined to rule out subluxation. Subluxation of the radius is most common in children from 2 to 4 years old. The child may complain of pain either in the elbow or the wrist. Passive range of motion is possible in all directions except supination. Subluxation of the shoulder is another occasional finding in the preschool child. It may be heralded by swelling, pain, and refusal to use that arm.

The elbow should also be inspected for increased carrying angle. This is frequently associated with gonadal dysgenesis, and is a danger signal that should alert the nurse-examiner to thoroughly investigate this possibility.

The nurse then examines one hand at a time carefully. Each should be checked for number of fingers, noting any polydactyly or syndactyly. (Polydactyly is frequently associated with Ellis-van Crevel syndrome and syndactyly with premature closure of the sutures.) The length of the fingers—long, narrow, short, stubby, or clubbed—is important. A short, broad, claw-like hand may indicate Hurler's syndrome; a trident hand (short, broad hands with the index, middle, and fourth fingers about equal length and a space between the thumb and first finger and between the

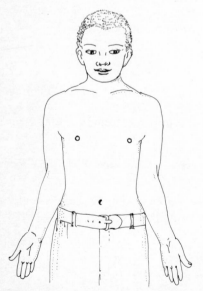

Figure 14-9 Child with increased carrying angle.

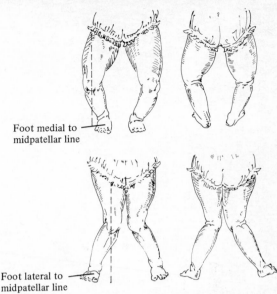

Foot medial to
midpatellar line

Foot lateral to
midpatellar line

Figure 14-10 Genu varum and genu valgum.

second and third fingers) is often associated with chondrodystrophy; short fingers, an incurved little finger, a low-set thumb and a simian crease should make the nurse investigate the possibility of Down's syndrome; digits may be unusually short in children with myositis ossificans or pseudohypoparathyroidism; macrodactyly or an enlarged digit may be normal or may be a sign of neurofibromatosis; an overlapping of the second and third fingers should make one think of trisomy 18 syndrome.

The creases of the palms are inspected. Although a simian crease is often associated with Down's syndrome, it is often found in normal individuals. There is an entire field of investigation called *dermatoglyphics* that is finding correlations between certain congenital anomalies and palmar crease patterns. The nurse should keep herself informed of the current findings from these studies.

The nurse then feels across the knuckles to ascertain the presence of 4 knuckles and gently runs her fingers up the length of the arm feeling and looking for radial pulses, widening of the wrist bones as seen in rickets, dryness, roughness or scaliness of the skin, skin color, as well as any bruises, scratches or bites, muscle wasting, swelling or lumps, and enlargement of epitrochlear lymph nodes at the elbow and axillary nodes at the axilla. The examiner then repeats this process with the other hand and checks both arms and hands for symmetry of length, width, and color.

In examining the lower extremities, the nurse observes the shape of the legs, noting the presence of genu varum (bowleggedness) or tibial

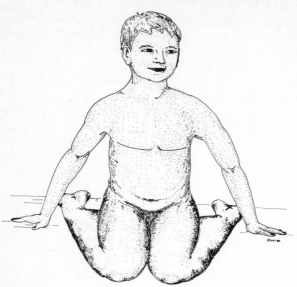

Figure 14–11 Child in the position called "TV squat."

torsion. Genu valgum is present if the medial malleoli are more than 1 inch apart when the knees are touching. Genu valgum may be normal in children between 2 and 3½ years of age. Genu varum is present when the medial malleoli are touching and the knees are more than 1 inch apart. Infants are frequently bowlegged until they have been walking for a year. However, severe genu varum may be due to such nutritional deficiencies as rickets. Tibial torsion is a twisting of the tibia which is sometimes initiated by an intrauterine position and aided by the child sitting in a TV squat (the buttocks on the floor with the knees and ankles flexed and flat against the floor to the side).

Tibial torsion can be tested for in one of three ways. The first way is to have the child lie on his back with his knees facing upward. The forefoot and hindfoot should be in line with the knees. The examiner places her thumb and index fingers on the lateral and medial malleoli. In an infant the four malleoli should be parallel to the table. In older children the external malleoli may rotate up to 20° and still be normal. The second way is to have the child sit on the examining table while the examiner draws a circle over the patellar and external malleoli. With the patella facing forward only the anterior edge of the malleolar circle should be seen. If one-half to three-fourths of the malleolar circle is seen, tibial torsion is present and the child needs to be referred. The third test requires the child to stand while a plumb line is drawn from the great iliac crest downward. The line should intersect the toes. If the medial malleoli are posterior and the lateral malleoli are anterior, the child needs to be referred to the physician.

The strength of the legs should be tested by having the child flex his legs while the examiner tries to straighten them. The nurse should check complete range of motion at the toes, ankles, knees, and hips. In infants it is especially important to check hip rotation to rule out congenital dislocation of the hip. Congenital dislocation of the hip is more common in girls than in boys and should be suspected if the mother complains of trouble in diapering the child due to the tight adductor muscles. A normal newborn should have hip rotation to almost 160 to 175 degrees, which means the flexed hips are almost flat on the bed. There are several methods of checking for hip rotation. One way is to check the leg length. As the femur rides upward above the acetabulum it shortens that leg and makes the opposite knee seem lower. When the feet are kept flat on the bed, with the knees flexed, and the examiner observes the height of the knees, it will be apparent if one knee is lower than the other. This is called the Allis's sign and indicates possible dislocation. The examiner should also check for unequal gluteal or leg folds. Although this is not a completely reliable sign of dislocated hip since most children have slightly asymmetrical folds, any significant asymmetry should be investigated thoroughly. Ortolani's sign is probably the most reliable test for dislocated hip. The examiner flexes the knees and abducts the hips up and out. A dislocated hip may be present if there is resistance to having the leg rotate the 175 degrees or if a click can be heard as the femur slips out of the acetabulum.

The lower extremities are also examined as the child stands. In this position the examiner can note foot arches. Pes cavus (a very high arch)

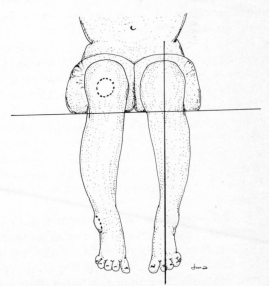

Figure 14–12 Testing for tibial torsion.

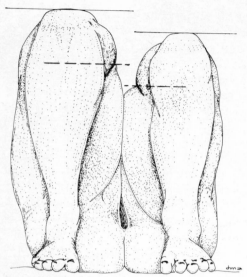

Figure 14-13   Allis's sign.

may be normal or a symptom of Friedreich's ataxia. All children have a fat pad under their medial arches until they have walked for 1 to 2 years, giving the appearance of flat feet. Many mothers are concerned about this in their young children, and the nurse-examiner should reassure the mother that flat feet are normal in a child of this age and that even if they are found in older children, there is no reason for concern unless the feet are causing symptoms. An easy way to test arches is to wet the child's feet and have him stand on two paper towels and then examine the imprints left on the paper.

As the child stands, his feet should point straight ahead. Pes valgus (toeing out) may be causing tibial torsion; pes varus (toeing in, pigeon-toed) may be causing or be caused by an anteverted femur or tibial torsion. Pes valgus and pes varus refer to the entire foot turning, while metatarsus varus refers to the turning in of the forefoot alone. When the child with metatarsus varus is standing, the heel is straight and in line with the leg, but the front half of the foot toes inward. This condition needs referral for treatment. In infancy many of these positions may be seen as a remnant of intrauterine life. If this is the case, passive manipulation will correct the deformity. If it cannot be corrected in this way, a referral is needed.

Such conditions as tibial torsion, genu valgum, and genu varus are apparent as the child stands. Looking at the child's shoes and their pattern of wear (e.g., is only the inside of the heel worn down?) may also give clues to the position of feet and legs. Finally, the child should walk, run, and skip while the examiner watches. Gait, balance, and stance should be observed. The new walker (between 12 to 18 months) has a wide-based gait and very little balance, but the older child has a very narrow-based gait and enough balance to stand on one leg for varying periods of time. Most children learn to skip fairly well by age 5 or 6.

The child's spine is observed and palpated when he is in the prone and standing positions. An infant is watched on his back and then turned over and observed for alignment and symmetry of movements, as well as for skin manifestations such as dimples, cysts, and tufts of hair and discoloration of the coccygeal area. The fingers are run down the spine to feel the lack or presence of the spinous processes. In older children the spine is also inspected in the upright position for masses, tenderness, stiffness, mobility, and posture. Posture is observed from the front, side, and back and when flexed. Normally the spine curves forward and backward but should have no side curves. If the forward and backward curves are exaggerated, they are considered pathologic. *Kyphosis* is the term given to an exaggerated concave curve in the thoracic region, and *lordosis* refers to an exaggerated convex curve in the lumbar region. *Scoliosis* is a lateral curvature of the spine and may be pathologic. Normally infants and small children with protuberant abdomens have a slight degree of lumbar lordosis which is normal. This is more pronounced in Black children. Some adolescents display rounded shoulders with slight

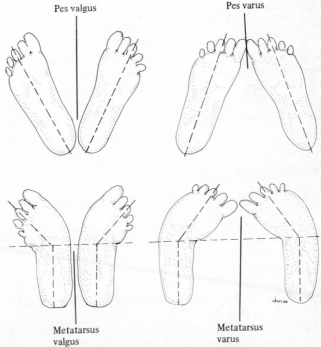

Pes valgus   Pes varus

Metatarsus   Metatarsus
valgus   varus

Figure 14–14 Child with pes valgus and pes varus, metatarsus varus and metatarsus valgus.

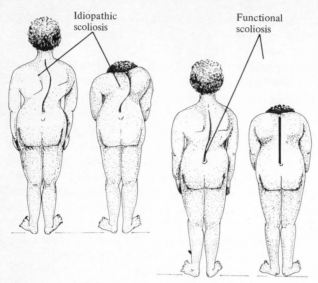

Figure 14-15 Child with functional scoliosis.

kyphosis. Usually this reflects a habitual posture rather than a permanent skeletal deformity. Some children develop a functional scoliosis. The fact that it is functional can be proved by having the child bend forward to touch his toes, as the examiner stands behind him and looks up the spine toward his head. Functional scoliosis will disappear under these conditions. If the scoliosis is not functional but due to a pelvic tilt, decreased vital capacity, or muscle contractures, the bent-over position will not correct it; in such case, the child needs to be referred.

Another orthopedic condition sometimes encountered is overlapping toes. In older children this may come from shoes that are too narrow. In infancy this is usually a hereditary condition. Sometimes strapping the toe into the correct position with a Band-Aid for 6 weeks will correct it.

BIBLIOGRAPHY

Adams, John C.: *Outline of Orthopaedics*, Baltimore: The Williams & Wilkins Company, 1967.

Barlow, T. G.: "Early Diagnosis and Treatment of Congenital Dislocation of the Hip," *Journal of Bone and Joint Surgery*, vol. 44B, no. 2, 1962, pp. 292–301.

Barness, Lewis A.: *Manual of Pediatric Physical Diagnosis*, Chicago: Year Book Medical Publishers, Inc., 1968, pp. 144–160.

Bick, Edgar M.: "Congenital Deformities of the Musculoskeletal System Noted in the Newborn," *American Journal of Diseases of Children*, vol. 100, no. 6, 1960, pp. 861–867.

Cattell, Hereward S., and David L. Filtzer: "Pseudosubluxation and Other Normal Variations in the Cervical Spine in Children," *Journal of Bone and Joint Surgery*, vol. 47A, no. 7, 1965, pp. 1295–1305.

Compere, Edward L.: "Foot Problems in Young Children," *Rocky Mountain Medical Journal*, vol. 47, October 1950, pp. 747–751.

DeGowin, Elmer, and Richard DeGowin: *Bedside Diagnostic Examination*, London: Macmillan & Co., Ltd., 1971, pp. 605–737.

Delp, Mahlon H., and Robert Manning: *Major's Physical Diagnosis*, Philadelphia: W. B. Saunders Company, 1968, pp. 242–272.

Green, Morris, and Julius Richmond: *Pediatric Diagnosis*, Philadelphia: W. B. Saunders Company, 1962, pp. 125–152.

Harris, Lloyd E., Paul R. Lipscomb, and John R. Hodgson: "Early Diagnosis of Congenital Dysplasia and Congenital Dislocation of the Hips," *Journal of the American Medical Association*, vol. 173, no. 3, 1960, pp. 229–233.

Hart, Vernon L.: "Congenital Dislocation of the Hip in the Newborn and Early Postnatal Life," *Journal of the American Medical Association*, vol. 143, no. 15, 1950, pp. 1299–1303.

Hollinshead, W. Henry: *Functional Anatomy of the Limbs and Back*, Philadelphia: W. B. Saunders Company, 1969.

James, J. I. P., G. C. Lloyd-Roberts, and M. F. Pilcher: "Infantile Structural Scoliosis," *Journal of Bone and Joint Surgery*, vol. 41B, no. 4, 1959, pp. 719–735.

Judge, Richard D., and George D. Zuidema: *Physical Diagnosis: A Physiologic Approach*, Boston: Little, Brown and Company, 1963, pp. 329–353.

Kite, J. Hiram: "Congenital Metatarsus Varus," *Journal of Bone and Joint Surgery*, vol. 32, no. 3, 1950, pp. 500–506.

Knight, Robert A.: "Developmental Deformities of the Lower Extremities," *Journal of Bone and Joint Surgery*, vol. 36A, no. 3, 1954, pp. 521–527.

Liebolt, Frederick L.: "Foot Problems in Children," *Surgery, Gynecology and Obstetrics*, vol. 90, January–June 1950, pp. 461–472.

Shifrin, Louis Z.: "Scoliosis: Current Concepts," *Clinical Pediatrics*, vol. 11, no. 10, 1972, pp. 594–602.

Von Rosen, Sophus: "Diagnosis and Treatment of Congenital Dislocation of the Hip in the Newborn," *Journal of Bone and Joint Surgery*, vol. 44B, no. 2, 1962, pp. 284–291.

Zausmer, Elizabeth: "Evaluation of Strength and Motor Development in Infants," *Physical Therapy Review*, vol. 33, no. 11, 1953, pp. 575–581.

SUGGESTED RESOURCES

1 Pamphlets

"The Extremities: Part I," Meade Johnson and Co. (Free)
"The Extremities: Part II," Meade Johnson and Co. (Free)

2 Films

"Diagnosis of Congenital Dislocated Hip"
    Color, 16 minutes
    Cost: Free

Ciba Pharmaceutical Co.
P.O. Box 1340
Newark, New Jersey 07101
"Gait and Musculoskeletal Disorders"
Color, 34 minutes
Cost: $5.00
Ciba Pharmaceutical Co.
P.O. Box 1340
Newark, New Jersey 07101

GLOSSARY

abduct   to move away from the medial line

acetabulum   the large, rounded cavity of the pelvis which holds the head of the femur

adduct   to move toward the medial line

Allis's sign   the equal height of the knees with the feet flat and the knees flexed; a test for dislocation of the hip

ankylosis   stabilization of a joint that should be moveable

atlas   the first cervical vertebra

axis   the second cervical vertebra

ball-and-socket joint   a rounded head of a bone fitted into a deep concave cavity, as seen in the hip joints

circumduction   rotation of one bone around a stationary disk

condyle   the rounded protuberance on the end of a bone

condyloid joint   a joint, such as the wrist, which allows flexion, extension, adduction, abduction, and circumduction but not axial rotation

dermatoglyphics   the study of the patterns of lines on the palms and fingers

dorsal   posterior, as of a surface, organ, or other area

epicondyle   a rounded protuberance above the condyle at the end of a bone

epiphysis   the end of the long bones which is cartilage during early childhood and ossifies during late childhood

everted   turning out and away from the median

false pelvis (greater pelvis)   the border of the pelvic girdle formed by the ilium and base of the sacrum

flaccid   flabby, weak, as an abnormal muscle

genu   the knee

genu valgum   knock-knees

genu varus   bowleggedness

gliding joints   a joint that allows a gliding motion between two flat surfaces, as in the carpal joints

ilium   the upper portion of hipbone

inverted   turning inward; toward the median line

ischium   the lower, posterior portion of the hipbone

kyphosis   an exaggerated concave curve in the thoracic region of the spine

ligament   the tough, fibrous tissue connecting two bones

lordosis   an exaggerated convex curve in the lumbar region of the spine

pes cavus a very high arch of the foot

pes valgus toeing out

pes varus toeing in

polydactyly extra digits on the hands or feet

pronation the position of the hand in which the palmar surface faces downward

pubis the pubic bone

sacrum the final section of the spinal cord, containing five bones

scoliosis a lateral curvature of the spine

subluxation a dislocation which is incomplete

supination the position of the hand in which the palmar surface faces upward

syndactyly the fusion or webbing of 2 or more phalanges

tendon the fibrous connective tissue joining muscle to bone

tibial torsion twisting of the tibia

true pelvis (lesser pelvis) the pelvic cavity bounded posteriorly by the sacrum and coccyx and anterolaterally by the pubis, the ischium and a small part of the ilium

ventral anterior, as of a surface, organ, or other area

The Neurologic Examination

WHY THE CHILD IS EXAMINED

Surely evaluation of the central nervous system is one of the most important assessments made during a physical examination. So many of the functions which give life its human quality are closely related to a healthy nervous system. Not only is gross neurologic impairment, such as severe cerebral palsy or meningomyelocele, important to the child's future life, but the more subtle defects, such as hyperactivity or the controversial "minimal brain dysfunction," will make a large qualitative difference in his general health and happiness. This is an area where preventive health measures and early recognition of problems are of the utmost importance.

WHAT TO EXAMINE: ANATOMY OF THE AREA

The nervous system is complex and delicately balanced. It is composed of a central nervous system and a peripheral nervous system. Each of these systems is composed of basic units, called *neurons*, and their protective

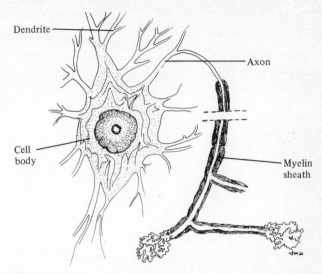

Dendrite

Axon

Cell body

Myelin sheath

Figure 15-1 A neuron.

coverings. Each neuron contains a nucleus, cell body, organelles, and inclusion bodies, as well as two types of processes: dendrites and axons. Dendrites are branches of the cell body cytoplasm, some of which are covered by myelin and some of which are not. Each neuron has one axon, but may have several dendrites. Impulses are received through the dendrites, travel into the cell body, and leave through the axon where they can be transmitted through a synapse to the dendrite of the next neuron. Axons may or may not be covered with a myelin sheath (a lipid material) and a neurilemma (sheath of Schwann).

There are two kinds of peripheral nerves: myelinated and unmyelinated. Myelinated nerves make up the spinal and cranial nerves; the unmyelinated nerves form the autonomic nervous system. Groups of nerves found outside the central nervous system are called *ganglia*; these can be either sensory or autonomic.

The central nervous system contains the brain (encephalon) and spinal cord (medulla spinalis). Parts of the brain can be described according either to layers or sections. The layers include bone, meninges, cortex (gray matter), and white matter. The bones covering the brain form the cranial cavity. These include the eight skull bones (1 parietal, 1 occipital, 2 frontal, 2 temporal, and 2 sphenoid) and many facial bones. The brain and spinal cord both are covered with three layers of membranes: the dura mater, the arachnoid, and the pia mater. The dura mater is composed of several layers of tough, fibrous connective tissue which lies directly beneath the periosteum of the bone. The arachnoid is a web-like, avascular membrane lying between the dura mater and the pia

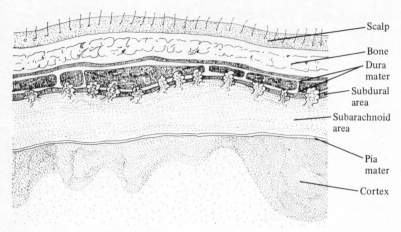

Figure 15–2 The meningeal layers.

mater. It is separated from the dura mater by the subdural space and the pia mater by the cerebrospinal fluid in the subarachnoid space. A spinal puncture in the lumbar region enters the subarachnoid space between the 3d and 4th lumbar vertebrae. The deepest layer of the meninges is the pia mater, which is a delicate, highly vascular layer attaching directly to the gray matter of the brain.

The next layer, or cortex, is actually the surface of the brain itself. Each hemisphere of the brain has a convex superior surface, a convex lateral surface, a medial surface which is flat, and an inferior (or basal) surface which is irregular. The entire surface is covered with irregular, convoluted grooves and fissures called *sulci*. These surfaces, generally called the *cortex*, are further divided into 11 areas thought to control specific functions.

The precentral cortex (or motor area) includes the precentral gyrus, the posterior frontal gyri, and the giant pyramidal cells of Betz. This area is located on the superior surface of the hemisphere and controls voluntary muscle contraction. Removal of this area causes paralysis.

The premotor area suppresses motor activity innervated by the other areas, and the frontal zone exerts some control over circulation, respiration and pupillary reaction. This is the area removed in the surgical procedure called *lobotomy* thought to improve severe psychotic problems.

The speech region (Broca's area) controls the ability to articulate speech. Motor aphasia can result from damage to this area.

The postcentral area receives stimulation from the spinal cord and controls the sensory areas of the body.

The visual sensory area (or striate area) integrates visual stimulation for size, form, motion, and color; the visual psychic (or parastriate) area recognizes, integrates, and associates visual images with past experiences.

The auditory sensory area integrates sound stimulus into pitch, quality, and loudness; the auditory psychic area recognizes and integrates these sound stimuli with past experiences.

The parietal area integrates several types of stimuli from various sensory areas.

The innermost layer of the brain is called the *basal ganglia* and contains several layers which will not be described here.

The central white matter (or centrum ovale) is the layer beneath the cortex; it is composed of three types of fibers: projection fibers, commissural fibers, and association fibers. The projection fibers contain both afferent and efferent fibers that connect the cortex, brain, and spinal cord; the commissural fibers connect the two hemispheres through the corpus callosum, anterior commissure, hippocampal commissure, fornix commissure, and posterior commissure. The association fibers connect different portions of the cortex to each other.

The brain can also be divided by sections: the cerebrum, the cerebellum, the pons, and the medulla oblongata. An important part of the brain is its system of ventricles called *ventricles of the brain* which is located within several of these sections. The cerebrum occupies the greatest area within the cranium and is divided into two hemispheres joined by the corpus callosum; it contains three sections called the *telencephalon, diencephalon*, and *mesencephalon*, each of which contains important structures.

The telencephalon contains part of the walls of the third ventricle. The diencephalon contains the thalamus, pineal body, hypothalamus, and

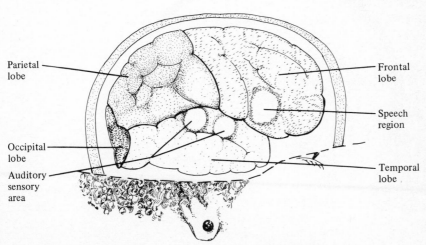

Figure 15–3 Areas of thought which control specific functions.

parts of the third ventricle. The thalamus is a large mass (about 4 cm) of gray matter, forming the lateral wall of the third ventricle which functions in the transmission of sensory impulses to the cortex. The pineal body lies posterior to the thalamus; its function is unclear but seems to be more active in childhood than in adult years. The hypothalamus is composed of gray matter and is located inferior to the thalamus. The optic chiasm is located in the hypothalamus, as are the mammillary bodies and a small bean-sized gland called the *hypophysis*. The hypothalamus has many functions, the most important of which are temperature control, water balance, and some visceral activities important in digestion.

The mesencephalon is a small constricted region joining the pons and cerebellum to the diencephalon.

The cerebellum is the next largest section of the brain. It is located between the occipital lobes of the cerebrum and the brainstem. The outer gray ridged cortex is divided into two lobes and covers a core of white matter. The cerebellum is important in the control of balance, movement, and posture.

The pons is a ventral protuberance of the brainstem. Several of the cranial nerves, such as the abducent, facial, trigeminal, and cochlear, arise in this area. Many descending and ascending nerve fibers come through the pons, and in general, it serves as a neural transmission center.

The medulla oblongata is a continuation of the spinal cord; it is tucked between the pons anteriorly and the cerebellum posteriorly. The

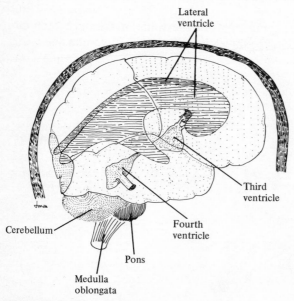

Figure 15–4 Areas of the brain.

rounded swelling on the anterior surface of the medulla contains the pyramid which holds many motor fibers. Some of these fibers cross the midline at the pyramidal decussation. The medulla performs many vital functions in addition to transmitting impulses along the spinal cord. It plays a major role in circulation and respiration; damage to this area often causes death. It also controls such activities as yawning, coughing, vomiting, and sneezing.

There are four ventricles of the brain: the two lateral ventricles, the third ventricle, and the fourth ventricle. A series of openings allow the cerebrospinal fluid to flow from ventricle to ventricle. The left and right lateral ventricles lie within the basal ganglia of the telencephalon. Fluid drains from these ventricles into the third ventricle via the foramen of Monro. The third ventricle lies midline between the right and left thalamus and communicates with the fourth ventricle via the aqueduct of Sylvius. The fourth ventricle lies in the cerebellum, pons, and superior portion of the medulla. The roof of the fourth ventricle contains three openings for spinal fluid to pass into the subarachnoid space. The brain and spinal cord are bathed in cerebrospinal fluid—a clear, watery liquid, which is formed in the ventricles, drains through the entire system of ventricles, and finally flows into the subarachnoid space.

The spinal cord is composed of a group of fibers running from the lumbar region to the medulla oblongata. Like the brain, it contains both gray and white matter. In the cord the gray matter forms two large lateral masses and one small midline strip that forms an H-shaped cross section. The areas are designated the *dorsal horn* (posterior column) and the *ventral horn* (anterior column). The dorsal horns receive and transmit impulses from the dorsal root fibers of the spinal nerves; the ventral horns transmit impulses from the peripheral nerves to muscles. The lateral horns are composed of preganglionic fibers of the sympathetic nervous system along the thoracic and lumbar regions; in the sacral region, they comprise part of the sympathetic nervous system.

The white matter contains myelinated and unmyelinated fibers and, like the gray matter, is divided into sections (or fasciculi) according to location. The dorsal part consists of 2 large ascending fasciculi, 1 small descending fasciculus, and 1 intersegmental fasciculus. Its main functions are muscle, tendon, and joint proprioception; tactile sensation; and fine discriminatory sensation.

The ventral funiculus contains 2 ascending tracts and 5 descending tracts. They transmit impulses of touch and pressure, visual reflexes, eye and head movements, and muscle tonus and equilibrium. The lateral funiculus contains ten tracts: 2 ascending and 8 descending. Proprioception, temperature, and pain impulses are transmitted via the lateral funiculus.

The peripheral nervous system consists of the cranial nerves, spinal nerves, and the autonomic nervous system. Afferent (sensory) fibers carry impulses from the organs to the central nervous system, while efferent (motor) fibers transmit impulses from the central nervous system to the organs.

There are 12 pairs of cranial nerves arising in the cranium.

1 Cranial nerve I: The olfactory nerves originate in the cranial cavity and emerge through the ethmoid bone into the nasal cavity. They terminate in a bundle of nerve fibers in the mucous membrane of the superior nasal tuberinates, and are needed for the sense of smell.

2 Cranial nerve II: The optic nerves arise in the cerebral peduncle, run along optic tracts past the optic chiasma (the convergence and divergence of the tracts), through the optic canal into the ganglionic layer of the retina. These nerves are needed for vision.

3 Cranial nerves III: The oculomotor nerves arise near the floor of the third ventricle of the brain and innervate several of the muscles surrounding the eye. They control the movement of the eye within the socket.

4 Cranial nerves IV: The trochlear nerves are the smallest cranial nerves arising from the cerebral aqueduct; they innervate the obliquus superior oculi muscle of the eye and control ocular movement.

5 Cranial nerves V: The trigeminal nerves are the largest of the cranial nerves containing somatic sensory, special visceral, efferent, and proprioceptive fibers. They arise near the pons and middle cerebellar peduncle and innervate the sensory portions of the face, the mucous membranes, and internal structures of the head; they also supply the muscles of mastication.

6 Cranial nerves VI: The abducent nerves originate near the floor of the fourth ventricle and innervate the rectus lateralis bulbi muscle of the eye. Stimulation of these nerves causes the muscles to rotate the corneal surface of the eye laterally.

7 Cranial nerves VII: The facial nerve has two roots originating in the pons. The larger roots control facial expression while the smaller roots supply the front two-thirds of the tongue with the sensation of taste; they also innervate sections of the external acoustic meatus, soft palate, and pharnyx. From this root, parasympathetic fibers control secretions from the submandibular, sublingual, lacrimal, nasal, and palatine glands.

8 Cranial nerves VIII: The acoustic nerves are each composed of two fibers—the cochlear branch concerned with hearing and the vestibular branch concerned with sensory and equilibratory functions. The cochlear branch innervates the organ of Corti within the internal ear, and the vestibular branch innervates the internal acoustic meatus at its superior lateral end.

9 Cranial nerves IX: The glossopharyngeal nerves consist of sensory and motor fibers which innervate the tongue and pharynx. They originate in the medulla oblongata.

10 Cranial nerve X: The vagus nerves are the longest of the cranial nerves; they originate in the medulla oblongata, wander through the neck and thorax, and terminate in the abdomen. Their somatic sensory fibers innervate the skin of the posterior surface of the external ear, and the external acoustic meatus, while the visceral afferent fibers control the mucous membrane of the pharynx, larynx, bronchi, lungs, heart, esophagus, stomach, kidneys, and intestines.

11 Cranial nerves XI: The accessory nerves originate in the medulla oblongata and each splits into the cranial section and the spinal section. The motor nerves of the cranial part innervate the pharnyx, larynx, and esophagus. The motor nerves of the spinal section innervate the trapezius and sternocleidomastoid muscles.

12 Cranial nerves XII: The hypoglossal nerves originate in the medulla oblongata and supply the motor fibers of the tongue.

Leaving the spinal cord between the cervical area and coccygeal area are 31 pairs of spinal nerves. There are five main divisions each of which contains several subdivisions. The primary divisions are 8 cervical pairs, 12 thoracic pairs, 5 lumbar pairs, 5 sacral pairs, and 1 coccygeal pair. Each spinal nerve contains a dorsal (posterior) root and a ventral (anterior) root. The dorsal roots attach to the cord along the lateral surfaces and carry impulses up the spinal cord from the body. The ventral roots attach to the cord along the anterior surface and carry impulses from the cord to the muscles. There are four main types of fibers carried via the cord: somatic afferent, visceral afferent, somatic efferent, and visceral efferent. Somatic afferent fibers carry sensations for pain, temperature, touch, and sensations from the muscles and joints to the dorsal root of the spinal cord; visceral afferent fibers carry reflex impulses to the cord; somatic efferent fibers carry motor impulses from the ventral roots of the spinal cord to the voluntary skeletal muscles; and visceral efferent fibers carry motor impulses from the ventral roots of the spinal cord to the involuntary muscles of the viscera, secretory glands, and blood vessels.

The peripheral of the autonomic nervous system is divided into the sympathetic (thoracolumbar) nervous system and the parasympathetic (craniosacral) nervous system. The two systems are frequently found in the same areas but are physiologically antagonistic toward each other. Generally, the sympathetic nervous system activates increased energy for bursts of activity, while the parasympathetic restores stability for quieter activity. The autonomic nervous system contains two types of fibers: visceral afferent and visceral efferent. The visceral afferent fibers carry impulses from the organs (mouth, pharynx, nose, thorax, etc.) to the central nervous system, while the visceral efferent fibers return impulses from the central nervous system to smooth muscles, cardiac muscle, and body glands.

The visceral efferent fibers of the thoracolumbar region and the sympathetic ganglia near the spinal cord form the sympathetic nervous system.

This system is divided into various branches and plexuses. The branches include spinal nerve branches, cranial nerve branches, arterial branches, and visceral branches. The plexuses (a tangle of nerves) include the cardiac plexus, the celiac plexus, and the pelvic plexus.

The visceral efferent fibers of the cranial and sacral portion of the spinal cord form the parasympathetic nervous system; its ganglia are located near specific viscera. As with the sympathetic system, the parasympathetic system is divided into various branches and plexuses.

WHERE TO EXAMINE

Like the nervous system itself, its examination encompasses all parts of the body, from the concentration of cranial nerves in the face and upper body to the permeation of the nervous network throughout the entire muscular system and body.

WHAT TO EXAMINE WITH

Although most of the neurologic examination depends on the clinician's skills and attentiveness, there are several pieces of equipment which may prove useful adjuncts. A reflex hammer of appropriate size (both a pediatric and adult size will be useful to the practitioner who deals with children from birth to 18 years). Even though the side of the hand can be used to obtain knee jerks, it is almost impossible when trying to obtain the triceps, biceps, or brachioradialis reflexes. Other necessary items for performing a complete neurologic examination are closed vials of peanut

Figure 15-5 Equipment needed to do a complete neurological examination.

a complete neurologic examination are closed vials of peanut butter, orange extract, or other easily recognizable odors; as well as a safety pin; cotton balls; two test tubes filled with hot and cold water; a tuning fork; containers of salt and sugar and an applicator stick for applying them to the tongue; a tongue blade for obtaining the gag reflex; an ophthalmoscope; a tape measure for comparing symmetry of muscle pairs; some objects of various shapes and textures (coins, bottle caps, different types of material); and an audiometer or other instrument or means for assessing hearing.

HOW TO EXAMINE AND WHAT TO EXAMINE FOR

A complete neurological examination is rather complex and time consuming, and the nurse will probably not wish to include the total system in every physical examination she does. However, it is vital that she be familiar with it, since it should be done if there is any questionable neurologic history or significant physical findings. She will always, however, wish to incorporate some of each part of the neurologic examination into every physical she does; if these few items are questionable, a more extensive work-up should be done.

Traditionally, the neurologic examination is divided into six tests: tests for cerebral function, for cranial nerve function, for cerebellar function, for motor system function, for sensory system function, and for reflex actions. This outline works very well for adults and older children, but the nervous system of younger children is less mature and much more difficult to evaluate. The authors will follow the traditional outline in discussing the neurologic examination, but will give specific references to the younger child and infant when possible.

Tests for Cerebral Function

Tests for cerebral function can be divided into those which test generalized types of functions and those which test specific functions. Generalized cerebral function is manifested in general behavior; level of consciousness, orientation, intellectual performance (including knowledge, judgment, calculation, memory, and thought content); and mood and behavior. In a child, these functions are more difficult to assess.

Knowledge of normal development and previous knowledge of the child's behavior are the most important aids in evaluating generalized cerebral functions. The one best test for these functions is a good developmental test. State of consciousness can be evaluated, although the important clues for a young child are primarily motor rather than verbal. (Is the infant or young child lethargic, drowsy, or even stuporous?) Excessive drowsiness, for instance, may indicate a metabolic problem, hypothalamic disease, or a diffuse brain tumor. Excitation or hyperactivity are also important. In the infant, orientation may be roughly assessed by recognition of the mother's face and later of familiar objects and people. Acute disorientation may result from inflammatory, toxic, metabolic, or traumatic brain disorders. Insidious loss of orientation may result from brain tumors. Generally, disorientation as to person or place is more serious than disorientation as to time. This is particularly true in children, since the time concept comes relatively late in the developmental sequence.

Immediate recall refers to brief retention of an idea, sound, or object. In general, a child of 4 years can be expected to repeat three digits or sounds after the examiner (e.g., "Johnny, see if you can say these numbers exactly as I do; now listen carefully '4 . . 2 . . 1'; OK; now you do it"). A child of 5 years can generally repeat four digits and a child of 6 years will usually be able to repeat five digits correctly. Loss of immediate recall is most often due to generalized cerebral disease or diseases of the primary projection area of the cortex.

Recent memory refers to memory which is required to hold an idea or image slightly longer. The child is shown an object and told that he will be asked later to tell what it was. About 5 minutes later, the examiner should ask him to recall what the object was. *Remote memory* refers to memory which holds for longer periods of time. The child may be asked what he had for dinner last night, for instance.

Specific functions of the cerebral cortex should also be tested when possible. There are three such localized functions. *Cortical sensory interpretation* refers to the ability to recognize objects through the different senses. *Cortical motor integration* refers to the integrative ability necessary to perform purposive, skilled acts. The lack of this ability is called *apraxia*. Finally, *language, both written and spoken* is a specific function of certain areas in the cerebral cortex. In both spoken and written language the child is required to have the ability to communicate by receiving and expressing ideas or commands. Lack of any of these abilities is called *aphasia*.

Many tests for these abilities can be incorporated into the developmental screening examination. Others can be turned into games which the child will enjoy. The ability to recognize objects through the different senses, for instance, can be tested with various games. The game of "find it" can be played to detect difficulties in visual perception; "Johnny, we're going to play a game to see how good you are at finding things. I'm going to put these five things out on my desk and when I name one you have to hand me that very one. OK? Now, hand me the apple." The examiner must be careful not to have the child himself name the object, since this involves not only recognition, but expressive language skills. *Stereogenesis* is the ability to recognize an object from its feel. This can also be assessed through games; "Now, Johnny, we're going to play another game. When you close your eyes, I'm going to put one of these three things in your hand; then I'm going to take it back, and when you open your eyes you must tell me which one it is." Objects such as bottle caps, coins, and buttons work well for this purpose. Children with cerebral palsy have particular difficulty with this sense. Difficulties with this sense also may be due to peripheral neuropathy, parietal lobe disorders, or posterior column disease.

Graphesthesia is the ability to identify shapes traced by the examiner on the palm or back of the child's hand. School children will usually be able to identify the numbers 0, 7, 3, 8, and 1; younger children do better when the examiner draws either geometric figures or parallel and crossing lines. This is done twice and the child is asked whether they are the same or different. It is usually best to do this first with the child's eyes open and then with them closed, to make sure he understands the game. If the test is consistently failed or if there is a great difference between the ability of the two hands, the results are most suspicious. Very young children who are still having difficulty with the concepts of "same" and "different" will be difficult to test accurately.

Kinesthesia is the ability to perceive weight or direction of movement. Children under about 5 years of age are developmentally too immature to be able to compare weights, but school-aged children should be able to do so fairly well. The child's directional sense is tested by playing the "up, down game." The child closes his eyes and must tell the examiner whether his finger is up or down. The examiner passively manipulates the digits to either an up or down position. Care must be taken to handle the digit by the sides so that the weight of the examiner's fingers does not give a clue. The younger children will again be too immature to have the concepts of up and down. Texture discrimination can be tested in the "rough, smooth game," in which the child closes his eyes and tells the examiner whether a piece of cloth (wool or silk) is rough or smooth.

Auditory agnosia is tested for by having the child identify sounds, such as a bell, a hand clap, or a knock on wood, with his eyes closed.

Problems of visual agnosia usually originate in the occipital lobe; problems of auditory agnosia, in the lateral and superior portions of the temporal lobe; tactile agnosia, in the parietal lobe; and agnosia of body parts and relationships, in the posteroinferior areas of the parietal lobe.

Cortical motor integration is tested by having the child perform a semicomplex skill, such as folding a piece of paper and sealing it in an envelope. Again, the developmental level must be kept in mind, and this type of integration is usually evident when doing any of the standard developmental screening tests.

Language is also usually tested with a developmental screening device. In the younger child, only spoken language will be tested. Screening tests for both speech and articulation are important, and the nurse should be familiar with them. Articulation requires fine motor coordination and can reflect neurologic difficulties. Separate tests for receptive and expressive abilities of speech are best for the neurologic evaluation of the child.

Although speech cannot be evaluated in the very young infant, the quality of his cry can have great neurologic significance. The normal cry should be loud and angry sounding. A high-pitched, whiny cry may indicate a central nervous system disorder, while a shrill, penetrating, high-pitched cry may be a result of intracranial damage. A cry that sounds like a cat screeching, especially in combination with microcephaly, micrognathia, oblique epicanthal folds, hypertelorism, or low-set ears, may indicate a chromosomal defect called *cri-du-chat* (cat's cry) *syndrome*. A weak cry, hoarseness, or aphonia is another danger sign the examiner should be alert for.

This group of functions is closely related to specific areas of the cortex. *Visual receptive aphasia (alexia)* is influenced by lesions of the occipitotemporal junction, while defects in the superior temporal cortex may result in *auditory receptive aphasia*. The lateral part of the temporal lobe may produce *nominal aphasia*, or inability to name objects, while lesions above the Sylvian fissure may cause difficulties in expressive language, which may be discovered with a speech-screening device. Difficulties in the occipital cortex may cause *visual agnosia*, while problems with tactile perception may result from lesions in the contralateral parietal lobe. Defects located in the nondominant parietal lobe may cause graphesthesia (see above).

Tests for cerebral function are difficult to perform on the infant, although levels of consciousness and general behavior should always be assessed.

Assessment of Cranial Nerves

The next section of the neurologic examination is the assessment of cranial nerve function. There are 12 pairs of cranial nerves and their anatomic location has already been discussed. The method of evaluating their function will be discussed in this section.

The test for Ist cranial nerve (olfactory nerve) is concerned with the sense of smell. The child is asked to identify familiar odors; peanut butter, oranges, or onions are a few which are usually familiar to young children. Each nostril is occluded in turn and closed vials of the peanut butter, orange, or onion extract are opened under the patient's nostril. Defects in either the olfactory bulb and tract or in the olfactory receptors in the nasal mucosa itself can interfere with smell. Many nonneurologic factors, such as colds or allergies, can also interfere with this sense. Some very young children may be able to smell accurately, but may not be able to name the smell.

The IId cranial nerve (optic nerve) is tested first by visual acuity screening tests as discussed in Chapter 5 and also by the test for visual fields. In this test, the examiner asks the child to cover each eye in turn and look at the examiner's nose. It is very difficult to get small children to maintain their stare at the examiner's nose, and sometimes a bright sticker or other object stuck on the end of the nose will aid the child's ability to keep his eyes focused steadily. While he is looking at the nurse's nose, the nurse starts at the periphery of each quadrant of vision and brings a finger in towards the center, asking the child to tell her when he can first see the finger. The examiner should stand 3 feet away, keeping her own right eye closed when the child's left eye is closed. In this way, she can compare her own visual fields with those of the child. Her finger should be midway between the child and her own face. After she has assessed the limits of the child's visual fields, she should recheck by asking him to tell her when her finger is moving and when it is still. Normally, visual fields extend 60 degrees on the nasal side, 100 degrees on the temporal side, and 130 degrees vertically. Care must be taken to repeat this test in all quadrants because specific defects will show up as

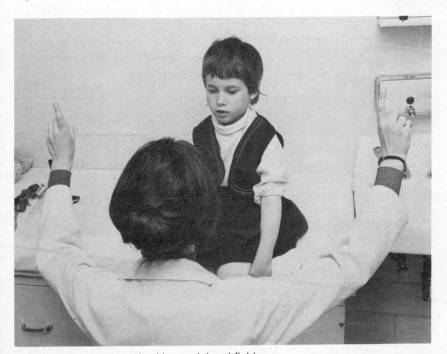

Figure 15-6 Examiner checking peripheral fields.

very localized limitations of visual fields. For instance, a lesion of one optic tract will result in blindness in the opposite half of both visual fields, while defects in the temporal lobe may result in blindness in the upper quadrants of both visual fields on the side contralateral to the defect. A parietal lobe impairment can produce similar defects, again contralateral to the defect. A parietal lobe impairment can produce similar contralateral blindness in the lower quadrants of both eyes, while a lesion located in the occipital lobe may cause blindness in the contralateral half of each eye, both upper and lower quadrants. It is easy to see from this how important it is to test separately all quadrants of vision of each eye. Funduscopic examination can be included at this point, and is discussed earlier in Chapter 5 "The Eye".

Cranial nerves III, IV, and VI (oculomotor, trochlear, and abducent) can be tested as a unit, since they all supply the various muscles which rotate the eyeball; the oculomotor nerve supplies the superior rectus, inferior rectus, medial rectus, inferior oblique, and levator palpebrae, as well as the muscles of the iris and ciliary body; the trochlear nerve innervates the superior oblique; and the abducent controls the lateral rectus muscle. The child is asked to follow the nurse's finger as it moves to all quadrants of vision. Any unequal movement of the pupils should be noted; at all times the pupillary light reflex should appear in corresponding spots on the two pupils. The eyes should also be observed for nystagmus. Very slight nystagmus, particularly at the far corners of the eyes, can be normal, but any sustained nystagmus should be referred. The pupillary examination, both direct and consensual, is also discussed in the chapter on the eyes.

The Vth cranial nerve (trigeminal nerve) has both a motor and a sensory division. The motor division innervates the masseter, temporalis, and pterygoid muscles, and its functions can be tested by asking the child to bite hard on a tongue blade while the nurse tries to pull it away; the jaw muscles are tense at this time and are palpated for symmetry and strength of contraction. Then, with the jaw relaxed and slightly open, the middle of the chin is tapped sharply with the reflex hammer. A sudden slight closing movement is the response expected in the normal child. This test is often difficult because it is hard for many children to relax their muscles when told to do so, and most will be unable to relax their jaws, thus invalidating the test.

There are three parts of the sensory division of the Vth cranial nerve: the opthalmic, maxillary, and mandibular. All are tested through various sensations. Wisps of cotton, warm and cold test tubes, and the point of a pin are used on the forehead, cheeks, and jaw to test for presence of sensation. The child is asked to close his eyes and tell the examiner when the gremlin touches him. This is done in all three areas on both sides. Presence and symmetry of response are noted. The corneal reflex is also tested by touching the tip of a wisp of cotton to the cornea. The normal response is a blink (Care must be taken to touch only the cornea.)

The VIIth cranial nerve (facial nerve) also has both a sensory and motor division. The sensory division innervates the sense of taste on the anterior two-thirds of the tongue, part of the sensation from the external ear canal and also the lacrimal, submaxillary, and sublingual glands. The motor division innervates most of the facial muscles. It is tested in the game "make a face," in which the nurse asks the child to make exactly the same faces as she does; she then looks at the ceiling, wrinkles her forehead, frowns, blows out her cheeks, purses her lips, smiles, and raises her eyebrows. The child's face is observed for any asymmetry that might indicate paralysis (minor asymmetry is almost always present and should be considered normal). The child is then asked to close his eyes and to keep them closed, even though the examiner will try to force them open. The examiner then pushes upward on the eyebrows while the child attempts to keep his eyes tightly shut. Equality of strength is noted. The sensory division can be tested by having the child stick out his tongue and to identify the taste of salt and sugar on the anterior sides of the it. Care must be taken to have the child keep his tongue out until the testing of each substance is finished or the substances will dissolve and travel to

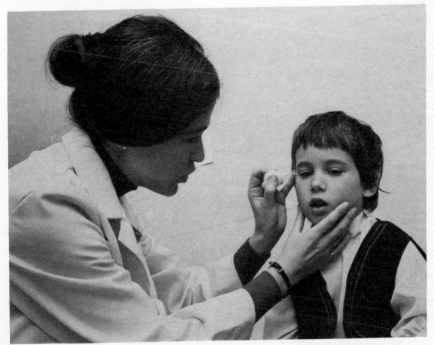

Figure 15–7 Examiner testing the corneal reflex with a wisp of cotton.

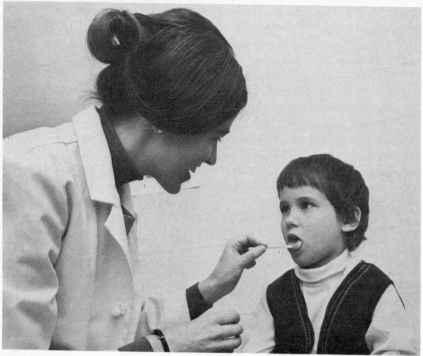

Figure 15–8 Examiner testing child's taste for salt and sugar.

both sides of the tongue. A glass of water should be taken between the salt and sugar.

The VIIIth cranial nerve (acoustic nerve) also has two divisions, the cochlear and the vestibular. The test for vestibular function is not routinely performed. It involves injecting 5 to 10 ml ice water into the ear canal. Vertigo and nystagmus are expected to occur. This test is impractical for the nurse-practitioner and if there is any indication that it should be done, the child should be referred. The cochlear division of the acoustic nerve is concerned with acuity of hearing and sound conduction. An audiogram or hearing screening test should be done and the nurse should be familiar with this procedure. A tuning fork may also be used for the Weber and Rinne tests. In the Weber, the vibrating tuning fork is placed in the middle of the head and the child is asked if he hears it louder in either ear or if it is the same in both ears. Normally, it will be the same in both ears. This decision is frequently hard for a child to make, particularly if he does not yet have the "same-different" concept, and his response is not always reliable. In the Rinne test, the vibrating fork is placed first on the mastoid process behind the ear and the child is asked to tell the nurse when he can no longer hear the sound; at that point, the fork

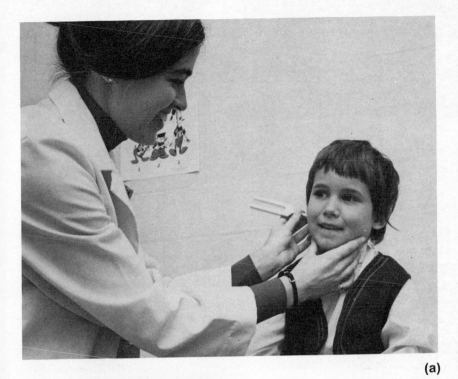

(a)

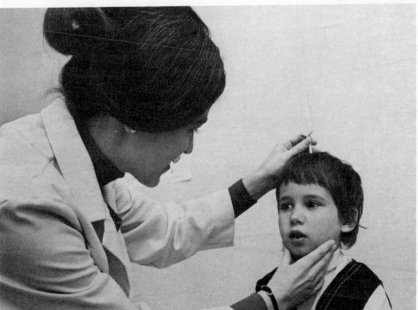

Figure 15–9 Examiner doing the Rinne (a) and Weber (b) tests.

(b)

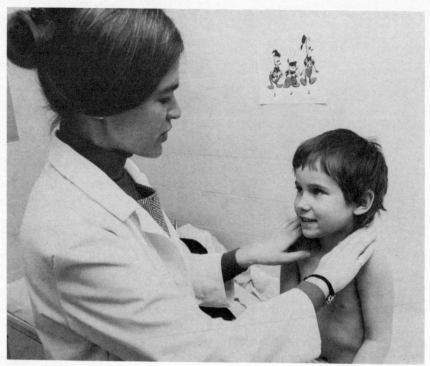

Figure 15–10 Examiner testing the strength of the trapezius muscle.

is brought around in front of the ear (not touching the child) and the child is asked if he can hear it then. Since air conduction should be about three times better than bone conduction, the child should reply that he does hear it when placed in front of his ear, even though the sound carried through the bone conduction from the mastoid process has stopped. This test seems to be easier than the Weber for most young children.

Cranial nerves IX and X (the glossopharyngeal and the vagus) are tested together. Both are involved in innervating the muscles involved in the mouth and throat area, although the distribution of the vagus is greater than this. The examiner should note any hoarseness of the voice, the ability to swallow, the movement of the uvula (when stroked with a tongue blade on each side of the uvula, it should rise and deviate to the stimulated side), the gag reflex and any dysarthria, dysphagia, or regurgitation of liquids through the nose.

Cranial nerve XI (accessory nerve) innervates the muscles of the upper shoulder. It is tested by checking the strength and symmetry of the sternocleidomastoid and trapezius. The child is asked to turn his head to one side; the examiner then pushes the child's chin in the same direction in which his head is turned while the child tries to push as hard as he can against this pressure. This will cause the sternocleidomastoid muscle on the opposite side to stand out, and it can be easily palpated. The process is then repeated on the other side. The trapezius is tested by having the child try to push his shoulders up against the examiner's hands while the examiner exerts pressure in a downward direction. Again, the muscles will tense and stand out where they can be easily inspected and palpated.

Finally, the XIIth cranial nerve (hypoglossal nerve), which innervates the muscles of the tongue is tested by first asking the child to stick his tongue out as far as he can. It should be observed for tremors or fasciculations. The nurse then places the tongue blade against one side of the tongue and pushes it in the other direction, instructing the child to try to push the stick away. This is then repeated on the other side, and the symmetry of muscle strength of each side of the tongue is assessed.

Most of these tests will be extremely difficult to do on the child under 2, although some symmetry of various muscles can be assessed by watching the child's movement. Even with an infant, some of the sensory tests, such as response to pain and touch, can sometimes be performed.

Tests for Cerebellar Function

The cerebellum functions primarily in regard to balance and coordination. In a child this may be reflected in the quality of skilled activity he is able

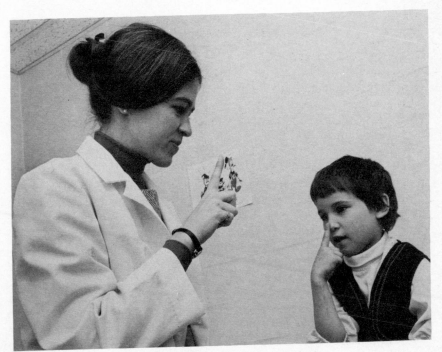

Figure 15–11 Examiner testing child with finger-to-nose test.

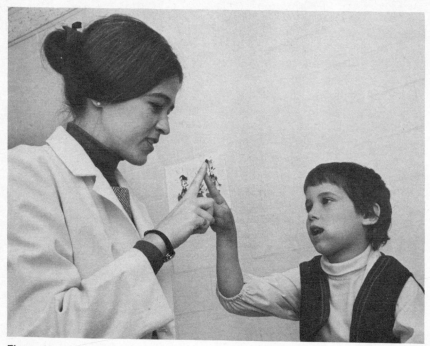

Figure 15–12 Examiner testing child with finger-to-finger test.

to perform. A developmental screening tool may be the most effective way to assess this quality. Motor skills, such as dressing, undressing, and buttoning, can be observed, as can block stacking, putting a raisin in a bottle, and throwing and kicking a ball. Handling a pencil is also important. When he draws a plus sign (+), can he cross the midline in one movement, or must he stop at the middle and change the pencil to the other hand? This kind of detail can be important in assessing the neurologic status of a child.

Other specific tests also are used. Can the child touch his nose first with a finger of one hand, then with the other, and finally with each hand in succession while his eyes are closed? Can he touch his finger to his nose and then to the examiner's finger, back to his nose and again to the examiner's finger in a new position? This sequence is done more rapidly the second and third time. There are no exact standards for this test, which are age-specific, but consistent past-pointing should arouse suspicion. The nurse will gain a general idea of how well each age group is able to do this after working with many children.

The child can be asked to pat his knees with the palm of his hand and then with the back of his hand. Again, this should be repeated several times fairly rapidly.

He can also be asked to touch each finger to the thumb of the same hand in rapid succession. He can further be asked to run each heel down

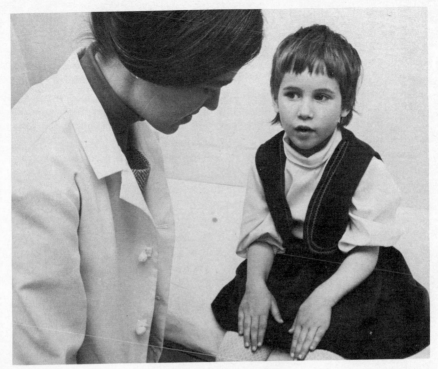

Figure 15–13 Child patting her knees with her hands.

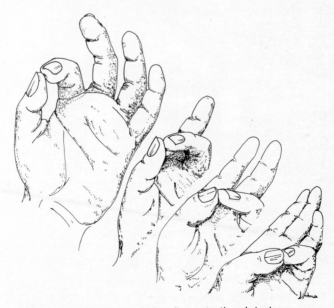

Figure 15–14 Child attempting finger-to-thumb test.

the contralateral shin, and to draw a figure 8 in the air with his foot while lying on his back.

When erect, he can be asked to stand straight, with feet together and eyes open and then closed. Walking in his normal gait with his eyes open and then closed and finally walking tandem may also be helpful. Many types of abnormal gait may indicate neurologic problems. Lesions in the cerebellar lobe may cause staggering and falling. This is different from the gait in which the child lifts his feet very high, placing them down with great force; this kind of abnormality is usually due to posterior column disease. Toe drop in which extreme plantarflexion is present will cause a similar gait. Hemiplegia, scissors gait, and the broad-based gait of muscular dystrophy should all be noted, although they are not specifically due to cerebellar disease or malfunction. Any abnormal gait should be referred; in order to do this effectively, the nurse must be well aware of developmental changes in gait such as the wide-based gait of the new walker or the knock-kneed gait of the preschooler.

Standing on one foot is another test for cerebellar function which is often useful. By the age of 4, a child should be able to do this for about 5 seconds; by the age of 6 he should be able to do it for 5 seconds with his arms folded across his chest; and by 7 he should be able to do it for 5 seconds with his eyes closed.

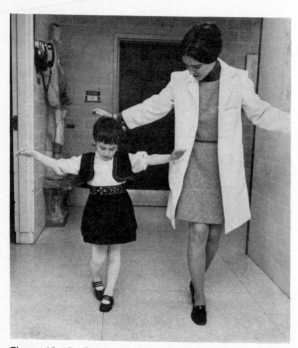

Figure 15-15 Child walking tandem.

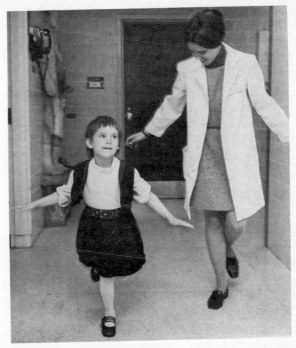

Figure 15–16   Child standing on one foot.

In an infant, cerebellar function is more difficult to evaluate, although coordination such as that seen in the sucking-swallowing movements and reaching and grasping development, are important.

Tests for Evaluating the Motor System

Evaluation of the motor system is an important part of the neurologic examination. Particular attention is paid to four aspects of the motor system: muscle size, muscle tone, muscle strength, and abnormal muscle movements.

Muscle size should be assessed as part of the physical examination of all children. Either hypertrophy or atrophy of the muscles should alert the examiner to the possibility of muscular dystrophy, particularly if it is coupled with a wide-based gait, difficulty in going up or down stairs, muscle weakness, or the characteristic method in which children with muscular dystrophy arise from the recumbent position, that is, by placing their hands on their legs and literally climbing up themselves. Generalized wasting can result from anterior horn cell disease, while localized wasting accompanied by a characteristic "rubbery" feel to the muscle mass can occur with lower motor neuron disease. If there is any suspicion of abnormality in muscle size, corresponding muscles should be measured with a tape measure at comparable places of both limbs. Any but very slight asymmetry should be considered abnormal, and the child should be referred to a physician.

Muscle tone is next evaluated through both passive range of motion and active movement. During passive range of motion, any involuntary resistance, spasticity, flaccidity, or rigidity should be noted, as should an increase or decrease in the expected range of motion. Assessment of muscle tone can be one of the most valuable clues to neurologic difficulty in the infant. For the first 2 months, an infant's muscle tone is expected to be primarily of the flexor type. After 2 months, extension gradually becomes more pronounced, beginning with the head and extending slowly to the feet. As the child's muscles enter this stage of extension, spasticity may begin to appear in the case of an infant with cerebral palsy. Spasticity is one of the earliest signs of most types of cerebral palsy, and certain maneuvers should be routinely done in order to elicit early signs of spasticity. When the examiner pushes the infant's head forward, a child with beginning signs of cerebral palsy will frequently resist this pressure and extend his neck back against the examiner's hand. Another useful sign is for the examiner to flex the infant's legs onto his abdomen and then quickly release them. In an infant with cerebral palsy, the legs may jump quickly back into extension and then adduction, perhaps even crossing. Any kind of crossing of this type, frequently referred to as "scissoring," should make the examiner highly suspicious. Another sign often encountered in an infant in the early stages of cerebral palsy is that when it is in the prone position and the examiner lifts his head, the infant will fail to extend his arms in the protective mechanism most infants display.

Muscle tone in infants is often most obvious from abnormal posturing, and the physical examination of an infant should always be begun by

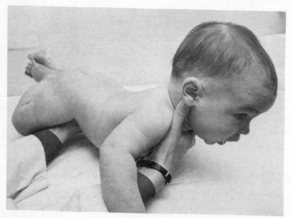

Figure 15–17 Normal infant held in ventral position.

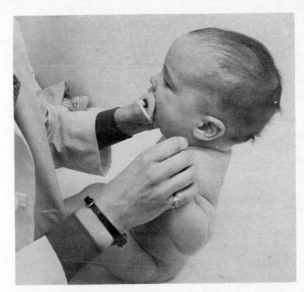

Figure 15–18 Head lag in a normal newborn.

observing his resting posture for a few minutes. The normal posture of a newborn is generally one of symmetry with limbs semiflexed and hips slightly abducted. The details will be influenced by the position he had assumed in utero. There are several abnormal postures which should serve as red flags to the examiner. The first of these is called the frog position in which the hips are held in abduction and are almost flat against the table while the hips are positioned in external rotation. This may be normal in a breech presentation, but in a vertex presentation, this should call for further neurologic investigation. It can be a sign of hypotonia, the so-called floppy infant syndrome. Opisthotonus, the position in which the back is arched and the neck is extended, may also be normal in a face presentation, but can have serious neurologic implications. Undue rotation of the head, extension of an arm, a hand held over the head, an infant who constantly holds both hands in front of his mouth, or a strikingly asymmetrical posture are examples of postures that may be clues to neurologic problems.

Muscle tone should also be assessed by holding the infant in certain positions. In ventral suspension, the examiner can support the baby with her hand held under the infant's chest, thus allowing an excellent view of the way the baby controls his head, trunk, arms and legs. A full-term infant should be expected to hold his head at a 45° angle or less from the horizontal line; his back should be straight or slightly flexed, arms flexed at the elbows and partially extended at the shoulder, and knees partly flexed. The floppy infant will have greater head lag than normal, a limp, floppy trunk, and dangling arms and legs.

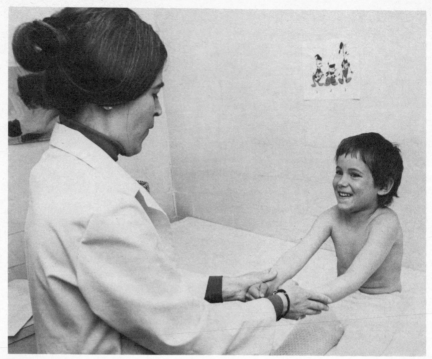

Figure 15–19 Examiner testing arm strength.

In the supine position, lying on the table, the examiner should pull the infant to a sitting position by his wrists. Even in premature infants, there will be some flexion of the head; usually in full-term infants, the head will be kept almost in the same plane as the body until the child reaches the sitting position; at this point, the head will balance for a second or two in line with the body and then bounce forward. The head of a floppy baby will lag notably, and will never balance atop the neck. In view of the importance of muscle tone in the neurologic assessment of the infant, the two maneuvers just described should be routinely incorporated into every physical examination of a young infant.

Muscle strength is evaluated next. This is usually tested by having the child push against some resistance offered by the examiner. For instance, strength of the flexor muscles of the fingers may be estimated by extending the child's fingers while he tries to resist and keep them flexed. He is then asked to keep them straight even though the examiner will attempt to flex them. With his arms straight out in front of him, the examiner can try to push them apart while the child attempts to keep them together; then with the arms extended to either side, the examiner tries to push them together while the child tries to resist this movement. Strength of various muscle groups can be checked in this same general way. Some can be checked by active movement without resistance; for instance, strength of the abdominal muscles can be assessed by having the child do several sit-ups. Muscle strength in the infant and toddler is slightly harder to assess, but can be judged fairly well from the newborn's suck and general motor activity and later by the speed with which motor skills develop.

The last part of the assessment of the motor system involves observation of various abnormal muscle movements. Swift jerking movements may be associated with extrapyramidal syndromes, while the slow, worm-like, irregular, movements may be a sign of athetoid cerebral palsy. Usually this type of movement does not develop until about the 18th month or so. Any kind of twistings, tics, choreiform movements, or tremors should be noted. Involuntary movements are more difficult to assess in the very young child, but an attempt should be made. Tremors are relatively common in the newborn, and if they are of high frequency and low amplitude, even though the child is not crying, they may be normal for the first few days. After the 4th day, this would be suspicious if it should occur anytime except during vigorous crying spells. Low-frequency, high-amplitude tremors are always suspicious, as are constant overshooting of movements, unusual rhythmic twitchings of the face, facial movements that seem to indicate paralysis, constant facial frowning, or tonic or clonic convulsions. Abnormal gaits have been previously discussed.

Tests for Evaluating the Sensory System

After an evaluation of the motor system, it is important to assess the sensory system. This is done in much the same way as when assessing the sensory division of some of the cranial nerves. There are two main divisions of tests used to assess the sensory system: those concerned with primary sensation and those concerned with cortical and discriminatory forms of sensation. In testing for primary sensation, all parts of the body can be tested, but a complete neurologic examination demands that at least the face, trunk, arms, and legs be tested and the borders of the various forms of sensation should be mapped out for each of them. At least five types of sensation must be tested: superficial tactile sensation, superficial pain, temperature, vibration, deep pressure pain, and some would include motion and position, which have already been discussed under the section on cerebellar functions. Normal sensitivity to superficial tactile sensation varies with the specific area of skin involved; therefore, symmetrical areas should be compared. With some types of damage to the sensory cortex, the child may be able to feel, but not be able to localize the feeling; it is wise, therefore, to have the child point to the spot where he feels the wisp of cotton, while keeping his eyes closed.

Superficial pain should be tested by alternating the sharp and blunt ends of a pin and asking the child to tell you which it is with his eyes closed. In certain conditions, such as tabes dorsalis or peripheral neuritis, the child will at first perceive dullness and then have an after image of sharpness. Again, it is most important to compare sides. Sensitivity may be found to be normal, reduced, or increased, but there are no objective standards for this and the judgment must be made after the examiner has tested many children and becomes subjectively familiar with the range of normal. If there is a deficit, temperature will usually be found to be defective also, since distribution of these two senses is very similar. If the results of the tests for pain are equivocal, temperature will frequently be more satisfactory standard. Temperature should be tested with test tubes filled with warm and cold water. The nurse must be careful to recheck frequently the temperature of the tubes, since the heat dissipates quickly.

The sense of vibration is also tested by means of a tuning fork, although it is really pressure receptors which are involved. The greatest sensitivity will be found between 200 and 400 cycles/second. A large tuning fork should be used since the vibration decay is slower than that of a small one, making it more useful. The sternum, elbows, knees, toes, and iliac crest should be tested. The examiner tells the child to say when the vibration stops. At that point, the examiner places the fork on his own body in an analogous area to see if he can still feel it. The patient's sides can also be compared in this way.

Deep pressure pain can also be tested. This should not be done unless there is definite indication that it is necessary, since rapport with the child frequently will be lost. Deep pressure pain can be tested over the eyeballs, testes, achilles tendon, and calf and forearm muscles.

Cortical and discriminatory forms of sensation can include two-point discrimination, point localization, texture discrimination, stereognostic sensation, graphesthesia, and the extinction phenomenon. In this discussion, the authors have chosen not to include texture discrimination, stereognostic sensation, and graphesthesia because they have been covered under cerebellar functions.

Two-point discrimination is the ability to tell without visual clues whether there are one or two points pressing on the skin. In the "mosquito game," the child is asked to close his eyes and tell whether he feels two mosquitoes or only one. Body areas differ in how sensitive they are to two-point discrimination. For instance, the average person can first distinguish two separate stimuli on his tongue when they are only 1 mm apart; on the fingertip, the stimuli need to be 2 to 8 mm apart; on the chest and forearm the normal individual will first sense two separate points at a distance at 75 mm. These are adult standards; there have been no standards worked out specifically for children, but the authors' clinical experience suggests that the distances are probably similar.

Point localization is similar to two-point discrimination, except that only one point is used. The child is asked to close his eyes and point to the spot where he feels something touch him. This can be incorporated into the testing for primary sensation by having the child point to the spot where the test tube or wisp of cotton or pin touches him.

Finally, the extinction phenomenon is tested. This is the situation in which two homologous parts are touched simultaneously; the child should be expected to know that there are two separate spots. Certain defects in the parietal lobe will cause the individual to experience only one stimulus even though two separate places are actually touched. The nurse should touch either the child's hand or cheek or both several times while his eyes are closed. He should be able to respond by telling where the touch is felt. For developmental reasons, this test is not always accurate under 6 years of age.

It is obvious that all these tests can easily be made into games and the children usually enjoy them immensely.

Very little of this testing is applicable to toddlers and infants. At times one can tell if a child this age responds to pain and touch but, in general, testing is unreliable.

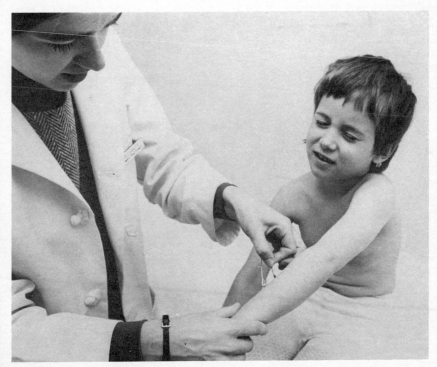

Figure 15–20 Examiner testing for two-point discrimination.

Assessing the Reflexes

The final traditional division of the neurologic examination to be discussed in this section is the assessment of reflexes. Reflexes are specific muscular responses to specific stimuli. They can be of various types. For adults and older children, they can be divided into three types: superficial, deep, and abnormal. For infants and very young children, some additional miscellaneous reflexes will be discussed.

There are many superficial reflexes, and four common examples will be given here. The abdominal reflexes are four in number. They consist of a movement of the abdominal musculature in the direction of a stimulus. They are obtained by stroking the four quadrants surrounding the umbilicus lightly with a pin or sharp point. This can be done in such a way that the scratches form either a square or a diamond on the abdomen. The expected response is for the umbilicus to move toward the quadrant which was stroked. In a newborn infant, this response is usually weak the first 2 days, but almost always present for the first 10 days. In general, however, there is great variability in this response and total lack does not indicate a pathologic condition. Asymmetry of response can be a danger sign, but in the clinical experience of the authors, asymmetry is frequently seen, probably as a result of an asymmetrical stimulus.

The cremasteric reflex is another superficial reflex relevant only in boys. The stimulus consists of stroking an inner thigh with a sharp object

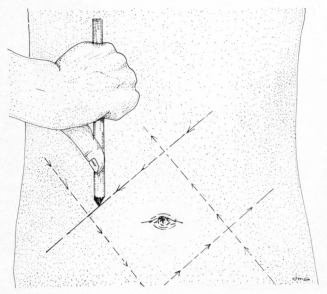

Figure 15–21 Examiner testing abdominal reflexes.

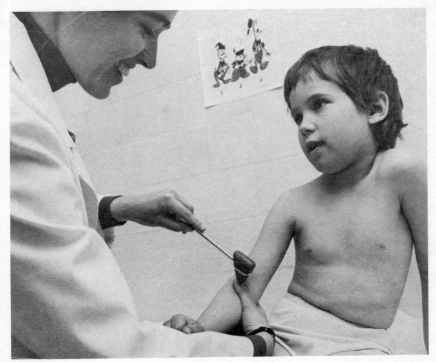

Figure 15-22 Examiner testing biceps reflex.

such as a pin. The expected response is for the testis on that side to be drawn from the scrotum up into the abdomen. This is a fairly reliable reflex, and its absence should make the investigator think of conditions such as spinal cord lesions. This response can also be elicited by cold or fear.

The plantar grasp reflex consists of a plantar flexion of the feet in response to the stimulus of pressure against the balls of the feet. This sometimes is elicited by mistake when the examiner attempts to elicit a Babinski reflex on a young infant. The plantar grasp reflex can also be absent as a result of spinal cord lesions.

The final example of a superficial reflex is the gluteal reflex. To obtain this, the nurse spreads the buttocks of the child and scratches the perianal area. The expected response is a quick contraction of the anal sphincter. If it causes low back pain, the examiner should worry about compression of the cauda equina.

Deep tendon reflexes are theoretically possible in any large muscle area; when the tendon is struck, contraction of the muscle is expected. Only the five most common reflexes will be discussed here: the biceps, triceps, brachioradialis, achilles, and patellar. The biceps reflex is obtained by flexing the child's arm over the examiner's arm while the

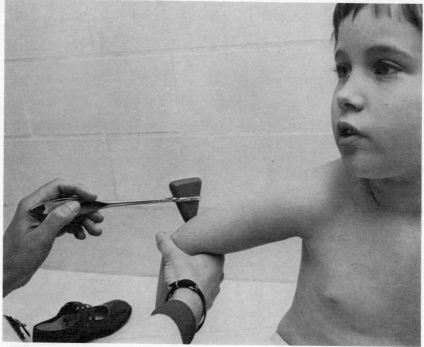

Figure 15–23 Examiner testing the triceps reflex.

examiner's thumb is pressed against the biceps tendon in the antecubital space. A tap of the reflex hammer onto the examiner's thumb should result in a quick, sharp contraction of the biceps. The triceps reflex is elicited again with the child's arm in the flexed position. This time, the reflex hammer is struck directly onto the triceps tendon behind the elbow. The authors find this reflex easiest to elicit if the child's upper arm is held straight out from the body and his lower arm is allowed to dangle loosely toward the floor. The expected response is contraction of the triceps, which should extend the elbow. The brachioradialis reflex is initiated by a sharp tap of the reflex hammer to the styloid process of the radius; this should result in flexion of the elbow and pronation of the forearm. The patellar reflex is obtained by striking the tendon immediately below the patella. This should result in extension of the knee, with a kicking action. This reflex can be strengthened by having the child lock the fingers of both hands and pull as hard as he can in an outward direction. Finally, the Achilles reflex is obtained by tapping the achilles tendon while the child's foot is held in the examiner's hand. Plantar flexion of the foot is expected. If the nurse-examiner has difficulty in obtaining the desired response, she should try different spots on the achilles tendon and vary the degree of flexion of the child's foot.

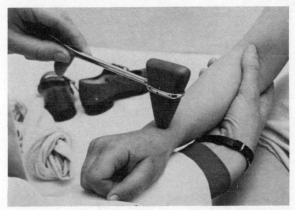

Figure 15–24   Examiner testing the brachioradialis reflex.

All reflexes should be evaluated as to their symmetry and strength, but there are some reflexes which just by their presence indicate abnormality. One of the most useful in older children is the Babinski reflex. The stimulus for the Babinski reflex is stroking the lateral aspect of the sole of the foot with a relatively sharp object, such as a pinpoint or fingernail.

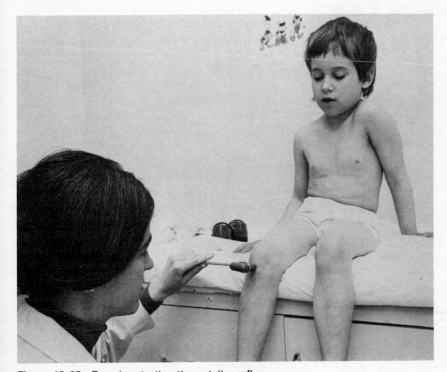

Figure 15–25   Examiner testing the patellar reflex.

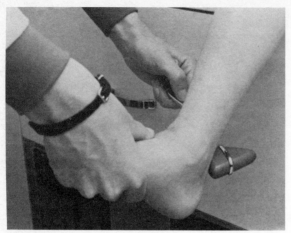

Figure 15–26 Examiner testing the Achilles reflex.

The stroke should begin at the heel, come up toward the little toe and across toward the big toe. The normal response is an incurving of the toes toward the stimulus. The abnormal response is a fanning of the toes, particularly of the big toe. Fanning is abnormal only after the child has begun to walk; however, before that time, the normal response is a fanning, and the abnormal response is a plantar flexion. This is a very useful reflex when it can be elicited. As pointed out before, however, the difficulty is that particularly on a young child the pressure used when applying the stimulus may cause the plantar flexion reflex to be elicited, thus invalidating the response. The other abnormal reflexes elicit the same response as the Babinski, but different stimuli are used. The Chaddock reflex is elicited by stroking the lateral aspect of the foot directly under

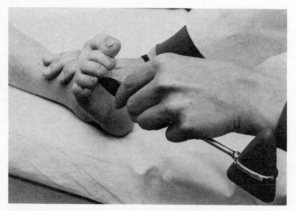

Figure 15–27 Examiner testing the Babinski reflex.

the lateral malleolus; the Oppenheim reflex is elicited by running the thumb and index finger briskly down the anteromedial surface of the tibial bone; and the Gordon reflex is elicited by tightly squeezing the belly of the calf muscle; the responses to all these reflexes are evaluated in the same way as the Babinski reflex.

These reflexes are also useful in assessing toddlers and infants; however, in infants, there are a host of other reflexes. Results of most of them are quite variable, and their usefulness is as yet not certain. However, a brief description of each will be given here along with a discussion of what is known about their significance when this is applicable.

Chvostek's reflex is elicited by briskly tapping the index finger over the parotid gland. In certain conditions, such as tetany and hypoglycemia, or in infants born of diabetic mothers, a facial twitching may occur.

The lip reflex is elicited by tapping the upper or lower lip sharply; the expected response is for the lips to pouch out or protrude. This response is impossible to achieve if the infant is crying or sucking.

The glabella reflex is obtained by tapping briskly on the glabella (the bridge of the nose). Normally the eyes will close tightly. The examiner should watch for lack of symmetry, possibly indicating paralysis.

The optical blink reflex can be elicited by shining a light suddenly at the baby's open eyes. The eyes should shut quickly, often accompanied by a quick dorsal flexion of the head. Absence of this response may indicate poor or no light perception.

The acoustic blink reflex is similar, but is elicited by a loud clap of the examiner's hands about 30 cm from the child's head. Care should be taken to avoid producing an air current which will strike the face. This is often hard to elicit the first 2 to 3 days of age, and if there is no response, it should be repeated after a few days later. If there is still no response, the question of auditory problems arise. Because the infant quickly gets used to this clapping after two or three times, he can be expected to fail to respond.

The tonic neck reflex is one of the more important reflexes. It can be considered both a posture and a reflex. The posture consists of turning the face to the side with the jaw over one shoulder. The arm and leg on the jaw side (the side toward which the face is pointing) will extend while the opposite arm and leg flex. This is the classic "fencer position." If the child is not lying in this position, the maneuver of turning his head to the extreme right or left should elicit it. This response will sometimes be present at birth, but its peak incidence is at about 2 to 3 months. An infant who never exhibits it should not be considered abnormal. The nurse should worry, however, about a child who displays this behavior constantly, particularly before 2 to 3 months of age, and who seems "locked" into this position. She should also worry if it lasts to a very late age; it would certainly be considered abnormal past 6 months, and if it were seen

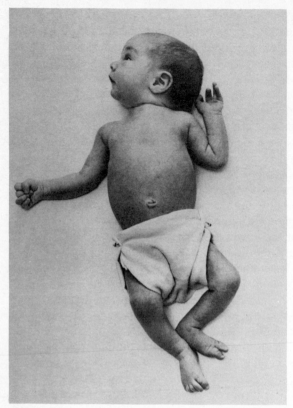

Figure 15-28 An infant displaying the tonic neck reflex. (*Mead Johnson, A Clinical Review of Concepts and Characteristics in Infant Development, vol. II, p. 1, 1972.*)

very often at 4 or 5 months, suspicion should be aroused. While a child is in this position, it is impossible for him to grasp with the arm extended toward the face side, and, of course, he cannot see the arm that is behind his head. Consequently, it is almost impossible for him to develop eye-hand coordination. It also seems to be impossible for most of these babies to bring their hands to midline or into their mouths; consequently, they are not usually able to roll over. The developmental ramifications of this problem are obvious.

Recoil of the arm is also an important reflex. To elicit this, the examiner should extend both of the infant's arms simultaneously by pulling them out by the wrists. The examiner then quickly lets go and observes the response. Normally, both arms should flex briskly at the elbows; this response should be strongest in the first 2 days of life, but it should persist through the entire neonatal period. The examiner should watch for asymmetry. In hypotonic or apathetic babies, there may be no response at all.

An attempt should also be made to elicit ankle clonus. This is done by pressing the thumbs sharply against the soles of the infant's feet, dorsiflexing the entire foot. The examiner then quickly releases this pressure and watches for clonus. Minor clonus may be normal, but any sustained clonus is suspect and further investigation is necessary.

The palmar grasp reflex is also tested. The examiner's fingers are pressed into the infant's palms from the ulnar side, being careful that the dorsal side is not stimulated. The normal response is for the infant's hands to grasp the examiner's fingers. She should watch for symmetry, being careful that the baby's head is in midline or a normal asymmetry may be felt. If the response is weak, the examiner should get the infant to suck, since sucking facilitates the grasp. This response is weaker during the first 2 days, and then becomes and remains strong until about 3 months. It should then gradually be replaced by a voluntary grasping.

A magnet reflex is elicited by light pressure to the soles of the feet. The legs should extend toward the pressure while the examiner inspects for asymmetries. This response may be absent in cases of lower spinal cord damage or may be weak with a breech presentation with flexed legs or in babies with sciatic nerve damage. A breech presentation accompanied by extended legs may have a stronger magnet response. This response may be normally more difficult to elicit in the first 2 days.

The crossed extensor reflex is obtained by extending one leg passively while pressing the knee of that leg to the table. With a pin, the sole of this foot is pricked. The response expected is for the other leg to extend and adduct slightly. This reflex is weak the first 2 days, but fairly constant after that; it may be absent in infants with spinal cord lesions and may be weak in those with peripheral nerve damage.

The withdrawal reflex is elicited by pricking the soles of the feet, one at a time. The leg of the foot which is pricked will flex at the hip, knee, and ankle. This response should be constant for the first 10 days, but it may be absent in cases of damaged spinal cords and weak in babies who have sciatic nerve damage or in those who have been delivered by breech presentation with their legs extended (in this case, the response may even be reversed and the baby will be seen to extend his leg rather than withdraw it). Again, asymmetries should be watched for.

The rooting reflex is well known to nurses. When the corners or the middle of the upper or lower lip are touched, the head should turn in the direction of the stimulation. If the upper lip is touched, the mouth should open and the head bend backward; if the lower lip is touched, the mouth should open while the lower jaw drops. The baby will often turn in the other direction if he is satiated. The response will usually be less vigorous the first 2 days of life, but if it is absent later, suspicion should be aroused that the baby may be in a depressed state, particularly if barbiturates have been used by the mother.

Sucking is another well-known reflex and vital to life. While the

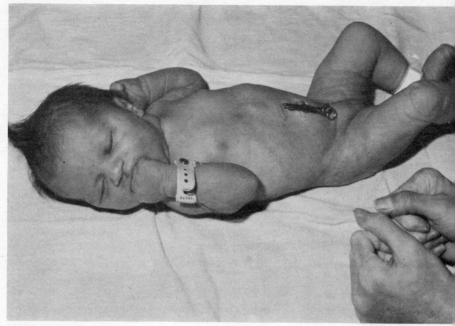

(a)

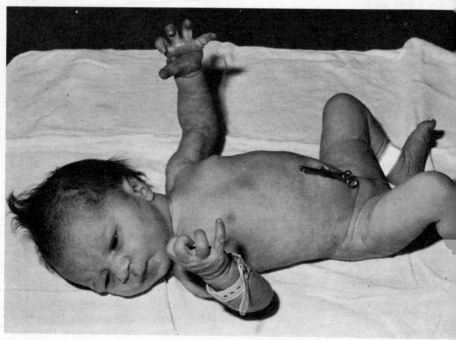

(b)

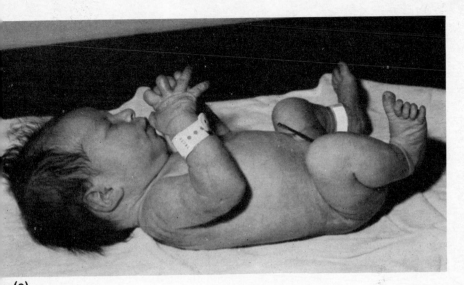

(c)

Figure 15–29   An infant demonstrating a complete Moro reflex.
(*From Clausen et al., Maternity Nursing Today, pp.
676, 677, and 679. Reproduced by permission of
the publisher.*)

infant sucks on the examiner's finger, four aspects of the sucking reflex
should be noted. The action of the tongue should be felt to push the finger
up and back, the rate should be fairly good, the pressure or strength
should be noted, and the pattern of grouping in the suck should be noted.
This is less intense in the first 3 to 4 days. Barbiturates, sometimes
transmitted in the breast milk, will depress sucking.

The masseter reflex is elicited by placing one index finger on the
lower chin of the infant and tapping it sharply with the index finger of the
other hand. A quick contraction of the masseter muscles will lift the chin;
this can frequently be felt better than it can be seen. It will normally be
weak in the first 2 days, but should be present for the first 10 days; its
absence may mean brainstem lesions or lesions of the Vth cranial nerve.

The Moro reflex is probably the most important reflex in the young
infant and should always be tested. There are several ways of eliciting a
response, but the most effective way is to hold the baby by supporting the
trunk with one hand (the baby is lying on his back) and supporting the
head and neck with the other hand. When the neck is relaxed, the head is
dropped backward a few centimeters. The expected response is an
abduction of the arm and shoulder; an extension of the arm at the elbow;
an extension of the fingers, with a C formed by the thumb and index
finger; and later, an adduction of the arm at the shoulder. The response

may have to be repeated three or four times for the examiner to be able to observe all components. It is expected to be present from birth to 3 or 4 months. If it lasts longer than 4 months, one should suspect a neurologic defect; if it lasts longer than 6 months, it should definitely be considered abnormal. It may be absent in the first weeks if there has been heavy sedation or cerebral trauma. If the response is present and then disappears, it may be one of the earliest signs of kernicterus. Again, the practitioner should watch for asymmetry.

Bauer's reflex is elicited with the infant lying prone. The examiner presses gently on the soles of the feet, and the baby should attempt to make crawling movements. This is difficult to get in the first 2 to 3 days.

Galant's reflex is seen when the examiner scratches a pin along the side of the spinal column, about 3 cm from midline, from the shoulder to the buttocks. The trunk should curve to the side of the scratch. If there is a spinal cord lesion, there will be an absence of response below the level of the lesion. This response is easiest to obtain at about 5 to 6 days of age.

The placing reflex may be difficult to elicit in the first 4 days. The examiner holds the baby upright in such a way that the dorsal side of the foot is gently touching the edge of the table. The infant's knees and hips

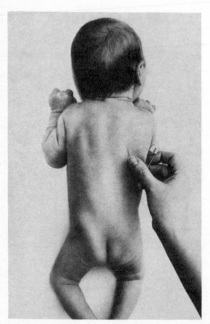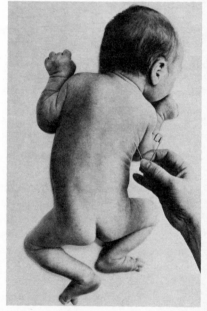

Figure 15–30 The examiner testing Galant's reflex. (*Mead Johnson, A Clinical Review of Concepts and Characteristics in Infant Development, vol. II, p. 3, 1972.*)

should flex and the foot should rise and be placed on the table. This response is absent in paralysis.

The stepping reflex is similar but has some differences. With the baby upright, the soles of the feet should touch the table surface. Alternating stepping movements should result. This is harder to elicit in the first 2 to 3 days and fades about the third or fourth week. It may be absent with breech delivery or with depression.

The rotation test is also done with the baby in the upright position facing the examiner. The examiner then spins around in such a way that she and the baby are spinning together in first one direction and then the other. When the baby's head is not held, it should turn in the direction toward which the baby is turning. When the head is restrained, the eyes should turn in that direction (the "doll's eye maneuver"). This is a vestibular reflex and may be abnormal if a vestibule of the ear is defective or a muscle paralysis exists.

The Landau reflex is obtained with the baby's abdomen supported on the examiner's hand, and his head and legs extending over either side of the hand. From 6 to 8 months until 3 years of age, the expected response is for the child to lift his head and extend his spine and legs. Lack of this response may be an indication of cerebral palsy.

The parachute reflex is one in which the infant is held prone and lowered slowly toward a surface. Normal babies will try to protect themselves by extending their arms and legs; children with cerebral palsy will often fail to do this. This response is normally present from 4 to 6 months on.

Positive supporting reactions are also important reflexes. When the ball of the foot touches the table, the baby will usually extend his legs and bear some weight. Infants who do extend their legs, but also cross them should be suspected of being afflicted with cerebral palsy.

Another important reflex is the neck righting reflex which is elicited by turning the head to one side. Normally, the body should follow in this same direction anytime between age of 3 months and 3 years. Many children with cerebral palsy cannot execute this maneuver and, consequently, never learn to turn over.

The protective side turning reflex is elicited by placing the baby in the prone position with the head in midline. Normal babies will protect themselves by turning their head to the side. Certain children with early signs of cerebral palsy will fail to do this.

Neurological "Soft" Signs

No discussion of a neurologic examination could be complete without mention of the "soft" signs so frequently referred to in pediatric neurology. Yet such a discussion is very difficult because of the controversy that exists in the literature regarding such signs. Different clinicians define these signs differently, and, in fact, some do not believe that they exist at all. Even those who believe they do exist do not agree as to exactly what they are or what they mean. In general, the term is used to refer to signs which are minimal and whose significance is not known. Clumsiness, hyperkinesis, language disturbances, perceptual developmental lags or inconsistencies, motor overflow, mirroring movements of the extremities (e.g., when one hand performs a motor task, the child cannot keep the other hand still), mixed or confused laterality, articulation defects, disturbance in balance, and short attention span are all examples of specific signs which some clinicians consider "soft." If these are associated with school difficulties, further investigation is necessary. Usually such problems appear in preschool children; if these signs are indeed predictions of future school problems, it would be desirable to intervene at that point. Although many clinicians feel this is the case, it certainly has not been firmly proved. The nurse-practitioner will probably want to read some of the articles in the bibliography and decide for herself what her policy will be in this regard.

BIBLIOGRAPHY

Amiel-Tison, C.: "Neurological Evaluation of the Maturity of Newborn Infants," *Archives of Disease in Childhood*, vol. 43: 1968, p. 89.

Barness, Lewis A.: *Manual of Pediatric Physical Diagnosis*, Chicago: Year Book Medical Publishers, Inc., 1968, pp. 161–173.

Barnett, Henry L.: *Pediatrics*, New York: Appleton Century Crofts, 1968, pp. 832–1020.

Bobath, K., and B. Bobath: "The Diagnosis of Cerebral Palsy in Infancy," *Archives of Diseases in Childhood*, vol. 31, 1956, p. 498.

Brown, Jr., "Feeding Reflexes in Infancy," *Developmental Medicine and Child Neurology*, vol. 11, October 1969, pp. 641–643.

Campbell, D., J. Koyer, and E. Lang, "Motor Activity in Early Life," *Biology of the Neonate*, vol. 18, 1971, pp. 108–120.

DeGowin, Elmer L., and Richard L. DeGowin, *Bedside Diagnostic Examination*, New York: The Macmillan Company, 1970, pp. 738–805.

Delp, Mahlon H., and Robert T. Manning: *Major's Physical Diagnosis*, Philadelphia: W. B. Saunders Company, 1968, pp. 173–299.

Goldie, L., and K. J. Hopkins: "Head Turning Towards Diffuse Light in the Neurological Examination of Newborn Infants," *Brain: Journal of Neurology*, vol. 87, 1946, p. 665.

Green, Morris, and Julius B. Richmond: *Pediatric Diagnosis*, Philadelphia: W. B. Saunders Company, 1962, pp. 152–175.

Hogan, G. R., and J. E. Milligan: "The Plantar Reflex of the Newborn," *New England Journal of Medicine*, vol. 285, August 1971, pp. 502–503.

Humphrey, T.: "Some Correlations between the Appearance of Human Fetal Reflexes and the Development of the Nervous System," *Progress in Brain Research*, 1964, pp. 4, 93.

Illingworth, R. S.: *An Introduction to Development and Assessment in the First Year*, London: William Heinemann, Ltd., 1966.

Judge, Richard D., and George D. Zuidema: *Physical Diagnosis: A Physiological Approach*, Boston: Little, Brown and Company, 1963, pp. 317–347.

Kempe, C. Henry, Henry K. Silver, and Donough O'Brien: *Current Pediatric Diagnosis and Treatment*, Los Altos, Calif.: Lange Medical Publications, 1970, pp. 392–458.

Korner, A. F.: "Neonatal Startles, Smiles, Erection, and Reflex Suck as Related to State, Sex, and Individuality," *Child Development*, vol. 40, December 1969, pp. 1039–1053.

Milligan, J. E., et al.: "Retention of Habituation of the Moro Response in the Newborn," *Developmental Medicine and Child Neurology*, vol. 12, February 1970, pp. 6–15.

Nelson, Waldo, *Textbook of Pediatrics*, Philadelphia: W. B. Saunders Company, 1964, pp. 1155–1250.

Parmalee, A. H., Jr.: "Sleep Studies for the Neurological Assessment of the Newborn," *Neuropaediatrie; Journal of Pediatric Neurobiology, Neurology and Neurosurgery* (Stuttgart), vol. 1, February 1970, pp. 351–353.

————, et al.: "Neurological Evaluation of the Premature Infant: A Follow-up Study," *Biology of the Neonate*, vol. 15, 1970, pp. 65–78.

Prechtl, Heinz, and David Beintema: *The Neurological Examination of the Full-term Newborn Infant*, The Lavenham Press, Ltd., England, 1965.

Prior, John, and Jack Silberstein: *Physical Diagnosis*, St. Louis: The C. V. Mosby Company, 1969, pp. 329–371.

Rabe, E. F.: "The Hypotonic Infant," *Journal of Pediatrics*, vol. 64, 1964, p. 422.

Robinson, R. J.: "Assessment of Gestational Age by Neurological Examination," *Archives of Disease in Childhood*, vol. 41, 1966, p. 437.

————, and J. P. M. Tizard: "The Central Nervous System in the Newborn," *British Medical Bulletin*, 1966, vol. 22, p. 49.

Schaeffer, Alexander J., and Mary Ellen Avery: *Diseases of the Newborn*, Philadelphia: W. B. Saunders Company, 1971, pp. 578–631.

Silver, Henry K., C. Henry Kempe, and Henry B. Bruyn, *Handbook of Pediatrics*, Los Altos, Calif.: Lange Medical Publications, 1965, pp. 382–414.

Soster, A. M., A. J. Sameroff, and A. J. Sostek: "Evidence for the Unconditionability of the Babinski Reflex in Newborns," *Child Development*, vol. 43, June 1972, pp. 509–519.

Thomas, A., and Y. Chesni: *The Neurological Examination of the Infant*, Little Clubs Clinics in Developmental Medicine, 1960.

Van Allen, M. W.: *Pictorial Manual of Neurologic Tests*, Chicago: Year Book Medical Publications, Inc., 1969.

Zelazo, P. R., N. A. Zelazo, and S. Kolb: "'Walking' in the Newborn," *Science*, vol. 176, April 21, 1972, pp. 314–315.

Ziai, Mohsen: *Pediatrics*, Boston: Little, Brown and Company, 1969, pp. 419–444.

SUGGESTED RESOURCES

1 Pamphlets

"Essentials of the Neurological Examination," Smith Kline and French Laboratories. (Free)

2 Films

"Cranial Nerves"
  Color, 35 minutes
  Cost: $5.00
  Ciba Pharmaceutical Co.
  P.O. Box 1340
  Newark, New Jersey 07101
"Hyperactive Child"
  Color, 34 minutes
  Cost: $5.00
  Ciba Pharmaceutical Co.
  P.O. Box 1340
  Newark, New Jersey 07101
"Mental Status Examination"
  Color, 20 minutes
  Cost: $2.00
  Ciba Pharmaceutical Co.
  P.O. Box 1340
  Newark, New Jersey 07101
"Neurological Examination of the Full-term Newborn"
  Color, 26 minutes
  Cost: Free
  National Medical Audiovisual Center (Annex)
  Station K
  Atlanta, Georgia 30324
"Otoneurological Examination for Vestibular Cerebellar Function"
  Color, 26 minutes
  Cost: Free
  Abbott Laboratories
  Abbott Park
  North Chicago, Illinois 60064
"Proprioceptive and Sensory Systems"
  Color, 29 minutes
  Cost: $5.00
  Ciba Pharmaceutical Co.
  P.O. Box 1340
  Newark, New Jersey 07101
"Recognition of Narcotic Withdrawal in the Newborn"
  Black and White, 15 minutes

Cost: $3.00
American Medical Association
535 North Dearborn Street
Chicago, Illinois 60610

GLOSSARY

abducent nerves the VIth cranial nerves which innervate the rectus lateralis muscle of the eye and cause the eye muscles to rotate laterally

accessory nerves the XIth cranial nerves which innervate parts of the pharynx, larynx, esophagus, trapezius, and sternocleidomastoid muscles

acoustic nerves the VIIIth cranial nerves composed of a cochlear branch concerned with hearing and a vestibular branch concerned with sensory functions and equilibrium

aqueduct of Sylvius the drainage system communicating between the third and fourth ventricle

arachnoid a web-like, avascular membrane lying between the dura mater and the pia mater, separated from the dura mater by the subdural space and from the pia mater by the subarachnoid space

association fibers a group of fibers in the centrum ovale which connect different portions of the cortex to each other

auditopsychic area the area of the brain involved in recognizing and integrating sound stimuli with past experience

auditory sensory area that area of the brain involved in integrating sound stimuli into pitch, quality, and loudness

axon an extension of a neuron whose function is to transmit impulses from the cell body outward to the rest of the body

basal ganglia the innermost layer of the brain

Broca's area that region involved in controlling the ability to articulate speech

central nervous system the part of the nervous system comprised of the brain and spinal cord

centrum ovale (white matter) the layer of the brain directly beneath the cortex which contains projection fibers, commissural fibers, and association fibers

cerebellum the second largest part of the brain located between the occipital lobes of the cerebrum and the brainstem which functions in controlling balance, movement, and posture

cerebrum the largest portion of the brain, containing the two hemispheres

commissural fibers a group of fibers in the centrum ovale which connect the two hemispheres through the corpus callosum, anterior commissure, hippocampal commissure, fornix commissure, and posterior commissure

corpus callosum that part of the brain which connects the two hemispheres of the cerebrum

cortex the outer layer of an organ; the outer layer of the brain

cranium the bony encasement of the brain; the skull

dendrite one of several extensions from the neuron whose function is to receive impulses and transmit them to the cell body

diencephalon   that part of the cerebrum which contains the thalamus, pineal body, hypothalamus, and parts of the third ventricle

dura mater   tough, fibrous connective tissue which lies directly beneath the periosteum of the cranium

encephalon   the brain

facial nerves   the VIIth cranial nerves which innervate the anterior two-thirds of the tongue, the external acoustic meatus, soft palate, and pharynx, as well as the secretions from the submandibular, sublingual, lacrimal, and palatine glands

glossopharyngeal nerves   the IXth cranial nerves which innervate the tongue and pharynx

hypoglossal nerves   the XIIth cranial nerves which innervate the tongue

hypothalamus   a small mass of gray matter located directly beneath the thalamus whose functions are involved in temperature control, water balance, and some digestive activities.

medulla oblongata   a continuation of the spinal cord located between the pons and the cerebellum, which serves to transmit impulses to the spinal cord and is concerned with circulation and respiration

medulla spinalis   the spinal cord

meninges   the three membranes covering the brain and spinal cord

mesencephalon   that small, constricted region of the cerebrum which joins the pons and cerebellum to the diencephalon

myelinated   describing or pertaining to certain nerves which are protected by a myelin sheath

neuron   the basic unit of the nervous system

oculomotor nerves   the IIId pair of cranial nerves involved in the movement of the eye within its socket

olfactory nerves   the Ist cranial nerves involved in the sense of smell

optic nerves   the IId cranial nerves involved in vision

parastriate area (visuopsychic area)   that area of the brain involved in recognizing, integrating, and associating visual images with past experiences

parietal area   that area of the brain involved in integrating several types of stimulation from various sensory areas

peripheral nervous system   the autonomic nervous system composed of the sympathetic and parasympathetic systems

pia mater   the deepest layer of the meninges, composed of delicate highly vascular tissue, which attaches directly to the gray matter of the brain

pineal gland   a small gland lying posterior to the thalamus which is more active in childhood than in adult years, and whose exact function is unknown

pons   a ventral protuberance of the brainstem, which serves as a neural transmission center

postcentral area   the area of the brain which receives stimuli from the spinal cord and controls the sensory areas of the body

precentral cortex (motor area)   that area of the surface of the brain, located on the superior portion of each hemisphere, which controls voluntary muscle contraction

premotor area   the area of the brain involved in suppressing motor activity as well as exerting some control over circulation, respiration, and pupillary reaction

projection fibers   a group of afferent and efferent fibers in the centrum ovale which connect the cortex, brain, and spinal cord

proprioception   the awareness of one's own bodily posture and movement

striate area   that area of the brain involved in integrating visual stimuli for size, form, motion, and color

telencephalon   that portion of the cerebrum which contains part of the wall of the third ventricle

thalamus   a large mass of gray matter forming the lateral wall of the third ventricle, which functions in the transmission of sensory impulses to the cortex

trigeminal nerves   the Vth cranial nerves which innervates the sensory portions of the face, the mucous membranes, and internal structures of the head as well as the muscles of mastication

trochlear nerves   the IVth cranial nerves which innervate the obliquus superior oculi muscles of the eye and control ocular movement

unmyelinated   a term referring to certain of the nerves which are not protected by a myelin sheath

vagus nerves   the Xth cranial nerves which innervate the skin of the posterior surface of the external ear, the external acoustic meatus, the pharynx, larynx, bronchi, lungs, heart, esophagus, stomach, kidneys, and intestines

ventricles of the brain   a system of small cavities in the brain, consisting of two lateral ventricles, a third ventricle, and a fourth ventricle

Index

Page numbers in *italic* indicate illustrations.